Fodor's

O'AHU

3rd Edition

Fodor's Travel Publications   New York, Toronto, London, Sydney, Auckland
www.fodors.com

Be a Fodor's Correspondent

Your opinion matters. It matters to us. It matters to your fellow Fodor's travelers, too. And we'd like to hear it. In fact, we need to hear it.

When you share your experiences and opinions, you become an active member of the Fodor's community. That means we'll not only use your feedback to make our books better, but we'll publish your names and comments whenever possible. Throughout our guides, look for "Word of Mouth," excerpts of your unvarnished feedback.

Here's how you can help improve Fodor's for all of us.

Tell us when we're right. We rely on local writers to give you an insider's perspective. But our writers and staff editors—who are the best in the business—depend on you. Your positive feedback is a vote to renew our recommendations for the next edition.

Tell us when we're wrong. We're proud that we update most of our guides every year. But we're not perfect. Things change. Hotels cut services. Museums change hours. Charming cafés lose charm. If our writer didn't quite capture the essence of a place, tell us how you'd do it differently. If any of our descriptions are inaccurate or inadequate, we'll incorporate your changes in the next edition and will correct factual errors at fodors.com immediately.

Tell us what to include. You probably have had fantastic travel experiences that aren't yet in Fodor's. Why not share them with a community of like-minded travelers? Maybe you chanced upon a beach or bistro or B&B that you don't want to keep to yourself. Tell us why we should include it. And share your discoveries and experiences with everyone directly at fodors.com. Your input may lead us to add a new listing or highlight a place we cover with a "Highly Recommended" star or with our highest rating, "Fodor's Choice."

Give us your opinion instantly at our feedback center at www.fodors.com/feedback. You may also e-mail editors@fodors.com with the subject line "O'ahu Editor." Or send your nominations, comments, and complaints by mail to O'ahu Editor, Fodor's, 1745 Broadway, New York, NY 10019.

You and travelers like you are the heart of the Fodor's community. Make our community richer by sharing your experiences. Be a Fodor's correspondent.
Aloha!

Tim Jarrell, Publisher

FODOR'S O'AHU
Editor: Rachel Klein

Editorial Contributors: Melissa Chang, Trina Kudlacek, Chad Pata

Production Editors: Astrid deRidder, Jennifer DePrima
Maps & Illustrations: David Lindroth, Ed Jacobus, William Wu, with additional cartography provided by Henry Columb, Mark Stroud, and Ali Baird, Moon Street Cartography; *cartographers;* Bob Blake, Rebecca Baer, *map editors;* William Wu, *information graphics*
Design: Fabrizio La Rocca, *creative director;* Guido Caroti, Siobhan O'Hare, *art directors;* Tina Malaney, Chie Ushio, Ann McBride, Jessica Walsh, *designers;* Melanie Marin, *senior picture editor*
Cover Photo (Rocky Point, North Shore): Sean Davey/Aurora Photos
Production Manager: Angela L. McLean

3rd Edition

ISBN 978-1-4000-0442-3

ISSN 1559-0771

SPECIAL SALES
This book is available at special discounts for bulk purchases for sales promotions or premiums. Special editions, including personalized covers, excerpts of existing books, and corporate imprints, can be created in large quantities for special needs. For more information, write to Special Markets/Premium Sales, 1745 Broadway, MD 6-2, New York, New York 10019, or e-mail specialmarkets@randomhouse.com.

AN IMPORTANT TIP & AN INVITATION
Although all prices, opening times, and other details in this book are based on information supplied to us at press time, changes occur all the time in the travel world, and Fodor's cannot accept responsibility for facts that become outdated or for inadvertent errors or omissions. So **always confirm information when it matters,** especially if you're making a detour to visit a specific place. Your experiences—positive and negative— matter to us. If we have missed or misstated something, **please write to us.** We follow up on all suggestions. Contact the O'ahu editor at editors@fodors.com or c/o Fodor's at 1745 Broadway, New York, NY 10019.

PRINTED IN CHINA

10 9 8 7 6 5 4 3 2 1

CONTENTS

Fodor's Features

MAPS

ABOUT
THIS BOOK

Our Ratings

Sometimes you find terrific travel experiences and sometimes they just find you. But usually the burden is on you to select the right combination of experiences. That's where our ratings come in.

As travelers we've all discovered a place so wonderful that its worthiness is obvious. And sometimes that place is so experiential that superlatives don't do it justice: you just have to be there to know. These sights, properties, and experiences get our highest rating, **Fodor's Choice** indicated by orange stars throughout this book.

Black stars highlight sights and properties we deem **Highly Recommended** places that our writers, editors, and readers praise again and again for consistency and excellence.

By default, there's another category: any place we include in this book is by definition worth your time, unless we say otherwise. And we will.

Disagree with any of our choices? Care to nominate a place or suggest that we rate one more highly? Visit our feedback center at www.fodors.com/feedback.

Budget Well

For attractions, we always give standard adult admission fees; reductions are usually available for children, students, and senior citizens. Want to pay with plastic? **AE, D, DC, MC, V** following restaurant and hotel listings indicate if American Express, Discover, Diner's Club, MasterCard, and Visa are accepted.

Restaurants

Unless we state otherwise, restaurants are open for lunch and dinner daily. We mention dress only when there's a specific requirement and reservations only when they're essential or not accepted—it's always best to book ahead.

Hotels

Hotels have private bath, phone, TV, and air-conditioning and operate on the European Plan (aka EP, meaning without meals), unless we specify otherwise.

Listings
- ★ Fodor's Choice
- ★ Highly recommended
- ✉ Physical address
- ✛ Directions or Map coordinates
- ⌖ Mailing address
- ☎ Telephone
- 🖷 Fax
- ⊕ On the Web
- ✉ E-mail
- 🎟 Admission fee
- ☉ Open/closed times
- Ⓜ Metro stations
- ▭ Credit cards

Hotels & Restaurants
- 🏨 Hotel
- Number of rooms
- ⚴ Facilities
- ❍ Meal plans
- ✕ Restaurant
- Reservations
- 👗 Dress code
- Smoking
- BYOB

Outdoors
- Golf
- Camping

Other
- Family-friendly
- ⇨ See also
- ✉ Branch address
- ☞ Take note

Experience
Oʻahu

WHAT'S WHERE

1 Honolulu. The capital city holds the nation's only royal palace, free concerts under the tamarind trees in the financial district, and the galleries and open markets of Nu'uanu and Chinatown.

2 Waikīkī. This city is the dream that sells Hawai'i as the place to surf, swim, and sail by day and dine, dance, and party by night.

3 Greater Honolulu and Pearl Harbor. Aside from visiting the most popular site on the island, there is much exploring to do, including taking a trip to the Bishop Museum, another attraction not to be missed.

4 Southeast O'ahu. Honolulu's main bedroom communities crawl up the steep-sided valleys. Also here are snorkelers' favorite Hanauma Bay and a string of wild and often hidden beaches.

5 Windward O'ahu. The offshore islands and remnants of ancient fishponds here are where the beach lovers live, along with many Native Hawaiians.

6 The North Shore. A mix of farmers and surfers call this part of the island home, where vacation rentals and plantation villages culminate in a tumble of black rocks at Ka'ena Point.

7 Central and West (Leeward) O'ahu. This part of the island includes the Central O'ahu highlands, the Leeward Coast, and the Hawaiian communities of Nānākuli and Wai'anae. It's finding a new identity as a "second city" of suburban homes and tech firms, coexisting with agriculture and traditional lifestyles.

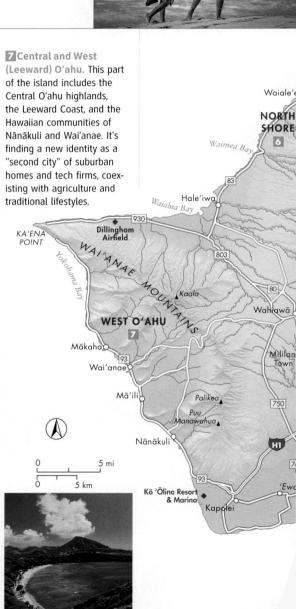

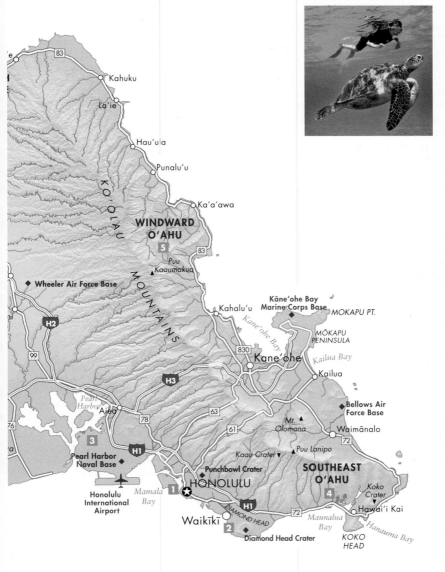

83

Kahuku

La'ie

Hau'ula

Punalu'u

Ka'a'awa

WINDWARD O'AHU

5

Puu
Kaaumakua

83

◆ Wheeler Air Force Base

K O ʻ O L A U

M O U N T A I N S

Kahalu'u

Kāne'ohe Bay
Marine Corps Base

Kane'ohe Bay

MOKAPU PT.

MŌKAPU
PENINSULA

H2

99

830

Kane'ohe

Kailua Bay

H3

Kailua

Pearl
Harbor

Aiea

78

63

Mt.
Olomana ▲

◆ Bellows Air
Force Base

Waimānalo

3

Pearl Harbor
Naval Base ◆

H1

61

Kaau Crater ▼

Puu Lanipo ▲

SOUTHEAST O'AHU

4

Koko
Crater

Honolulu
International
Airport

*Mamala
Bay*

1 ★ **HONOLULU**

◆ Punchbowl Crater

Hawai'i Kai

72

Waikīkī

H1

DIAMOND HEAD

2

72

*Maunalua
Bay*

◆ Diamond Head Crater

KOKO
HEAD

Hanauma Bay

76

O'AHU AND HAWAI'I TODAY

O'ahu—where Honolulu and Waikīkī are—is the third-largest Hawaiian Island and has 75% of the state's population. Honolulu is the perfect place to experience the state's indigenous culture, the hundred years of immigration that resulted in today's blended society, and the tradition of aloha. The museums and historic and cultural sites will ground you, at least a bit, in Hawai'i's history. The widest range of restaurants as well as the best nightlife in the Islands is here, too.

But O'ahu is not just Honolulu and Waikīkī. It is looping mountain trails on the western Wai'anae and eastern Ko'olau ranges. It is monster waves breaking on the golden beaches of the North Shore. It is country stores and beaches where turtles are your swimming companions.

Hawaiian culture and tradition here have experienced a renaissance over the last few decades. There's a real effort to revive traditions and to respect history as the Islands go through major changes. New developments often have a Hawaiian cultural expert on staff to ensure cultural sensitivity and to educate newcomers.

Nonetheless, development remains a huge issue for all Islanders—land prices are skyrocketing, putting many areas out of reach for the native population. Traffic is becoming a problem on roads that were not designed to accommodate all the new drivers, and the Islands' limited natural resources are being seriously tapped. The government, though sluggish to respond at first, is trying to make development in Hawai'i as sustainable as possible.

Sustainability

Prior to Western contact, Hawai'i's native dwellers were 100% sustainable. For a place so well endowed with the richest natural resources, contemporary Hawai'i is a far cry from its past. This great challenge also presents a great opportunity. Hawai'i's climate and renewable resources—the sun, the wind, and the waves—can be developed for the greater good and provide almost every conceivable kind of alternative energy.

Although sustainability is an effective buzzword and authentic direction for the island's dining establishments, 90% of Hawai'i's food and energy is imported. Most of the land is used for monocropping of pineapples or sugarcane, which have both severely declined in the past decades. Sugarcane is now only produced commercially on Maui, while pineapple production has dropped by half. Dole, once the largest pineapple company in Hawai'i, closed its plants in 1991, and after 90 years, Del Monte stopped pineapple production in 2008. The next year, Maui Land and Pineapple Company also ceased its Maui Gold pineapple operation, although in early 2010 a group of executives took over one third of the land and created a new company. Low cost of labor and transportation from Latin American and Southeast Asian countries are factors for the industry's demise. Although this proves daunting, it also sets the stage for great agricultural change to be explored.

Back-to-Basics Agriculture

Emulating how the Hawaiian ancestors lived and returning to their simple ways of growing and sharing a variety of foods has become a statewide initiative. Hawai'i has the natural conditions and talent to produce far more diversity in agriculture than it currently does.

The seed of this movement thrives through various farmers' markets and partnerships between restaurants and local farmers. Localized efforts such as the Hawai'i

Farm Bureau Federation are collectively leading the organic and sustainable agricultural renaissance. From home-cooked meals and casual plate lunches to fine-dining cuisine, these sustainable trailblazers enrich the culinary tapestry of Hawai'i and uplift the island's overall quality of life.

Tourism and the Economy

The over-$10 billion tourism industry represents a third of Hawai'i's state income. Naturally, this dependency causes economic hardship as the financial meltdown of recent years affects tourists' ability to visit and consume. One way the industry has made changes has been to adopt more eco-conscious practices, as many Hawaiians feel that planning shouldn't happen without regard for impact to local communities and their natural environment.

Belief that an industry based on the Hawaiians' *aloha* should protect, promote, and empower local culture and provide more entrepreneurial opportunities for local people has become more important to tourism businesses. More companies are incorporating authentic Hawaiiana in their programs and aim not only to provide a commercially viable tour but also to ensure that the visitor leaves feeling connected to his or her host. The concept of *kuleana*, a word for both privilege and responsibility, is upheld. Having the privilege to live in such a sublime place comes with the responsibility to protect it.

Sovereignty

Political issues of sovereignty continue to divide the natives of Hawai'i with myriad organizations, each operating with separate agendas but collectively lacking one defined goal. Ranging from achieving complete and utter independence to solidifying a nation within a nation, existing sovereignty models remain fractured and their future unresolved. The introduction of the Native Hawaiian Government Reorganization Act of 2009 attempts to set up a legal framework in which Native Hawaiians can attain federal recognition and coexist as a self-governed entity. Also known as the Akaka Bill after Senator Daniel Akaka of Hawai'i, this pending bill has been presented before Congress and is still evolving at the time of this writing.

Rise of Hawaiian Pride

After Hawai'i received statehood in 1959, a process of Americanization transpired. Traditions were duly silenced in the name of citizenship. Hawaiian language and arts were banned from schools and children were distanced from their local customs. But Hawaiians are resilient, and with the rise of the civil rights movement they began to reflect on their own national identity, bringing an astonishing renaissance of the Hawaiian culture to fruition. The people rediscovered language, the hula, the chant or *mele*, and the traditional Polynesian art of canoe building and wayfinding (navigation by the stars). This cultural resurrection is now firmly established in today's Hawaiian culture, with a palpable pride that exudes from Hawaiians young and old.

The election of President Barack Obama has fueled not only Hawaiian pride but also wider hope for a better future. The president's connection and commitment to Hawaiian values of diversity, spirituality, family, and conservation have restored confidence that Hawai'i can inspire a more peaceful, tolerant, and environmentally conscious world.

O'AHU PLANNER

When You Arrive

Honolulu International Airport is 20 minutes (40 during rush hour) from Waikīkī. Car rental is across the street from baggage claim. An inefficient airport taxi system requires you to line up to a taxi wrangler who radios for cars (about $25 to Waikīkī). Other options: TheBus ($2, one lap-size bag allowed) or public airport shuttle ($8). Ask the driver to take H1, not Nimitz Highway, at least as far as downtown, or your introduction to paradise will be Honolulu's industrial backside.

Visitor Information

Before you go, contact the O'ahu Visitors Bureau (OVB) for a free vacation planner and map. For general information, contact the Hawai'i Visitors and Convention Bureau. The HVCB Web site has a calendar that allows you to see what local events will be taking place during your stay.

Contacts **Hawai'i Visitors and Convention Bureau** (✉ 2270 Kalakaua Ave., Suite 801, Honolulu ☎ 808/923–1811, 800/464–2924 for brochures ⊕ www.gohawaii. com).**O'ahu Visitors Bureau** (✉ 733 Bishop St., Suite 1520, Honolulu ☎ 808/524–0722, ⊕ www.visit-oahu.com).

Getting Here and Around

If you plan on getting outside of Waikīkī and Honolulu, renting a car is a must. But renting a Mustang convertible is a sure sign that you're a tourist and practically begs "Come burglarize me." A good rule of thumb: When the car is out of your sight even for a moment, it should be empty of anything you care about. But there are other added bonuses of opting out of your Hawai'i dream machine—you'll save some money and won't be hassled by constantly having to put the top down during one of the island's intermittent rain showers.

Reserve your vehicle in advance, especially during the Christmas holidays. This will not only ensure that you get a car but also that you get the best rates. ⇨ See "Travel Smart O'ahu" for more information on renting a car and driving.

ISLAND DRIVING TIMES

It might not seem as if driving from your hotel in Waikīkī to the North Shore, say, would take very much time. But it will take longer than you'd think from glancing at a map, and roads are subject to some pretty heavy traffic.

Be aware that areas around Honolulu can have traffic jams that would rival Southern California, so plan your movements accordingly. Heavy traffic toward downtown Honolulu begins as early as 6:30 AM and lasts until 9 AM. In the afternoon, expect traffic departing downtown to back up beginning around 3 PM until approximately 7 PM.

Here are average driving times—without traffic—that will help you plan your excursions accordingly.

Waikīkī to Kō'Ōlina	1 hour
Waikīkī to Hale'iwa	45 minutes
Waikīkī to Hawai'i Ka	25 minutes
Waikīkī to Kailua	30 minutes
Waikīkī to Downtown Honolulu	10 minutes
Waikīkī to Airport	25 minutes
Kane'ohe to Turtle Bay	1 hour
Hawai'i Kai to Kailua	25 minutes
Hale'iwa to Turtle Bay	20 minutes

Money-Saving Tips

There are ways to travel to paradise even on a budget. Pick up free publications at the airport and at racks all over the island; many of them are filled with money-saving coupons.

Access to beaches and most hiking trails on the island is free to the public.

Grocery stores and Wal-Mart generally stock postcards and souvenirs; they can be less expensive here than at hotel gift shops.

For inexpensive fresh fruit and produce, check out farmers' markets and farm stands along the road—they'll often let you try before you buy.

Dining and Lodging on O'ahu

Hawai'i is a melting pot of cultures, and nowhere is this more apparent than in its cuisine. From lū'au and "plate lunch" to sushi and steak, there's no shortage of interesting flavors and presentations.

Whether you're looking for a quick snack or a multicourse meal, turn to Chapter 8 to find the best eating experiences the island has to offer. Jump in and enjoy!

Choosing vacation lodging is a tough decision, but fret not—our expert writers and editors have done most of the legwork.

Looking for a tropical forest retreat, a big resort, or a private vacation rental? Chapter 9 will give you all the details you need to book a place that suits your style. Quick tips: Reserve your room far in advance. Be sure to ask about discounts and special packages (hotel Web sites often have Internet-only deals).

WHAT IT COSTS

	¢	$	$$	$$$	$$$$
Restaurants	under $10	$10–$17	$18–$26	$27–$35	over $35
Hotels		under $100	$100–$180	$181–$260	$261–$340	over $340

Restaurant prices are for a main course at dinner. Hotel prices are for two people in a standard double room in high season. Condo price categories reflect studio and one-bedroom rates.

Seeing Pearl Harbor

Pearl Harbor is a must-see for many, but there are things to know before you go. Consider whether you want to see only the USS *Arizona* Memorial, or the USS *Bowfin* and USS *Missouri* as well. Allow approximately an hour and 15 minutes for the USS *Arizona* tour.

Plan to arrive early—tickets for the USS *Arizona* Memorial (free) are given out on a first-come, first-served basis and can disappear within an hour.

There are restrictions on what you can bring with you, including purses, backpacks, and camera cases (although cameras are allowed). Baggage lockers are available for a small fee. Also, don't forget ID.

Note that children under 4 are not allowed on the USS *Bowfin* and may not enjoy the crowds and waiting in line at other sights.

Older kids are likely to find the more experiential, hands-on history of the USS *Bowfin* and USS *Missouri* memorable.

The USS *Arizona* Memorial visitor's center is open from 7:30 AM to 5 PM. For more information, visit ⊕ *www.gohawaii. about.com/cs/pearlharbor.*

TOP O'AHU EXPERIENCES

That Beach
(A) Kailua is the beach you came to Hawai'i for: wide and gently sloped, glowing golden in the sun, outfitted with a couple of well-placed islets to gaze at, and fronted by waters in ever-changing shades of turquoise. The waves are gentle enough for children. Kayakers are drawn to the Mokulua Islands offshore. Small convenience stores and restaurants are within walking distance. And there's just enough wind to keep you from baking. It's paradise, but civilized.

Finding Shangri La
(B) Wealth allowed heiress Doris Duke to acquire the lavish seaside estate she called Shangri La. For most, that would have been enough. But Duke had a passion—Islamic art and architecture—and determination as well as money. She had a vision of courtyards and pleasure gardens and rooms that are themselves works of art. And she presided over every detail

of the never-quite-finished project. The property, now a center for Islamic studies, is utterly unique and quite simply not to be missed.

O'ahu After Hours
(C) Yes, you can have an umbrella drink at sunset. But in the multicultural metropolis of Honolulu, there's so much more to it than that. Sip a glass of wine and listen to jazz at Formaggio, join the beach-and-beer gang at Duke's Canoe Club, or head to Zanzabar, where DJs spin hip-hop and techno. Sample the sake at an *izakaya* (Japanese tavern) or listen to a performance by a Hawaiian musician. Snack on *pūpū* (hors d'oeuvres), and begin your journey toward that unforgettable tropical sunrise.

Hiking to Ka'ena Point
(D) If we had but one day to spend in rural O'ahu, we'd spend it walking the back road along the rocky shore at the island's northern tip. Ka'ena, a state park as well

1

as a protected natural area, is composed of 850 acres of undeveloped coastline that centers on the point where it is said the souls of the ancient dead leapt into the eternal darkness. The views are incomparable; shells can be scavenged in keyhole coves in calm weather; whales spout offshore during winter; and threatened native plants flourish. It's a trek that will change your mind about O'ahu being "too crowded."

Catching a Wave

(E) Taking a surfing lesson from a well-muscled beach boy has been a Honolulu must-do since the first gay divorcée stepped off the first cruise ship. Waikīkī, with its well-shaped but diminutive waves, remains the perfect spot for *grommets* (surfing newbies), though surf schools operate at beaches (and many hotels) around the island. Most companies guarantee at least one standing ride in the course of a lesson. And catching that first wave? We guarantee you'll never forget it.

Exploring Chinatown

(F) Chinatown is like one of those centerpiece lazy Susans: Turn it this way, and you find one thing; turn it another, and there's something else. Each of the various guided tours of this compact and busy neighborhood offers up a different dish: One focuses on food and restaurants, another shines a light on cultural attractions, and the occasional architect-led AIA Tour delves into the area's design character. Take your pick or wander on your own. Just don't miss this unique mixed plate.

Hula with Heart

(G) Professional hula dancers—the ones in poolside hotel shows and dinner extravaganzas—are perfection: hands like undulating waves, smiles that never waiver. But if you want to experience hula with heart, scan the newspapers for a hula

school fund-raiser, or ask the activities desk about local festivals. You may see some missteps and bumbles, but you'll also experience different hula styles and hear songs and chants deeply rooted in the culture, all the while surrounded by the scents of a hundred homemade lei.

A Sail on the Wild Side

(H) Who wouldn't want these memory snapshots to take home: the unblinking and seemingly amused eye of a spinner dolphin as it arcs through the wake of the catamaran in which you're riding; the undulating form of an endangered green sea turtle swimming below you; the slap and splash and whoosh of a humpback whale breaching in full view on indigo seas. Wild Side Specialty Tours can't promise these specific encounters, but their ecologically conscious daily excursions in a quiet, uncrowded catamaran do guarantee good memories.

A Day on the North Shore

(I) "Hanohano Hale'iwa," the song says—beautiful Hale'iwa. Also fun, funky, fast-moving, family-friendly, Hale'iwa is an easy place in which to while away half a day. Visit the quirky surf museum, wander through the surf shops, choose from half a dozen good but cheap restaurants, suck up some refreshing shave ice, find one-of-a-kind clothes and gifts, and charter a catamaran or fishing boat. Then head back the long way to town (along the east side of the island) by way of a route that takes you past world-renowned surf spots.

A Trip to Japan

(J) Little known outside O'ahu's growing community of Japanese nationals is a class of small restaurant/bars called *izakaya,* or Japanese taverns. Even newer on the scene are *okonomi,* hip spots that specialize in Osaka-style grilled omelets and potent Japanese spirits. Both are like a visit to Japan, minus the long plane ride, and,

1

though pricey, the à la carte menus are unfailingly excellent—if distinctly odd—a must-notch in any foodie's belt.

A Plate-Lunch Picnic

(K) Take a break the way the locals do: Get a *plate lunch* (typically meat with two scoops of macaroni salad and two scoops of rice), then find a park or beach. Don't pack a ton of stuff, don't stick to a schedule. Eat, *talk story* (local slang for chatting), take a nap, or people watch—then explore, walk, swim, or snorkel. Some options: Mitsu-Ken Catering, then a picnic on the grounds of the nearby Bishop Museum; Fukuya Delicatessen, then Kāhala Beach Park; Diamond Head Market and Grill, then Waikīkī Beach or Kapi'olani Park; L&L Drive-Inn, then Kailua Beach.

Walking in the Rain Forest or to a Waterfall

Wend your way through the hillside neighborhood of 'Aiea, northwest of Honolulu, and suddenly you're in a cool, green park, scented with astringent eucalyptus. This is the 3½-mi 'Aiea Loop Trail, and if you're committed to squeezing a hike into a short O'ahu stay, you couldn't do better for glimpses of hidden valleys and the experience of an island forest.

(L) If waterfalls are more your speed, then head straight to the back of Mānoa Valley, 3 mi *mauka* (toward the mountains from Waikīkī) and you'll find a 1½-mi trail along a well-worn path following Mānoa stream through native trees and flowers to the Mānoa Falls.

GREAT ITINERARIES

To experience even a fraction of O'ahu's charms, you need a minimum of four days and a bus pass. Five days and a car is better: Waikīkī is at least a day, Honolulu and Chinatown another, Pearl Harbor the better part of another. Each of the rural sections can swallow a day each, just for driving, sightseeing, and stopping to eat. And that's before you've taken a surf lesson, hung from a parasail, hiked a loop trail, or visited a botanical garden. The following itineraries will take you to our favorite spots on the island.

First Day in Waikīkī

You'll be up at dawn due to the time change and dead on your feet by afternoon due to jet lag. Have a dawn swim, change into walking gear, and head east along Kalākaua Avenue to Monsarrat Avenue, and climb Diamond Head. After lunch, nap in the shade, do some shopping, or visit the nearby East Honolulu neighborhoods of Mō'ili'ili and Kaimukī, rife with small shops and good little restaurants. End the day with an early, interesting, and inexpensive dinner at one of these neighborhood spots.

Southeast and Windward Exploring

For sand, sun, and surf, follow H1 east to keyhole-shaped Hanauma Bay for picture-perfect snorkeling, then round the southeast tip of the island with its windswept cliffs and the famous Hālona Blowhole. Fly a kite or watch bodysurfers at Sandy Beach. Take in Sea Life Park. In Waimānalo, stop for local-style plate lunch, or punch on through to Kailua, where there's intriguing shopping and good eating.

The North Shore

Hit H1 westbound and then H2 to get to the North Shore. You'll pass through pineapple country, then drop down a scenic winding road to Waialua and Hale'iwa. Stop in Hale'iwa town to shop, to experience shave ice, and to pick up a guided dive or snorkel trip. On winding Kamehameha Highway, stop at famous big-wave beaches, take a dip in a cove with a turtle, and buy fresh Island fruit at roadside stands.

Pearl Harbor

Pearl Harbor is almost an all-day investment. Be on the grounds by 7:30 AM to line up for USS *Arizona* Memorial tickets. Clamber all over the USS *Bowfin* submarine. Finally, take the free trolley to see the "Mighty Mo" battleship. If it's Wednesday or Saturday, make the five-minute drive *mauka* (toward the mountains) for bargain-basement shopping at the sprawling Aloha Stadium Swap Meet.

Town Time

If you are interested in history, devote a day to Honolulu's historic sites. Downtown, see 'Iolani Palace, the Kamehameha Statue, and Kawaiaha'o Church. A few blocks east, explore Chinatown, gilded Kuan Yin Temple, and artsy Nu'uanu with its galleries. On the water is the informative Hawai'i Maritime Center. Hop west on H1 to the Bishop Museum, the state's anthropological and archaeological center. And 1 mi up Pali Highway is Queen Emma Summer Palace, whose shady grounds were a royal retreat. The Foster Botanical Garden is worth a visit for plant lovers.

THE HAWAIIAN ISLANDS

O'ahu. The state's capital, Honolulu, is on O'ahu; this is the center of Hawai'i's economy and by far the most populated island in the chain—900,000 residents add up to 71% of the state's population. At 597 square mi, O'ahu is the third-largest island in the chain; most residents live in or around Honolulu, so the rest of the island still fits neatly into the tropical, untouched vision of Hawai'i. Situated southeast of Kaua'i and northwest of Maui, O'ahu is a central location for island hopping. Surfing contests on the legendary North Shore, in Pearl Harbor, and on iconic Waikīkī Beach are all here.

Maui. The second-largest island in the chain, Maui is northwest of the Big Island and close enough to be visible from its beaches on a clear day. The island's 729 square mi are home to only 119,000 people but host approximately 2.5 million tourists every year. With its restaurants and lively nightlife, Maui is the only island that competes with O'ahu in terms of entertainment. Its charm lies in that, although entertainment is available, Maui's towns still feel like island villages compared to the heaving modern city of Honolulu.

Hawai'i (The Big Island). The Big Island has the second-largest population of the Islands (167,000) but feels sparsely settled due to its size. It's 4,038 square mi and growing—all the other islands could fit onto the Big Island, and there would still be room left over. The southernmost island in the chain (slightly southeast of Maui), the Big Island is home to Kīlauea, the most active volcano on the planet. It percolates within Volcanoes National Park, which draws 2.5 million visitors every year.

Kaua'i. The northernmost island in the chain (northwest of O'ahu), Kaua'i is, at approximately 550 square mi, the fourth-largest of all the Islands and the least populated of the larger islands, with just under 63,000 residents. Known as the Garden Isle, Kaua'i claims the title "Wettest Spot on Earth," with an annual average rainfall of about 450 inches. The island is a favorite with honeymooners and others wanting to get away from it all—lush and peaceful, it's the perfect escape from the modern world.

Moloka'i. North of Lāna'i and Maui, and east of O'ahu, Moloka'i is Hawai'i's fifth-largest island, encompassing 260 square mi. On a clear night, the lights of Honolulu are visible from Moloka'i's western shore. Moloka'i is sparsely populated, with just under 7,400 residents, the majority of whom are native Hawaiians. Most of the island's 85,000 annual visitors travel from Maui or O'ahu to spend the day exploring its beaches, cliffs, and former leper colony on Kalaupapa Peninsula.

Lāna'i. Lying just off Maui's western coast, Lāna'i looks nothing like its sister islands, with pine trees and deserts in place of palm trees and beaches. Still, the tiny 140-square-mi island is home to nearly 3,000 residents and draws an average of 90,000 visitors each year to two resorts (one in the mountains and one at the shore), both operated by Four Seasons.

Hawai'i's Geology

The Hawaiian Islands consist of more than just the islands inhabited and visited by humans. A total of 19 islands and atolls constitute the State of Hawai'i, with a total land mass of 6,423.4 square mi.

The Islands are actually exposed peaks of a submersed mountain range called the Hawaiian Ridge-Emperor Seamounts

chain. The range was formed as the Pacific Plate moved very slowly (about 32 mi every million years) over a hot spot in the earth's mantle. Because the plate moved northwestwardly, the Islands in the northwest portion of the archipelago are older, which is also why they're smaller—they have been eroding longer.

The Big Island is the youngest, and thus the largest, island in the chain. It is built from seven different volcanoes, including Mauna Loa, which is the largest shield volcano on the planet. Mauna Loa and Kīlauea are the only Hawaiian volcanoes still erupting with any sort of frequency. Mauna Loa last erupted in 1984. Kīlauea has been continuously erupting since 1983.

Mauna Kea (Big Island), Hualālai (Big Island), and Haleakalā (Maui) are all in what's called the postshield stage of volcanic development—eruptions decrease steadily for up to 250,000 years before ceasing entirely. Kohala (Big Island), Lāna'i (Lāna'i), and Wai'anae (O'ahu) are considered extinct volcanoes, in the erosional stage of development; Ko'olau (O'ahu) and West Maui (Maui) volcanoes are extinct volcanoes in the rejuvenation stage—after lying dormant for hundreds of thousands of years, they began erupting again, but only once every several thousand years.

There is currently an active undersea volcano called Lo'ihi that has been erupting regularly. If it continues its current pattern, it should breach the ocean's surface in tens of thousands of years.

Hawai'i's Flora and Fauna

Hawai'i boasts 11 of the world's 13 climates. The Islands have wine-growing regions, cactus-speckled ranchlands, icy mountaintops, and rainforests.

More than 90% of Hawaiian plants and animals are endemic, like the koa tree and the yellow hibiscus. Long-dormant volcanic craters are perfect hiding places for rare native plants. The silversword, a rare cousin of the sunflower, grows on Hawai'i's three tallest peaks—Haleakalā, Mauna Kea, and Mauna Loa—and nowhere else on Earth. 'Ōhi'a trees—thought to be the favorite of Pele, the volcano goddess—bury their roots in fields of once-molten lava and sprout ruby pom-pom-like lehua blossoms. The deep yellow petals of 'ilima (once reserved for royalty) are tiny discs, which make the most elegant lei.

Most of the plants you see while walking around aren't Hawaiian at all but came from Tahitian, Samoan, or European visitors. Plumeria creeps over all of the Islands; orchids run rampant on the Big Island; bright orange 'ilima light up the mountains of O'ahu. These flowers give the Hawaiian lei their color and fragrance.

Hawai'i's state bird, the nēnē goose, is making a comeback from its former endangered status. It roams freely in parts of Maui, Kaua'i, and the Big Island. Rare Hawaiian monk seals breed in the northwestern Islands. With only 1,500 left in the wild, you probably won't catch many lounging on the beaches, though they have been spotted on the shores of Kaua'i in recent years. Spinner dolphins and sea turtles can be found off the coast of all the Islands; and every year from December to May, the humpback whales migrate to Hawai'i in droves.

WHEN TO GO

Long days of sunshine and fairly mild year-round temperatures make Hawai'i an all-season destination. Most resort areas are at sea level, with average afternoon temperatures of 75°F to 80°F during the coldest months of December and January; during the hottest months of August and September, the temperature often reaches 90°F. Higher upcountry elevations typically have cooler and often misty conditions. Only at mountain summits does it reach freezing.

Moist trade winds drop their precipitation on the north and east sides of the Islands, creating tropical climates, whereas the south and west sides remain hot and dry with desert-like conditions. Rainfall can be high in winter, particularly on the north and east shores.

Most travelers head to the Islands in winter, specifically from mid-December through mid-April. This high season means that fewer travel bargains are available; room rates average 10% to 15% higher during this season than the rest of the year.

Winter on O'ahu is whales (November through March) and waves (surf competitions December through February). In September, the Aloha Festivals celebrate island culture. In summer, the Islands honor the king who made them a nation, Kamehameha I, on June 11, with parades and events on all islands. O'ahu's one-of-a-kind Pan-Pacific Festival follows the Kamehameha Day, bringing together hundreds of performers from Japan's seasonal celebrations.

Hawaiian Holidays

If you happen to be in the Islands on March 26 or June 11, you'll notice light traffic and busy beaches—these are state holidays not celebrated anywhere else.

March 26 recognizes the birthday of Prince Jonah Kūhiō Kalaniana'ole, a member of the royal line who served as a delegate to Congress and spearheaded the effort to set aside homelands for Hawaiian people. June 11 honors the first island-wide monarch, Kamehameha I; locals drape his statues with lei and stage elaborate parades. May 1 isn't an official holiday, but it's the day when schools and civic groups celebrate the quintessential Island gift, the flower lei, with lei-making contests and pageants. Statehood Day is celebrated on the third Friday in August (admission to the Union was August 21, 1959). Most Japanese and Chinese holidays are widely observed. On Chinese New Year, homes and businesses sprout bright red good-luck mottoes, lions dance in the streets, and everybody eats *gau* (steamed pudding) and *jai* (vegetarian stew). Good Friday is a state holiday in spring, a favorite for family picnics.

Climate

The following are average maximum and minimum temperatures for Honolulu; the temperatures throughout the Hawaiian Islands are similar.

HAWAIIAN HISTORY

Hawaiian history is long and complex; a brief survey can put into context the ongoing renaissance of native arts and culture.

The Polynesians

Long before both Christopher Columbus and the Vikings, Polynesian seafarers set out to explore the vast stretches of the open ocean in double-hulled canoes. From western Polynesia, they traveled back and forth between Samoa, Fiji, Tahiti, the Marquesas, and the Society Isles, settling on the outer reaches of the Pacific, Hawaiʻi, and Easter Island, as early as AD 300. The golden era of Polynesian voyaging peaked around AD 1200, after which the distant Hawaiian Islands were left to develop their own unique cultural practices and subsistence in relative isolation.

The Islands' symbiotic society was deeply intertwined with religion, mythology, science and artistry. Ruled by an *aliʻi*, or chief, each settlement was nestled in an *ahupuaʻa*, a pyramid-like land division from the uplands where the aliʻi lived, through the valleys and down to the shores where the commoners resided. Everyone contributed, whether it was by building canoes, catching fish, making tools, or farming land.

A United Kingdom

When the British explorer Captain James Cook arrived in 1778, he was revered as a god upon his arrival and later killed over a stolen boat. With guns and ammunition purchased from Cook, the Big Island chief, Kamehameha, gained a significant advantage over the other aliʻi. He united Hawaiʻi into one kingdom in 1810, bringing an end to the frequent interisland battles that dominated Hawaiian life.

Tragically, the new kingdom was beset with troubles. Native religion was abandoned, and *kapu* (laws and regulations) were eventually abolished. The explorers brought foreign diseases with them, and within a few short years the Hawaiian population was cut in half.

New laws regarding land ownership and religious practices eroded the underpinnings of precontact Hawaii. Each successor to the Hawaiian throne sacrificed more control over the island kingdom. As Westerners permeated Hawaiian culture, Hawaii became more riddled with layers of racial issues, injustice, and social unrest.

Modern Hawaii

Finally in 1893, the last Hawaiian monarch, Queen Liliʻuokalani, was overthrown by a group of Americans and European businessmen and government officials, aided by an armed militia. This led to the creation of the Republic of Hawaiʻi, and it became a U.S. territory for the next 60 years. The loss of Hawaiian sovereignty and the conditions of annexation have haunted the Hawaiian people since the monarchy was toppled.

Pearl Harbor was attacked in 1941, which engaged the United States immediately into World War II. Tourism, from its beginnings in the early 1900s, flourished after the war and naturally inspired rapid real estate development in Waikīkī. In 1959, Hawaiʻi officially became the 50th state. Statehood paved the way for Hawaiians and Hawaiʻi's immigrants to participate in the American democratic process.

HAWAIIAN PEOPLE AND THEIR CULTURE

By July 2009, Hawai'i's population was more than 1.3 million with the majority of residents living on O'ahu. Twenty-five percent are Hawaiian or part Hawaiian, more than 40% are Asian-American, and about 20% Caucasian. More than a fifth of the population list two or more races, making Hawai'i the most diverse state in the United States. Among individuals 18 and older, about 89% finished high school, half attained some college, and a little shy of 30% completed a bachelor's degree or higher.

The Role of Tradition

The kingdom of Hawaii was ruled by a spiritual class system. Although the *ali'i*, or chief, was believed to be the direct descendent of a deity or god, the high priest, known as the *kahuna*, presided over every imaginable life ceremony and *kapu* that strictly governed the commoners. Each part of nature and ritual was connected to a deity—Kane was the highest of all deities, symbolizing sunlight and creation; Ku was the god of war; Lono represented fertility, rainfall, music, and peace; Kanaloa was the god of the underworld or darker spirits; and there is Pele, the goddess of fire. The kapu not only provided social order, they also swayed the people to act with reverence for the environment. Any abuse was met with extreme punishment, often death, as it put the land and people's *mana*, or spiritual power, in peril.

Ancient deities play a huge role in Hawaiian life today—not just in daily rituals, but in the Hawaiians' reverence for their land. Gods and goddesses tend to be associated with particular parts of the land, and most of them are connected with many places, thanks to the body of stories built up around each.

One of the most important ways the ancient Hawaiians showed respect for their gods and goddesses was through the hula. Various forms of the hula were performed as prayers to the gods and as praise to the chiefs. Performances were taken very seriously, as a mistake was thought to invalidate the prayer, or even to offend the god or chief in question. Hula is still performed both as entertainment and as prayer; it is not uncommon for a hula performance to be included in an official government ceremony.

Who Are the Hawaiians Today?

To define the Hawaiians in a page, let alone a paragraph, is nearly impossible. First, there are Hawaiians by residence, similar to Californians, New Yorkers, or Texans. Those considered to be indigenous Hawaiians are descendents of the ancient Polynesians who crossed the vast ocean and settled Hawai'i. According to the government, there are Native Hawaiians or native hawaiians (note the change in capitalization) depending on their blood makeup.

Federal and state agencies apply different methods to determine Hawaiian lineage, from measuring blood percentage to mapping genealogy. This has caused turmoil within the community for the simple fact that it excludes so many. It almost guarantees that, as races intermingle, even those considered Native Hawaiian now will eventually disappear on paper, displacing generations to come.

Modern Hawaiian Culture

Perfect weather aside, Hawai'i might be the warmest place anyone can visit. The Hawai'i experience begins and ends with *aloha*, a word that envelops love, affection, and mercy, and has become a salutation for hello and goodbye. Broken down,

alo means "presence" and *ha* means "breath"—the presence of breath. It's to live with love and respect for self and others with every breath. Past the manicured resorts and tour buses, aloha is a spirit and moral compass that binds all of Hawai'i's people.

Hawaiians have been blessed with some of the most unspoiled natural wonders, and aloha extends to the land, or *'aina*. People are raised outdoors and have strong ties to nature. They realize as children that the ocean and land are the delicate source of all life. Even ancient gods were embodied by nature, and this reverence has been passed down to present generations who believe in *kuleana,* their privilege and responsibility.

Hawaiians' diverse cultures unfold in a beautiful montage of customs and arts—including music, to dance, to food. Musical genres range from slack key to *Jawaiian* (Hawaiian reggae) to *hapa-haole* (Hawaiian music with English words). From George Kahumoku's Grammy-worthy laid-back strumming, to the late Iz Kamakawiwo'ole's "Somewhere over the Rainbow," to Jack Johnson's more mainstream tunes, contemporary Hawaiian music has definitely carved its ever-evolving niche. The Merrie Monarch Festival is celebrating almost 50 years of worldwide hula competition and education. The fine-dining culinary scene, especially in Honolulu, has a rich tapestry of ethnic influences and talent. But the real gems are the humble hole-in-the-wall eateries that serve authentic cuisines of many ethnic origins in one plate, a deliciously mixed plate indeed.

And perhaps, the most striking quality in today's Hawaiian culture is the sense of family, or *ohana*. Sooner or later, almost everyone you meet becomes an uncle or auntie, and it is not uncommon for near-strangers to be welcomed into a home as a member of the family. Until the late 1950s, the practice of *hanai*, in which a family essentially adopts a child, usually a grandchild, without formalities, was still prevalent. The *hanai*, which means to feed or nourish, still resonates within most families and communities.

How to Act Like a Local

Adopting local customs is a firsthand introduction to the Islands' unique culture. So live in T-shirts and shorts. Wear cheap rubber flip-flops, but call them slippers. Wave people into your lane on the highway, and, when someone lets you in, give them a wave of thanks in return. Never, ever blow your horn, even when the pickup truck in front of you is stopped for a long session of "talk story" right in the middle of the road.

Holoholo means to go out for the fun of it—an aimless stroll, ride, or drive. "Wheah you goin', braddah?" "Oh, holoholo." It's local-speak for Sunday drive, no plan, it's not the destination but the journey. Try setting out without an itinerary. Learn to *shaka*: pinky and thumb extended, middle fingers curled in, waggle sideways. Eat white rice with everything. When someone says, "Aloha!" answer, "Aloha no!" ("And a real big aloha back to you"). And, as the locals say, "No make big body" ("Try not to act like you own the place").

KIDS AND FAMILIES

With dozens of adventures, discoveries, and fun-filled beach days, Hawai'i is a blast with kids. Even better, the things to do here do not appeal only to small fry. The entire family, parents included, will enjoy surfing, discovering a waterfall in the rain forest, and snorkeling with sea turtles. And there are plenty of organized activities for kids that will free parents' time for a few romantic beach strolls.

Choosing a Place to Stay

Resorts: All the big resorts make kids' programs a priority, and it shows. When you are booking your room, ask about "kids eat free" deals and the number of kids' pools at the resort. Also check out the size of the groups in the children's programs, and find out whether the cost of the programs includes lunch, equipment, and activities.

In Waikīkī, your best bet for kids is the Hilton Hawaiian Village, where there's a large beach and loads of kids' programs. Another good choice is the Waikīkī Beach Marriott Resort, which has a variety of programs for kids as well. Other options include the Waikīkī Beach Hotel and the Sheraton Princess Kaiulani.

Condos: Condo and vacation rentals are a fantastic value for families vacationing in Hawai'i. You can cook your own food, which is cheaper than eating out and sometimes easier (especially if you have a finicky eater in your group), and you'll get twice the space of a hotel room for about a quarter of the price. If you decide to go the condo route, be sure to ask about the size of the complex's pool (some try to pawn off a tiny soaking tub as a pool) and whether barbecues are available. One of the best parts of staying in your own place is having a sunset family barbecue by the pool or overlooking the ocean.

For the ultimate condo experience on O'ahu, Marriott's Ko Olina Beach Club can't be beat. Sheltered beaches, four pools, barbecues, and children's play areas, combined with large kitchens and an on-site grocery store make this the best condo option for families. In Waikīkī, the Castle Waikīkī Shore is the only beachfront condo property. Outrigger Luana offers barbecues, a pool, and recreational areas near Fort DeRussy on Waikīkī Beach.

Ocean Activities

Hawai'i is all about getting your kids outside—away from TV and video games. And who could resist the turquoise water, the promise of spotting dolphins or whales, and the fun of Boogie boarding or surfing?

On the Beach: Most people like being in the water, but toddlers and school-age kids tend to be especially enamored of it. The swimming pool at your condo or hotel is always an option, but don't be afraid to hit the beach with a little one in tow. There are several beaches in Hawai'i that are nearly as safe as a pool—completely protected bays with pleasant white-sand beaches. As always, use your judgment, and heed all posted signs and lifeguard warnings.

In Waikīkī, your best bets for young children are Kūhiō Beach Park and Fort DeRussy Beach Park. Both have water protected from a strong shore break and a wide stretch of sand. On the Windward side, your best bets are Kailua Beach Park with its shade trees and good bathroom and shower facilities or ultracalm Lanikai Beach. North Shore beaches are recommended for children only in the summer months, and of these, Waimea Bay's wide stretch of sand and good facilities ranks

as the best for kids. On the Leeward side of the island, Kō'Ōlina's protected beaches are great for families with small children.

On the Waves: Surf lessons are a great idea for older kids, especially if mom and dad want a little quiet time. Beginner lessons are always on safe and easy waves and last anywhere from two to four hours.

Waikīkī is *the* place for everyone to learn to surf, including kids. Some hotels, including the Waikīkī Beach Marriott Resort & Spa, offer in-house surf schools. Or, for a unique experience, try Hawaiian Fire, Inc. These off-duty Honolulu firefighters teach water safety in addition to surfing in their two-hour lessons near Barber's Point (starting at $97).

The Underwater World: If your kids are ready to try snorkeling, Hawai'i is a great place to introduce them to the underwater world. Even without the mask and snorkel, they'll be able to see colorful fish darting this way and that, and they may also spot turtles and dolphins at many of the island beaches.

On O'ahu the quintessential snorkeling experience can be had at Hanauma Bay. After viewing an educational film about Hawai'i's underwater world, and descending into a half-submerged volcano, kids have an opportunity not only to see hundreds of species of fish in protected waters but to enjoy a wide stretch of beach as well. In summer months only, Shark's Cove on the North Shore is an interesting experience for older kids who have learned the basics of snorkeling at Hanauma Bay.

Land Activities

In addition to beach experiences, Hawai'i has rain forests, botanical gardens, numerous aquariums (O'ahu and Maui take the cake), and even petting zoos and hands-on children's museums that will keep your kids entertained and out of the sun for a day.

O'ahu is fortunate to have the largest variety of land-based experiences in the Islands. Kids can visit the Honolulu Zoo for a sleepover, touch fishy friends at the Waikīkī Aquarium, help in a dolphin training session at Sea Life Park, or even learn to husk a coconut at the Polynesian Culture Center. For kids who need some room to roam, Ho'omaluhia Botanical Garden offers wide-open spaces and a pond complete with ducks, while Kualoa Ranch is the place for horseback riding.

After Dark

At night, younger kids get a kick out of lū'au, and many of the shows incorporate young audience members, adding to the fun. The older kids might find it all a bit lame, but there is a handful of new shows in the Islands that are more modern, incorporating acrobatics, lively music, and fire dancers. If you're planning on hitting a lū'au with a teen in tow, we highly recommend going the modern route.

Cirque du Soleil's Waikīkī production will keep even teens in your family entertained, while the Paradise Cove Lū'au offers fire dancers and kid-friendly games.

O'AHU'S BEST BEACHES

Just as there are many different words for the many kinds of rain in Hawai'i, there are numerous kinds of beaches: rocky, coral rubble, and white-, green- and black-sand. Some beaches require a hike; others you can drive to. Some are in the city, others in the country. The end result: There's one—or more—just right for you.

Makapu'u Beach

This beach boasts O'ahu's possibly most breathtaking scenic view—with a hiking trail to an historic lighthouse, offshore views of two rocky islets that are home to thousands of nesting seabirds, and hang gliders launching off nearby cliffs.

Although the white-sand beach and surroundings adorn many postcards, the treacherous ocean's currents invite experienced body boarders only.

Word of Mouth: "I thought the beaches on the East Shore/SE side of Oahu were positively stunning. Makapu'u Beach Park was gorgeous. Looks like you could get there by the #22 bus from Waikīkī." —Andrew

Kailua Beach Park

This is a true family beach, offering something for everyone: a long stretch of sand for walking, turquoise seas set against cobalt skies for impressive photographs, a sandy-bottom shoreline for ocean swimming, and grassy expanses underneath shade trees for picnics.

You can even rent a kayak and make the short paddle to Popia (Flat) Island. This is windward O'ahu, so expect wind—all the better if you're an avid windsurfer or kiteboarder.

Word of Mouth: "Kailua Bay is my favorite place in the world so far, let alone Hawaii." —karameli

Waimea Bay

This is the beach that makes Hawai'i famous every winter when monster waves and the world's best surfers roll in. Show up to watch, not partake. If the rest of us want to get in the water here, we have to wait until summer when the safe on-shore break is great for novice bodysurfers.

Word of Mouth: "Waimea Beach Park. The view of the curved bay with the tower of St. Peter and Paul Catholic Mission in the background is awesome. If the lot fills up quickly on the weekend, there's roadside parking. Waimea is usually where the best of the best come to surf the big waves but that's usually in the winter." —tina

White Plains

This beach is equal parts Kailua Beach Park, with its facilities and tree-shaded barbecue areas, and Waikīkī, with its numerous surf breaks—minus the crowds and high-rises.

Pack for the day—cooler with food and drink, snorkel gear, inflatables, and body board—as this destination is 35 minutes from downtown Honolulu.

TOP 10 HAWAIIAN FOODS TO TRY

Food in Hawai'i reflects the state's diverse cultural makeup and tropical location. Fresh seafood, organic fruits and vegetables, free-range poultry and meat, and locally grown products are the hallmarks of Hawai'i regional cuisine. Its preparations are drawn from across the Pacific Rim, including Japan, the Philippines, Korea, and Thailand—and now, "Hawaiian food" is a cuisine in its own right.

Saimin

The ultimate hangover cure and the perfect comfort food during Hawai'i's mild winters, *saimin* ranks at the top of the list of local favorites. In fact, it's one of the few dishes deemed truly local, having been highlighted in cookbooks since the 1930s. *Saimin* is an Asian-style noodle soup so ubiquitous, it's even on McDonald's menus statewide. In mom-and-pop shops, a large melamine bowl is filled with homemade *dashi* (Japanese soup stock) or chicken broth and wheat-flour noodles and then topped off with strips of omelet, green onions, bright pink fish cake, and *char siu* (Chinese roast pork) and/or canned luncheon meat, such as SPAM. Add *shoyu* (soy sauce) and chili pepper water, lift your chopsticks, and slurp away.

SPAM

Speaking of SPAM, Hawaii's most prevalent grab-and-go snack is SPAM *musubi*. Often displayed next to cash registers at groceries and convenience stores, the glorified rice ball is rectangular, topped with a slice of fried SPAM and wrapped in *nori* (seaweed). Introduced back in the plantation days by Japanese field workers, musubi is a minimeal in itself. But just like sushi, the rice part hardens when refrigerated. So it's best to gobble it up right after purchase.

Hormel Company's SPAM actually deserves its own recognition—way beyond a mere musubi topping. About five million cans are sold per year in Hawaii and the Aloha State even hosts a festival in its honor. One local claims she can stretch a can of SPAM into three separate meals for a family of five. The spiced luncheon meat gained popularity in World War II days, when fish was rationed. Gourmets and those with aversions to salt, high cholesterol, and high blood pressure may cringe at the thought of eating it, but SPAM is here to stay in Hawai'i.

Manapua

Another savory snack is *manapua*, fist-sized dough balls fashioned after Chinese *bao* (bun) and stuffed with fillings such as char siu pork and then steamed. Many mom-and-pop stores sell them in commercial steamer display cases along with pork hash and other dim sum. Modern-day fillings include curry chicken.

Fresh 'Ahi or Tako

There's nothing like fresh 'ahi or *tako* (octopus) *poke* to break the ice at a backyard party, except, of course, the cold beer handed to you from the cooler. The perfect pūpū, *poke* (pronounced poh-kay) is basically raw seafood cut into bite-size chunks and mixed with everything from green onions to roasted and ground kukui nuts. Other variations include round onion, sesame oil, seaweed, and chili pepper water. Shoyu is the constant. These days, grocery stores sell a rainbow of varieties such as kim chee crab and anything goes, from adding mayonnaise to tobiko caviar. Fish lovers who want to take it to the next level order sashimi, the best cuts of 'ahi sliced and dipped in a mixture of shoyu and wasabi.

Tropical Fruits

Tropical fruits such as apple banana and strawberry papaya are plucked from trees in island neighborhoods and eaten for breakfast—plain or with a squeeze of fresh lime. Locals also love to add their own creative touches to exotic fruits. Green mangoes are pickled with Chinese five-spice powder, Maui Gold pineapples are topped with *li hing mui* (salty dried plum) powder (heck, even margarita glasses are rimmed with it!). Green papaya is tossed in a Vietnamese salad with fish paste and fresh prawns.

Plate Lunch

It would be remiss not to mention the plate lunch as one of the most beloved dishes in Hawai'i. It generally always includes two scoops of white steamed rice; a side of macaroni and/or macaroni-potato salad, heavy on the mayo; and perhaps *kimchee* or *koko* (salted cabbage). There are countless choices of main protein, such as chicken katsu, fried mahimahi, and beef tomato. The king of all plate lunches is the Hawaiian plate. The main item is *laulau* (pork, beef, and fish or chicken with taro leaves wrapped and steamed in ti leaves) or kalua pig and cabbage along with poi, lomilomi salmon, chicken long rice, and steamed white rice.

Bento Box

The bento box gained popularity back in the plantation days, when workers toiled in the sugarcane fields. No one brought sandwiches to work then. Instead it was a lunch box with the ever-present steamed white rice, pickled *ume* (plum) to preserve the rice, and main meats such as fried chicken or fish. In the Hawai'i of today, many stores sell prepackaged bentos, or you may go to an *okazuya* (Japanese tavern) with a hot buffet counter and create your own.

Malasadas

The Portuguese have contributed much to Hawaiian cuisine in the form of sausage, soup, and sweetbread. But their most revered food is *malasadas*, hot, deep-fried doughnuts rolled in sugar. Malasadas are crowd pleasers. Buy them by the dozen, hot from the wok and placed in brown bags to absorb the grease. Or bite into gourmet malasadas at restaurants, filled with vanilla or chocolate cream.

Shave Ice

Much more than just a snow cone, shave ice is what locals crave after a blazing day at the beach or a hot-as-hades game of soccer. If you're lucky, you'll find a neighborhood store that hand-shaves the ice, but it's rare. Either way, the counter person will ask you first if you'd like ice cream and/or adzuki beans scooped into the bottom of the cone or cup. Then they shape the ice into a giant mound and add colorful fruit syrups. First-timers should order the Rainbow, of course.

Crack Seed

There are dozens of varieties of crack seed in dwindling specialty shops and at drugstores. Chinese call the preserved fruits and nuts "see mui" but somehow the pidgin English version is what Hawaiians prefer. Those who like hard candy and salty foods will love li hing mangoes and rock salt plums, and those with an itchy throat will feel relief from the lemon strips. Peruse large glass jars of crack seed sold in bulk or smaller hanging bags—the latter make good gifts for friends back home.

HAWAI'I AND THE ENVIRONMENT

Sustainability. It's a word rolling off everyone's tongues these days. In a place known as one of the most remote on Earth (check your globe), Hawai'i is relies heavily on the outside world for food and material goods—estimates put the percentage of food arriving on container ships as high as 90. Like many places, though, efforts are afoot to change that. And you can help.

Shop Local Farms and Markets

From Hilo to Hanalei, farmers' markets are cropping up, providing a place for growers to sell fresh fruits and vegetables. There is no reason to buy imported mangoes, papayas, avocadoes, and bananas at grocery stores, when the ones you'll find at farmers' markets are not only fresher and bigger but tastier, too. Some markets allow the sale of fresh-packaged foods— salsa, say, or smoothies—and the on-site preparation of food—like pork laulau or roasted corn on the cob—so you can make your run to the market a dining experience.

Not only is the locavore movement vibrantly alive at farmers' markets, but Hawai'i's top chefs are sourcing more of their produce—and fish, beef, chicken, and cheese—from local providers as well. You'll notice this movement on restaurant menus, featuring Ki'lauea greens or Hamakua tomatoes or locally caught mahimahi.

And while most people are familiar with Kona coffee farm tours on Big Island, if you're interested in the growing slow-food movement in Hawai'i, you'll be heartened to know many farmers are opening up their operations for tours—as well as sumptuous meals.

Support Hawai'i's Merchants

Food isn't the only sustainable effort in Hawai'i. Buying local goods like art and jewelry, Hawaiian heritage products, crafts, music, and apparel is another way to "green up" the local economy. The County of Kaua'i helps make it easy with their Kaua'i Made program (⊕ www.kauaimade.net), which showcases products made on Kaua'i, by Kaua'i people, using Kaua'i materials. The Maui Chamber of Commerce does something similar with its Made in Maui program (⊕ www.madeinmaui.com). Think of both as the Good Housekeeping Seal of Approval for locally made goods.

Then there the crafty entrepreneurs who are diverting items from the trash heap by repurposing garbage. Take Muumuu Heaven (⊕ www.muumuuheaven.com) on O'ahu. They got their start by reincarnating vintage aloha apparel into hip new fashions. Kini Beach (⊕ www.Kinibeach.com) collects discarded grass mats and plastic inflatables from Waikīkī hotels and uses them to make pricey bags and totes.

Choose Green Tour Operators

Conscious decisions when it comes to island activities go a long way to protecting Hawai'i's natural world. The Hawai'i Ecotourism Association (⊕ www.hawaiiecotourism.org) recognizes tour operators for, among other things, their environmental stewardship. The Hawai'i Tourism Authority (⊕ www.hawaiitourismauthority.org) recognizes outfitters for their cultural sensitivity. Winners of these awards are good choices when it comes to guided tours and activities.

O'AHU'S BEST OUTDOOR ADVENTURES

In a place surrounded by the ocean, water sports abound. Surfing. Snorkeling. Scuba diving. Hawai'i has it all—and more. But that's just the sea. Interior mountains and valleys offer a never-ending stream of other outdoor adventures. Here are our picks for the best water and land adventures.

Dive and Snorkel at Shark's Cove

Some of the best things in life require a wait. That's the case with Shark's Cove—you have to wait for summer until it's safe to enter the water and swim with an amazing array of marine life, thanks to the large boulders and coral heads dotting the seafloor and forming small caves and ledges.

This is both a spectacular shore dive and snorkeling destination in one—perfect for the diver–snorkeler couple.

Word of Mouth: "Let's see, stop at Shark's Cove, and snorkel. This is a don't-miss. Look for sea turtles there." —CindyW

Bike the 'Aiea Loop Trail

This 4.5-mile, single-track, loop trail offers some of the most fun mountain biking in central O'ahu. Although it's listed as an intermediate trail, some sections are a bit technical with steep drop-offs.

We recommend it for the weekend warrior who has a bit more experience. Caution: Do not attempt in wet weather.

Golf at Luana Hills Country Club

Carved out of the middle of a tropical rain forest, this peaceful setting offers an antidote to the hustle and bustle of Waikīkī.

Bring your A game and a full bag, because club selection is key here. You'll want to hit every fairway.

Learn to Surf at Waikīkī Beach

You've heard the age-old saying that goes, "When in Rome, do what the Romans do"? Well, when in Hawai'i, surf. The sport that was once reserved for *ali'i* (royalty) knows no class barrier these days. And there is no better place to learn than Waikīkī, with its long and gentle rolling swells.

Word of Mouth: "I had decided that the perfect last day in Waikīkī would be spent learning to surf. Waikīkī Beach has the reputation for being the best place in the world to learn to surf, and the weather was beautiful." —annabellefreddie

Hike to Ka'ena Point

For a raw and rugged look at O'ahu's coastline, head to hot, dry Ka'ena Point. The 5-mi round-trip hike—rather, walk—ends at the westernmost tip of the island, known in Hawaiian culture as the jumping-off point for souls departing this world for the next. Today, Laysan albatrosses nest here.

ONLY IN HAWAII

Traveling to Hawai'i is as close as an American can get to visiting another country while staying within the United States. There's much to learn and understand about the state's indigenous culture, the hundred years of immigration that resulted in today's blended society, and the tradition of aloha that has welcomed millions of visitors over the years.

Aloha Shirt

To go to Hawai'i without taking an aloha shirt home is almost sacrilege. The first aloha shirts from the 1920s and 1930s were classic canvases of art and tailored for the tourists. Popular culture caught on in the 1950s, and they became a fashion craze. With the 1960s' more subdued designs, the Aloha Friday was born, and the shirt became appropriate clothing for work, play, and formal occasions. Because of its soaring popularity, cheaper and mass-produced versions became available.

Hawaiian Quilt

Although ancient Hawaiians were already known to produce fine *kapa* (bark) cloth, the actual art of quilting originated from the missionaries. Hawaiians have made the designs to reflect their own aesthetic, and bold patterns evolved over time. They can be pricey, but only because the quilts are intricately made by hand and can take years to finish. These masterpieces are considered precious heirlooms that reflect the history and beauty of Hawai'i.

Popular Souvenirs

Souvenir shopping can be intimidating. There's a sea of island-inspired and often kitschy merchandise, so we'd like to give you a breakdown of popular and fun gifts that you might encounter and consider bringing home.

Hula doll. The hula dancer has been immortalized and commodified in many ways, from the classic dashboard bobble hip to the newer hula girl desktop duster.

Grass skirts and coconut bras. Sometimes bought as a set and sometimes as separates, either way this costume will definitely elicit a smile or ten at a lū'au.

Home accessories. Relive your spa treatment at home with Hawaiian bath and body products, or deck out the kitchen in festive lū'au style with bottle openers, pineapple mugs, tiki glasses, shot glasses, slipper and surfboard magnets, and salt-and-pepper shakers.

Lei and shell necklaces. From silk or polyester flower lei to kukui or puka shell necklaces, lei have been traditionally used as a welcome offering to guests (although the artificial ones are more for fun, as real flowers are always preferable).

Lauhala products. Lauhala weaving is a traditional Hawaiian art. The leaves come from the Hala or Pandanus tree and handwoven to create lovely gift boxes, baskets, bags, and picture frames.

Vintage Hawai'i. You can find vintage photos, reproductions of vintage postcards or paintings, heirloom jewelry, and vintage aloha wear in many specialty stores.

Warrior helmets. Traditionally called *makaki'i* or *makini* after ancient Hawaiian warriors, these helmets are miniature masks adorned with feathers. They're popular among a younger crowd and hung on the car's rearview mirror or doorway for protection.

Lū'au

The lū'au's origin is traced back in 1819 when King Kamehameha II broke a great taboo and shared a feast with women and commoners. The name came from

a traditional dish of chicken wrapped in taro leaves and baked in coconut milk. In the olden days, lu'au were enjoyed sitting on the floor where woven lauhala mats were laid and covered with ti leaves and tropical flowers. Platters of *kalua pu'a* (pig baked in the *imu*, or underground oven), salted fish, sweet potatoes and *poi* (pounded taro and a staple in Hawaiian cuisine) were shared in the gathering.

Over time, the hula, fire knife dance and other Polynesian dances became part of the celebration. Today, the lu'au usually commemorates a child's first birthday or graduation. Offered in many elaborate presentations, it remains a Hawaiian experience that most visitors enjoy.

Nose flutes

The nose flute is an instrument used in ancient times to serenade a lover. For the Hawaiians, the nose is romantic, sacred and pure. The Hawaiian word for kiss is *honi*. Similar to an Eskimo's kiss, the noses touch on each side sharing one's spiritual energy or breath. The Hawaiian term, *'ohe hano ihu*, simply translated to "bamboo," with which the instrument is made; "breathe," because one has to gently breathe through it to make soothing music; and "nose," as it is made for the nose and not the mouth.

Slack Key Guitar and the Paniolos

Kiho'alu, or slack key music, evolved in the early 1800s when King Kamehameha III brought in Mexican and Spanish vaqueros to manage the overpopulated cattle that had run wild on the islands. The vaqueros brought their guitars and would play music around the campfire after work. When they left, supposedly leaving their guitars to their new friends, the Hawaiian *paniolos,* or cowboys, began to infuse what they learned from

the vaqueros with their native music and chants, and so the art of slack key music was born.

Today, the paniolo culture thrives where ranchers have settled. Slack key music has also enjoyed international recognition and garnered Grammy Awards numerous times for the Hawaiian music genre.

'Ukulele

The 'ukulele or 'uke literally translates to the "the jumping flea" and came to Hawaii in the 1880s by way of the Portuguese and Spanish. Once a fading art form, today it brings international kudos as a solo instrument, thanks to tireless musicians and teachers who have worked hard to keep it by our fingertips.

One such teacher is Roy Sakuma. Founder of four 'ukulele schools and a legend in his own right, Sakuma and his wife Kathy produced O'ahu's first 'Ukulele Festival in 1971. Since then, they've brought the tradition to the Big Island, Kaua'i, and Maui. The free event annually draws thousands of artists and fans all over the globe.

Hula

"Hula is the language of the heart, therefore the heartbeat of the Hawaiian people." — Kalākaua I, the Merrie Monarch. Thousands—from tots to seniors—devote hours each week to hula classes. All these dancers need some place to show off their stuff. The result is a network of hula competitions (generally free or very inexpensive) and free performances in malls and other public spaces. Many resorts offer hula instruction or "hula-cise."

To watch hula, especially in the ancient style, is to understand that this was a sophisticated culture—skilled in many arts, including not only poetry, chant, and dance but also in constructing instruments and fashioning adornments.

WEDDINGS AND HONEYMOONS

There's no question that Hawaiʻi is one of the country's foremost honeymoon destinations. Romance is in the air here, and the white, sandy beaches and turquoise water and swaying palm trees and balmy tropical breezes and perpetual summer sunshine put people in the mood for love. It's easy to understand why Hawaiʻi is fast becoming a popular wedding destination as well, especially as the cost of airfare has gone down, and new resorts and hotels entice visitors. A destination wedding is no longer exclusive to celebrities and the superrich. You can plan a traditional ceremony in a place of worship followed by a reception at an elegant resort, or you can go barefoot on the beach and celebrate at a lūʻau. There are almost as many wedding planners in the islands as real estate agents, which makes it oh-so-easy to wed in paradise, and then, once the knot is tied, to stay and honeymoon as well.

The Big Day

Choosing the Perfect Place. When choosing a location, remember that you really have two choices to make: the ceremony location and where to have the reception, if you're having one. For the former, there are beaches, bluffs overlooking beaches, gardens, private residences, resort lawns, and, of course, places of worship. It really depends on you. As for the reception, there are these same choices, as well as restaurants and even lūʻau. If you decide to go outdoors, remember the seasons—yes, Hawaiʻi has seasons. If you're planning a winter wedding outdoors, be sure you have a backup plan (such as a tent), in case it rains. Also, if you're planning an outdoor wedding at sunset—which is very popular—be sure you match the time of your ceremony to the time the sun sets at that time of year. If you choose indoors, be sure to ask for pictures of the environs

when you're planning. You don't want to plan a pink wedding, say, and wind up in a room that's predominantly red. Or maybe you do. The point is, it should be your choice.

Finding a Wedding Planner. If you're planning to invite more than a minister and your loved one to your wedding ceremony, seriously consider an on-island wedding planner who can help select a location, help design the floral scheme and recommend a florist as well as a photographer, help plan the menu and choose a restaurant, caterer, or resort, and suggest any Hawaiian traditions to incorporate into your ceremony. And more: Will you need tents, a cake, music? Maybe transportation and lodging? Many planners have relationships with vendors, providing packages—which mean savings.

If you're planning a resort wedding, most have on-site wedding coordinators; however, there are many independents around the island and even those who specialize in certain types of ceremonies—by locale, size, religious affiliation, and so on. A simple "Hawaiʻi weddings" Google search will reveal dozens. What's important is that you feel comfortable with your coordinator. Ask for references—and call them. Share your budget. Get a proposal—in writing. Ask how long they've been in business, how much they charge, how often you'll meet with them, and how they select vendors. Request a detailed list of the exact services they'll provide. If your idea of your wedding doesn't match their services, try someone else. If you can afford it, you might want to meet the planner in person.

Getting Your License. The good news about marrying in Hawaiʻi is no waiting period, no residency or citizenship requirements,

and no blood tests or shots are required. However, both the bride and groom must appear together in person before a marriage license agent to apply for a marriage license. You'll need proof of age—the legal age to marry is 18. (If you're 19 or older, a valid driver's license will suffice; if you're 18, a certified birth certificate is required.) Upon approval, a marriage license is immediately issued and costs $60, cash only. After the ceremony, your officiant will mail the marriage license to the state. Approximately 120 days later, you will receive a copy in the mail. (For $10 extra, you can expedite this process. Ask your marriage-license agent when you apply for your license.) For more detailed information, visit ⊕ *www.hawaii.gov* or call ☎ *808/274-3100*.

Also—this is important—the person performing your wedding must be licensed by the Hawai'i Department of Health, even if he or she is a licensed minister. Be sure to ask.

Wedding Attire. In Hawai'i, basically anything goes, from long, formal dresses with trains to white bikinis. Floral sundresses are fine, too. For the men, tuxedos are not the norm; a pair of solid-colored slacks with a nice aloha shirt is. In fact, tradition in Hawai'i for the groom is a plain white aloha shirt (they do exist) with slacks or long shorts and a colored sash around the waist. If you're planning a wedding on the beach, barefoot is the way to go.

If you decide to marry in a formal dress and tuxedo, you're better off making your selections on the mainland and hand-carrying them aboard the plane. Yes, it can be a pain, but ask your wedding-gown retailer to provide a special carrying bag. After all, you don't want to chance losing your wedding dress in a wayward piece of luggage.

As for fittings, again, that's something to take care of before you arrive in Hawai'i.

Local customs. When it comes to traditional Hawaiian wedding customs, the most obvious is the lei exchange in which the bride and groom take turns placing a lei around the neck of the other—with a kiss. Bridal lei are usually floral, whereas the groom's is typically made of *maile*, a green leafy garland that drapes around the neck and is open at the ends. Brides often also wear a *haku* lei—a circular floral headpiece. Other Hawaiian customs include the blowing of the conch shell, hula, chanting, and Hawaiian music.

The Honeymoon

Do you want champagne and strawberries delivered to your room each morning? A maze of a swimming pool in which to float? A five-star restaurant in which to dine? Then a resort is the way to go. If, however, you prefer the comforts of a home, try a bed-and-breakfast. A bed-and-breakfast is also good if you're on a tight budget or don't plan to spend much time in your room. On the other hand, maybe you want your own private home in which to romp naked—or just laze around recovering from the wedding planning. Maybe you want your own kitchen in which to whip up a gourmet meal for your loved one. In that case, a private vacation-rental home is the answer. Or maybe a condominium resort. That's another beautiful thing about Hawai'i: The lodging accommodations are almost as plentiful as the beaches, and there's one to match your tastes and your budget.

CRUISING THE ISLANDS

Cruising has become extremely popular in Hawai'i. For first-time visitors, it's an excellent way to get a taste of all the islands; and if you fall in love with one or even two islands, you know how to plan your next trip. It's also a comparatively inexpensive way to see Hawai'i.

The limited amount of time in each port can be an argument against cruising—there's enough to do on any island to keep you busy for a week, so some folks feel shortchanged by cruise itineraries.

Cruising to Hawai'i

Carnival Cruises. They call them "fun ships" for a reason—Carnival is all about keeping you busy and showing you a good time, both onboard and onshore. Great for families, Carnival always plans plenty of kid-friendly activities, and their children's program rates high with the little critics. Carnival offers itineraries starting in Ensenada, Vancouver, and Honolulu. Their ships stop on Maui (Kahului and Lahaina), the Big Island (Kailua-Kona and Hilo), O'ahu, and Kaua'i. ☎ 888/227–6482 ⊕ www.carnival.com.

Holland America. The grande dame of cruise lines, Holland America has a reputation for service and elegance. Holland America's Hawai'i cruises leave and return to San Diego, California, with a brief stop at Ensenada. In Hawai'i, the ship ties up at port in Maui (Lahaina), the Big Island (Kailua-Kona and Hilo), O'ahu, and for half a day on Kaua'i. Holland America also offers longer itineraries (30-plus days) that include Hawai'i, Tahiti, and the Marquesas. ☎ 877/932–4259 ⊕ www. hollandamerica.com.

Princess Cruises. Princess strives to offer affordable luxury. Their prices start out a little higher, but you get more bells and whistles (more affordable balcony rooms, nice decor, more restaurants to choose from, personalized service). They're not fantastic for kids, but they do a great job of keeping teenagers occupied. Princess's Hawaiian cruise is 14 days, round-trip from Los Angeles, with a service call in Ensenada. The *Island Princess* stops in Maui (Lahaina), the Big Island (Hilo and Kailua-Kona), O'ahu, and Kaua'i. For the cruise-goer looking for the epic voyage, Princess Cruises offers a Sydney, Australia, to Los Angeles route, which includes stops in Hawai'i and Tahiti. ☎ 800/774–6237 ⊕ www.princess.com.

Cruising Within Hawai'i

Norwegian Cruise Lines. Norwegian is the only major operator to offer interisland cruises in Hawai'i. Several of their ships cruise the islands. The main one is *Pride of America* (Vintage Americana theme, very new, big family focus with lots of connecting staterooms and suites), which offers seven-day or longer itineraries within the Islands, stopping on Maui, O'ahu, the Big Island, and overnighting in Kaua'i. ☎ 800/327–7030 ⊕ www.ncl.com.

Hawai'i Nautical. Offering a completely different sort of experience, Hawai'i Nautical provides private multiple-day interisland cruises on their catamarans, yachts, and sailboats. Prices are higher, but service is completely personal, right down to the itinerary. ☎ 808/234–7245 ⊕ www. hawaiinautical.com.

Exploring O'ahu

WORD OF MOUTH

"I had a blast during my one day in O'ahu and I thought Waikīkī was great fun. I think it would be a perfect vacation spot for people who love Vegas glitz; big city excitement; shopping; and beautiful beaches."

—Songdoc

Updated By
Trina Kudlacek

Oʻahu is one-stop Hawaiʻi—all the allure of the Islands in a chop-suey mix that has you kayaking around offshore islets by day and sitting in a jazz club 'round midnight, all without ever having to take another flight or repack your suitcase. It offers both the buzz of modern living in jam-packed Honolulu (the state's capital) and the allure of slow-paced island life on its northern and eastern shores. It is, in many ways, the center of the Hawaiian universe.

There are more museums, staffed historic sites, and walking tours here than you'll find on any other island. And only here do a wealth of renovated buildings and well-preserved neighborhoods so clearly spin the story of Hawaiʻi's history. It's the only place to experience island-style urbanity, since there are no other true cities in the state. And yet you can get as lost in the rural landscape and be as laid-back as you wish.

Oʻahu is home to Waikīkī, the most famous Hawaiian beach with some of the world's most famous surf on the North Shore and the Islands' best known historical site—Pearl Harbor. If it's isolation, peace, and quiet you want, Oʻahu is probably not for you, but if you'd like a bit of spice with your piece of paradise, this island provides it.

GEOLOGY

Encompassing 597 square mi, Oʻahu is the third-largest island in the Hawaiian chain. Scientists believe the island was formed about 4 million years ago by two volcanoes: Waiʻanae and Koʻolau. Waiʻanae, the older of the two, makes up the western side of the island, whereas Koʻolau shapes the eastern side. Central Oʻahu is an elevated plateau bordered by the two mountain ranges, with Pearl Harbor to the south. Several of Oʻahu's most famous natural landmarks, including Diamond Head and Hanauma Bay, are tuff rings and cinder cones formed during a renewed volcanic stage (roughly 1 million years ago).

FLORA AND FAUNA

Due to its elevation, the eastern (Koʻolau) side of Oʻahu is much cooler and wetter than the western side of the island, which tends to be dry and arid. The island's official flower, the little orange *ilima,* grows predominantly in the east, but leis throughout the island incorporate *ilima.* Numerous tropical fish call the reef at Hanauma Bay home, migrating humpback whales can be spotted off the coast past Waikīkī and Diamond Head from December through April, spinner dolphins pop in and out of the island's bays, and dozens of islets off Oʻahu's eastern coast provide refuge for endangered seabirds.

HISTORY

Oʻahu is the most populated island because early tourism to Hawaiʻi started here. Although Kīlauea volcano on Hawaiʻi was a tourist attraction in the late 1800s, it was the building of the Moana Hotel on Waikīkī

Kick back in a hammock in Waikīkī and gaze off at Diamond Head in the distance.

Beach in 1901 and subsequent advertising of Hawai'i to wealthy San Franciscans that really fueled tourism in the islands. O'ahu was drawing tens of thousands of guests yearly when, on December 7, 1941, Japanese Zeros appeared at dawn to bomb Pearl Harbor. Though tourism understandably dipped during the war (Waikīkī Beach was fenced with barbed wire), the subsequent memorial only seemed to attract more visitors, and O'ahu remains hugely popular with tourists to this day.

HONOLULU

Here is Hawai'i's only true metropolis, its seat of government, center of commerce and shipping, entertainment and recreation mecca, a historic site and an evolving urban area—conflicting roles that engender endless debate and controversy. For the visitor, Honolulu is an everyman's delight: hipsters and scholars, sightseers and foodies, nature lovers and culture vultures all can find their bliss.

Once there was the broad bay of Mamala and the narrow inlet of Kou, fronting a dusty plain occupied by a few thatched houses and the great Pakaka *heiau* (shrine). Nosing into the narrow passage in the early 1790s, British sea captain William Brown named the port Fair Haven. Later, Hawaiians would call it Honolulu, or "sheltered bay." As shipping traffic increased, the settlement grew into a Western-style town of streets and buildings, tightly clustered around the single freshwater source, Nu'uanu Stream. Not until piped water became available in the early 1900s did Honolulu spread across the greening plain. Long before that, however, Honolulu gained importance when King Kamehameha

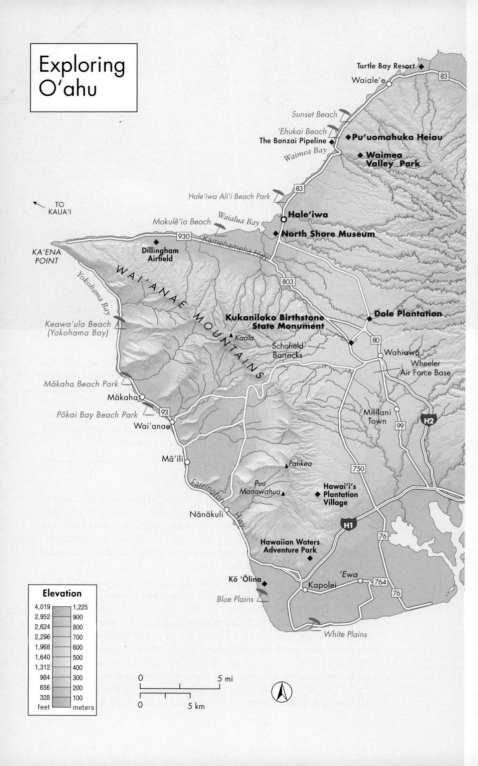

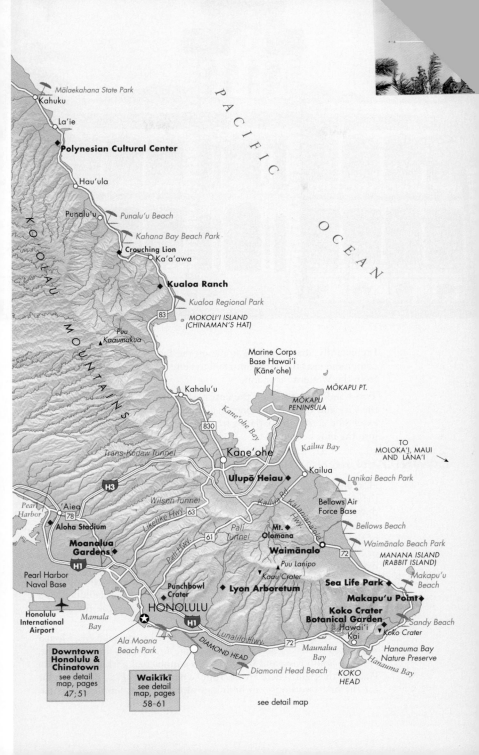

PACIFIC

OCEAN

Mālaekahana State Park
Kahuku

La'ie

Polynesian Cultural Center

Hau'ula

Punalu'u   *Punalu'u Beach*

Kahana Bay Beach Park
Crouching Lion
Ka'a'awa

Kualoa Ranch

Kualoa Regional Park
83
MOKOLI'I ISLAND
(CHINAMAN'S HAT)

Puu
Kaaumakua

Marine Corps
Base Hawai'i
(Kāne'ohe)

MŌKAPU PT.

MŌKAPU
PENINSULA

Kahalu'u

830

Kane'ohe Bay

Kailua Bay

TO
MOLOKA'I, MAUI
AND LĀNA'I

Kane'ohe

Trans-Ko'olau Tunnel

Ulupō Heiau ◆   Kailua

Lanikai Beach Park

KO'OLAU   MOUNTAINS

H3

Wilson Tunnel

63

Kailua Rd

Kalanianaole Hwy

Bellows Air
Force Base

Bellows Beach

Pearl
Harbor

'Aiea
78
Aloha Stadium ◆

Likelike Hwy.

*Pali
Tunnel*

61

Mt. ◆
Olamana

Waimānalo   72   *Waimānalo Beach Park*

MANANA ISLAND
(RABBIT ISLAND)

**Moanalua
Gardens** ◆

H1

Pali Hwy.

Puu Lanipo

Kaau Crater

*Makapu'u
Beach*

Pearl Harbor
Naval Base

Punchbowl
Crater

◆ **Lyon Arboretum**

Sea Life Park ◆

Makapu'u Point ◆

Honolulu
International
Airport

*Mamala
Bay*

HONOLULU
★

H1

Hawai'i
Kai

**Koko Crater
Botanical Garden** ◆   *Sandy Beach*
▼ Koko Crater

**Downtown
Honolulu &
Chinatown**
see detail
map, pages
47; 51

*Ala Moana
Beach Park*

DIAMOND HEAD

Lunalilo Hwy.

72

*Maunalua
Bay*

Hanauma Bay
Nature Preserve

Waikīkī
see detail
map, pages
58–61

Diamond Head Beach

KOKO
HEAD

Hanauma Bay

see detail map

Take a guided tour of 'Iolani Palace, said to be America's only royal residence, built in 1882.

I reluctantly abandoned his home on the Big Island to build a chiefly compound near the harbor in 1804 to better protect Hawaiian interests from the Western incursion.

Two hundred years later, the entire island is, in a sense, Honolulu—the City and County of Honolulu. The city has no official boundaries, extending across the flatlands from Pearl Harbor to Waikīkī and high into the hills behind.

DOWNTOWN HONOLULU

Honolulu's past and present play a delightful counterpoint throughout the downtown sector. Postmodern glass-and-steel office buildings look down on the Aloha Tower, built in 1926 and, until the early 1960s, the tallest structure in Honolulu. Hawai'i's history is told in the architecture of these few blocks: the cut-stone turn-of-the-20th-century storefronts of Merchant Street, the gracious white-columned American-Georgian manor that was the home of the Islands' last queen, the jewel-box palace occupied by the monarchy before it was overthrown, the Spanish-inspired stucco and tile-roofed Territorial Era government buildings, and the 21st-century glass pyramid of the First Hawaiian Bank Building.

GETTING HERE AND AROUND

To reach Downtown Honolulu from Waikīkī by car, take Ala Moana Boulevard to Alakea Street and turn right; three blocks up on the right, between South King and Hotel; there's a municipal parking lot in Ali'i Place on the right. There are also public parking lots (75¢ per half hour for the first two hours) in buildings along Alakea, Smith, Beretania, and Bethel streets (Gateway Plaza on Bethel Street is a good choice). The best parking downtown, however, is street parking along Punchbowl Street—when you can find it. Another option is to take route 19 or 20 of highly popular and convenient TheBus to the Aloha Tower Marketplace, or take a trolley from Waikīkī.

TIMING

Plan a couple of hours for exploring downtown's historic buildings, more if you're taking a guided tour or walk. The best time to visit is in the cool and relative quiet of morning or on the weekends when downtown is all but deserted except for the historic sites.

TOP ATTRACTIONS

❹ Fodor'sChoice ★ **'Iolani Palace.** America's only official state residence of royalty was completed in 1882 on the site of an earlier palace, and it contains the thrones of King Kalākaua and his successor (and sister) Queen Lili'uokalani. Bucking the stereotype of the primitive islander, the palace had electric lighting installed even before the White House. Downstairs galleries showcase the royal jewelry and kitchen and offices of the monarchy. The palace is open for guided or self-guided audio tours; reservations are essential. ■TIP→ If you're set on taking a guided tour, call for reservations a few days in advance. The gift shop and ticket office are located in what was formerly the 'Iolani Barracks, built to house the Royal Guard. ⊠ *King and Richards Sts., Downtown* ☎ *808/522–0832* ⊕ *www.iolanipalace.org* ☑ *$12, $20 guided tour, $1 for audio tour, $6 downstairs galleries only* ⊙ *Tues.–Sat. 9–2, guided tours every 15 mins 9–11:15, self-guided audio tours 11:45–3:30, Galleries 9–5.*

❺ **Kamehameha I Statue.** Paying tribute to the Big Island chieftain who united all the warring Hawaiian Islands into one kingdom at the turn of the 18th century, this statue, which stands with one arm outstretched in welcome, is one of three originally cast in Paris, France, by American sculptor T. R. Gould. The original statue, lost at sea and replaced by this one, was eventually salvaged and is now in Kapa'au, on the Big Island, near the king's birthplace. Each year on the king's birthday, June 11, the more famous copy is draped in fresh lei that reach lengths of 18 feet and longer. A parade proceeds past the statue, and Hawaiian civic clubs, the women in hats and impressive long *holokū* dresses and the men in sashes and cummerbunds, pay honor to the leader whose name means "The Lonely One." ⊠ *417 S. King St., outside Ali'iōlani Hale, Downtown.*

❾ **Kawaiaha'o Church.** Fancifully called Hawai'i's Westminster Abbey, this 14,000-coral-block house of worship witnessed the coronations, weddings, and funerals of generations of Hawaiian royalty. Each of the building's coral blocks was quarried from reefs offshore at depths of more than 20 feet and transported to this site. Interior woodwork was created from the forests of the Ko'olau Mountains. The upper gallery has an exhibit of paintings of the royal families. The graves of missionaries and of King Lunalilo are adjacent. Services in English and Hawaiian are held each Sunday, and the church members are exceptionally welcoming, greeting newcomers with lei; their affiliation is United Church of Christ. Although there are no guided tours, you can look around the church at no cost. ⊠ 957 Punchbowl St., at King St., Downtown ☏ 808/522–1333 ⊡ Free ☉ English and Hawaiian service Sun. at 9 AM.

WORTH NOTING

❷ Aloha Tower Marketplace. Two stories of shops and kiosks sell island-inspired clothing, jewelry, art, and home furnishings. The Marketplace also has indoor and outdoor restaurants and live entertainment. For a bird's-eye view of this working harbor, take a free ride up to the observation deck of Aloha Tower. Cruise ships dock at Piers 9 and 10 alongside the Marketplace and are often greeted and sent out to sea with music and hula dancing at the piers' end. ⊠ 1 Aloha Tower Dr., at Piers 10 and 11, Downtown ☏ 808/528–5700; 808/566–2337 entertainment info ⊕ www.alohatower.com ☉ Mon.–Sat. 9–9, Sun. 9–6; restaurants open later.

QUICK BITES

In a vintage brick building at the corner of Nu'uanu Street and Merchant, **Murphy's Bar & Grill** (⊠ 2 Merchant St., Downtown ☏ 808/531–0422) is an old-fashioned Irish pub, sports bar, and kamā'aina-style family restaurant. Comfort food is the order of the day.

❸ Hawai'i State Art Museum. Hawai'i was one of the first states in the nation to legislate that a portion of the taxes paid on commercial building projects be set aside for the purchase of artwork. A few years ago, the state purchased an ornate period-style building (built to house the headquarters of a prominent developer) and dedicated 12,000 feet on the second floor to the art of Hawai'i in all its ethnic diversity. The **Diamond Head Gallery** features new acquisitions and thematic shows from the Art in Public Places Collection and the Hawaii State Foundation on Culture and the Arts. The **'Ewa Gallery** houses more than 150 works documenting Hawai'i's visual-arts history since becoming a state in 1959. Also included are a sculpture gallery and educational meeting rooms. For lunch, join the local business crowd at popular **Downtown @ the HiSam** (⇨ see Where to Eat); reservations are essential. ⊠ 250 S. Hotel St., 2nd fl., Downtown ☏ 808/586–0900 museum; 808/536–5900 restaurant ⊕ www.hawaii.gov/sfca ⊡ Free ☉ Tues.–Sat. 10–4.

❻ Hawai'i State Capitol. The capitol's architecture is richly symbolic: the columns resemble palm trees, the legislative chambers are shaped like volcanic cinder cones, and the central court is open to the sky, representing Hawai'i's open society. Cast bronzes of the Hawai'i state seal, each weighing 7,500 pounds, hang above both its entrances. The building,

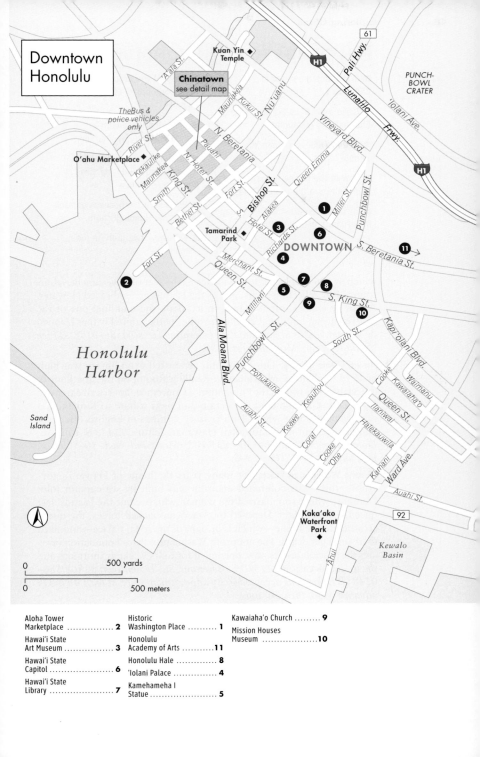

Downtown Honolulu

Kuan Yin Temple

Chinatown see detail map

PUNCH-BOWL CRATER

TheBus & police vehicles only

O'ahu Marketplace

DOWNTOWN

Tamarind Park

Honolulu Harbor

Sand Island

Kaka'ako Waterfront Park

Kewalo Basin

0   500 yards
0   500 meters

FUN THINGS TO DO IN HONOLULU

- Grab some green tea in Chinatown.

- Tickle a tiki at La Mariana Sailing Club bar and restaurant.

- Visit a goddess at Kuan Yin Temple.

- Bow to the throne in the only royal palace in the United States.

- Encounter an artist at First Friday in Nu'uanu's gallery district.

- Shop 'til you drop in the funky neighborhoods of Mō'ili'ili and Kaimukī.

- Study the Hawaiian stars at Bishop Museum planetarium.

- Hum along with a Hawaiian hymn during Sunday services at Kawaiaha'o Church.

- Hang from the heavens parasailing off the Honolulu shore.

- Eat Navy-style grub on the "Mighty Mo."

which in 1969 replaced 'Iolani Palace as the seat of government, is surrounded by reflecting pools, just as the Islands are embraced by water. A pair of statues, often draped in lei, flank the building: one of the beloved queen Lili'uokalani and the other of the sainted Father Damien de Veuster. ⊠ *215 S. Beretania St., Downtown* ☎ *808/586–0178* ⊠ *Free* ⊙ *Guided tours Mon. and Fri. 1:30.*

❼ Hawai'i State Library. This beautifully renovated main library was built in 1913. Its Samuel M. Kamakau Reading Room, on the first floor in the Mauka (Hawaiian for "mountain") Courtyard, houses an extensive Hawai'i and Pacific book collection and pays tribute to Kamakau, a missionary student whose 19th-century writings in English offer rare and vital insight into traditional Hawaiian culture. ⊠ *478 S. King St., Downtown* ☎ *808/586–3500* ⊠ *Free* ⊙ *Mon. and Wed. 10–5, Tues., Fri., and Sat. 9–5, Thurs. 9–8.*

❶ Historic Washington Place. For many years the home of Hawai'i's governors, this white-columned mansion was built by sea captain John Dominis, whose son married the woman who became the Islands' last queen, Lili'uokalani. Deposed by American-backed forces, the queen returned to the home—which is in sight of the royal palace—and lived there until her death. The nonprofit Washington Place Foundation operates the gracious estate now, opening it for tours weekday mornings and on special occasions. ⊠ *320 S. Beretania St., Downtown* ☎ *808/586–0248* ⊠ *Donations accepted* ⊙ *By appointment only, at least 48 hrs in advance Mon. thru Fri. only.*

⓫ Honolulu Academy of Arts. Originally built around the collection of a Honolulu matron who donated much of her estate to the museum, the academy is housed in a maze of courtyards, cloistered walkways, and quiet low-ceilinged spaces. An impressive permanent collection includes Hiroshige's *ukiyo-e* Japanese prints, donated by James Michener; Italian Renaissance paintings; and American and European art. The newer Luce Pavilion complex, nicely incorporated into the more traditional architecture of the place, has a traveling-exhibit gallery, a Hawaiian

Waikīkī and Honolulu, looking west to Diamond Head, as seen from above.

gallery, an excellent café, and a gift shop. The Academy Theatre screens art films. This is also the jumping-off place for tours of Doris Duke's estate, Shangri La. Call or check the Web site for special exhibits, concerts, and films. ✉ *900 S. Beretania St., Downtown* ☎ *808/532–8700* ⊕ *www.honoluluacademy.org* ✐*$10, free 1st Wed. and 3rd Sun. of month* ☉ *Tues.–Sat. 10–4:30, Sun. 1–5.*

8 **Honolulu Hale.** This Mediterranean Renaissance–style building was constructed in 1929 and serves as the center of city government. Stroll through the shady, open-ceiling lobby with exhibits of local artists, and time your visit to coincide with one of the free concerts sometimes offered in the evening, when the building stays open late. During the winter holiday season, the Hale becomes the focal point for the annual Honolulu City Lights, a display of lighting and playful holiday scenes spread around the Honolulu Hale campus. ✉ *530 S. King St., Downtown* ☎ *808/768–6622* ✐ *Free* ☉ *Weekdays 8–4:30.*

Kaka'ako Waterfront Park. Rolling hills carpeted in lush green grass greet the visitor to Kaka'ako park. Popular with local families and perfect for watching the sunset or the Friday evening sailboat races, it has a seaside promenade following a lava-rock wall. Though it has no beach access, the Diamond Head end of the promenade is a great spot to watch surfers and Friday evening fireworks off of Waikīkī. ✉ *677 Ala Moana Blvd., Kaka'ako* ☎*No phone* ☉ *7–7 daily.*

10 **Mission Houses Museum.** The determined Hawai'i missionaries arrived in 1820, gaining royal favor and influencing every aspect of island life. Their descendants became leaders in government and business. You can walk through their original dwellings, including Hawai'i's oldest

O'AHU SIGHTSEEING TOURS

Guided tours are convenient; you don't have to worry about finding a parking spot or getting admission tickets. Most of the tour guides have taken special classes in Hawaiian history and lore, and many are certified by the state of Hawai'i. On the other hand, you won't have the freedom to proceed at your own pace, nor will you have the ability to take a detour trip if something else catches your attention.

BUS AND VAN TOURS
Polynesian Adventure. ☎ 808/833-3000 ⊕ www.polyad. com.

Roberts Hawai'i. ☎ 808/539-9400 ⊕ www.robertshawaii.com.

THEME TOURS
Discover Hawaii Tours. ☎ 808/877-9588 ⊕ www. discoverhawaiitours.com.

E Noa Tours. Certified tour guides conduct Circle Island, Pearl Harbor, and shopping tours. ☎ 808/591-2561 ⊕ www.enoa.com.

Home of the Brave Hawaii Victory Tour. Perfect for military history buffs, narrated tours visit O'ahu's military bases and the National Memorial Cemetery of the Pacific. Also includes a visit to their private museum including artifacts and memorabilia from World War II. Day or evening itineraries available. ☎ 808/396-8112 ⊕ www. pearlharborhq.com.

Matthew Gray's Hawai'i Food Tours. Get a taste of Hawai'i's culture by going on the "Hole in the Wall Tour" culinary tour. Includes discussion of Hawai'i food ways and history of culinary diversity in the Islands, along with samplings of a variety of local favorites at local ethnic restaurants, markets, and bakeries as you walk through Chinatown. A great way to get a taste of Hawai'i's culture. ☎ 808/926-3663 ⊕ www.hawaiifoodtours.com.

Polynesian Cultural Center. An advantage of this tour is that you don't have to drive yourself back to Waikīkī after dark if you take in the evening show. Call regarding different packages as some include luaus. ☎ 808/293-3333 or 808/923-1861 ⊕ www.polynesia.com.

WALKING TOURS
American Institute of Architects (AIA) Downtown Walking Tour. See Downtown Honolulu from an architectural perspective. Saturdays only. ☎ 808/545-4242 ⊕ www. aiahonolulu.org.

Hawai'i Geographic Society. A number of Downtown Honolulu historic-temple and archaeology walking tours are available. ☎ 808/538-3952.

wooden structure, a white frame house that was prefabricated in New England and shipped around the Horn. Docents give an excellent picture of what mission life was like; certain areas of the museum may be seen only on a one-hour guided tour. Rotating displays showcase such arts as Hawaiian quilting, portraits, even toys. The museum also hosts special local tours and other events. Check the Web site for current programs. The gift shop has many locally made crafts. There is also an on-site café. ⊠ *553 S. King St., Downtown* ☎ *808/447-3910*

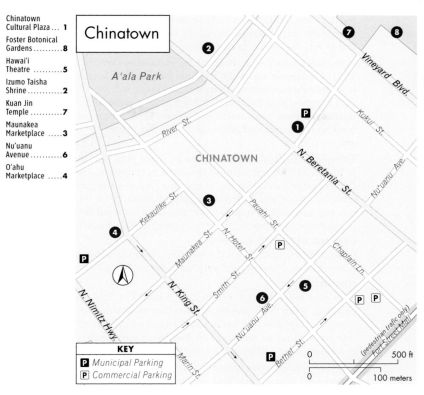

Chinatown

A'ala Park

River St.

CHINATOWN

Kekaulike St.

Maunakea St.

N. Hotel St.

Pauahi St.

Smith St.

N. King St.

Nu'uanu Ave.

Marin St.

Bethel St.

N. Nimitz Hwy.

N. Beretania St.

Nu'uanu Ave.

Kukui St.

Vineyard Blvd.

Chaplain Ln.

(pedestrian trafic only) Fort Street Mall

KEY
P *Municipal Parking*
P *Commercial Parking*

0   500 ft
0   100 meters

⊕ *www.missionhouses.org* ✉ *$10* ⊗ *Tues.–Sat. 10–4; guided tours at 11, 1, and 2:45.*

CHINATOWN

Chinatown's original business district was made up of dry-goods and produce merchants, tailors and dressmakers, barbers, herbalists, and dozens of restaurants. The meat, fish, and produce stalls remain, but the mix is heavier now on gift and curio stores, lei stands, jewelry shops, and bakeries, with a smattering of noodle makers, travel agents, Asian-language video stores, and dozens of restaurants.

The name *Chinatown* here has always been a misnomer. Though three-quarters of O'ahu's Chinese lived closely packed in these 25 acres in the late 1800s, even then the neighborhood was half Japanese. Today, you hear Vietnamese and Tagalog as often as Mandarin and Cantonese, and there are voices of Japan, Singapore, Malaysia, Korea, Thailand, Samoa, and the Marshall Islands, as well.

Perhaps a more accurate name is the one used by early Chinese: *Wah Fau* ("Chinese port") signifying a landing and jumping-off place. Chinese laborers, as soon as they completed their plantation contracts, hurried into the city to start businesses here. It's a launching point for today's immigrants, too: Southeast Asian shops almost outnumber Chinese; stalls carry Filipino specialties like winged beans and goat meat; and in one tiny space, knife-wielding Samoans skin coconuts to order.

In the half century after the first Chinese laborers arrived in Hawai'i in 1851, Chinatown was a link to home for the all-male cadre of workers who planned to return to China rich and respected. Merchants not only sold supplies, they held mail, loaned money, wrote letters, translated documents, sent remittances to families, served meals, offered rough bunkhouse accommodations, and were the center for news, gossip, and socializing.

Though much happened to Chinatown in the 20th century—beginning in January 1900, when almost the entire neighborhood was burned to the ground to halt the spread of bubonic plague—it remains a bustling, crowded, noisy, and odiferous place bent primarily on buying and selling, and sublimely oblivious to its status as a National Historic District or the encroaching gentrification on nearby Nu'uanu Avenue.

GETTING HERE AND AROUND

Chinatown occupies 15 blocks immediately north of downtown Honolulu—it's flat, compact, and very walkable.

TIMING

This area is easily explored in half a day. The best time to visit is morning, when the *popos* (grandmas) shop—it's cool out, and you can enjoy a cheap dim-sum breakfast. Chinatown is a seven-days-a-week operation. Sundays are especially busy with families sharing dim sum in raucous dining hall–size restaurants.

If you're here between January 20 and February 20, check local newspapers for Chinese New Year activities. Bakeries stock special sweets, stores and homes sprout bright-red scrolls, and lion dancers cavort through the streets feeding on *li-see* (money envelopes). The Narcissus Queen is chosen, and an evening street fair draws crowds.

TOP ATTRACTIONS

❶ Chinatown Cultural Plaza. This sprawling multistory shopping square surrounds a courtyard with an incense-wreathed shrine and Moongate stage for holiday performances. The Chee Kung Tong Society has a beautifully decorated meeting hall here; a number of such *tongs* (meeting places) are hidden on upper floors in Chinatown. Outside, near the canal, local members of the community play cards and mah-jongg. ⊠ *100 N. Beretania, Chinatown.*

❷ Izumo Taisha Shrine. From Chinatown Cultural Plaza, cross a stone bridge to visit Okuninushi No Mikoto, a *kami* (god) who is believed in Shinto tradition to bring good fortune if properly courted (and thanked afterward). ⊠ *N. Kukui and Canal, Chinatown.*

❼ Kuan Yin Temple. A couple of blocks *mauka* (toward the mountains) from Chinatown is the oldest Buddhist temple in the Islands. Mistakenly called a goddess by some, Kuan Yin, also known as Kannon, is a bodhisattva—one who chose to remain on earth doing good even after achieving enlightenment. Transformed from a male into a female figure centuries ago, she is credited with a particular sympathy for women.

SHOPPING IN CHINATOWN

Chinatown is rife with ridiculously inexpensive gifts: folding fans for $1 and coconut purses for $5 at **Maunakea Marketplace**, for example.

Curio shops sell everything from porcelain statues to woks, ginseng to Mao shoes. If you like to sew, or have a yen for a brocade cheongsam, visit the Hong Kong Supermarket in the Wo Fat Chop Sui building (at the corner of N. Hotel and Maunakea) for fresh fruit, crack seed (Chinese dried fruit popular for snacking), and row upon row of boxed, tinned delicacies with indecipherable names.

Chinatown Cultural Plaza offers fine-quality jade. Chinatown is Honolulu's lei center, with shops strung along Beretania and Maunakea; every local has a favorite shop where they're greeted by name. In spring, look for gardenia nosegays wrapped in ti leaves.

You see representations of her all over the Islands: holding a lotus flower (symbolizing beauty in the form of the flower which grows from the mud of human frailty), as at the temple; pouring out a pitcher of oil (like mercy flowing); or as a sort of Madonna with a child. Visitors are permitted, but be aware this is a practicing place of worship. ⊠ *170 N. Vineyard, Downtown* ☎ *No phone.*

❸ **Maunakea Marketplace.** On the corner of Maunakea and Hotel streets is this plaza surrounded by shops, an indoor market, and a food court. Within the Marketplace, the **Hawaiian Chinese Cultural Museum and Archives** (🎟 *$2* ⊙ *Mon.–Sat. 10–2*) displays historic photographs and artifacts.■ TIP→ If you appreciate fine tea, visit the Tea Hut, an unpretentious counter inside a curio shop. ⊠ *1120 Maunakea St., Chinatown* ☎ *808/524–3409.*

❹ **O'ahu Marketplace.** Here is a taste of old-style Chinatown, where you're
★ likely to be hustled aside as a whole pig, ready for roasting, is carried through the crowd and where glassy-eyed fish of every size and hue lie stacked on ice. Try the bubble tea (juices and flavored teas mixed with beadlike tapioca) or pick up a magenta dragonfruit for breakfast. ⊠ *N. King St. at Kekaulike, Chinatown.*

WORTH NOTING

❽ **Foster Botanical Garden.** Some of the trees in this botanical garden, open since 1931, date back to 1853 when Queen Kalama allowed a young German doctor to lease a portion of her land. Over 150 years later, you can see these trees and countless others along with bromeliads, orchids, and other tropical plants, some of which are rare or endangered. Look out in particular for the cannonball tree and the redwood-size Quipo tree. A docent-led tour is available Monday–Saturday at 1 PM (call for reservations). ⊠ *50 N. Vineyard Blvd., Chinatown* ☎ *808/522–7066* ⊕ *www.honolulu.gov/parks/hbg* 🎟 *$5* ⊙ *Daily 9–4.*

❺ **Hawai'i Theatre.** Opened in 1922, this theater earned rave reviews for its neoclassical design, with Corinthian columns, marble statues, and plush carpeting and drapery. Nicknamed the "Pride of the Pacific," the facility was rescued from demolition in the early 1980s and underwent a $30 million renovation. Listed on both the State and National Register of Historic Places, it has become the centerpiece of revitalization efforts of Honolulu's downtown area. The 1,400-seat venue hosts concerts, theatrical productions, dance performances, and film screenings. ⊠ *1130 Bethel St., Chinatown* ☎ *808/528–0506* ✉ *$5* ⊘ *1-hr guided tours Tues. at 11; call ahead.*

❻ Nuʻuanu Avenue. Here on Chinatown's southern border and on Bethel Street, which runs parallel, are clustered art galleries, restaurants, a wine shop, an antiques auctioneer, a dress shop or two, one tiny theater space (the Arts at Mark's Garage), and one historic stage (the Hawaiʻi Theatre). **First Friday** art nights, when galleries stay open until 9 PM, draw crowds. If you like art and people-watching and are fortunate enough to be on Oʻahu the first Friday of the month, this event shouldn't be missed. ⊠ *Nuʻuanu Ave., Chinatown.*

> ## BEST SNACKS IN CHINATOWN
>
> A world of small, inexpensive restaurants exists within Chinatown, among them:
>
> ■ **Golden Palace:** $1.50 dim sum
>
> ■ **Yusura:** Homey Japanese
>
> ■ **Ba-Le:** Vietnamese sandwiches
>
> ■ **Urumi:** Japanese noodles
>
> ■ **Grand Café & Bakery:** Retro diner
>
> ■ **Mabuhay:** Filipino standards
>
> ■ **Sweet Basil:** Thai buffet

WAIKĪKĪ

A short drive from downtown Honolulu, Waikīkī is Oʻahu's primary resort area. A mix of historic and modern hotels and condos front the sunny 2 ½-mi stretch of beach, and many have clear views of Diamond Head to the west. The area is home to much of the island's dining, nightlife, and shopping scene—from posh boutiques to hole-in-the-wall eateries to craft booths at the International Marketplace.

Waikīkī was once a favorite retreat for Hawaiian royalty. In 1901 the Moana Hotel debuted, introducing Waikīkī as an international travel destination. The region's fame continued to grow when Duke Kahanamoku helped popularize the sport of surfing, offering lessons to visitors at Waikīkī. You can see Duke immortalized in a bronze statue, with a surf board, on Kuhio Beach. Today, there is a decidedly "urban resort" vibe here; streets are clean, gardens are manicured, and the sand feels softer than at beaches farther down the coast. There isn't much of a local culture—it's mainly tourist crowds—but you'll still find the relaxed surfy vibe that has drawn people here for more than a century.

Diamond Head Crater is perhaps Hawaiʻi's most recognizable natural landmark. It got its name from sailors who thought they had found precious gems on its slopes; these later proved to be calcite crystals, or fool's gold. Hawaiians saw a resemblance in the sharp angle of the crater's seaward slope to the oddly shaped head of the ʻahi fish and so called it Lēʻahi, though later they Hawaiianized the English name to

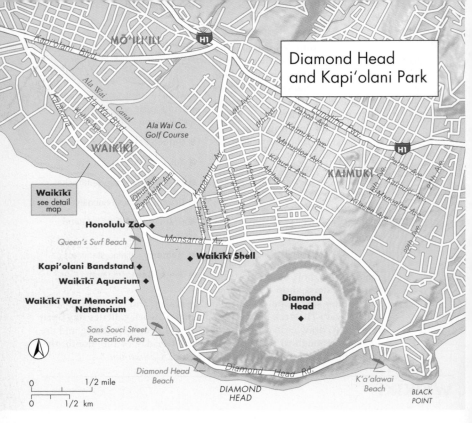

Diamond Head
and Kapiʻolani Park

Kaimana Hila. It is commemorated in a widely known hula—*"A ʻike i ka nani o Kaimana Hila, Kaimana Hila, kau mai i luna"* ("We saw the beauty of Diamond Head, Diamond Head set high above").

Kapiʻolani Park lies in the shadow of the crater. King David Kalākaua established the park in 1887, named it after his queen, and dedicated it "to the use and enjoyment of the people." Kapiʻolani Park is a 500-acre expanse where you can play all sorts of field sports, enjoy a picnic, see wild animals at the Honolulu Zoo, or hear live music at the Waikīkī Shell or the Kapiʻolani Bandstand.

GETTING HERE AND AROUND

Bounded by the Ala Wai Canal on the north and west, the beach on the south, and the Honolulu Zoo to the east, Waikiki is compact and easy to walk around. TheBus runs multiple routes here from the airport and downtown Honolulu. By car, finding Waikiki from H1 can be tricky; look for the Punahou exit for western Waikiki, and the King Street exit for eastern Waikiki.

TOP ATTRACTIONS

Diamond Head State Monument and Park. Panoramas from this 760-foot extinct volcanic peak, once used as a military fortification, extend from Waikīkī and Honolulu in one direction and out to Koko Head in the other, with surfers and windsurfers scattered like confetti on the cresting

Continued on page 63

Return Policy

With a sales receipt or Barnes & Noble.com packing slip, a full refund in the original form of payment will be issued from any Barnes & Noble Booksellers store for returns of undamaged NOOKs, new and unread books, and unopened and undamaged music CDs, DVDs, and audio books made within 14 days of purchase from a Barnes & Noble Booksellers store or Barnes & Noble.com with the below exceptions:

A store credit for the purchase price will be issued (i) for purchases made by check less than 7 days prior to the date of return, (ii) when a gift receipt is presented within 60 days of purchase, (iii) for textbooks, or (iv) for products purchased at Barnes & Noble College bookstores that are listed for sale in the Barnes & Noble Booksellers inventory management system.

YOU MAY ALSO LIKE...

INS & OUTS OF WAIKĪKĪ

Waikīkī is all that is wonderful about a resort area, and all that is regrettable. On the wonderful side: swimming, surfing, parasailing, and catamaran-riding steps from the street; the best nightlife in Hawai'i;

shopping from designer to dime stores; and experiences to remember: the heart-lifting rush the first time you stand up on a surfboard, watching the old men play cutthroat checkers in the beach pavilions, eating fresh grilled snapper as the sun slips into the sea. As to the regrettable: clogged streets, body-lined beaches, $5 cups of coffee, tacky T-shirts, $20 parking stalls, schlocky artwork, the same street performers you saw in Atlantic City, drunks, cease-less construction—all rather brush the bloom from the plumeria.

Modern Waikīkī is nothing like its original self, a network of streams, marshes, and islands that drained the inland valleys. The Ala Wai Canal took

care of that in the 1920s. More recently, new landscaping, walkways, and a general attention to infrastructure have brightened a façade that had begun distinctly to fade.

But throughout its history, Waikīkī has retained its essential character: an enchantment that cannot be fully explained and one that, though diminished by high-rises, traffic, and noise, has not yet disappeared. Hawaiian royalty came here, and visitors continue to follow, falling in love with sharp-prowed Diamond Head, the sensuous curve of shoreline with its baby-safe waves, and the strong-footed surfers like moving statues in the golden light.

WAIKĪKĪ WEST

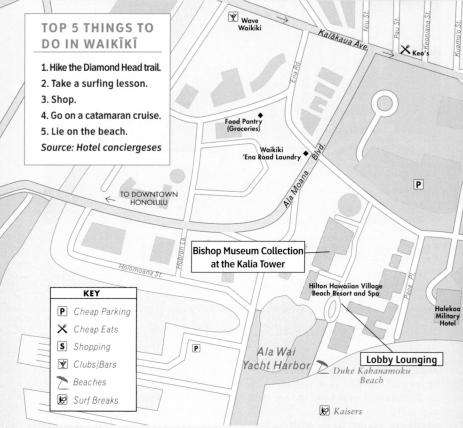

TOP 5 THINGS TO DO IN WAIKĪKĪ

1. Hike the Diamond Head trail.
2. Take a surfing lesson.
3. Shop.
4. Go on a catamaran cruise.
5. Lie on the beach.

Source: Hotel conciergeses

TO DOWNTOWN HONOLULU

Wave Waikiki

Kalākaua Ave

Niu St.

Pau St.

Keoniana St.

Kuamo'o St.

Keo's

Ena Rd

Food Pantry (Groceries)

Waikiki 'Ena Road Laundry

Ala Moana Blvd.

P

Hotomoana St.

Hobron La.

Bishop Museum Collection at the Kalia Tower

Hilton Hawaiian Village Beach Resort and Spa

Paoa Pl.

Halekoa Military Hotel

KEY

P	*Cheap Parking*
✕	*Cheap Eats*
S	*Shopping*
☼	*Clubs/Bars*
◿	*Beaches*
🏄	*Surf Breaks*

P

Ala Wai Yacht Harbor

Lobby Lounging

Duke Kahanamoku Beach

🏄 *Kaisers*

CHEAP EATS

Keo's, 2028 Kūhiō: Breakfast.

Pho Old Saigon, 2270 Kūhiō: Vietnamese.

Japanese noodle shops: Try Menchanko-Tei, Waikīkī Trade Center; Ezogiku, 2164 Kalākaua.

■ TIP→ Thanks to the many Japanese nationals who stay here, Waikīkī is blessed with lots of cheap, authentic Japanese food, particularly noodles. Plastic representations of food in the window are an indicator of authenticity and a help in ordering.

SHOP, SHOP, SHOP/PARTY, PARTY, PARTY

2100 Kalākaua: Select high-end European boutiques (Chanel, Gucci, Yves Saint Laurent).

Island Treasures Antique Mall: Hawaiian collectibles from precious to priceless. 2301 Kūhiō Ave. 808/922-8223.

Zanzabar: Upscale Zanzabar is a different club every night–Latin, global, over 30, under 18. Waikīkī Trade Center, 2255 Kūhiō Ave. 808/924-3939.

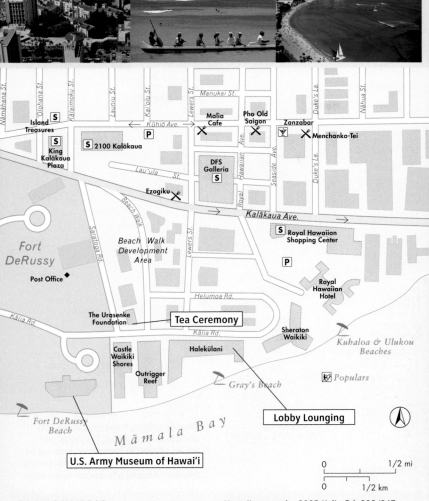

RAINY DAY IDEAS

Lobby Lounging: Among Waikīkī's great gathering spots are Halekūlani's tranquil courtyards with gorgeous flower arrangements and glimpses of the famous and the Hilton Hawaiian Village's flagged pathways with koi ponds, squawking parrots, and great shops.

Bishop Museum Collection at the Kalia Tower, Hilton Hawaiian Village: 8,000-square-foot branch of Hawai'i's premier cultural archive illuminates life in Waikīkī through the years and the history of the

Hawaiian people. 2005 Kalia Rd. 808/947–2458. $7. Daily 10–5.

Tea Ceremony, Urasenke Foundation: Japan's mysterious tea ceremony is demonstrated. 245 Saratoga Rd. 808/923–3059. $3 donation. Wed., Fri. 10–noon.

U.S. Army Museum of Hawai'i: Exhibits, including photographs and military equipment, trace the history of Army in the Islands. Battery Randolph, Kalia Rd., Fort DeRussy. 808/955–9552. Free. Tues.–Sun. 10–4:15.

WAIKĪKĪ EAST

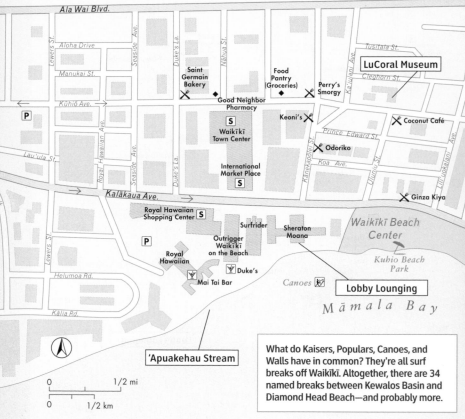

Ala Wai Blvd.

Lewers St. • Aloha Drive • Seaside Ave. • Manukai St. • Kūhiō Ave. • Royal Hawaiian Ave. • Seaside Ave. • Duke's Ln. • Lau'ula St. • Kalākaua Ave.

Duke's Ln. • Nāhua St.

Saint Germain Bakery ◆ Good Neighbor Pharmacy

Food Pantry (Groceries) ◆

Perry's Smorgy

LuCoral Museum

Tusitala St. • Cleghorn St. • Kai'ulani Ave.

Keoni's

Prince Edward St.

Coconut Café

S Waikīkī Town Center

Odoriko

Kānekapōlei St. • Koa Ave. • Uluniu St.

S International Market Place

Ginza Kiya

Lili'uokalani Ave.

Royal Hawaiian Shopping Center S

P

Royal Hawaiian

Outrigger Waikīkī on the Beach

Surfrider

Sheraton Moana

Waikīkī Beach Center

Kuhio Beach Park

Helumoa Rd.

Mai Tai Bar

Duke's

Canoes

Lobby Lounging

Mā mala Bay

Kālia Rd.

'Apuakehau Stream

0 — 1/2 mi
0 — 1/2 km

What do Kaisers, Populars, Canoes, and Walls have in common? They're all surf breaks off Waikīkī. Altogether, there are 34 named breaks between Kewalos Basin and Diamond Head Beach—and probably more.

CHEAP EATS
Coconut Café, 2441 Kūhiō: Burgers, sandwiches under $5; fresh fruit smoothies.

Ginza Kiya, 2464 Kalākaua: Japanese noodle shop.

Keoni's, Outrigger East Hotel, 150 Kaiulani Ave.: Breakfasts at rock-bottom prices.

Odoriko, King's Village, 131 Kāiulani Ave.: Japanese noodle shop.

Perry's Smorgy Restaurant, 2380 Kūhiō: family-friendly American food; brunch under $10.

■ TIP→ To save money, go inland. Kūhiō, one block toward the mountains from the main drag of Kalākaua, is lined with less expensive restaurants, hotels, and shops.

SHOP, SHOP, SHOP/PARTY, PARTY, PARTY
Sheraton Moana Surfrider: Pick up a present at Noeha Gallery or Sand People. Then relax with a drink at the venerable Banyan Veranda. The radio program *Hawai'i Calls* first broadcast to a mainland audience from here in 1935.

Duke's Canoe Club, Outrigger Waikīkī: Beach party central.

Mai Tai Bar at the Royal Hawaiian: Birthplace of the Mai Tai.

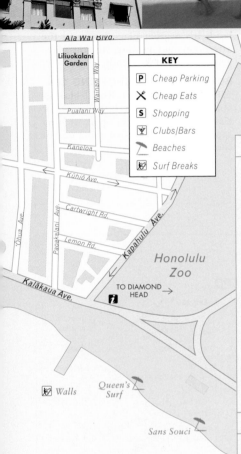

KEY

P	*Cheap Parking*
✕	*Cheap Eats*
S	*Shopping*
🍸	*Clubs/Bars*
⌐	*Beaches*
🏄	*Surf Breaks*

WHAT THE LOCALS LOVE

Paid-parking–phobic Islanders usually avoid Waikīkī, but these attractions are juicy enough to lure locals:

■ **Auntie Genoa Keawe**, old-style lūʻau music Thursdays at the Waikīkī Beach Marriott Resort and Spa.

■ **Pan-Pacific Festival-Matsuri in Hawaii**, a summer cultural festival that's as good as a trip to Japan.

■ **Aloha Festivals in September**, the legendary floral parade and evening show of contemporary Hawaiian music.

■ **The Wildest Show in Town**, $1 summer concerts at the Honolulu Zoo.

■ **Sunset on the Beach**, free films projected on an outdoor screen at Queen's Beach, with food and entertainment.

ʻAPUAKEHAU STREAM

Wade out just in front of the Outrigger Waikīkī on the Beach and feel a current of chilly water curling around your ankles. This is the last remnant of three streams that once drained the inland valleys behind you, making of Waikīkī a place of swamps, marshes, taro and rice paddies, and giving it the name "spouting water." High-ranking chiefs surfed in a legendary break gouged out by the draining freshwater and rinsed off afterward in the stream whose name means "basket of dew." The Ala Wai Canal, completed in the late 1920s, drained the land, reducing proud ʻApuakehau Stream to a determined phantom passing beneath Waikīkī's streets.

RAINY DAY IDEAS

Lobby lounging: Check out the century-old, period-furnished lobby and veranda of the Sheraton Moana Surfrider Hotel on Kalākaua.

LuCoral Museum: Exhibit and shop explores the world of coral and other semi-precious stones; wander about or take $2 guided tour and participate in jewelry-making activity. 2414 Kūhiō.

WHAT'S NEW & CHANGING

Waikīkī, which was looking a bit shop-worn, is in the midst of many make-overs. Ask about noise, disruption, and construction when booking.

In addition to fresh landscaping and period light fixtures along Kalākaua and a pathway that encircles Ala Wai Canal, expect:

BEACH WALK: After ten years of planning, the Waikīkī Beach Walk—a pedestrian walkway lined with restaurants and shops—opened in 2007 to rave reviews. It was a massive project for the city, costing about $535 million and taking up nearly 8 acres of land. It's a great place to spend the afternoon, but be warned: this place gets packed on weekends.

ROYAL HAWAIIAN SHOPPING CENTER: The fortress-like Royal Hawaiian Shopping Center in the center of Kalākaua Avenue is an open, inviting space with a palm grove and a mix of shops and restaurants.

GETTING THERE

It can seem impossible to figure out how to get to Waikīkī from H-1. The exit is far inland, and even when you follow the signs, the route jigs and jogs; it sometimes seems a wonder that more tourists aren't found starving in Kaimuki.

FROM EASTBOUND H-1 (COMING FROM THE AIRPORT):

1. To western Waikīkī (Ft. DeRussy and most hotels): Take the Punahou exit from H-1, turn right on Punahou and get in the center lane. Go right on Beretania and almost immediately left onto Kalākaua, which takes you into Waikīkī.

2. To eastern Waikīkī (Kapiʻolani Park): Take the King Street exit, and stay on King for two blocks. Go right on Kapahulu, which takes you to Kalākaua.

FROM WESTBOUND H-1:

Take the Kapiʻolani Boulevard exit. Follow Kapiʻolani to McCully, and go left on McCully. Follow McCully to Kalākaua, and you're in Waikīkī.

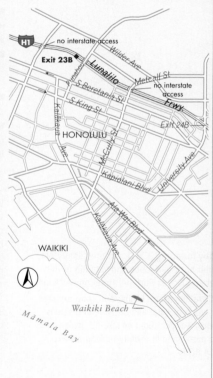

waves below. This 360-degree perspective is a great orientation for first-time visitors. On a clear day, look to your left past Koko Head to glimpse the outlines of the islands of Maui and Molokaʻi. To enter the park from Waikīkī, take Kalākaua Avenue east, turn left at Monsarrat Avenue, head a mile up the hill, and look for a sign on the right. Drive through the tunnel to the inside of the crater. The ¾-mi trail to the top begins at the parking lot. New lighting inside the summit tunnel and a spiral staircase eases the way, but be aware that the hike to the crater is a strenuous upward climb; if you aren't in the habit of getting much

> ## WAIKIKI'S BEST FREE ENTERTAINMENT
>
> Waikīkī's entertainment scene isn't just dinner shows and lounge acts. There are plenty of free or nearly free offerings right on the beach and at Kapiʻolani Park. Queen's Surf Beach hosts the popular Sunset on the Beach, which brings big-screen showings of recent Hollywood blockbusters to the great outdoors. Also, during the summer months, the Honolulu Zoo has weekly concerts, and admission is just $1.

exercise, this might not be for you. Take bottled water to ensure that you stay hydrated under the tropical sun. ■TIP→ To beat the heat and the crowds, rise early and do the hike before 8 AM. As you walk, note the color of the vegetation; if the mountain is brown, Honolulu has been without significant rain for a while; but if the trees and undergrowth glow green, you'll know it's the wet season (winter) without looking at a calendar. This is when rare Hawaiian marsh plants revive on the floor of the crater. Keep an eye on your watch if you're there at day's end, because the gates close promptly at 6. ⊠ *Diamond Head Rd. at 18th Ave., Waikīkī* ☎ *808/587–0285* ⊕ *www.hawaiistateparks.org* ⊠ *$1 per person, $5 per vehicle* ☉ *Daily 6–6.*

☕ **Honolulu Zoo.** To get a glimpse of the endangered *nēnē*, the Hawaiʻi state bird, check out the Kipuka Nēnē Sanctuary. Though many animals prefer to remain invisible, the monkeys appear to enjoy being seen and are a hoot to watch. It's best to get to the zoo right when it opens, since the animals are livelier in the cool of the morning. There are bigger and better zoos, but this one, though showing signs of neglect due to budget constraints, is a lush garden and has some great programs. The Wildest Show in Town, a series of concerts ($2 donation), takes place on Wednesday evenings in summer. You can have a family sleepover inside the zoo during Snooze in the Zoo on a Friday or Saturday night every month. Or just head for the petting zoo, where kids can make friends with a llama or stand in the middle of a koi pond. There's an exceptionally good gift shop. On weekends, the Zoo Fence Art Mart, on Monsarrat Avenue on the Diamond Head side outside the zoo, has affordable artwork by contemporary artists. Metered parking is available all along the *makai* (ocean) side of the park and in the lot next to the zoo. TheBus, Oʻahu's only form of public transportation, makes stops here along the way to and from Ala Moana Center and Sea Life Park (routes 22 and 58). ⊠ *151 Kapahulu Ave., Waikīkī* ☎ *808/971–7171* ⊕ *www.honoluluzoo.org* ⊠ *$12* ☉ *Daily 9–4:30.*

Kapi'olani Bandstand. Victorian-style Kapi'olani Bandstand, which was originally built in the late 1890s, is Kapi'olani Park's stage for community entertainment and concerts. The nation's only city-sponsored band, the Royal Hawaiian Band, performs free concerts on Sunday afternoons. Local newspapers list event information. ⊠ *Near intersection of Kalākaua and Monsarrat Aves., Waikīkī.*

☺ **Waikīkī Aquarium.** This amazing little attraction harbors more than 3,000 organisms and 500 species of Hawaiian and South Pacific marine life, endangered Hawaiian monk seals, sharks, and the only chambered nautilus living in captivity. The Edge of the Reef exhibit showcases five different types of reef environments found along Hawai'i's shorelines. Check out the Northwestern Hawaiian Islands exhibit (scheduled to open summer 2010), the Hawaiian Streams Exhibit (opening fall 2010) Ocean Drifters jellyfish exhibit, outdoor touch pool, and the self-guided audio tour, which is included with admission. The aquarium offers programs of interest to adults and children alike, including the Aquarium After Dark when visitors grab a flashlight and view fish going about their rarely observable nocturnal activities. Plan to spend at least an hour at the aquarium, including 10 minutes for a film in the Sea Visions Theater. ⊠ *2777 Kalākaua Ave., Waikīkī* 🕾 *808/923–9741* ⊕ *www.waquarium.org* 🎫 *$9* ⊙ *Daily 9–4:30.*

Waikīkī Shell. Locals bring picnics and grab one of the 6,000 "grass seats" (lawn seating) for music under the stars (there are actual seats, as well). Concerts are held May 1 to Labor Day, with a few winter dates, weather permitting. Check newspaper Friday entertainment sections to see who is performing. ⊠ *2805 Monsarrat Ave., Waikīkī* 🕾 *808/591–2211* ⊕ *www.blaisdellcenter.com.*

Waikīkī War Memorial Natatorium. This 1927 World War I monument, dedicated to the 102 Hawaiian servicemen who lost their lives in battle, stands proudly—its 20-foot archway, which was completely restored in 2002, is floodlighted at night. Despite a face-lift in 2000, the 100-meter saltwater swimming pool, the training spot for Olympians Johnny Weissmuller and Buster Crabbe and the U.S. Army during World War II, is closed, as the pool needs repair. The city has commissioned a study of the Natatorium's future while a nonprofit group fights to save the facility. ⊠ *2777 Kalākaua Ave., Waikīkī.*

GREATER HONOLULU AND PEARL HARBOR

Downtown Honolulu and Chinatown can easily swallow up a day's walking, sightseeing, and shopping. Another day's worth of attractions surrounds the city's core. To the north, just off H1 in the tightly packed neighborhood of Kalihi, explore a museum gifted to the Islands in memory of a princess. Immediately *mauka*, off Pali Highway, are a renowned resting place and a carefully preserved home where royal families retreated during the doldrums of summer. To the south, along King Street and Wai'alae Avenue, are a pair of neighborhoods chockablock with interesting restaurants and shops. Down the shore a bit from Diamond Head, visit O'ahu's ritziest address and an equally upscale shopping center.

One reason to venture farther afield is the chance to glimpse Honolulu's residential neighborhoods. Species of classic Hawai'i homes include the tiny green-and-white plantation-era house with its corrugated tin roof, two windows flanking a central door and small porch; the breezy bungalow with its swooping Thai-style roofline and two wings flanking screened French doors through which breezes blow into the living room. Note the tangled "Grandma-style" gardens and many *ohana* houses—small homes in the backyard of a larger home or built as apartments perched over the garage, allowing extended families to live together. Carports, which rarely house cars, are the Island version of rec rooms, where parties are held and neighbors sit to "talk story." Sometimes you see gallon jars on the flat roofs of garages or carports: these are pickled lemons fermenting in the sun. Also in the neighborhoods, you find the folksy restaurants and takeout spots favored by Islanders.

GETTING HERE AND AROUND

For those with a Costco card, the cheapest gas on the island is at the Costco station on Arakawa Street between Dillingham Boulevard and Nimitz Highway.

TOP ATTRACTIONS

★ **Bishop Museum.** Founded in 1889 by Charles R. Bishop as a memorial to his wife, Princess Bernice Pauahi Bishop, the museum began as a repository for the royal possessions of this last direct descendant of King Kamehameha the Great. Today it's the Hawai'i State Museum of Natural and Cultural History. Its five exhibit halls house almost 25 million items that tell the history of the Hawaiian Islands and their Pacific neighbors. The latest addition to the complex is a natural-science wing with state-of-the-art interactive exhibits. The recently renovated Hawaiian Hall, also with state-of-the art and often interactive displays, teaches about the Hawaiian culture. Hawaiian artifacts—lustrous feather capes, bone fish hooks, the skeleton of a giant sperm whale, photography and crafts displays, and an authentic, well-preserved grass house—are displayed inside a three-story 19th-century Victorian-style gallery. Also check out the planetarium, daily tours, hula and science demonstrations, special exhibits, and the Shop Pacifica. The building alone, with its huge Victorian turrets and immense stone walls, is worth seeing. ✉ *1525 Bernice St., Kalihi* ☎ *808/847–3511* ⊕ *www.bishopmuseum. org* ☜ *$15.95* ☉ *Daily 9–5.*

The Contemporary Art Museum. In the exclusive Makīkī Heights neighborhood just minutes from downtown Honolulu, the Contemporary Art Museum houses collections of modern art dating from 1940. It is in the 3.5-acre Alice Cooke Spalding home and estate, built in 1925. In addition to its ever-changing exhibitions, the museum has a peaceful sculpture garden beneath shade trees with breathtaking views of Diamond Head and Waikīkī. A fun gift shop features jewelry and other art by local artists. The Contemporary Café is popular with locals for lunch. ✉ *2411 Makīkī Heights Dr., Makīkī Heights* ☎ *808/526–1322* ⊕ *www.tcmhi.org* ☜ *$5* ☉ *Tues.–Sat. 10–4, Sun. noon–4.*

Pearl Harbor. *See highlighted feature in this chapter.*

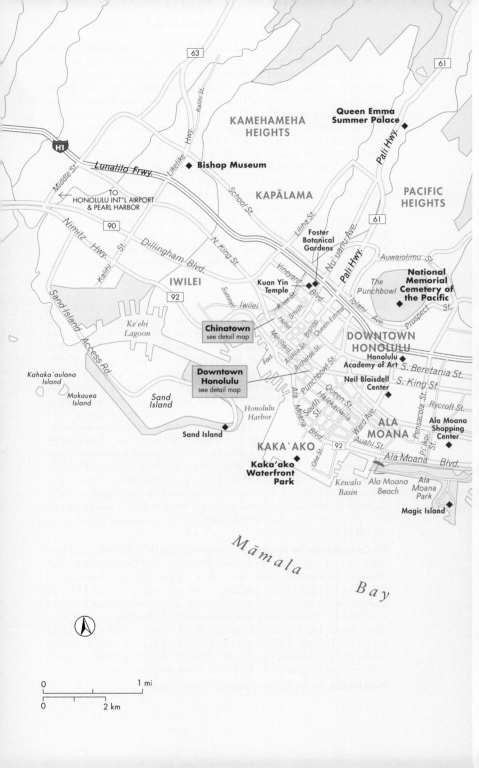

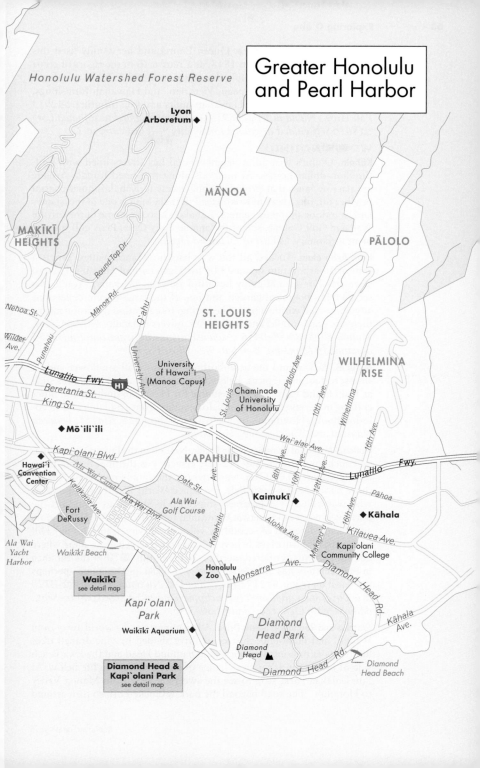

Greater Honolulu and Pearl Harbor

Honolulu Watershed Forest Reserve

Lyon
Arboretum ◆

MĀNOA

PĀLOLO

MAKĪKĪ
HEIGHTS

ST. LOUIS
HEIGHTS

WILHELMINA
RISE

Round Top Dr.

Nehoa St.

Mānoa Rd.

Wilder
Ave.

Punahou

O'ahu

University Ave.

Lunalilo Fwy.

H1

Beretania St.

King St.

University
of Hawai'i
(Manoa Capus)

St. Louis

Chaminade
University
of Honolulu

Pālolo Ave.

10th Ave.

Wilhelmina

16th Ave.

◆ Mō'ili'ili

Kapi'olani Blvd.

Wai'alae Ave.

Hawai'i
Convention
Center

KAPAHULU

Lunalilo Fwy.

Ala Wai Canal

Karakaua Ave.

Ala Wai Blvd.

Date St.

Ave.

8th Ave.

10th Ave.

12th Ave.

Pāhoa

Fort
DeRussy

Ala Wai
Golf Course

Kaimukī ◆

◆ Kāhala

16th Ave.

Ala Wai
Yacht
Harbor

Waikīkī Beach

Kapahulu

Alohea Ave.

Makapu'u

Kīlauea Ave.

Kapi'olani
Community College

Waikīkī
see detail map

Honolulu
Zoo ◆

Monsarrat   Ave.

Diamond Head Rd.

Kāhala
Ave.

Kapi'olani
Park

Waikīkī Aquarium ◆

Diamond
Head Park

Diamond Head & Kapi'olani Park
see detail map

Diamond
Head ▲

Diamond Head Rd.

Diamond
Head Beach

Queen Emma Summer Palace. Queen Emma and her family used this stately white home, built in 1848, as a retreat from the rigors of court life in hot and dusty Honolulu during the mid-1800s. It has an eclectic mix of memorabilia, European, Victorian, and Hawaiian furnishings, and excellent examples of Hawaiian quilts and koa furniture. ⊠ *2913 Pali Hwy., Nu'uanu* ☎ *808/595–3167* ⊕ *www.daughtersofhawaii.org* ⊡ *$6* ☉ *Self-guided or guided tours daily 9–4; last entry at 3.*

WORTH NOTING

Kāhala. O'ahu's wealthiest neighborhood has streets lined with multimillion-dollar homes. At intervals along tree-lined Kāhala Avenue are narrow lanes that provide public access to Kāhala's quiet coastal beaches offering views of Koko Head. Kāhala Mall is one of the island's largest indoor shopping centers. Kāhala is also the home of the private Wai'alae Golf Course, site of the annual Sony Open PGA golf tournament in January. ⊠ *East of Diamond Head.*

Lyon Arboretum. Tucked all the way back in Manoa Valley, this is a gem of an arboretum operated by the University of Hawai'i. Hike to a waterfall or sit and enjoy beautiful views of the valley. You'll also see an ethnobotanical garden and one of the largest palm collections anywhere—all within a park-like setting. Its educational mission means there are regular talks and walks with university faculty. ⊠ *Manoa Rd, Manoa* ☎ *808/988–0456* ⊕ *www.hawaii.edu/lyonarboretum* ⊡ *$5 donation* ☉ *Mon.–Fri. 8–4; Sat. 9–3; Closed Sun.*

Mō'ili'ili. Packed into the neighborhood of Mō'ili'ili are flower and lei shops, restaurants (Spices, Fukuya Delicatessen), and little stores such as Kuni Island Fabrics, a great source for Hawaiian quilting and other crafting materials; Siam Imports, for goodies from Thailand; and Revolution Books, Honolulu's only leftist book shop. ⊠ *S. King St., between Hausten and Wai'alae Ave., Honolulu.*

National Memorial Cemetery of the Pacific. Nestled in the bowl of Puowaina, or Punchbowl Crater, this 112-acre cemetery is the final resting place for more than 50,000 U.S. war veterans and family members. Among those buried here is Ernie Pyle, the famed World War II correspondent who was killed by a Japanese sniper on Ie Shima, an island off the northwest coast of Okinawa. Puowaina, formed 75,000–100,000 years ago during a period of secondary volcanic activity, translates as "Hill of Sacrifice." Historians believe this site once served as an altar where ancient Hawaiians offered sacrifices to their gods. ■TIP➜ The entrance to the cemetery has unfettered views of Waikīkī and Honolulu—perhaps the finest on O'ahu. ⊠ *2177 Puowaina Dr., Nu'uanu* ☎ *808/532–3720* ⊕ *www.cem.va.gov/cem/cems/nchp/nmcp.asp* ⊡ *Free* ☉ *Mar.–Sept., daily 8–6:30; Oct.–Feb., daily 8:30–5:30.*

Tantalus and Round Top Scenic Drive. A few minutes and a world away from Waikīkī and Honolulu, this scenic drive shaded by vine-draped trees has frequent pullouts with views of Diamond Head and the Ewa Beach side of Honolulu. It's a nice change of pace from urban life below. At Puu Ualakaa Park, stop to see the sweeping view from Manoa Valley to Honolulu. The road beyond the park is blocked off, so turn around

Continued on page 75

USS *West Virginia* (BB48), 7 December 1941

PEARL HARBOR

December 7, 1941. Every American then alive recalls exactly what he or she was doing when the news broke that the Japanese had bombed Pearl Harbor, the catalyst that brought the United States into World War II.

Although it was clear by late 1941 that war with Japan was inevitable, no one in authority seems to have expected the attack to come in just this way, at just this time. So when the Japanese bombers swept through a gap in Oʻahu's Koʻolau Mountains in the hazy light of morning, they found the bulk of America's Pacific fleet right where they hoped it would be: docked like giant stepping stones across the calm waters of the bay named for the pearl oysters that once prospered there. More than 2,000 people died that day, including 49 civilians. A dozen ships were sunk. And on the nearby air bases, virtually every American military aircraft was destroyed or damaged. The attack was a stunning success, but it lit a fire under America, which went to war with "Remember Pearl Harbor" as its battle cry. Here, in what is still a key Pacific naval base, the attack is remembered every day by thousands of visitors, including many curious Japanese, who for years heard little World War II history in their own country. In recent years, the memorial has been the site of reconciliation ceremonies involving Pearl Harbor veterans from both sides.

GETTING AROUND

Pearl Harbor is both a working military base and the most-visited O'ahu attraction. Four distinct destinations share a parking lot and are linked by footpath, shuttle, and ferry.

The USS *Arizona* visitor center is accessible from the parking lot. The *Arizona* Memorial itself is in the middle of the harbor; get tickets for the ferry ride at the visitor center. The USS *Bowfin* is also reachable from the parking lot.

The USS *Missouri* is docked at Ford Island, a restricted area of the naval base. Vehicular access is prohibited. To get there, take a shuttle bus from the station near the *Bowfin*.

ARIZONA MEMORIAL

Snugged up tight in a row of seven battleships off Ford Island, the USS *Arizona* took a direct hit that December morning, exploded, and rests still on the shallow bottom where she settled.

A visit to the *Arizona* Memorial begins prosaically—a line, a ticket that assigns you to a group and tour time, a wait filled with shopping, visiting the museum, and strolling the grounds. When your number is called, you watch a 23-minute documentary film then board the ferry to the memorial. The swooping, stark-white memorial, which straddles the wreck of the USS *Arizona*, was designed by Honolulu architect Alfred Preis to represent both the depths of the low-spirited, early days of the war, and the uplift of victory. After the carnival-like courtyard, a somber, contemplative mood descends upon visitors during the ferry ride; this is a place where 1,177 crewmen lost their lives died. Gaze at the names of the dead carved into the wall of white marble.

Scatter flowers (but no lei—the string is bad for the fish). Salute the flag. Remember Pearl Harbor.

808/422–0561
www.nps.gov/usar

USS *MISSOURI* (BB63)

Together with the *Arizona* Memorial, the *Missouri's* presence in Pearl Harbor perfectly bookends America's WWII experience that began December 7, 1941, and ended on the "Mighty Mo's" starboard deck with the signing of the Terms of Surrender.

Surrender of Japan, USS *Missouri*, 2 September 1945

In the parking area behind the USS *Bowfin* Museum, board a jitney for a breezy, eight-minute ride to Ford Island and the teak decks and towering superstructure of the *Missouri*, docked for good in the very harbor from which she first went to war on January 2, 1945. The last battleship ever built, the *Missouri* famously hosted the final act of WWII, the signing of the Terms of Surrender. The commission that governs this floating museum has surrounded her with buildings tricked out in WWII style—a canteen that serves as an orientation space for tours, a WACs and WAVEs lounge with a flight simulator the kids will love ($5 for one person, $18 for four), Truman's Line restaurant serving Navy-

style meals, and a Victory Store housing a souvenir shop and covered with period mottos ("Don't be a blabateur"). ■TIP→ Definitely hook up with a tour guide (additional charge) or purchase an audio tour ($2)—these add a great deal to the experience.

The *Missouri* is all about numbers: 209 feet tall, six 239,000-pound guns, capable of firing up to 23 mi away. Absorb these during the tour, then stop to take advantage of the view from the decks. The Mo is a work in progress, with only a handful of her hundreds of spaces open to view.

808/423–2263 or 888/877–6477
www.ussmissouri.org

USS *BOWFIN* (SS287)

SUBMARINE MUSEUM & PARK

Launched one year to the day after the Pearl Harbor attack, the USS *Bowfin* sank 44 enemy ships during WWII and now serves as the centerpiece of a museum honoring all submariners.

Although the *Bowfin* no less than the *Arizona* Memorial commemorates the lost, the mood here is lighter. Perhaps it's the childlike scale of the boat, a metal tube just 16 feet in diameter, packed with ladders, hatches, and other obstacles, like the naval version of a jungle gym. Perhaps it's the World War II-era music that plays in the covered patio. Or it might be the museum's touching displays—the penciled sailor's journal, the Vargas girlie posters. Aboard the boat nicknamed "Pearl Harbor Avenger," compartments are fitted out as though "Sparky" was away from the radio room just for a moment, and "Cooky" might be right back to his pots and pans. The museum includes many artifacts to spark family conversations, among them a vintage dive suit that looks too big for Shaquille O'Neal. A caution: The *Bowfin* could be hazardous for very young children; no one under four allowed.

808/423–1341
www.bowfin.org

THE PACIFIC AVIATION MUSEUM

This new museum opened on December 7, 2006, as phase one of a four-phase tribute to the air wars of the Pacific. Located on Ford Island in Hangar 37, an actual seaplane hangar that survived the Pearl Harbor attack, the museum is made up of a theater where a short film on Pearl Harbor kicks off the tour, an education center, a shop, and a restaurant. Exhibits—many of which are interactive and involve sound effects—include an authentic Japanese Zero in a diorama setting a chance to don a flight suit and play the role of a World War II pilot using one of six flight simulators. Various aircrafts are employed to narrate the great battles: the Doolittle Raid on Japan, the Battle of Midway, Guadalcanal, and so on. The actual Stearman N2S-3 in which President George H. W. Bush soloed is another exhibit. ☎ 808/441–1000 ⊕ www.pacificaviationmuseum.org ✈ $14.

PLAN YOUR PEARL HARBOR DAY
LIKE A MILITARY CAMPAIGN

DIRECTIONS

Take H–1 west from Waikīkī to Exit 15A and follow signs. Or take TheBus route 20 or 47 from Waikīkī. Beware high-priced private shuttles. It's a 30-minute drive from Waikīkī.

WHAT TO BRING

Picture ID is required during periods of high alert; bring it just in case.

You'll be standing, walking, and climbing all day. Wear something with lots of pockets and a pair of good walking shoes. Carry a light jacket, sunglasses, hat, and sunscreen.

No purses, packs, or bags are allowed. Take only what fits in your pockets. Cameras are okay but without the bags. A private bag storage booth is located in the parking lot near the visitors' center. Leave nothing in your car; theft is a problem despite bicycle security patrols.

HOURS

Hours are 8 AM to 5 PM for all attractions. However, the *Arizona* Memorial starts giving out tickets on a first-come, first-served basis at 7:30 AM; the last tickets are given out at 3 PM. Spring break, summer, and holidays are busiest, and tickets sometimes run out by noon.

TICKETS

Arizona: Free. Add $5 for museum audio tours.

Aviation: $14 adults, $7 children. Add $7 for aviator's guided tour.

Missouri: $16 adults, $8 children. Add $6 for chief's guided tour or audio tour; add $33 for in-depth, behind-the-scenes tours.

Bowfin: $10 adults, $4 children. Add $2 for audio tours. Children under 4 may go into the museum but not aboard the *Bowfin*.

KIDS

This might be the day to enroll younger kids in the hotel children's program. Preschoolers chafe at long waits, and attractions involve some hazards for toddlers. Older kids enjoy the *Bowfin* and *Missouri,* especially.

MAKING THE MOST OF YOUR TIME

Expect to spend at least half a day; a whole day is better.

At the *Arizona* Memorial, you'll get a ticket, be given a tour time, and then have to wait anywhere from 15 minutes to 3 hours. You must pick up your own ticket so you can't hold places. If the wait is long, skip over to the *Bowfin* to fill the time.

SUGGESTED READING

Pearl Harbor and the USS Arizona Memorial, by Richard Wisniewski. $5.95. 64-page magazine-size quick history.

Bowfin, by Edwin P. Hoyt. $14.95. Dramatic story of undersea adventure.

The Last Battleship, by Scott C. S. Stone. $11.95. Story of the Mighty Mo.

If you're a snorkeler, head straight for Hanauma Bay, the bset and most popular place to snorkel on O'ahu.

here to head back to Honolulu. To start the drive, go to Punchbowl Memorial Cemetery and follow Tantalus Drive as it climbs uphill.

SOUTHEAST O'AHU

Driving southeast from Waikīkī on busy four-lane Kalaniana'ole Highway, you'll pass a dozen bedroom communities tucked into the valleys at the foot of the Ko'olau Range, with just fleeting glimpses of the ocean from a couple of pocket parks. Suddenly, civilization falls away, the road narrows to two lanes, and you enter the rugged coastline of Koko Head and Ka Iwi.

This is a cruel coastline: dry, windswept, and rocky shores, with untamed waves that are notoriously treacherous. While walking its beaches, do not turn your back on the ocean, don't venture close to wet areas where high waves occasionally reach, and do heed warning signs.

At this point, you're passing through Koko Head Regional Park. On your right is the bulging remnant of a pair of volcanic craters that the Hawaiians called Kawaihoa, known today as Koko Head. To the left is Koko Crater and an area of the park that includes a hiking trail, a dryland botanical garden, a firing range, and a riding stable. Ahead is a sinuous shoreline with scenic pullouts and beaches to explore. Named the Ka Iwi Coast (*iwi*, "ee-vee," are bones—sacred to Hawaiians and full of symbolism) for the channel just offshore, this area was once home to a ranch and small fishing enclave that were destroyed by a tidal wave in the 1940s.

EXPLORING

Koko Crater Botanical Garden. If you've visited any of O'ahu's other botanical gardens, this one will be in stark contrast. Inside the tallest tuff cone on O'ahu, in one of the hottest and driest areas on the island, Koko Crater botanical garden allows visitors the opportunity to see dryland species of plants including baobab trees, cacti, plumeria, and bougainvillea. ✉ *Kealahou St.* ☎ *808/848–5555* ⊕ *www.honolulu.gov/parks/hbg* ✍ *Free* ☉ *Sunrise–sunset.*

QUICK BITES   Stop for shave ice on the South Shore? President Barack Obama did while visiting the island in December 2008. Kokonuts Shave Ice and Snacks in Koko Marina Center serves, arguably, the best shave ice this side of Hale'iwa. ✉ 7192 *Kalaniana'ole Hwy.* ☎ *808/396–8809* ☉ *10:30* AM–9 PM.

Hālona Blowhole. Below a scenic turnout along the Koko Head shoreline, this oft-photographed lava tube sucks the ocean in and spits it out. Don't get too close, as conditions can get dangerous. ■TIP→ Look to your right to see the tiny beach below that was used to film the wavewashed love scene in From Here to Eternity. In winter this is a good spot to watch whales at play. Offshore, the islands of Moloka'i and Lāna'i call like distant sirens, and every once in a while Maui is visible in blue silhouette. Take your valuables with you and lock your car, because this scenic location is a hot spot for petty thieves. ✉ *Kalaniana'ole Hwy., 1 mi east of Hanauma Bay.*

♺ Fodor's Choice ★

Hanauma Bay Nature Preserve. The exterior wall of a volcanic crater collapsed thousands of years ago, opening it to the sea and thereby giving birth to O'ahu's most famous snorkeling destination. Even from the overlook, the horseshoe-shape bay is a beauty, and you can easily see the reefs through the clear aqua waters. The wide beach is a great place for sunbathing and picnics. This is a marine conservation district, and regulations prohibit feeding the fish. Visitors are required to go through the Education Center and view a nine-minute orientation before trekking down to the bay. The center and film provide a cultural history of the area and exhibits about the importance of protecting its marine life. Check out the "Today at the Bay" exhibit for up-to-date information on daily tides, ocean safety warnings, and activities. Food concessions and equipment rentals are also on-site. ■TIP→ Between the hours of 10 and 1 the parking lot gets full as the number of vehicles allowed to park is limited. Also note that the bay is best in the early hours before the waters are churned up. Call for current conditions. Thursday evening lectures, and Summer Saturday night Hanauma Bay by Starlight events (extending opening hours to 10 PM), are held regularly. Take Bus #22 from Waikīkī to Hanauma Bay's parking lot. ✉ *7455 Kalaniana'ole Hwy.* ☎ *808/396–4229* ⊕ *www.honolulu.gov/parks/facility/hanaumabay/index.htm* ✍ *$7.50; parking $1; mask, snorkel,*

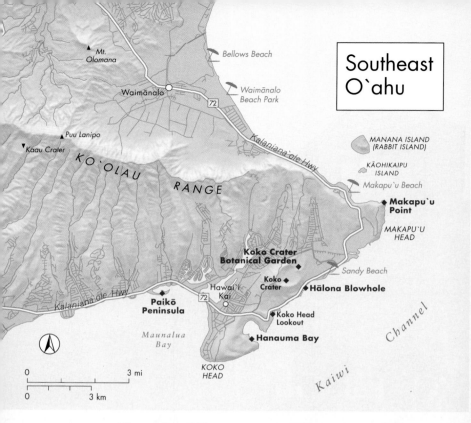

and fin rental available, prices vary; tram from parking lot $1.75 round-trip ⊙ *Wed.–Mon. 6–6.*

Scenic lookout. Just past Hanauma Bay as you head toward Makapu‘u Point, you'll see a turnout with some fine views of the coastline and, in winter, you'll have an opportunity to see storm-generated waves crashing against lava cliffs. This is also a popular place for winter whale-watching so bring your binoculars, some sunscreen, and a picnic lunch and join the small crowd scanning for telltale white spouts of water only a few hundred yards away. ⊠ *Kalaniana‘ole Hwy., just past Hanauma Bay, Koko Head.*

Makapu‘u Point. This spot has breathtaking views of the ocean, mountains, and the Windward islands. The point of land jutting out in the distance is **Mōkapu Peninsula,** site of a U.S. Marine base. The spired mountain peak is **Mt. Olomana.** In front of you on the long pier is part of the **Makai Undersea Test Range,** a research facility that's closed to the public. Offshore is **Manana Island (Rabbit Island),** a picturesque cay said to resemble a swimming bunny with its ears pulled back. Coincidentally, Manana Island was once overrun with rabbits, thanks to a rancher who let a few hares run wild on the land. They were eradicated in 1994 by biologists who grew concerned that the rabbits were destroying the island's native plants.

Nestled in the cliff face is the **Makapu'u Lighthouse,** which became operational in 1909 and has the largest lighthouse lens in America. The lighthouse is closed to the public, but near the Makapu'u Point turnout you can find the start of 1-mi-long paved road (closed to traffic). Hike up to the top of the 647-foot bluff for a closer view of the lighthouse and, in winter, a great whale-watching vantage point. ⊠ *Kalaniana'ole Hwy., 2 mi past Sandy Beach, Koko Head.*

WINDWARD O'AHU

Looking at Honolulu's topsy-turvy urban sprawl, you would never suspect the Windward side existed. It's a secret Oahuans like to keep, so they can watch the awe on the faces of their guests when the car emerges from the tunnels through the mountains and they gaze for the first time on the panorama of turquoise bays and emerald valleys watched over by the knife-edged Ko'olau ridges. Jaws literally drop. Every time. And this just a 15-minute drive from downtown.

It is on this side of the island that many Native Hawaiians live. Evidence of traditional lifestyles is abundant in crumbling fishponds, rock platforms that once were altars, taro patches still being worked, and thrownet fishermen posed stock-still above the water (though today, they're invariably wearing polarized sunglasses, the better to spot the fish).

Here, the pace is slower, more oriented toward nature. Beach-going, hiking, diving, surfing, and boating are the draws, along with a visit to the Polynesian Cultural Center, and poking through little shops and wayside stores.

GETTING HERE AND AROUND

For a driving experience you won't soon forget, take the H3 freeway from the Leeward side (the side including Waikīkī and Honolulu) over to the Windward side. As you pass through the tunnels, be prepared for one of the most breathtaking stretches of road anywhere. Flip a coin before you leave to see who will drive and who will gape.

TIMING

You can easily spend an entire day exploring Windward O'ahu, or you can just breeze on through, nodding at the sights on your way to the North Shore. Waikīkī to Windward is a drive of less than half an hour; to the North Shore via Kamehameha Highway along the Windward Coast is one hour, minimum.

TOP ATTRACTIONS

Byodo-In Temple. Tucked away in the back of the Valley of the Temples cemetery is a replica of the 11th-century Temple at Uji in Japan. A 2-ton carved wooden statue of the Buddha presides inside the main temple building. Next to the temple building are a meditation pavilion and gardens set dramatically against the sheer green cliffs of the Ko'olau Mountains. You can ring the 5-foot, 3-ton brass bell for good luck and feed some of the hundreds of carp that inhabit the garden's pond. ⊠ *47-200 Kahekili Hwy., Kāne'ohe* ☎ *808/239–9844* ⊠ *$3* ☉ *Daily 9–5.*

★ **Kailua Beaches.** Ready for a beach break? Head straight on Kailua Road to the 35-acre, 2½-mi-long **Kailua Beach Park,** which many people

Shangri La

The marriage of heiress Doris Duke, at age 23, to a much older man didn't last. But their around-the-world honeymoon did leave her with two lasting loves: Islamic art and architecture, which she first encountered on that journey; and Hawai'i, where the honeymooners made an extended stay while Doris learned to surf and befriended Islanders unimpressed by her wealth.

Today visitors to her beloved Islands— where she spent most winters—can share both loves by touring her home. The sought-after tours, which are coordinated by and begin at the downtown Honolulu Academy of Arts, start with a visit to the Arts of the Islamic World Gallery. A short van ride then takes small groups on to the house itself, on the far side of Diamond Head.

In 1936 Duke bought 5 acres at Black Point, down the coast from Waikīkī, and began to build and furnish the first home that would be all her own. She called it **Shangri La**. For more than 50 years, the home was a work in progress as Duke traveled the world, buying art and furnishings, picking up ideas for her Mughul garden, for the Playhouse in the style of a 17th-century Irani pavilion, and for the water terraces and tropical gardens. When she died in 1993, Duke left instructions that her home was to become a public center for the study of Islamic art.

To walk through the house and its gardens—which have remained much as Duke left them with only some minor conservation-oriented changes—is to experience the personal style of someone who saw everything as raw material for her art.

With her trusted houseman, Jin de Silva, she helped build the elaborate Turkish Room, trimming tiles and painted panels to retrofit the existing space (including raising the ceiling and lowering the floor) and building a fountain of her own design. Among many aspects of the home inspired by the Muslim tradition is the entry: an anonymous gate, a blank white wall, and a wooden door that bids you "Enter herein in peace and security" in Arabic characters. Inside, tiles glow, fountains tinkle, and shafts of light illuminate artworks through arches and high windows. This was her private world, entered only by trusted friends.

The house is open by guided tour; tours take 2½ hours. Children under 12 are not admitted. All tours begin at the Honolulu Academy of Arts.

✉ *Academy of Arts, 900 S. Beretania, Kahala* ☎ *808/532–3853 Honolulu Academy of Arts* ⊕ *www.honoluluacademy.org* ✉ *Tours $25* ☉ *Tours Wed.–Sat. by reservation; first tour 8:30 AM, last tour 1:30 PM.*

---

consider the best on the island. South of the Kailua Beach is **Lanikai,** originally a summer-beach-house community for O'ahu's wealthy; the beach here (there are public access trails) is narrow but less used. Both beaches have won Best Beach awards. Take Kailua Road to South Kalaheo, turn right and continue as the road veers left, cross the bridge and enter the park on the left. To get to Lanikai, continue on as South Kalaheo becomes Kawailoa, turn left at the dead end and enter the

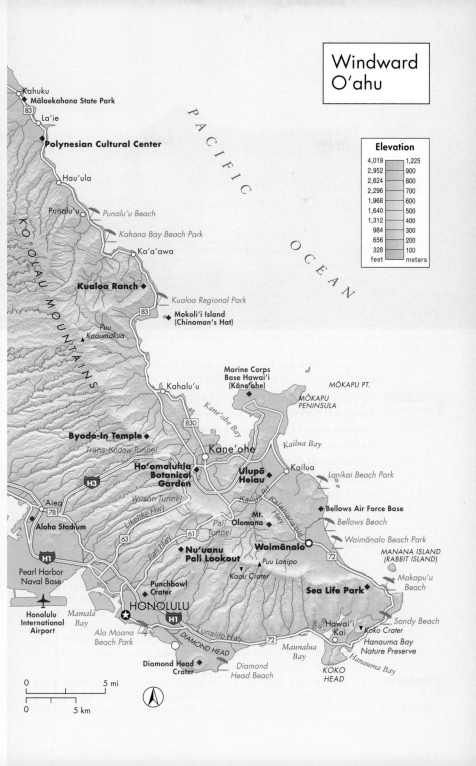

Windward O'ahu

Elevation

feet	meters
4,019	1,225
2,952	900
2,624	800
2,296	700
1,968	600
1,640	500
1,312	400
984	300
656	200
328	100

PACIFIC OCEAN

KO'OLAU MOUNTAINS

Kahuku
Mālaekahana State Park
83
La'ie
Polynesian Cultural Center
Hau'ula
Punalu'u
Punalu'u Beach
Kahana Bay Beach Park
Ka'a'awa
Kualoa Ranch
Kualoa Regional Park
83
Mokoli'i Island
(Chinaman's Hat)
Puu Kaaumakua
Marine Corps Base Hawai'i (Kāne'ohe)
MŌKAPU PT.
MŌKAPU PENINSULA
Kahalu'u
Kane'ohe Bay
830
Byodo-In Temple
Trans-Koolau Tunnel
Kane'ohe
Kailua Bay
Ho'omaluhia Botanical Garden
Ulupō Heiau
Kailua
Lanikai Beach Park
H3
Wilson Tunnel
Kailua Rd.
'Aiea
78
Likelike Hwy.
Pali Tunnel
Mt. Olomana
Kalanianaole Hwy.
Bellows Air Force Base
Bellows Beach
Aloha Stadium
63
61
Nu'uanu Pali Lookout
Waimānalo Beach Park
H1
Pali Hwy.
Puu Lanipo
72
MANANA ISLAND (RABBIT ISLAND)
Pearl Harbor Naval Base
Punchbowl Crater
Kaau Crater
Waimānalo
Makapu'u Beach
Honolulu International Airport
Mamala Bay
HONOLULU
Sea Life Park
H1
Hawai'i Kai
Sandy Beach
Ala Moana Beach Park
Lunalilo Hwy.
72
Koko Crater
Hanauma Bay Nature Preserve
DIAMOND HEAD
Maunalua Bay
Hanauma Bay
Diamond Head Crater
Diamond Head Beach
KOKO HEAD

0   5 mi

0   5 km

You can catch a great sunset over Manana Island, otherwise known as Rabbit Island, located on the windward side of O'ahu.

A'alapapa/Mokulua Drive loop. Park on Mokulua Drive (be sure not to park in the bike lane) and look for beach access. ⊠ *Kawailoa Rd.*

QUICK BITES

Generations of children have purchased their beach snacks and sodas at **Kalapawai Market** (⊠ *306 S. Kalāheo Ave.*), near Kailua Beach. A Windward landmark since 1932, the green-and-white market has distinctive charm. You'll see slipper-clad locals sitting in front sharing a cup of coffee and talking story at picnic tables or in front of the market. It's a good source for your carryout lunch, since there's no concession stand at the beach. Or, grab a cup of coffee and have a seat at the wooden tables outside. With one of the better selections of wine on the island, the market is also a great place to pick up a bottle.

Nu'uanu Pali Lookout. This panoramic perch looks out to Windward O'ahu. It was in this region that King Kamehameha I drove defending forces over the edges of the 1,000-foot-high cliffs, thus winning the decisive battle for control of O'ahu. ■ TIP→ From here you can see views that stretch from Kāne'ohe Bay to Mokoli'i ("little lizard"), a small island off the coast, and beyond. Temperatures at the summit are several degrees cooler than in warm Waikīkī, so bring a jacket along. Hang on tight to any loose possessions; it gets extremely windy at the lookout. Lock your car and take valuables with you; break-ins are common. ⊠ *Top of Pali Hwy.* ☉ *Daily 9–4.*

EN ROUTE

As you drive the Windward and North Shores along Kamehameha Highway, you'll note a number of interesting geological features. At Kualoa look to the ocean and gaze at the uniquely shaped little island of

Mokoliʻi ("little lizard"), a 206-foot-high sea stack also known as Chinaman's Hat. According to Hawaiian legend, the goddess Hiʻiaka, sister of Pele, slew the dragon Mokoliʻi and flung its tail into the sea, forming the distinct islet. Other dragon body parts—in the form of rocks—are scattered along the base of nearby Kualoa Ridge. ■TIP➔ In Lāʻie, if you turn right on Anemoku Street, and right again on Naupaka, you come to a scenic lookout where you can see a group of islets, dramatically washed by the waves.

2

☺ **Polynesian Cultural Center.** Re-created individual villages showcase the island lifestyles and traditions of Hawaiʻi, Tahiti, Samoa, Fiji, New Zealand, and Tonga. Focusing on individual islands within its 42-acre center, 35 mi from Waikīkī, the Polynesian Cultural Center was founded in 1963 by the Church of Jesus Christ of Latter-day Saints. It houses restaurants, hosts lūʻaus, and demonstrates cultural traditions such as tribal tattooing, fire dancing, and ancient customs and ceremonies. The expansive open-air shopping village carries Polynesian handicrafts. ■TIP➔ If you're staying in Honolulu, see the center as part of a bus tour so you won't have to drive home late at night after the 90-minute evening show. Various packages are available, from basic admission to an all-inclusive deal. Every May, the PCC hosts the World Fire Knife Dance Competition, an event that draws the top fire-knife dance performers from around the world. ✉ 55-370 Kamehameha Hwy., Lāʻie ☎ 808/293–3333 or 800/367–7060 ⊕ www.polynesia.com ☞ $45–$225 ⊙ Mon.–Sat. 12:30–9:30. Islands exhibit closes at 5:30.

Windward Villages. Tiny villages—generally consisting of a sign, store, a beach park, possibly a post office, and not much more—are strung along Kamehameha Highway on the Windward side. Each has something to offer. In **Waiahole,** look for fruit stands and an ancient grocery store. In **Kaʻaʻawa,** there's a lunch spot and convenience store/gas station. In **Punaluʻu,** stop at the gallery of fanciful landscape artist Lance Fairly and the woodworking shop, Kahaunani Woods & Crafts, plus venerable Ching General Store or the Shrimp Shack. Kim Taylor Reece's photo studio, featuring haunting portraits of hula dancers, is between Punaluʻu and Hauʻula. **Hauʻula** has Hauʻula Gift Shop and Art Gallery, formerly yet another Ching Store, now a clothing shop where sarongs wave like banners, and, at Hauʻula Kai Shopping Center, Tamura Market, with excellent seafood and the last liquor before Mormon-dominated Lāʻie.

WORTH NOTING

Kualoa Ranch. Set on 4,000 acres, and a 45-minute drive from Waikīkī, this working ranch offers a wide range of activities—from ATV and horseback tours to hula lessons or jungle expeditions in six-wheel-drive vehicles. The mountains, which serve as the backdrop of this scenic ranch, may seem familiar as the ranch has served as the set for movies such as *Jurassic Park* and *Wind Talkers,* and TV shows *Magnum PI* and

Lost. ⊠ *Kamehameha Highway, Ka'a'awa* ☎ *808/237–7321* ⊕ *www. kualoa.com* ⊠ *Admission varies based on activity* ⊙ *Book activities 2–3 days in advance.*

ℭ **Sea Life Park.** Dolphins leap and spin, penguins frolic, and a "whalfin" performs impressive tricks at this marine-life attraction 15 mi from Waikīkī at scenic Makapu'u Point. What's a "whalfin"? She's one-quarter false killer whale and three-quarters bottle-nosed dolphin— the only one of her kind in existence. The park has a 300,000-gallon Hawaiian reef aquarium, the Hawaiian Monk Seal Care Center, and a breeding sanctuary for Hawai'i's endangered *Honu* sea turtle. Swim with the sea lions, trek to the bottom of the reef aquarium to help divers feed the fish, or get up close and personal with three different dolphin encounters. ⊠ *41-202 Kalaniana'ole Hwy., Waimānalo* ☎ *808/259–7933 or 886/365–7446* ⊕ *www.sealifeparkhawaii.com* ⊠ *$29* ⊙ *Daily 10:30–5.*

Ho'omaluhia Botanical Garden. The name, which means "to make a place of peace and tranquillity," describes the serenity and feeling of endless space you find in this verdant garden framed by the stunning Ko'olau mountain range. Inside its 400 acres are plant collections from such tropical areas as the Americas, Africa, Melanesia, the Philippines, and Hawai'i. Not just for the botanist, Ho'omaluhia also has a pond and open lawns ideal for picnicking. ⊠ *45-680 Luluku Rd., he'ohe* ☎ *808/233–7323* ⊕ *www.honolulu.gov/parks/hbg* ⊠ *Free* ⊙ *Daily 9–4.*

Ulupō Heiau. Though they may look like piles of rocks to the uninitiated, *heiau* are sacred stone platforms for the worship of the gods and date from ancient times. Ulupō means "night inspiration," referring to the legendary *Menehune*, a mythical race of diminutive people who are said to have built the heiau under the cloak of darkness. ⊠ *Kalaniana'ole Hwy. and Kailua Rd., behind YMCA.*

Waimānalo. The biggest draws of this modest little seaside town flanked by chiseled cliffs are its beautiful beaches, with glorious views to the Windward side. **Bellows Beach** is great for swimming and bodysurfing, and **Waimānalo Beach Park** is also safe for swimming. Down the side roads as you head *mauka* are little farms that grow a variety of fruits and flowers. Toward the back of the valley are small ranches with grazing horses. ■ TIP➔ If you see any trucks selling corn and you're staying at a place where you can cook it, be sure to get some in Waimānalo. It may be the sweetest you'll ever eat, and the price is the lowest on O'ahu. ⊠ *Kalaniana'ole Hwy.*

THE NORTH SHORE

An hour from town and a world away in atmosphere, O'ahu's North Shore, roughly from Kahuku Point to Ka'ena Point, is about small farms and big waves, tourist traps and otherworldly landscapes. Parks and beaches, roadside fruit stands and shrimp shacks, a bird sanctuary, and a valley preserve offer a dozen reasons to stop between the one-time plantation town of Kahuku and the surf mecca of Hale'iwa.

Stroll along Kailua Beach, which many consider to be O'ahu's best beach, as well as the hottest place to windsurf on the island.

Hale'iwa has had many lives, from resort getaway in the 1900s to plantation town through the 20th century to its life today as a surf and tourist magnet. Beyond Hale'iwa is the tiny village of Waialua, a string of beach parks, an airfield where gliders, hang-gliders, and parachutists play, and, at the end of the road, Ka'ena Point State Recreation Area, which offers a brisk hike, striking views, and whale-watching in season.

Pack wisely for a day's North Shore excursion: swim and snorkel gear, light jacket and hat (the weather is mercurial, especially in winter), sunscreen and sunglasses, bottled water and snacks, towels and a picnic blanket, and both sandals and close-toed shoes for hiking. A small cooler is nice; you may want to pick up some fruit or fresh corn. As always, leave valuables in the hotel safe and lock the car whenever you park.

GETTING HERE AND AROUND
From Waikīkī, the quickest route to the North Shore is H1 east to H2 north and then the Kamehameha Highway past Wahiawā; you'll hit Hale'iwa in less than an hour. The Windward route (H1 east, H3, Like Like or Pali Highway, through the mountains, or Kamehameha Highway north) takes at least 90 minutes to Hale'iwa.

TIMING
It's best to dedicate and entire day for an excursion to the North Shore, as it's about an hour from downtown Honolulu, depending on traffic.

TOP ATTRACTIONS

Haleʻiwa. During the 1920s this seaside hamlet boasted a posh hotel at the end of a railroad line (both long gone). During the 1960s, hippies gathered here, followed by surfers from around the world. Today Haleʻiwa is a fun mix of old general stores and contemporary boutiques, galleries, and eateries. Be sure to stop in at **Liliʻuokalani Protestant Church,** founded by missionaries in the 1830s. It's fronted by a large, stone archway built in 1910 and covered with night-blooming cereus. ✉ *Follow H1 west from Honolulu to H2 north, exit at Wahiawā, follow Kamehameha Hwy. 6 mi, turn left at signaled intersection, then right into Haleʻiwa* ⊕ *www.haleiwamainstreet.com.*

QUICK BITES

For a real slice of Haleʻiwa life, stop at Matsumoto's (✉ **66-087 Kamehameha Hwy.** ☎ **808/637–4827** ⊕ *www.matsumotoshaveice.com*), a family-run business in a building dating from 1910, for shave ice in every flavor imaginable. For something different, order a shave ice with adzuki beans—the red beans are boiled until soft, mixed with sugar, and then placed in the cone with the ice on top.

Kaʻena Point State Recreation Area. The name means "the heat" and, indeed, this windy barren coast lacks both shade and fresh water (or any man-made amenities). Pack water, wear sturdy closed-toe shoes, don sunscreen and a hat, and lock the car. The hike is along a rutted dirt road, mostly flat and 3 mi long, ending in a rocky, sandy headland. It is here that Hawaiians believed the souls of the dead met with their family gods, and, if judged worthy to enter the afterlife, leapt off into eternal darkness at Leinaakaʻuane, just south of the point. In summer and at low tide, the small coves offer bountiful shelling; in winter, don't venture near the water. Rare native plants dot the landscape. November through March, watch for humpbacks spouting and breaching. Binoculars and a camera are highly recommended. ✉ *North end of Kamehameha Hwy.*

☾ **Waimea Valley Park.** Waimea may get lots of press for the giant winter
★ waves in the bay, but the valley itself is a newsmaker and an ecological treasure in its own right. If you visit one botanical garden on Oʻahu, this is the one to see. The Office of Hawaiian Affairs is working to conserve and restore the natural habitat. Follow the Kamananui Stream up the valley through the 1,800 acres of gardens. The botanical collections here include more than 5,000 species of tropical flora, including a superb gathering of Polynesian plants. It's the best place on the island to see native species, such as the endangered Hawaiian moorhen. You can also see the remains of the Hale O Lono *heiau* (temple) along with other ancient archaeological sites; evidence suggests that the area was an important spiritual center. At the back of the valley, **Waihī Falls** plunges 45 feet into a swimming pond. Daily activities between 10 and 2 include hula lessons, native plant walks, lei-making lessons and kapa cloth–making demonstrations ■ TIP➔ Bring your suit—a swim is the perfect way to end your hike. There's a lifeguard and changing room. Be sure to bring mosquito repellent, too; it gets buggy. ✉ *59-864 Kamehameha*

Continued on page 91

Imagine picking your seat for free at the Super Bowl or wandering the grounds of Augusta National at no cost during The Masters, and you glimpse the opportunity you have when attending the Vans Triple Crown of Surfing on the North Shore.

NORTH SHORE SURFING & THE TRIPLE CROWN

10-FOOT WAVES.
10,000 FANS.
TOP 50 SURFERS.

Long considered the best stretch of surf breaks on Earth, the North Shore surf area encompasses 6 mi of coastline on the northwestern tip of O'ahu from Hale'iwa to Sunset Beach. There are over 20 major breaks within these 6 mi. Winter storms in the North Pacific send huge swells southward which don't break for thousands of miles until they hit the shallow reef of O'ahu's remote North Shore. This creates optimum surfing all winter long and was the inspiration for having surf competitions here each holiday season.

Every November and December the top 50 surfers in world rankings descend on "The Country" to decide who is the best all-around surfer in the world. Each of the three invitation-only contests that make up the Triple Crown has its own winner; competitors also win points based on the final standings. The surfer who excels in all three contests, racking up the most points overall, wins the Vans Triple Crown title. The first contest is held at **Hale'iwa Beach,** the second at **Sunset Beach.** The season reaches its crescendo at the most famous surf break in the world, the **Banzai Pipeline.**

The best part is the cost to attend the events—nothing; your seat for the show—wherever you set down your beach towel. Just park your car, grab your stuff, and watch the best surfers in the world tame the best waves in the world.

> The only surfing I understand involves a mouse.

The contests were created not only to fashion an overall champion, but to attract the casual fan to the sport. Announcers explain each ride over the loudspeakers, discussing the nuances and values being weighed by the judges. A scoreboard displays points and standings during the four days of each event.

If this still seems incomprehensible to you, the action on the beach can also be exciting as some of the most beautiful people in the world are attracted to these contests.

For more information, see www.triplecrownofsurfing. com

What should I bring?

Pack for a day at the Triple Crown the way you would for any day at the beach–sun block, beach towel, bottled water, and if you want something other than snacks, food.

These contests are held in rural neighborhoods (read: few stores), so pack anything you might need during the day. Also, binoculars are suggested, especially for the contest at Sunset. The pros will be riding huge outside ocean swells, and it can be hard to follow from the beach without binoculars. Hale'iwa's breaks and Pipeline are considerably closer to shore, but binoculars will let you see the intensity on the contestants' faces.

Hale'iwa Ali'i Beach Park
Vans Triple Crown Contest #1: OP Pro Hawaii

The Triple Crown gets underway with high-performance waves (and the know-how to ride them) at Hale'iwa. Though lesser known than the other two breaks of the Triple Crown, it is the perfect wave for showing off: the contest here is full of sharp cutbacks (twisting the board dramatically off the top or bottom of the wave), occasional barrel rides, and a crescendo of floaters (balancing the board on the top of the cresting wave) before the wave is destroyed on the shallow tabletop reef called the Toilet Bowl. The rider who can pull off the most tricks will win this leg, evening the playing field for the other two contests, where knowledge of the break is the key. Also, the beach park is walking distance from historic Hale'iwa town, a mecca to surfers worldwide who make their pilgrimage here every winter to ride the waves. Even if you are not a fan, immersing yourself in their culture will make you one by nightfall.

Sunset Beach
Vans Triple Crown Contest #2: O'Neill World Cup of Surfing

At Sunset, the most guts and bravado win the day. The competition is held when the swell is at 8 to 12 feet and from the northwest. Sunset gets the heaviest surf because it is the exposed point on the northern tip of O'ahu. Surfers describe the waves here as "moving mountains." The choice of waves is the key to this contest as only the perfect one will give the competitor a ride through the jigsaw-puzzle outer reef, which can kill a perfect wave instantly, all the way into the inner reef. Big bottom turns (riding all the way down the face of the wave before turning dramatically back onto the wave) and slipping into a super thick tube (slowing down to let the wave catch you and riding inside its vortex) are considered necessary to carry the day.

Banzai Pipeline
Vans Triple Crown Contest #3: Rip Curl Pipeline Masters

It is breathtaking to watch the best surfers in the world disappear into a gaping maw of whitewash for a few seconds only to emerge from the other side unscathed. Surfing the Pipeline showcases their ability to specialize in surfing, to withstand the power and fury of a 10-foot wave from within its hollow tube.

How does the wave become hollow in the first place? When the deep ocean floor ascends steeply to the shore, the waves that meet it will pitch over themselves sharply, rather than rolling. This pitching causes a tube to form, and in most places in the world that tube is a mere couple of feet in diameter. In the case of Pipeline, however, its unique, extremely shallow reef causes the swells to open into 10-foot-high moving hallways that surfers can pass through. Only problem: a single slip puts them right into the raggedly sharp coral heads that caused the wave to pitch in the first place. Broken arms and boards are the rule rather than the exception for those who dare to ride and fail.

■ TIP→ The Banzai Pipeline is a surf break, not a beach. The best place to catch a glimpse of the break is from 'Ehukai Beach.

When Are the Contests?

The first contests at Hale'iwa begin the second week of November, and the Triple Crown finishes up right before Christmas.

Surfing, more so than any other sport, relies on Mother Nature to allow competition. Each contest in the Triple Crown requires only four days of competition, but each is given a window of twelve days. Contest officials decide by 7 AM of each day whether the contest will be held or not, and they release the information to radio stations and via a hotline (whose number changes each year, unfortunately). By 7:15, you will know if it is on or not. Consult the local paper's sports section for the hotline number or listen to the radio announcement. The contests run from 8:30 to 4:30, featuring half-hour heats with four to six surfers each.

If big crowds bother you, go early on in the contests, within the first two days of each one. While the finale of the Pipeline Masters may draw about 10,000 fans, the earlier days have the same world class surfers with less than a thousand fans.

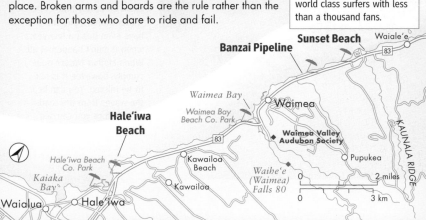

How Do I Get There?

If you hate dealing with parking and traffic, take TheBus. It will transport you from Waikīkī to the contest sites in an hour for two bucks and no hassle.

If you must drive, watch the news the night before. If they are expecting big waves that night, there is a very good chance the contest will be on in the morning. Leave by 6 AM to beat the crowd. When everybody else gets the news at 7:15 AM that the show is on, you will be parking your car and taking a snooze on the beach waiting for the surfing to commence.

Parking is limited so be prepared to park alongside Kamehameha Highway and trek it in.

But I'm not coming until Valentine's Day.

There doesn't need to be a contest underway for you to enjoy these spots from a spectator's perspective. The North Shore surf season begins in October and concludes at the end of March. Only the best can survive the wave at Pipeline. You may not be watching Kelly Slater or Andy Irons ripping, but, if the waves are up, you will still see surfing that will blow your mind. Also, there are surf contests year-round on all shores of O'ahu, so check the papers to see what is going on during your stay. A few other events to be on the lookout for:

Buffalo's Annual Big Board Surfing Classic
Generally held in March at

legendary waterman "Buffalo" Keaulana's home beach of Mākaha, this is the Harlem Globetrotters of surfing contests. You'll see tandem riding, headstands, and outrigger canoe surfing. The contest is more about making the crowds cheer than beating your competitors, which makes it very accessible for the casual fan.

Converse Hawaiian Open
During the summer months, the waves switch to the south shore, where there are surf contests of one type or another each week. The Open is one of the biggest and is a part of the US Professional Longboard Surfing Championships. The best shoot it out every August on the waves Duke Kahanamoku made famous at Queen's Beach in Waikīkī.

Quiksilver in Memory of Eddie Aikau Big Wave Invitational
The granddaddy of them all is a one-day, winner-take-all contest in 25-foot surf at Waimea Bay. Because of the need for huge waves, it can be held only when there's a perfect storm. That could be at any time in the winter months, and there have even been a few years when it didn't happen at all. When Mother Nature does comply, however, it is not to be missed. You can hear the waves from the road, even before you can see the beach or the break.

Hwy., Hale'iwa ☎ *808/638–7766* ⊕ *www.audubon.org* 🖃 *$10, parking $2* ⊙ *Daily 9–5.*

The chocolate-*haupia* (coconut) pie at Ted's Bakery (🖃 *59-024 Kamehameha Hwy., near Sunset Beach* ☎ *808/638–8207*) is legendary. Stop in for a take-out pie or for a quick plate lunch or sandwich.

WORD OF MOUTH

"The Waimea Audubon Center [now known as Waimea Valley Park] was very nice. It has paved trails through beautiful gardens; there are also some other trails. It was very peaceful! Peacocks run around the property." —Kerry392

WORTH NOTING

North Shore Surf and Cultural Museum. Shop-owner and curator Hurricane Bob displays more than 30 vintage surfboards dating back to the 1930s, a shrine dedicated to legendary surfer Duke Kahanamoku, video presentations, surf memorabilia, and even a motorized surfboard that served as the forerunner to the Jet Ski. 🖃 *66-250 Kamehameha Hwy., Hale'iwa* ☎ *808/637–8888* 🖃 *Donations accepted* ⊙ *Wed.–Mon. 11:30–6.*

Pu'uomahuka Heiau. Worth a stop for its spectacular views from a bluff high above the ocean overlooking Waimea Bay, this sacred spot was once the site of human sacrifices. It's now on the National Register of Historic Places. 🖃 *½-mi north of Waimea Bay, from Rte. 83 turn right on Pūpūkea Rd. and drive 1 mi uphill.*

CENTRAL AND WEST (LEEWARD) O'AHU

O'ahu's central plain is a patchwork of old towns and new residential developments, military bases, farms, ranches, and shopping malls, with a few visit-worthy attractions and historic sites scattered about. Central O'ahu encompasses the Moanalua Valley, residential Pearl City, and the old plantation town of Wahiawā, on the uplands halfway to the North Shore.

West (or Leeward) O'ahu has the island's fledgling "second city"—the planned community of Kapolei, where the government hopes to attract enough jobs to lighten inbound traffic to downtown Honolulu—then continues on past a far-flung resort to the Hawaiian communities of Nānākuli and Wai'anae, to the beach and the end of the road at Keawe'ula, aka Yokohama Bay.

A couple of cautions as you head to the Leeward side: Highway 93 is a narrow, winding two-lane road notorious for accidents. There's an abrupt transition from freeway to highway at Kapolei, and by the time you reach Nānākuli, it's a country road, so slow down. ⚠ Car break-ins and beach thefts are common here.

GETTING HERE AND AROUND

For central Oahu, all sights are most easily reached by either the H1 or H2 freeway. West O'ahu begins at folksy Waipahu and continues past Makakilo and Kapolei on H1 and Highway 93, Farrington Highway.

FUN THINGS TO DO AROUND O'AHU

■ Loop a mountain trail high above the city.

■ Play Hawaiian checkers at the Paradise Cove lū'au.

■ Walk to the ends of the earth at Ka'ena Point.

■ Watch winter's house-size waves on the North Shore.

■ Kayak to Kapapa off the Kualoa shore.

■ Lose yourself in a tropical maze at Dole Plantation.

■ Pick up a papaya at a roadside stand.

■ Let the wind whip your cares away on Nu'uanu Pali Overlook.

TIMING

If you've got to leave one part of this island for the next trip, this is the part to skip. It's a longish drive to West O'ahu by island standards—45 minutes to Kapolei from Waikīkī and 90 minutes to Wai'anae—and Central O'ahu has little to offer. The attraction most worth the trek to West O'ahu is Hawai'i's Plantation Village in Waipahu, about a half hour out of town; it's a living-history museum built from actual homes of turn-of-the-20th-century plantation workers. In Central O'ahu, check out the Dole Plantation for all things pineapple.

TOP ATTRACTIONS

Dole Plantation. Celebrate Hawai'i's famous golden fruit at this promotional center with exhibits, a huge gift shop, a snack concession, educational displays, and the world's largest maze. Take the self-guided Garden Tour, plant your own pineapple or hop aboard the *Pineapple Express* for a 20-minute train tour to learn a bit about life on a pineapple plantation. Kids love the 3-plus-acre Pineapple Garden Maze, made up of 14,000 tropical plants and trees. This is about a 40-minute drive from Waikīkī, a suitable stop on the way to or from the North Shore. ✉ *64-1550 Kamehameha Hwy., Wahiawā* ☎ *808/621–8408* ⊕ *www. dole-plantation.com* ▣ *Pavilion free, maze $6, train $7.75, garden tour $4* ⊙ *Daily 9–5:30; train, maze, and garden close at 5.*

Mākaha Beach Park. Famous as a surfing-and-boogie-boarding park, Mākaha hosts an annual surf meet and draws many scuba divers in summer, when the waves are calm, to explore underwater caverns and ledges. It's popular with families year-round, but in winter watch for riptides and currents; Mākaha means "fierce," and there's a reason for that. ✉ *84-369 Farrington Hwy., Wai'anae.*

WORTH NOTING

Kūkaniloko Birthstone State Monument. In the cool uplands of Wahiawā is haunting Kūkaniloko, where noble chieftesses went to give birth to high-ranking children. One of the most significant cultural sites on the island, the lava-rock stones here were believed to possess the power to ease the labor pains of childbirth. The site is marked by approximately 180 stones covering about a half-acre. It's about a 40- to 45-minute drive from Waikīkī. ✉ *Kamehameha Hwy. and Whitmore Ave., north side of Wahiawā town, Wahiawā.*

Moanalua Gardens. This lovely park is the site of the internationally acclaimed Prince Lot Hula Festival on the third weekend in July. Throughout the year, the Moanalua Gardens Foundation sponsors 3-mi guided hikes into Kamananui Valley, usually on Sunday; call for times. Self-guided tour booklets ($5) are also available from the Moanalua

Gardens Foundation office. To reach Moanalua Gardens, take the Moanalua Freeway westbound (78). Take the Tripler exit, then take a right on Mahiole Street. Pineapple Place is just after Moanalua Elementary School. ⊠ *1352 Pineapple Pl., Honolulu* ☎ *808/833–1944* ⊕ *www. mgf-hawaii.com* ⊠ *Free, guided hikes $5* ⊙ *Weekdays 8–4:30.*

☺ **Wet and Wild Hawaii.** This 25-acre family attraction has waterslides, water cannons, and waterfalls. ⊠ *400 Farrington Hwy., off H1 at Exit 1, Kapolei* ☎ *808/674–9283* ⊕ *www.hawaiianwaters.com* ⊠ *$40* ⊙ *10:30–3:30 weekend 10:30–4.*

Hawai'i's Plantation Village. Starting in the 1800s, immigrants seeking work on the sugar plantations came to these islands like so many waves against the shore. At this living museum 30 minutes from downtown Honolulu, visit authentically furnished buildings, original and replicated, that re-create and pay tribute to the plantation era. See a Chinese social hall; a Japanese shrine, sumo ring, and saimin stand; a dental office; and historic homes. The village is open for guided tours only. ⊠ *Waipahu Cultural Gardens Park, 94-695 Waipahu St., Waipahu* ☎ *808/677–0110* ⊕ *www.hawaiiplantationvillage.org* ⊠ *$13* ⊙ *Tours on the hr, Mon.–Sat. 10–2.*

Keawa'ula Beach (Yokohama Bay). The last sandy beach, and the last stop, on Farrington Highway is both a surfing beach and a sunbathing spot far, far from the madding crowd. Just down the road is the western end of the undeveloped Ka'ena Point State Recreation Area; you can hike to Ka'ena Point from here, but it's a rugged trek. ⊠ *End of Farrington Hwy., Wai'anae.*

Ko Olina. Among the many amenities at this resort that are open to the public is the challenging (and pricey) Ted Robinson–designed golf course *(*⇨ *see Chapter 5, Golf, Hiking and Outdoor Activities)*, two nice, sit-down lunch spots—Roy's Ko Olina at the golf course and the Naupaka Terrace at the JW Marriott Ko Olina Resort & Spa—and a couple of man-made swimming lagoons surrounded by lush lawns with changing and bathroom facilities. ⊠ *Farrington Hwy., at Ali'inui Dr., Kapolei* ☎ *808/676–5300 Ko Olina Golf Club; 808/676–7697 Roy's Ko Olina; 808/679–0079 Naupaka Terr.* ⊕ *www.koolinagolf.com.*

Pōkai Bay Beach Park. This gorgeous swimming and snorkeling beach is protected by a long breakwater left over from a now-defunct boat harbor. The beach's entire length is sand, and a reef creates smallish waves perfect for novice surfers. ⊠ *85-027 Wai'anae Valley Rd., off Farrington Hwy., Wai'anae.*

3

Beaches

WORD OF MOUTH

"Lanikai is arguably the best beach on O'ahu; IMHO, it's probably the nicest beach in all of Hawai'i. The semi-white, powdery sand; shallow, turquoise waters; two picturesque islands to view offshore; gorgeous sunrise."

—bluefan

Updated By
Chad Pata

Tropical sun mixed with cooling trade winds and pristine waters make O'ahu's shores a literal heaven on earth. But contrary to many assumptions, the island is not one big beach. There are miles and miles of coastline without a grain of sand, so you need to know where you are going to fully enjoy the Hawaiian experience.

Much of the island's southern and eastern coast is protected by inner reefs. The reefs provide still coastline water but not much as far as sand is concerned. However, where there are beaches on the south and east shores, they are mind-blowing. In West O'ahu and on the North Shore you can find the wide expanses of sand you would expect for enjoying the sunset. Sandy bottoms and protective reefs make the water an adventure in the winter months. Most visitors assume the seasons don't change a thing in the Islands, and they would be right—except for the waves, which are big on the South Shore in summer and placid in winter. It's exactly the opposite on the north side where winter storms bring in huge waves, but the ocean goes to glass come May and June.

HONOLULU

The city of Honolulu has only one beach, the monstrous Ala Moana. It hosts everything from Dragon Boat competitions to the Aloha State Games.

☾ ★ **Ala Moana Beach Park.** Ala Moana has a protective reef, which makes it ostensibly a ½-mi-wide saltwater swimming pool. After Waikīkī, this is the most popular beach among visitors. To the Waikīkī side is a peninsula called Magic Island, with shady trees and paved sidewalks ideal for jogging. Ala Moana also has playing fields, tennis courts, and a couple of small ponds for sailing toy boats. This beach is for everyone, but only in the daytime. It's a high-crime area after dark. ⊠ *Honolulu, near Ala Moana Shopping Center and Ala Moana Blvd. From Waikīkī take Bus 8 to shopping center and cross Ala Moana Blvd.* ⚲ *Lifeguard, toilets, showers, food concession, picnic tables, grills, parking lot.*

WAIKĪKĪ

The 2½-mi strand called Waikīkī Beach extends from Hilton Hawaiian Village on one end to Kapi'olani Park and Diamond Head on the other. Although it's one contiguous piece of beach, it's as varied as the people that inhabit the Islands. Whether you're an old-timer looking to enjoy the action from the shade or a sports nut wanting to do it all, you can find every beach activity here without ever jumping in the rental car.

■ TIP→ **If you're staying outside the area, our best advice is to park at either end of the beach and walk in.** Plenty of parking exists on the west end at the Ala Wai Marina, where there are myriad free spots on the beach as

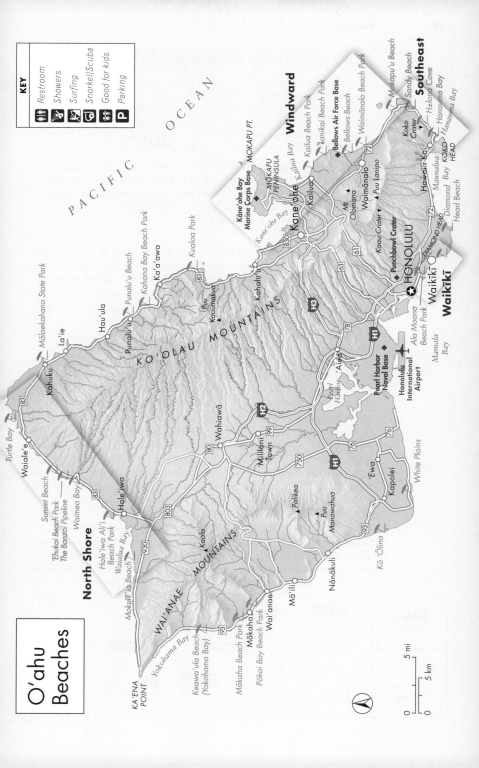

SURF WITH THE WHOLE FAMILY

Outrigger canoes are a simple, cheap, but oft-overlooked way to have fun in Waikīkī. Everyone clamors to be on the water off Waikīkī, and most people go for pricey sailing trips or surf lessons.

The long, funny-looking boats in front of Duke's Canoe Club allow you to get out on the water for much less money. At $10 for three rides, the price hasn't changed in a

decade, and the thrill hasn't changed in centuries. You can get a paddle, but no one expects you to use it—the beach boys negotiate you in and out of the break as they have been doing all their lives.

If you think taking off on a wave on a 10-foot board is a rush, wait until your whole family takes off on one in a 30-foot boat!

well as metered stalls around the harbor. For parking on the east end, Kapiʻolani Park and the Honolulu Zoo both have metered parking for $1 an hour—more affordable than the $10 per hour the resorts want.

Duke Kahanamoku Beach. Named for Hawaiʻi's famous Olympic swimming champion, Duke Kahanamoku, this is a hard-packed beach with the only shade trees on the sand in Waikīkī. It's great for families with young children because there are plenty of shaded areas and because it has Waikīkī's calmest waters, thanks to a rock wall that creates a semi-protected cove. The ocean clarity here is not as brilliant as elsewhere on Waikīkī because of the stillness of the surf, but it's a small price to pay for peace of mind about youngsters. ⊠ *In front of Hilton Hawaiian Village Beach Resort and Spa* ⊂ *Toilets, showers, food concession.*

Fort DeRussy Beach Park. Even before you take the two newly refurbished beach parks into account, this is one of the finest beaches on the south side of Oʻahu. Wide, soft, ultrawhite beaches with gently lapping waves make it a family favorite for running/jumping/frolicking fun (this also happens to be where the NFL used to hold its rookie sand football game every year). Add to that the heavily shaded grass grilling area, sand volleyball courts, and aquatic rentals, and this becomes a must for the active visitor. ⊠ *In front of Fort DeRussy and Hale Koa Hotel* ⊂ *Lifeguard, toilets, showers, food concession, picnic tables, grills, playground.*

Gray's Beach. A little lodging house called Gray's-by-the-Sea stood here in the 1920s; now it's a gathering place for eclectic beach types from sailing pioneers like George Parsons to the "bird men" of Waikīkī: stop and watch the show as up to six parrots are placed on the heads,

If you've never been on a surfboard before, O'ahu is the place to give it a try, just like these students on Waikīkī Beach.

shoulders, and arms of squealing tourists waiting impatiently for their photos to be taken. The tides often put sand space at a premium, but if you want a look back into old Waikīkī, have a mai tai at the Shorebird and check out a time gone by. ⊠ *In front of Halekūlani* ☞ *Lifeguard, toilets, showers, food concession.*

Kahaloa and Ulukou Beaches. The beach widens out again here, creating the "it" spot for the bikini crowd. Beautiful bodies abound. This is where you find most of the sailing-catamaran charters for a spectacular sail out to Diamond Head or surfboard and outrigger-canoe rentals for a ride on the rolling waves of the surf break. Great music and outdoor dancing beckon the sand-bound visitor to Duke's Canoe Club where shirt and shoes not only aren't required, they're discouraged. ⊠ *In front of Royal Hawaiian Hotel and Sheraton Moana Surfrider* ☞ *Lifeguard, toilets, showers, food concession.*

Ⓒ **Kūhiō Beach Park.** This beach has experienced a renaissance after a recent face-lift. Now bordered by a landscaped boardwalk, it's great for romantic walks any time of day. Check out the Kūhiō Beach hula mound Tuesday to Sunday at 6:30 for free hula and Hawaiian-music performances and a torch-lighting ceremony at sunset. Surf lessons for beginners are available from the beach center every half hour. ⊠ *Past Sheraton Moana Surfrider Hotel to Kapahulu Ave. pier* ☞ *Lifeguard, toilets, showers, food concession.*

Ⓒ **Queen's Surf.** So named because it was once the site of Queen Lili'uokalani's beach house, this beach draws a mix of families and gay couples—and it seems as if someone is always playing a steel drum. Many weekends, movie screens are set up on the sand, and major motion pictures are

Not a water baby? Come to Sandy Beach—otherwise known as Breack Neck Beach—to watch the massive ocean swells and awesome pounding surf.

shown after the sun sets (⊕ *www.sunsetonthebeach.net*). In the daytime, banyan trees provide shade and volleyball nets attract pros and amateurs alike (this is where Misty May and Kerri Walsh play while in town). The water fronting Queen's Surf is an aquatic preserve, providing the best snorkeling in Waikīkī. ⊠ *Across from entrance to Honolulu Zoo* ☞ *Lifeguard, toilets, showers, picnic tables, grills.*

Sans Souci. Nicknamed Dig-Me Beach because of its outlandish display of skimpy bathing suits, this small rectangle of sand is a good sunning spot for all ages. Children enjoy its shallow, safe waters that are protected by the walls of the historic Natatorium, an Olympic-size saltwater swimming arena. Serious swimmers and triathletes also swim in the channel here, beyond the reef. Sans Souci is favored by locals wanting to avoid the crowds while still enjoying the convenience of Waikīkī. ⊠ *Across from Kapi'olani Park, between New Otani Kaimana Beach Hotel and Waikīkī War Memorial Natatorium* ☞ *Lifeguard, toilets, showers, picnic tables.*

Diamond Head Beach. You have to like hiking to like Diamond Head Beach. This beautiful, remote spot is at the base of Diamond Head crater. The beach is just a small strip of sand with lots of coral in the water. This said, the views looking out from the point are breathtaking, and it's amazing to watch the windsurfers skimming along, driven by the gusts off the point. From the parking area, look for an opening in the wall where an unpaved trail leads down to the beach. Even for the unadventurous, a stop at the lookout point is well worth the time. ⊠ *At base of Diamond Head. Park at the crest of Diamond Head Rd. and walk down* ☞ *Showers, parking lot.*

SOUTHEAST O'AHU

Much of Southeast O'ahu is surrounded by reef, making most of the coast uninviting to swimmers, but the spots where the reef opens up are true gems. The drive along this side of the island is amazing, with its sheer lava-rock walls on one side and deep-blue ocean on the other. There are plenty of restaurants in the suburb of Hawai'i Kai, so you can make a day of it, knowing that food isn't far away.

Hanauma Bay Nature Preserve. Picture this as the world's biggest open-air aquarium. You come here to see fish, and fish you'll see. Due to their exposure to thousands of visitors every week, these fish are more like family pets than the skittish marine life you might expect. An old volcanic crater has created a haven from the waves where the coral has thrived. There's an educational center where you must watch a nine-minute video about the nature preserve before being allowed down to the bay. ■ TIP➜ The bay is best early in the morning (around 7), before the crowds arrive; it can be difficult to park later in the day. Smoking is not allowed, and the beach is closed on Tuesday.

Hālona Cove. Also known as From Here to Eternity Beach and "Pounders," this little beauty is never crowded due to the short treacherous climb down to the sand. But for the intrepid, what a treat this spot can be. It's in a break in the ocean cliffs, with the surrounding crags providing protection from the wind. Open-ocean waves roll up onto the beach (thus the second nickname), but unlike at Sandy Beach, a gently sloping sand bottom takes much of the punch out of them before they hit the shore. ⚠ The current is mellow inside the cove but dangerous once you get outside of it. Turtles frequent the small cove, seeking respite from the otherwise blustery coast. It's great for packing a lunch and holing up for the day. ✉ Below Hālona Blow Hole Lookout parking lot ☞ No facilities.

★ **Sandy Beach.** Probably the most popular beach with locals on this side of O'ahu, the broad, sloping beach is covered with sunbathers who come to watch The Show and soak up rays. The Show is a shore break that's unlike any other in the Islands. Monster ocean swells rolling into the beach combined with the sudden rise in the ocean floor causes waves to jack up and crash magnificently on the shore. Expert surfers and body boarders young and old brave this danger to get some of the biggest barrels you can find for bodysurfing. But keep in mind that ⚠ the beach is nicknamed "Break-Neck Beach" for a reason: many neck and back injuries are sustained here each year. Use extreme caution when swimming here,

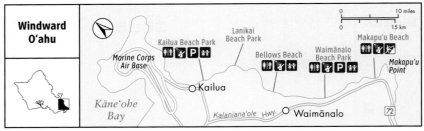

or just kick back and watch the drama unfold from the comfort of your beach chair. ⊠ *Makai of Kalaniana'ole Hwy., 2 mi east of Hanauma Bay* ☞ *Lifeguard, toilets, showers, picnic tables.*

WINDWARD O'AHU

The Windward side lives up to its name with ideal spots for windsurfing and kiteboarding, or for the more intrepid, hang gliding. For the most part the waves are mellow, and the bottoms are all sand—making for nice spots to visit with younger kids. The only drawback is that this side does tend to get more rain. But the vistas are so beautiful that a little sprinkling of "pineapple juice" shouldn't dampen your experience; plus, it benefits the waterfalls that cascade down the Ko'olaus. Beaches are listed from south to north.

Fodor'sChoice
★

Makapu'u Beach. A magnificent beach protected by Makapu'u Point welcomes you to the Windward side. Hang gliders circle above the beach, and the water is filled with body boarders. Just off the coast you can see Bird Island, a sanctuary for aquatic fowl, jutting out of the blue. The currents can be heavy, so check with a lifeguard if you're unsure of safety. Before you leave, take the prettiest (and coldest) outdoor shower available on the island. Being surrounded by tropical flowers and foliage while you rinse off that sand is a memory you will cherish from this side of the rock. ⊠ *Across from Sea Life Park on Kalaniana'ole Hwy., 2 mi south of Waimānalo* ☞ *Lifeguard, toilets, showers, picnic tables, grills.*

🄲 **Waimānalo Beach Park.** One of the most beautiful beaches on the island, Waimānalo is a "local" beach, busy with picnicking families and active sports fields. Expect a wide stretch of sand; turquoise, jade, and deep-blue seas; and gentle shore-breaking waves that are fun for all ages. Theft is an occasional problem, so lock your car. ⊠ *South of Waimānalo town, look for signs on Kalaniana'ole Hwy.* ☞ *Lifeguard, toilets, showers, picnic tables.*

Bellows Beach. Bellows is the same beach as Waimānalo, but it's under the auspices of the military, making it friendlier for visitors. The park area is excellent for camping, and ironwood trees provide plenty of shade. ■TIP→ **The beach is best before 2 PM. After 2 the trade winds bring clouds that get hung up on steep mountains nearby, causing overcast skies until mid-afternoon.** There are no food concessions, but McDonald's and other take-out fare, including *huli huli* (rotisserie) chicken on weekends, are right outside the entrance gate. ⊠ *Entrance on Kalaniana'ole*

Kailua Beach is an ideal place for a picnic, as nearby pavilions and palm trees provide a break from the strong Hawaiian sun.

Hwy., near Waimānalo town center ⚘ *Lifeguard, toilets, showers, picnic tables, grills.*

★ **Lanikai Beach Park.** Think of the beaches you see in commercials: peaceful jade-green waters, powder-soft white sand, families and dogs frolicking mindlessly, offshore islands in the distance. It's an ideal spot for camping out with a book. Though the beach hides behind multimillion-dollar houses, by state law there is public access every 400 yards. ■**TIP➜ Look for walled or fenced pathways every 400 yards, leading to the beach. Be sure not to park in the marked bike and jogging lane.** There are no shower or bathroom facilities here—they are a two-minute drive away at Kailua Beach Park. ✉ *Past Kailua Beach Park; street parking on Mokulua Dr. for various public-access points to beach* ⚘ *No facilities.*

Fodor's Choice
★ **Kailua Beach Park.** A cobalt-blue sea and a wide continuous arc of powdery sand make Kailua Beach Park one of the island's best beaches, illustrated by the crowds of local families that spend their weekend days here. This is like a big Lanikai Beach, but a little windier and a little wider, and a better spot for spending a full day. Kailua Beach has calm water, a line of palms and ironwoods that provide shade on the sand, and a huge park with picnic pavilions where you can escape the heat. This is the "it" spot if you're looking to try your hand at wind- or kiteboarding. **You can rent kayaks nearby at Kailua Sailboards and Kayaks** (✉ *130 Kailua Rd.* ☎ *808/262–2555*) **and take them to the Mokulua Islands for the day.** ✉ *Near Kailua town, turn right on Kailua Rd. at market, cross bridge, then turn left into beach parking lot* ⚘ *Lifeguard, toilets, showers, picnic tables, grills, playground, parking lot.*

SUN SAFETY ON O'AHU

Hawai'i's weather—seemingly never-ending warm, sunny days with gentle trade winds—can be enjoyed year-round with good sun sense. Because of Hawai'i's subtropical location, the length of daylight here changes little throughout the year. The sun is particularly strong, with a daily UV average of 14. Visitors should take extra precaution to avoid sunburns and long-term cancer risks due to sun exposure.

The Hawai'i Dermatological Society recommends these sun safety tips:

■ Plan your beach, golf, hiking, and other outdoor activities for the early morning or late afternoon, avoiding the sun between 10 AM and 4 PM when it's the strongest.

■ Apply a broad-spectrum sunscreen with a sun protection factor (SPF) of at least 15. Hawai'i lifeguards use sunscreens with an SPF of 30. Cover areas that are most prone to burning like your nose, shoulders, tops of feet and ears. And don't forget to use sun-protection products on your lips.

■ Apply sunscreen at least 30 minutes before you plan to be outdoors and reapply every two hours, even on cloudy days. Clouds scatter sunlight so you can still burn on an overcast day.

■ Wear light, protective clothing, such as a long-sleeve shirt and pants, broad-brimmed hat and sunglasses.

■ Stay in the shade whenever possible—especially on the beach—by using an umbrella. Remember that sand and water can reflect up to 85% of the sun's damaging rays.

■ Children need extra protection from the sun. Apply sunscreen frequently and liberally on children over six months of age and minimize their time in the sun. Sunscreen is not recommended for children under six months.

Kualoa Park. Grassy expanses border a long, narrow stretch of beach. While the shallow water is more suited for wading than swimming, the spectacular views of Kāne'ohe Bay and the Ko'olau Mountains make Kualoa one of the island's most beautiful picnic, camping, and beach areas. Dominating the view is an islet called Mokoli'i, better known as Chinaman's Hat, which rises 206 feet above the water. You can swim in the shallow areas year-round. The one drawback is that it's usually windy, but the wide-open spaces are ideal for kite flying. ⊠ *North of Waiāhole, on Kamehameha Hwy.* ⚲ *Toilets, showers, picnic tables, grills.*

☺ **Kahana Bay Beach Park.** Local parents often bring their children here to wade in safety in the very shallow, protected waters. This pretty beach cove, surrounded by mountains, has a long arc of sand that is great for walking and a cool, shady grove of tall ironwood and pandanus trees that is ideal for a picnic. An ancient Hawaiian fishpond, which was in use until the 1920s, is visible nearby. The water here is not generally a clear blue due to the runoff from heavy rains in the valley. ⊠ *North of Kualoa Park on Kamehameha Hwy.* ⚲ *Toilets, showers, picnic tables.*

Punalu'u Beach Park. If you're making a circle of the island, this is a great stopping point to jump out of your car and stretch your legs. It's easy, because the sand literally comes up to your parked car, and nice, because there is a sandy bottom and mostly calm conditions. Plus there are full facilities and lots of shade trees. Often overlooked, and often overcast, Punaluʻu can afford you a moment of solitude and fresh air before you get back to your sightseeing. ⊠ *In Punaluʻu, on Kamehameha Hwy.* ☞ *Toilets, showers, picnic tables.*

Mālaekahana Beach Park. The big attraction here is tiny Goat Island, a bird sanctuary just offshore. At low tide the water is shallow enough—never more than waist-high—so that you can wade out to it. Wear sneakers or aqua socks so you don't cut yourself on the coral. The beach itself is fairly narrow but long enough for a 20-minute stroll, one-way. The waves are never too big, and sometimes they're just right for the beginning body-surfer. The entrance gates, which close at 6:45 PM, are easy to miss and you can't see the beach from the road. Families love to camp in the groves of ironwood trees at Mālaekahana State Park. Cabins are also available here, making a perfect rural getaway. ⊠ *Entrance gates ½ mi north of Lāʻie on Kamehameha Hwy.* ☞ *Toilets, showers, picnic tables, grills.*

NORTH SHORE

"North Shore, where the waves are mean, just like a washing machine," sing the Kaʻau Crater Boys about this legendary side of the island. And in winter they are absolutely right. At times the waves overtake the road, stranding tourists and locals alike. When the surf is up, there are signs on the beach telling you how far to stay back so that you aren't swept out to sea. The most prestigious big-wave contest in the world, the Eddie Aikau, is held at Waimea Bay on waves the size of a six-story building. The Triple Crown of Surfing roams across three beaches in the winter months.

All this changes come summer when this tiger turns into a kitten, with water smooth enough to water-ski on and ideal for snorkeling. The fierce Banzai Pipeline surf break becomes a great dive area, allowing you to explore the coral heads that, in winter, have claimed so many lives on the ultrashallow but big, hollow tubes created here. Even with the monster surf subsided, this is still a time for caution: Lifeguards are more scarce, and currents don't subside just because the waves do.

That said, it's a place like no other on earth and must be explored. From the turtles at Mokulēʻia to the tunnels at Shark's Cove, you could spend your whole trip on this side and not be disappointed.

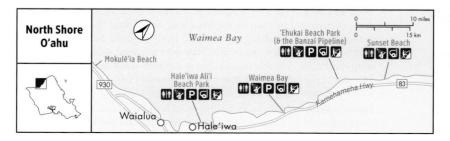

Sunset Beach on O'ahu's North Shore is known for its ample supply of puka shells, which are a staple of Hawaiian jewelry.

Turtle Bay. Now known more for its resort than its magnificent beach, Turtle Bay is mostly passed over on the way to the better-known beaches of Sunset and Waimea. But for the average visitor with the average swimming capabilities, this is the place to be on the North Shore. The crescent-shape beach is protected by a huge sea wall. You can see and hear the fury of the northern swell, while blissfully floating in cool, calm waters. The convenience of this spot is also hard to pass up—there is a concession selling sandwiches and sunblock right on the beach. The resort has free parking for beach guests. ⊠ *4 mi north of Kahuku on Kamehameha Hwy.; turn into resort and let guard know where you are going.* ☞ *Toilets, showers, food concessions, picnic tables.*

★ **Sunset Beach.** The beach is broad, the sand is soft, the summer waves are gentle, and the winter surf is crashing. Many love searching this shore for the puka shells that adorn the necklaces you see everywhere. Carryout truck stands selling shave ice, plate lunches, and sodas usually line the adjacent highway. ⊠ *1 mi north of 'Ehukai Beach Park on Kamehameha Hwy.* ☞ *Lifeguard, toilets, showers, picnic tables.*

'Ehukai Beach Park. What sets 'Ehukai apart is the view of the famous **Banzai Pipeline,** where the winter waves curl into magnificent tubes, making it an experienced wave-rider's dream. It's also an inexperienced swimmer's nightmare, though spring and summer waves are more accommodating to the average swimmer. Except when the surf contests are going on, there's no reason to stay on the central strip. Travel in either direction from the center, and the conditions remain the same but the population thins out, leaving you with a magnificent stretch of sand

BEACH SAFETY ON O'AHU

Hawai'i's world-renowned, beautiful beaches can be extremely dangerous at times due to large waves and strong currents—so much so that the state rates wave hazards using three signs: a yellow square (caution), a red stop sign (high hazard), and a black diamond (extreme hazard). Signs are posted and updated three times daily or as conditions change.

Visiting beaches with life guards is strongly recommended, and you should swim only when there's a normal caution rating. Never swim alone or dive into unknown water or shallow breaking waves. If you're unable to swim out of a rip current, tread water and wave your arms in the air to signal for help.

Even in calm conditions, there are other dangerous things in the water to be aware of, including razor-sharp coral, jellyfish, eels, and sharks, to name a few.

Jellyfish cause the most ocean injuries, and signs are posted along beaches when they're present. Reactions to a sting are usually mild (burning sensation, redness, welts); however, in some cases they can be severe (breathing difficulties). If you're stung, pick off the tentacles, rinse the affected area with water and apply ice.

The chances of getting bitten by a shark in Hawaiian waters are very low; sharks attack swimmers or surfers three or four times per year. Of the 40 species of sharks found near Hawai'i, tiger sharks are considered the most dangerous because of their size and indiscriminate feeding behavior. They're easily recognized by their blunt snouts and vertical bars on their sides.

Here are a few tips to reduce your shark-attack risk:

■ Swim, surf, or dive with others at beaches patrolled by lifeguards.

■ Avoid swimming at dawn, dusk and night, when some shark species may move inshore to feed.

■ Don't enter the water if you have open wounds or are bleeding.

■ Avoid murky waters, harbor entrances, areas near stream mouths (especially after heavy rains), channels or steep drop-offs.

■ Don't wear high-contrast swimwear or shiny jewelry.

■ Don't swim near dolphins, which are often prey for large sharks.

■ If you spot a shark, leave the water quickly and calmly; never provoke or harass a shark, no matter how small.

The Web site ⊕ *oceansafety.soest. hawaii.edu* provides statewide beach hazard maps as well as weather and surf advisories, listings of closed beaches, and safety tips.

all to yourself. ⊠ *Parking lot borders Kamehameha Hwy., 1 mi north of Foodland at Pūpūkea ⌖ Lifeguard, toilets, showers, parking lot.*

Fodor's Choice **Waimea Bay.** Made popular in that old Beach Boys song "Surfin' U.S.A.,"
★ Waimea Bay is a slice of big-wave heaven, home to king-size 25- to 30-foot winter waves. Summer is the time to swim and snorkel in the calm waters. The shore break is great for novice bodysurfers. Due to its popularity, the postage-stamp parking lot is quickly filled, but everyone

parks along the side of the road and walks in. ⊠ *Across from Waimea Valley, 3 mi north of Hale'iwa on Kamehameha Hwy.* ☞ *Lifeguard, toilets, showers, picnic tables, parking lot.*

Hale'iwa Ali'i Beach Park. The winter waves are impressive here, but in summer the ocean is like a lake, ideal for family swimming. The beach itself is big and often full of locals. Its broad lawn off the highway invites volleyball and Frisbee games and groups of barbecuers. This is also the opening break for the Triple Crown of Surfing, and the grass is often filled with art festivals or carnivals. ⊠ *North of Hale'iwa town center and past harbor on Kamehameha Hwy.* ☞ *Lifeguard, toilets, showers, picnic tables.*

Mokulē'ia Beach Park. There is a reason why the producers of the TV show *Lost* chose this beach for their set. On the remote northwest point of the island, it is about 10 mi from the closest store or public restroom; you could spend a day here and not see another living soul. And that is precisely its beauty—all the joy of being stranded on a desert island without the trauma of the plane crash. The beach is wide and white, the waters bright blue (but a little choppy) and full of sea turtles and other marine life. Mokulē'ia is a great secret find, just remember to pack supplies and use caution, as there are no lifeguards. ⊠ *East of Hale'iwa town center, across from Dillingham Airfield* ☞ *No facilities.*

WEST LEEWARD O'AHU

The North Shore may be known as "Country," but the west side is truly the rural area on O'ahu. There are commuters from this side to Honolulu, but many are born, live, and die on this side with scarcely a trip to town. For the most part, there's less hostility and more curiosity toward outsiders. Occasional problems have flared up, mostly due to drug abuse that has ravaged the fringes of the island. But the problems have generally been car break-ins, not violence. So, in short, lock your car, don't bring valuables, and enjoy the amazing beaches.

The beaches on the west side are expansive and empty. Most O'ahu residents and tourists don't make it to this side simply because of the drive; in traffic it can take almost 90 minutes to make it to Ka'ena Point from Downtown Honolulu. But you'll be hard-pressed to find a better sunset anywhere.

Fodor's Choice
★
White Plains. Concealed from the public eye for many years as part of the Barbers Point Naval Air Station, this beach is reminiscent of Waikīkī but without the condos and the crowds. It is a long, sloping beach with numerous surf breaks, but it is also mild enough at shore for older children to play freely. It has views of Pearl Harbor and, over that, Diamond Head. Although the sand lives up to its name, the real joy of this beach comes from its history as part of a military property for the better part of a century, leaving it unchanged. Expansive parking, great restroom facilities, and numerous tree-covered barbecue areas make it a great day-trip spot. As a bonus, a Hawaiian monk seal takes up residence here several months out of the year (seals are rarely seen anywhere in the Islands). ⊠ *Take the Makakilo exit off H1 west, turn*

left. Follow it into the base gates, turn left. Follow blue signs to the beach ☞ Lifeguard, toilets, showers, picnic tables.

☺ **Kō'Ōlina.** This is the best spot on the island if you have small kids. The ★ resort commissioned a series of four man-made lagoons, but, as they are required by law to provide public beach access, you are the winner. Huge rock walls protect the lagoons, making them into perfect spots for the kids to get their first taste of the ocean without getting bowled over. The large expanses of seashore grass and hala trees that surround the semicircle beaches are made-to-order for naptime. A 1½-mi jogging track connects the lagoons. Due to its appeal for *keiki* (children), Kō'Ōlina is popular and the parking lot fills up quickly when school is out and on weekends, so try to get there before 10 AM. The biggest parking lot is at the farthest lagoon from the entrance. ⊠ *23 mi west of Honolulu. Take Kō'Ōlina exit off H1 west and proceed to guard shack ☞ Toilets, showers, food concession.*

Papaoneone Beach. You have to do a little exploring to find Papaoneone Beach, which is tucked away behind three condos. Duck through a wide, easy-to-spot hole in the fence, and you find an extremely wide, sloping beach that always seems to be empty. The waters are that eerie blue found only on the west side. The waves can get high here (it faces the same direction as the famed Mākaha Beach), but, for the most part, the shore break makes for great easy rides on your boogie board or belly. The only downside is that, with the exception of a shower, all the facilities are for the condos, so it's just you and the big blue. ⊠ *In Mākaha, just across from Jade St. ☞ Showers.*

Mākaha Beach Park. This beach provides a slice of local life most visitors don't see. Families string up tarps for the day, fire up hibachis, set up lawn chairs, get out the fishing gear, and strum 'ukuleles while they "talk story" (chat). Legendary waterman Buffalo Keaulana can be found in the shade of the palms playing with his grandkids and spinning yarns of yesteryear. In these waters Buffalo invented some of the most outrageous methods of surfing and raised his world-champion son Rusty. He also made Mākaha the home of the world's first international surf meet in 1954 and still hosts his Big Board Surfing Classic. With its long, slow-building waves, it's a great spot to try out long boarding. The swimming is generally decent in summer, but avoid the big winter waves. ⊠ *35 mi (1½ hrs) west of Honolulu on H1, then Farrington Hwy. ☞ Lifeguards, toilets, showers, picnic tables, grills.*

Yokohama Bay. You'll be one of the few outsiders at this Wai'anae Coast beach at the very end of the road. If it weren't for the little strip of paved road, it would feel like a deserted isle: no stores, no houses, just a huge sloping stretch of beach and some of the darkest-blue water off the island. Locals come here to fish and swim in waters that are calm enough for children in summer. Early morning brings with it spinner dolphins by the dozens just offshore. Though Makua Beach up the road is the best spot to see these animals, it's not nearly as beautiful or sandy as "Yokes." ⊠ *Northern end of Farrington Hwy., about 7 mi north of Mākaha ☞ Toilets, showers.*

4

Water Sports and Tours

WORD OF MOUTH

"Just wanted to add a comment about Shark's Cove. Excellent snorkeling! Saw an amazing array of fish and the butt of a big sea turtle as he swam behind a rock."

—Sandra_E

Updated By
Chad Pata

There's more to the beach than just lying on it. O'ahu is rife with every type of activity you can imagine. Most of the activities are offered in Waikīkī, right off the beach. On the sand in front of your hotel, the sights and sounds of what is available will overwhelm you. Rainbow-colored parachutes dot the horizon as parasailers improve their vantage point on paradise. The blowing of conch shells announces the arrival of the beach catamarans that sail around Diamond Head Crater. Meanwhile, the white caps of Waikīkī are being sliced by all manner of craft, from brilliant-red outrigger canoes to darting white surf boards. Enjoy observing the flurry of activity for a moment, then jump right in.

As with all sports, listen to the outfitter's advice—they're not just saying it for fun. Caution is always the best bet when dealing with "mother" ocean. She plays for keeps and forgives no indiscretions. That being said, she offers more entertainment than you can fit into a lifetime, much less a vacation. So try something new and enjoy.

A rule of thumb is that the ocean is much more wily and unpredictable on the north- and west-facing shores, but that's also why those sides have the most famous waves on earth. So plan your activity side according to your skill level.

BOAT TOURS AND CHARTERS

Hawai'i Nautical. It's a little out of the way, but the experiences with this local company are worth the drive. Catamaran cruises lead to snorkeling with dolphins, gourmet dinner cruises head out of beautiful Kō'Ōlina harbor, and sailing lessons are available on a 20-foot sailboat and a 50-foot cat. If you're driving out from Waikīkī, you may want to make a day of it, with sailing in the morning, then 18 holes on the gorgeous resort course in the afternoon. Three-hour cruise rates with snacks and two drinks begin at $110 per person. ⊠ *Kō'Ōlina Harbor, Kō'Ōlina Marriott Resort, Kapolei* ☎ *808/234–7245* ⊕ *www. hawaiinautical.com.*

Fodor's Choice **KanDoo Island.** This activity defies description as it has been anchored
★ off Waikīkī Beach since August of 2009. Is it a sail? Well, it is a 148-foot catamaran, but it stays stationary there from 9 AM to 9 PM allowing people to swim, or lounge and enjoy its three bars. There are also waterslides, water trampolines, banana boat rides and ultimate parasailing, as well as snorkeling, Jet Skiing and, for the educationally minded, marine-conservation classes. Shuttle boats run out of Kewalo Basin

Beaches on the leeward side of O'ahu are some of the quietest and most deserted—and have picture perfect sunsets.

every 20 minutes so you can stay for as short or as long as you wish. As if all that wasn't enough, after 9 PM it turns into a floating rock-and-roll club for the adults only. ⊠ *Kewalo Basin, Honolulu* ☎ *808/526–1133* ⊕ *www.gokandoo.com.*

Paradise Cruises. One-stop shopping for specialty cruises. Offerings run the gamut from day cruises around Diamond Head with snorkeling, kayaking, and windsurfing to fine-dining night cruises with lobster and live entertainment, to winter whale-watching cruises. You can learn lei-making or coconut frond–weaving, or you can take a 'ukulele or hula lesson. They also offer seminars on Hawaiian history and culture, and there are artifact displays onboard the boat. Two-hour dinner-cruise rates begin at $61 per person. ⊠ *Pier 5, Honolulu Harbor, Honolulu* ☎ *808/983–7700* ⊕ *www.starofhonolulu.com.*

Sashimi Fun Fishing. A combination trip suits those who aren't quite ready to troll for big game in the open-ocean swells. Sashimi Fun Fishing runs a party cruise with fishing and music. They keep close enough to shore to still see O'ahu while jigging for a variety of reef fish. The cruise includes a local barbecue dinner. The four-hour fishing-cruise rates with hotel transportation begin at $63 per person. They also do a rock-and-roll booze cruise from 9 PM to midnight for just $38. ☎ *808/955–3474* ⊕ *www.808955fish.com.*

Tradewind Charters. Tradewind specializes in everything from weddings to funerals. They offer half-day private-charter tours for sailing, snorkeling, and whale-watching. Traveling on these luxury yachts not only gets you away from the crowds but also gives you the opportunity to "take the helm" if you wish. The cruise includes snorkeling at an exclusive anchorage as well as hands-on snorkeling and sailing instruction. Charter prices are approximately $495 for up to six passengers. ⌧ *796 Kalanipuu St., Honolulu* ☎ *800/829–4899* ⊕ *www.tradewindcharters.com.*

BODYBOARDING AND BODY SURFING

Bodyboarding (or sponging) has become a popular alternative to surfing for a couple of reasons. First, the start-up cost is much less—a usable board can be purchased for $30 to $40 or can be rented on the beach for $5 an hour. Second, it's a whole lot easier to ride a bodyboard than to tame a surfboard. For beginner bodyboarding all you must do is paddle out to the waves, turn toward the beach, and kick like crazy when the wave comes.

Most grocery and convenience stores sell bodyboards. Though the boards do not rival what the pros use, you won't notice a difference in their handling on smaller waves. ■ **TIP→** Another small investment you'll want to make is surf fins. These smaller, sturdier versions of dive fins sell for $25 to $35 at surf and dive stores, sporting-goods stores, and even Wal-Mart. Most beach stands do not rent fins with the boards. Though they are not necessary for bodyboarding, fins do give you a tremendous advantage when you are paddling into waves. If you plan to go out in bigger surf, we would also advise you to get fin leashes to prevent loss. For bodysurfing, you definitely want to invest in fins. Check out the same spots as for bodyboarding.

If the direction of the current or dangers of the break are not readily apparent to you, don't hesitate to ask a lifeguard for advice.

BEST SPOTS

Bodyboarding and bodysurfing can be done anywhere there are waves, but, due to a paddling advantage surfers have over spongers, it's usually more fun to go to exclusively bodyboarding spots.

Kūhiō Beach Park (⌧ *Waikīkī, past Sheraton Moana Surfrider Hotel to Kapahulu Ave. pier*) is an easy spot for the first-timer to check out the action. Try **The Wall**, a break so named for the breakwall in front of the beach. It's a little crowded with kids, but it's close enough to shore to keep you at ease. There are dozens of breaks in Waikīkī, but the Wall is the only one solely occupied by spongers. Start out here to get the hang of it before venturing out to **Canoes** or **Kaiser Bowl's.**

Makapu'u Beach (⌧ *Across from Sea Life Park, 2 mi south of Waimānalo on Kalaniana'ole Hwy.*) on the Windward side is a sponger's dream beach with its extended waves and isolation from surfers. If you're a little more timid, go to the far end of the beach to **Keiki's,** where the waves are mellowed by Makapu'u Point, for an easier, if less thrilling, ride. Although the main break at Makapu'u is much less dangerous than Sandy's, check out the ocean floor—the sands are always shifting, sometimes exposing coral heads and rocks. Also always check the

A top choice among bodyboarders and bodysurfers is Break Neck Beach, for its big surf.

currents: they can get strong. But for the most part, this is the ideal beach for both bodyboarding and bodysurfing.

★ The best spot on the island for advanced bodyboarding is **Sandy Beach** (⊠ *2 mi east of Hanauma Bay on Kalaniana'ole Hwy.*) on the Windward side. It's a short wave that goes right and left, but the barrels here are unparalleled for pure sponging. The ride is intense and breaks so sharply that you actually see the wave suck the bottom dry before it crashes on to it. That's the reason it's also called "Break Neck Beach." It's awesome for the advanced, but know its danger before enjoying the ride.

EQUIPMENT

There are more than 30 rental spots on Waikīkī Beach, all offering basically the same prices. But if you plan to bodyboard for more than just an hour, we would suggest buying a board for $20 to $30 at an ABC convenience store and giving it to a kid when you're preparing to end your vacation. It will be more cost-effective for you and will imbue you with the aloha spirit while making a kid's day.

DEEP-SEA FISHING

The joy of fishing in Hawai'i is that there isn't really a season; it's good year-round. Sure, the bigger yellowfin tuna ('ahi) are generally caught in summer, and the coveted spearfish are more frequent in winter, but you can still catch them any day of the year. You can also find dolphin fish (mahimahi), wahoo (ono), skip jacks, and the king—Pacific blue marlin—ripe for the picking on any given day.

When choosing a fishing boat in the Islands, keep in mind the immensity of the surrounding ocean. Look for the older, grizzled captains who have been trolling these waters for half a century. All the fancy gizmos in the world can't match an old tar's knowledge of the waters.

The general rule for the catch is an even split with the crew. Unfortunately, there are no "freeze-and-ship" providers in the state, so, unless you plan to eat the fish while you're here, you'll probably want to leave it with the boat. Most boats do offer mounting services for trophy fish; ask your captain.

Besides the gift of fish, a gratuity of 10% to 20% is standard but use your own discretion depending on how you felt about the overall experience.

BOATS AND CHARTERS

Hawaii Fishing Adventures. Based out of Kō'Ōlina resort, Captain Jim and his crew try to bring the full Hawaiian experience to their fishing trips. While most fishing boats head straight out to the open ocean, Captain Jim trolls along the Leeward coast giving visitors a nice sense of the island while stalking the fish. They also offer an overnighter to Molokai's Penguin Banks, reputed to be some of Hawai'i's best fishing grounds. The six-hour tour runs $650 with the overnighter booking at $2,500. ☎ 808/520–4852 ⊕ www.webconsole.net/hifi/index.shtml.

Inter-Island Sportfishing. The oldest-running sportfishing company on O'ahu also boasts the largest landed Blue Marlin—more than 1,200 pounds. With two smaller boats and the 53-foot *Maggie Joe* (which can hold up to 25), they can manage any small party with air-conditioned cabins and cutting-edge fishing equipment. They also work with Grey's Taxidermy, the world's largest marine taxidermist, to mount the monster you reel in. Half-day exclusive charter rates for groups of six begin at $650. ☎ 808/591–8888 ⊕ www.maggiejoe.com.

Magic Sportfishing. The awards Magic has garnered are too many to mention here, but we can tell you their magnificent 50-foot *Pacifica* fishing yacht is built for comfort, whether you're fishing or not. Unfortunately, Magic can accommodate only up to six. Full-day exclusive charter rates begin at $975. ☎ 808/596–2998 ⊕ www.magicsportfishing.com.

JET SKIING, WAKEBOARDING, AND WATERSKIING

Aloha Parasail/Jet Ski. Jet Ski in the immense Ke'ehi Lagoon as planes from Honolulu International take off and land right above you. After an instructional safety course, you can try your hand at navigating their buoyed course. They provide free pickup and drop-off from Waikīkī. The Waverunners run about $40 per person for 45 minutes of riding time. ☎ 808/521–2446.

Hawai'i Sports Wakeboard and Water Ski Center. Hawai'i Sports turns Maunalua Bay into an action water park with activities for all ages. While Dad's learning to wakeboard, the kids can hang on for dear life on bumper tubes, and Mom can finally get some peace parasailing over the bay

with views going to Diamond Head and beyond. There a
boats that will ride six, Jet Skis for two, and scuba missio.
Jet Ski–rental rates begin at $49 per person, and packa
available. ⊠ *Koko Marina Shopping Center, 7192 Kalaniana*
Hawai'i Kai ☎ *808/395–3773* ⊕ *www.hawaiiwatersceni*

KAYAKING

Kayaking is quickly becoming a top choice for visitors to the Islands.
Kayaking alone or with a partner on the open ocean provides a vantage
point not afforded by swimming and surfing. Even amateurs can travel
long distances and keep a lookout on what's going on around them.
This ability to travel long distances can also get you into trouble. ⚠ **Experts agree that rookies should stay on the Windward side.** Their reasoning is
simple: if you tire, break or lose an oar, or just plain pass out, the onshore
winds will eventually blow you back to the beach. The same cannot be
said for the offshore breezes of the North Shore and West O'ahu.

Kayaks are specialized: some are better suited for riding waves while
others are designed for traveling long distances. Your outfitter can
address your needs depending on your activities. Sharing your plans
with your outfitter can lead to a more enjoyable experience.

BEST SPOTS

★ If you want to try your hand at surfing kayaks, **Bellows Beach** (near
Waimānalo town center, entrance on Kalaniana'ole Hwy.) on the Windward side and **Mokulē'ia Beach** (across from Dillingham Airfield) on the
North Shore are two great spots. Hard-to-reach breaks, the ones that
surfers exhaust themselves trying to reach, are easily accessed by kayak.
The buoyancy of the kayak also allows you to catch the wave earlier
and get out in front of the white wash. One reminder on these spots: if
you're a little green, stick to Bellows with those onshore winds. Generally speaking, you don't want to be catching waves where surfers are;
in Waikīkī, however, pretty much anything goes.

For something a little different try **Kahana River** (⊠ *empties into Kahana
Bay, 8 mi east of Kāne'ohe*), also on the Windward side. The river may
not have the blue water of the ocean, but the Ko'olau Mountains, with
waterfalls aplenty when it's raining, are magnificent in the background.
It's a short jaunt, about 2 mi round-trip, but it is packed with rain-forest
foliage and the other rain-forest denizen, mosquitoes. Bring some repellent and enjoy this light workout.

The hands-down winner for kayaking is **Lanikai Beach** (⊠ *Past Kailua
Beach Park; street parking on Mokulua Dr. for various public-access
points to beach*) on the Windward side. This is perfect amateur territory with its still waters and onshore winds. If you're feeling more
adventurous, it's a short paddle out to the Mokes. This pair of islands
off the coast has beaches, surf breaks on the reef, and great picnicking
areas. Due to the distance from shore (about 1 mi), the Mokes usually
afford privacy from all but other intrepid kayakers. Lanikai is great
year-round, and most kayak-rental companies have a store right up
the street in Kailua.

O'AHU'S TOP FOUR WATER ACTIVITIES

Sailing

Tour Company/ Outfitter	Length	AM/ PM	Departure Point	Adult/kid Price	Ages	Snack vs. Meal	Alcoholic Beverages	Boat Type	Worth Noting
Pirate Bar Cruise	2 hrs	PM	Honolulu	Free	Adults only	N/A	Yes	80-foot maxi	Departs from Kewalo Basin, sail is free, drinks to be purchased
Hawaii Nautical	3 hrs	AM/ PM	West Side	$99	All ages	Snack	Yes	50-foot cat	Leaves from Kō' Ōlina resort, lots of whales in the wintertime
Makani	2 hrs	AM/ PM	South Shore	$35	All ages	Snack	Yes	65-foot catamaran	Offers all variety of sails, from sunset to snorkel sails
Hawaii Sailing Adventure	2 hrs	PM	South Shore	$119	Adults	Full dinner	All drinks included	80-foot single hull	Luxury cruise
Tradewind Charters	Half day	AM/ PM	South Shore	$495 for 6 people	All Ages	Upon request	Yes	Variety of vessels	Great for weddings or private parties

Deep Sea Fishing

Tour Company/ Outfitter	Length	AM/ PM	Departure Point	Adult/kid Price	Ages	Snack vs. Meal	Alcoholic Beverages	Boat Type	Worth Noting
Maggie Joe	Half day	AM	South Side	$700	N/A	N/A	BYOB	53-foot deep sea fishing boat	Oldest running sports-fishing company on O'ahu
Magic Sportfishing	Full day	AM	South Side	$950	N/A	N/A	BYOB	50-foot fishing yacht	Boat is built for comfort
Sashimi Fun Fishing	4 hrs	PM	South Side	$63 a person	N/A	Meal	BYOB	Variety of vessels	Reef fishing for those not ready for the open ocean

Deep Sea Fishing cont'd.

							BYOB		
Hawaii Fishing Charters	6 hrs	AM/PM	West Side	$625	N/A	N/A	BYOB	44-foot luxury boat	Sails out of Kō'Ōlina Resort
Diving									
Captain Bruce's Hawaii	2 hrs	AM/PM	West/East Shore	$110	N/A	Snack	N/A	Pro 42 Jet Boat	Hot showers on board
Ocean Concepts Hawaii	2 hrs	AM/PM	West Shore	$110	N/A	N/A	N/A	All variety	Only full-service diving company on Leeward side
Reeftrekkers	2 hrs	AM/PM	All Shores	$95	N/A	N/A	N/A	All variety	Reader's Choice award past four years
Oahu Diving	2 hrs	AM/PM	South Shore	$95	N/A	N/A	N/A	44-foot catamaran	Good for first-time divers
Surf-N-Sea	2 hrs	AM/PM	North Shore	$110	N/A	N/A	N/A	All variety	Cameraman available to shoot your dive
Sailing									
Pirate Bar Cruise	2hrs	PM	Honolulu	Free	Adults only	N/A	Yes	80-foot maxi	Departs from Kewalo Basin, sail is free, drinks to be purchased

DID YOU KNOW?

Inexperienced kayakers should stick to Windward O'ahu, where calmer waters allow you to relax and check out what's down below.

EQUIPMENT, LESSONS AND TOURS

Go Bananas. Staffers make sure that you rent the appropriate kayak for your abilities, and they outfit the rental car with soft racks to transport the boat to the beach. The store also carries clothing and kayaking accessories. Full-day rates begin at $30 for single kayaks, and $45 for doubles. ⊠ *799 Kapahulu Ave., Honolulu* ☎ *808/737–9514.*

Prime Time Sports. This is one of many stands renting kayaks right on Waikīkī Beach. The prices among the different stands are pretty much the same. The convenience of Prime Time's central location is their primary drawing card. Hourly rates begin at $12 for single kayaks, and $25 for doubles. ⊠ *Fort DeRussy Beach, Waikīkī* ☎ *808/949–8952.*

KAYAKING TO THE MOKES

"The Mokes," the two islands off Lanikai Beach, are a perfect kayaking destination. Both islands have small beach areas, and you will feel a little like Robinson Crusoe on a weekday, so long as you don't look at the multimillion-dollar homes looming on the hillsides of Lanikai. There are guided tours, which pretty much consist of simply escorting you out to the islands. But, as the water between the Mokes and Lanikai is calm and as it would be impossible to miss them, spend your money on suntan oil and snacks instead and enjoy the paddle.

Surf 'N Sea. This outfitter is located right on the beach, so you don't have to worry about transporting your boat—just rent it and start paddling. They also offer everything from paddleboats to windsurfing lessons. Keep in mind that their yellow boats are great in summer when the ocean turns peaceful, but winter on the North Shore is hazardous for even the hard-core fan. From spring to fall, however, kayaks are great for getting to outside reef-snorkeling spots or surfing the reduced waves. Full-day rates begin at $60 for single kayaks. ⊠ *62-595 Kamehameha Hwy., North Shore* ☎ *808/637–9887* ⊕ *www.surfnsea.com.*

Twogood Kayaks Hawai'i. The one-stop shopping outfitter for kayaks on the Windward side offers rentals, lessons, guided kayak tours, and even weeklong camps if you want to immerse yourself in the sport. Guides are trained in history, geology, and birdlife of the area. Kayak a full day with a guide for $119; this includes lunch, snorkeling gear, and transportation from Waikīkī. Although their rental prices are about $10 more than average, they do deliver the boats to the water for you and give you a crash course in ocean safety. It's a small price to pay for the convenience and for peace of mind when entering new waters. Full-day rates begin at $49 for single kayaks, and $59 for doubles. ⊠ *345 Hahani St., Kailua* ☎ *808/262–5656* ⊕ *www.twogoodkayaks.com.*

KITEBOARDING

See Windsurfing and Kiteboarding, below.

PARASAILING

Parasailing is the training-wheels approach to extreme sports—you think you want to try something crazy, but you're not ready to step out of an airplane quite yet. Generally you fly about 500 feet off the water, enjoying a bird's-eye view of everything, while also enjoying the silence that envelops you at that height. As we said, it's a nice alternative to leaping from planes that still gets you seeing the sights.

Hawai'i X–Treme Parasailing. Reputed to be the highest parasail ride on O'ahu, rides here actually pull people as high as 1,200 feet for 15 minutes. They offer pickups from Waikīkī, making it convenient to try this combo of water skiing and parachuting. Rates run from $47 to $79. ⊠ *Kewalo Basin Harbor, Honolulu* ☎ *808/330–8308.*

SAILING

For a sailing experience in O'ahu, you need go no farther than the beach in front of your hotel in Waikīkī. Strung along the sand are seven beach catamarans that will provide you with one-hour rides during the day and 90-minute sunset sails. Pricewise look for $12 to $15 for day sails and $15 to $20 for sunset rides. ■TIP→ They all have their little perks, and they're known for bargaining so feel free to haggle, especially with the smaller boats. Some provide drinks for free, some charge for them, and some let you pack your own, so keep that in mind when pricing the ride.

Mai Tai Catamaran. Taking off from in front of the Sheraton Hotel, this cat is the fastest and sleekest on the beach. If you have a need for speed and enjoy a slightly more upscale experience, this is the boat for you. ☎ *808/922–5665.*

Na Hoku II Catamaran. The diametric opposite of Mai Tai, this is the Animal House of catamarans with reggae music and cheap booze. Their motto is "Cheap drinks, Easy Crew." They're beached right out in front of Duke's Barefoot Bar at the Outrigger Waikīkī Hotel and sail five times daily. ☎ *No phone* ⊕ *www.nahokuii.com.*

Makani Catamaran. If you want to take your catamaran experience to the next level, give the team at Makani a call. Built from the water up in St Criox by Captain Jon Jepson, this vessel is the tops in Hawaii for luxury—from its Bose stereo system and LCD TVs to its freshwater bathrooms. It sails out of Kewalo Basin three times daily. ☎ *808/591–9000* ⊕ *www.sailmakani.com.*

SCUBA DIVING

All the great stuff to do atop the water sometimes leads us to forget the real beauty beneath the surface. Although snorkeling and snuba (more on that later) do give you access to this world, nothing gives you the freedom of scuba.

The diving on O'ahu is comparable with any you might do in the tropics, but its uniqueness comes from the isolated environment of the Islands. There are literally hundreds of species of fish and marine life that you can find only in this chain. Adding to the singularity of diving off O'ahu is the human history of the region. Military activities and tragedies of the 20th century filled the waters surrounding O'ahu with wreckage that the ocean creatures have since turned into their homes.

Although instructors certified to license you in scuba are plentiful in the Islands, we suggest that you get your PADI certification before coming as a week of classes may be a bit of a commitment on a short vacation. ■ TIP→ You can go on introductory dives without the certification, but the best dives require it.

BEST SPOTS

Hanauma Bay (⊠ *7455 Kalaniana'ole Hwy.*) is an underwater state park and a popular dive site in Southeast O'ahu. The shallow inner reef of this volcanic crater bay is filled with snorkelers, but its floor gradually drops from 10 to 70 feet at the outer reef where the big fish prefer the lighter traffic. It's quite a trek down into the crater and out to the water so you may want to consider a dive-tour company to do your heavy lifting. Expect to see butterfly fish, goatfish, parrot fish, surgeonfish, and sea turtles.

Just off Diamond Head, a collection of volcanic boulders creates a series of caves known as **Hundred Foot Hole.** Once a fishing ground reserved for royalty, it now serves as a great spot for everyone to get Hawaiian lobsters. A dive light is a good idea here because much of the area is shaded, and you don't want to miss such sea life as octopus, manta rays, and white-tip sharks. It is shore accessible.

The **Mahi Wai'anae,** a 165-foot minesweeper, was sunk in 1982 in the waters just south of Wai'anae on O'ahu's leeward coast to create an artificial reef. It's intact and penetrable, but you'll need a boat to access it. In the front resides an ancient moray eel who is so mellowed that you can pet his barnacled head without fearing for your hand's safety. Goatfish, tame lemon-butterfly fish, and blue-striped snapper hang out here, but the real stars are the patrols of spotted eagle rays that are always cruising by. It can be a longer dive as it's only 90 feet to the hull.

East of Diamond Head, **Maunalua Bay** has several boat-access sites, including Turtle Canyon, with lava-flow ridges and sandy canyons teeming with green sea turtles of all sizes; *Kāhala Barge,* a penetrable, 200-foot sunken vessel; Big Eel Reef, with many varieties of moray eels; and Fantasy Reef, a series of lava ledges and archways populated with barracuda and eels. There's also the sunken Corsair. It doesn't boast much sea life, but there's something special about sitting in the cockpit of a plane 100 feet below the surface of the ocean.

Here in the warm waters off the coast of O'ahu, there's a good chance you'll find yourself swimming alongside a green sea turtle.

Fodor's Choice The best shore dive on O'ahu is **Shark's Cove** (✉ *across from Foodland in Pūpūkea*) on the North Shore, but unfortunately it's accessible only during the summer months. Novices can drift along the outer wall, watching everything from turtles to eels. Veterans can explore the numerous lava tubes and tunnels where diffused sunlight from above creates a dreamlike effect in spacious caverns. It's 10- to 45-feet deep, ready-made for shore diving with a parking lot right next to the dive spot. **Three Tables** is just west of Shark's Cove, enabling you to have a second dive without moving your car. Follow the three perpendicular rocks that break the surface out to this dive site, where you can find a variety of parrot fish and octopus, plus occasional shark and ray sightings at depths of 30 to 50 feet. It's not as exciting as Shark's Cove, but it is more accessible for the novice diver.

Increase your caution the later in the year you come to these sights; the waves pick up strength in fall, and the reef can be turned into a washboard for you and your gear. Both are null and void during the winter surf sessions.

EQUIPMENT, LESSONS, AND TOURS

Captain Bruce's Hawai'i. Captain Bruce's focuses on the west and east shores, covering the *Mahi* and the Corsair. This full-service company has refresher and introductory dives as well as more advanced drift and night dives. No equipment is needed; they provide it all. Most importantly, this is the only boat on O'ahu that offers hot showers onboard. Two-tank boat-dive rates begin at $110 per person. ☎ *808/373–3590 or 800/535–2487* ⊕ *www.captainbruce.com.*

Hanauma Bay Dive Tours. You can guess the specialty here. They o. introductory dives in the federally protected reserve for those aged 1. and above, with snuba available to those eight years old and up. The charge is $115 for a one-tank dive. ☎ *808/256–8956.*

Reeftrekkers. The owners of the slickest dive Web site in Hawai'i are also the *Scuba Diving* Reader's Choice winners for the past four years. Using the dive descriptions and price quotes on their Web site, you can plan your excursions before ever setting foot on the island. Two-tank boat-dive rates begin at $115 per person. ☎ *808/943–0588* ⊕ *www. reeftrekkers.com.*

Surf-N-Sea. The North Shore headquarters for all things water-related is great for diving that side as well. There is one interesting perk—the cameraman can shoot a video of you diving. It's hard to see facial expressions under the water, but it still might be fun for those who need documentation of all they do. Two-tank boat-dive rates begin at $135 per person. ☎ *808/637–3337* ⊕ *www.surfnsea.com.*

SNORKELING

One advantage that snorkeling has over scuba is that you never run out of air. That and the fact that anyone who can swim can also snorkel without any formal training. A favorite pastime in Hawai'i, snorkeling can be done anywhere there's enough water to stick your face in. Each spot will have its great days depending on the weather and time of year, so consult with the purveyor of your gear for tips on where the best viewing is that day. Keep in mind that the North Shore should be attempted only when the waves are calm, namely in the summertime.

■ **TIP➜** Think of buying a mask and snorkel as a prerequisite for your trip— they make any beach experience better. Just make sure you put plenty of sunblock on your back because once you start gazing below, your head may not come back up for hours.

BEST SPOTS

As Waimea Bay is to surfing, **Hanauma Bay** (✉ *7455 Kalaniana'ole Hwy.*) in Southeast O'ahu is to snorkeling. By midday it can get crowded, but with more than a half-million fish to observe, there's plenty to go around. Due to the protection of the narrow mouth of the cove and the prodigious reef, you will be hard-pressed to find a place in which you will feel safer while snorkeling.

Right on the edge of Waikīkī, **Queen's Surf** is a marine reserve located between the break wall and the Queen's pier. It's not as chock-full of fish as Hanauma, but it has its share of colorful reef fish and the occasional sea turtle just yards from shore. It's a great spot for an escape if you're stuck in Waikīkī and have grown weary of watching the surfers.

Directly across from the electric plant outside of Kō'Ōlina resort, **Electric Beach** (✉ *1 mi west of Kō'Ōlina*) in West O'ahu has become a haven for tropical fish. The expulsion of hot water from the plant warms the ocean water, attracting all kinds of wildlife. Although the visibility is not always the best, the crowds are thin, and the fish are guaranteed. Just park next to the old train tracks and enjoy this secret spot.

Great shallows right off the shore with huge reef protection make **Shark's Cove** (✉ *across from Foodland in Pūpūkea*) on the North Shore a great spot for youngsters in the summertime. You can find a plethora of critters from crabs to octopi, in waist-deep or shallower water. The only caveat is that once the winter swell comes, this becomes a human pinball game rather than a peaceful cove.

EQUIPMENT AND TOURS

Hanauma Bay Rental Stand. You can get masks, fins, and snorkels right at the park. ☏ *808/395–4725.*

Hanauma Bay Snorkeling Excursions. For those who are a little more timid about entering these waters, this outfitter provides a tour with a guide to help alleviate your fears. They'll even pick you up in Waikīkī and provide you with equipment and knowledge for around $25. ☏ *808/373–5060.*

Kahala Kai. The *Kahala Kai* sails out of Kewalo Basin in Honolulu— very convenient if you have other plans in town. Take a two-hour sail out to sea-turtle breeding grounds where 50-foot-plus visibility makes for great snorkeling with loads of sea life from turtles and reef fish to dolphins and, in the wintertime, whales. Rates for a three-hour sail, all equipment included, begin at $75 per person. ☏ *808/239–3900.*

Ko Olina Kat. The dock in Kō'Ōlina harbor is a little more out of the way, but this is a much more luxurious option than the town snorkel cruises. Three-hour tours of the west side of O'ahu are punctuated with stops for observing dolphins from the boat and a snorkel spot well populated with fish. All gear, snacks, sandwiches, snorkel gear to keep and two alcoholic beverages make for a more complete experience but also a pricier one (starting at $110 per person). ☏ *808/234–7245.*

Snorkel Bob's. We suggest buying your gear, unless it's going to be a one-day affair. Either way, Snorkel Bob's has all the stuff you'll need (and a bunch of stuff you won't) to make your water adventures enjoyable. Also feel free to ask the staff about the good spots at the moment, as the best spots can vary with weather and seasons. ✉ *702 Kapahulu Ave.* ☏ *808/735–7944.*

SNUBA

Snuba, the marriage of scuba and snorkeling, gives the nondiving set their first glimpse into the freedom of scuba. Snuba utilizes a raft with a standard airtank on it and a 20-foot air hose that hooks up to a regulator. Once attached to the hose, you can swim, unfettered by heavy tanks and weights, up to 15 feet down to chase fish and examine reef for as long as you fancy. If you ever get scared or need a rest, the raft is right there, ready to support you. Kids eight years and older can use the equipment. It can be pricey, but, then again, how much is it worth to be able to sit face to face with a 6-foot-long sea turtle and not have to rush to the surface to get another breath?

At **Hanauma Bay Snuba Dive** (☏ *808/256–8956*), a three-hour outing (with 45 minutes in the water), costs $115.

Continued on page 132

SNORKELING IN HAWAI'I

The waters surrounding the Hawaiian Islands are filled with life—from giant manta rays cruising off the Big Island's Kona Coast to humpback whales giving birth in Maui's Mā'alaea Bay. Dip your head beneath the surface to experience a spectacularly colorful world: pairs of milletseed butterflyfish dart back and forth, red-lipped parrotfish snack on coral algae, and spotted eagle rays flap past like silent spaceships. Sea turtles bask at the surface while tiny wrasses give them the equivalent of a shave and a haircut. The water quality is typically outstanding; many sites afford 30-foot-plus visibility. On snorkel cruises, you can often stare from the boat rail right down to the bottom.

Certainly few destinations are as accommodating to every level of snorkeler as Hawai'i. Beginners can tromp in from sandy beaches while more advanced divers descend to shipwrecks, reefs, craters, and sea arches just offshore. Because of Hawai'i's extreme isolation, the island chain has fewer fish species than Fiji or the Caribbean—but many of the fish that are here exist nowhere else. The Hawaiian waters are home to the highest percentage of endemic fish in the world.

The key to enjoying the underwater world is slowing down. Look carefully. Listen. You might hear the strange crackling sound of shrimp tunneling through coral, or you may hear whales singing to one another during winter. A shy octopus may drift along the ocean's floor beneath you. If you're hooked, pick up a waterproof fishkey from Long's Drugs. You can brag later that you've looked the Hawaiian turkeyfish in the eye.

Picasso Triggerfish

Milletseed Butterflyfish

Yellow Tang

Moorish Idol

Hawaiian Whitespotted Toby

Saddleback Wrasse*

Red Lipped Parrotfish

Hawaiian Turkeyfish

Zebra Moray Eel

Stocky Hawkfish

Green Sea Turtle Honu

Spotted Eagle Ray

*endemic to Hawai'i

POLYNESIA'S FIRST CELESTIAL NAVIGATORS: HONU

Honu is the Hawaiian name for two native sea turtles, the hawksbill and the green sea turtle. Little is known about these dinosaur-age marine reptiles, though snorkelers regularly see them foraging for *limu* (seaweed) and the occasional jellyfish in Hawaiian waters. Most female honu nest in the uninhabited Northwestern Hawaiian Islands, but a few sociable ladies nest on Maui and Big Island beaches. Scientists suspect that they navigate the seas via magnetism—sensing the earth's poles. Amazingly, they will journey up to 800 miles to nest—it's believed that they return to their own birth sites. After about 60 days of incubation, nestlings emerge from the sand at night and find their way back to the sea by the light of the stars.

SUBMARINE TOURS

★ **Atlantis Submarines.** This is the underwater venture for the unadventurous. Not fond of swimming but want to see what you have been missing? Board this 64-passenger vessel for a ride down past ship wrecks, turtle breeding grounds, and coral reefs galore. Unlike a trip to the aquarium, this gives you a chance to see nature at work without the limitations of mankind. The tours, which leave from the pier at the Hilton Hawaiian Village, are available in several languages and run from $99 to $115. ✉ *Hilton Hawaiian Village Beach Resort and Spa, 2005 Kālia Rd., Waikīkī, Honolulu* ☎ *808/973–1296.*

SURFING

Perhaps no word is more associated with Hawai'i than surfing. Every year the best of the best gather here to have their Super Bowl: Vans Triple Crown of Surfing. The pros dominate the waves for a month, but the rest of the year belongs to people like us, just trying to have fun and get a little exercise.

O'ahu is unique because it has so many famous spots: Banzai Pipeline, Waimea Bay, Kaiser Bowls, and Sunset Beach resonate in young surfers' hearts the world over. The renown of these spots comes with a price: competition for those waves. The aloha spirit lives in many places but not on premium waves. As long as you follow the rules of the road and concede waves to local riders, you should not have problems. Just remember that locals view these waves as their property, and everything should be all right.

If you're nervous and don't want to run the risk of a confrontation, try some of the alternate spots listed below. They may not have the name recognition, but the waves can be just as great.

BEST SPOTS

If you like to ride waves in all kinds of craft, try **Mākaha Beach** (✉ *1½ hrs west of Honolulu on H1 and Farrington Hwy.*). It has interminable rights that allow riders to perform all manner of stunts: from six-man canoes with everyone doing headstands to bully boards (oversize bodyboards) with Dad's whole family riding with him. Mainly known as a long-boarding spot, it's predominantly local but not overly aggressive to the respectful outsider. The only downside is that it's way out on the west shore. Use caution in the wintertime as the surf can get huge.

If you really need to go somewhere people have heard of, your safest bet on the North Shore is **Sunset Beach** (✉ *1 mi north of 'Ehukai Beach Park on Kamehameha Hwy.*). There are several breaks here including **Kammie's** on the west side of the strip and **Sunset Point,** which is inside of the main Sunset break. Both of these tend to be smaller and safer rides for the less experienced. For the daring, Sunset is part of the Triple Crown for a reason. Thick waves and long rides await, but you're going to want to have a thick board and a thicker skull. The main break is very local, so mind your Ps and Qs.

In Waikīkī, try getting out to **Populars,** a break at **Ulukou Beach** (⊠ *Waikīkī, in front of Royal Hawaiian Hotel*). Nice and easy, Populars never breaks too hard and is friendly to both the rookie and the veteran. The only downside here is the ½-mi paddle out to the

break, but no one ever said it was going to be easy, plus the long pull keeps it from getting overcrowded.

White Plains Beach (⊠ *In former Kalaeloa Military Installation*) is a spot where trouble will not find you. Known among locals as "mini-Waikīkī," it breaks in numerous spots, preventing the logjam that happens with many of O'ahu's more popular breaks. As part of a military base in West O'ahu, the beach was closed to the public until a couple of years ago. It's now occupied by mostly novice to intermediate surfers, so egos are at a minimum, though you do have to keep a lookout for loose boards.

EQUIPMENT AND LESSONS

C&K Beach Service. To rent a board in Waikīkī, visit the beach fronting the Hilton Hawaiian Village. Rentals cost $10 to $15 per hour, depending on the size of the board, and $18 for two hours. Small-group lessons are $50 per hour with board, and trainers promise to have you riding the waves by lesson's end. ☎ *No phone.*

Hans Hedemann Surf Hawaii. Hans Hedemann spent 17 years on the professional surfer World Tour circuit. He and his staff offer surfing and bodysurfing instruction, four-day intensive surf camps on the North Shore and in Waikīkī, and fine-tuning courses with Hans himself. One-hour group-lesson rates begin at $75 per person, $150 per person for a private lesson. ☎ *808/924–7778* ⊕ *www.hhsurf.com.*

Ⓒ **Hawaiian Fire, Inc.** Off-duty Honolulu firefighters—and some of Hawai'i's most knowledgeable water-safety experts—man the boards at one of Hawai'i's hottest new surfing schools. Lessons include equipment, safety and surfing instruction, and two hours of surfing time (with lunch break) at a secluded beach near Barbers Point. Transportation is available from Waikīkī. Two-hour group-lesson rates begin at $99 per person, $187 per person for a private lesson. ☎ *808/737–3473* ⊕ *www. hawaiianfire.com.*

North Shore Eco-Surf Tours. The only prerequisites here are "the ability to swim and the desire to surf." North Shore Eco-Surf has a more relaxed view of lessons, saying that the instruction will last somewhere between 90 minutes and four hours. The group rate begins at $78 per person, $135 for a private lesson. ☎ *808/638–9503* ⊕ *www.ecosurf-hawaii.com.*

★ **Surf-n-Sea.** This is the Wal-Mart of water for the North Shore. Rent a short board for $6 an hour or a long board for $7 an hour ($24 and $30 for full-day rentals). Lessons cost $85 for three hours. Depending on how you want to attack your waves, you can also rent bodyboards

This surfer is doing a stellar job of surfing the infamous Bonzai Pipeline on O'ahu's North Shore.

or kayaks. ✉ *62-595 Kamehameha Hwy.* ☎ *808/637–9887* ⊕ *www. surfnsea.com.*

WHALE-WATCHING

November is marked by the arrival of snow in much of America, but in Hawai'i it marks the return of the humpback whale. These migrating behemoths move south from their North Pacific homes during the winter months for courtship and calving, and they put on quite a show. Watching males and females alike throwing themselves out of the ocean and into the sunset awes even the saltiest of sailors. Newborn calves riding gently next to their two-ton mothers will stir you to your core. These gentle giants can be seen from the shore as they make a splash, but there is nothing like having your boat rocking beneath you in the wake of a whale's breach.

Hawai'i Sailing Adventures and Hawai'i Nautical both run whale-watching charters during the winter months. At Hawai'i Sailing Adventures, two-hour whale-watching cruise rates with dinner start at $119. At Hawai'i Nautical, three-hour whale-watching cruise rates with snacks start at $100.

★ **Wild Side Specialty Tours.** Boasting a marine-biologist crew, this west-side tour boat takes you to undisturbed snorkeling areas. Along the way you can view dolphins, turtles, and, in winter, whales. The tours leave early (7 AM) to catch the wildlife still active, so it's important to plan ahead as they're an hour outside Honolulu. Three-hour whale-watching

SURF SMART

A few things to remember when surfing in O'ahu:

■ The waves switch with the seasons—they're big in the south in summer, and they loom large in the north in winter. If you're not experienced, it's best to go where the waves are small. There will be fewer crowds, and your chances of injury dramatically decrease.

■ Always wear a leash. It may not look the coolest, but when your board gets swept away from you and you're swimming a half mile after it, you'll remember this advice.

■ Watch where you're going. Take a few minutes and watch the surf from the shore. Observe how big it is, where it's breaking, and how quickly the sets are coming. This knowledge will allow you to get in and out more easily and to spend more time riding waves and less time paddling.

cruise rates with Continental breakfast start at $105. ⊠ *Wai'anae Boat Harbor, Slip A11, Wai'anae Boat Harbor* ☎ *808/306–7273.*

WINDSURFING AND KITEBOARDING

Those who call windsurfing and kiteboarding cheating because they require no paddling have never tried hanging on to a sail or kite. It will turn your arms to spaghetti quicker than paddling ever could, and the speeds you generate . . . well, there's a reason why these are considered extreme sports.

Windsurfing was born here in the Islands. For amateurs, the Windward side is best because the onshore breezes will bring you back to land even if you don't know what you're doing. The new sport of kiteboarding is tougher but more exhilarating as the kite will sometimes take you in the air for hundreds of feet. We suggest only those in top shape try the kites, but windsurfing is fun for all ages.

EQUIPMENT AND LESSONS

Kailua Sailboard and Kayaks Company. The appeal here is that they offer both beginner and high-performance gear. They also give lessons, either at $119 for a four-hour group lesson or $109 for a one-hour individual lesson. ■ TIP➔ Since both options are around the same price, we suggest the one-hour individual lesson; then you have the rest of the day to practice what they preach. Full-day rentals for the more experienced run from $59 for the standard board to $79 for a high-performance board. ⊠ *130 Kailua Rd., Kailua* ☎ *808/262–2555* ⊕ *www.kailuasailboards.com.*

Naish Hawai'i. If you like to learn from the best, try out world-champion Robby Naish and his family's services. Not only do they build and sell boards, rent equipment, and provide accommodation referrals, but they also offer their windsurfing and kiteboarding expertise. A four-hour package, including 90 minutes of instruction and a three-hour board rental, costs $75. ⊠ *155A Hamakua Dr., Kailua* ☏ *808/261–6067* ⊕ *www.naish.com.*

★ **Hawaiian Watersports.** Although this company has stores in town and in Kailua, the wind and kite surfing is all done on the windward side of the island, naturally. Check their Web site for regular deals, with prices starting at $79 for a group rate with two hours of instruction and two hours of practice, or $149 for a private lesson. ⊠ *354 Hahani St., Kailua* ☏ *808/262–5483* ⊕ *www.hawaiianwatersports.com.*

Golf, Hiking, and Outdoor Activities

WORD OF MOUTH

"We played the Ko' Olilna golf course, which was fairly easy and beautiful—lots of waterfalls, ponds, and swans."

—dolciani

Updated By
Chad Pata

Although much is written about the water surrounding this little rock known as O'ahu, there is as much to be said for the rock itself. It's a wonder of nature, thrust from the ocean floor a hundred millennia ago by a volcanic hot spot that is still spitting out islands today. This is the most remote island chain on earth, and there are creatures and plants that can be seen here and nowhere else. And there are dozens of ways for you to check it all out.

From the air you can peer down into nooks and crannies in the mountains—where cars cannot reach and hikers don't dare. Whether flitting here and there amidst a helicopter's rush and roar, or sailing by in the silence of a glider's reverie, you glimpse sights that few have experienced. Or if you would rather, take a step back in time and take off from the waters of Ke'ehi Lagoon in a World War II–era seaplane. Follow the flight path flown by the Japanese Zeros as they attempted to destroy Pearl Harbor and the American spirit. On the North Shore, you can even throw yourself from an airplane and check out the unique reef formations as you hurtle toward earth at 120 mph.

Would you prefer the ground tour, where gravity and you are no longer at odds? O'ahu is covered in hikes that vary from tropical rain forest to arid desert. Even when in the bustling city of Honolulu, you are but 10 minutes from hidden waterfalls and bamboo forests. Out west you can wander a dusty path that has long since given up its ability to accommodate cars but is perfect for hikers. You can splash in tidal pools, admire sea arches, and gape at caves opened by the rock slides that closed the road. You can camp out for free on most of these treks and beaches. You might end up swearing that being homeless in Hawai'i is better than living in the houses back home.

If somewhat less rugged and less vigorous exploration is more your style, how about letting horses or SUVs do your dirty work? You can ride them on the beaches and in the valleys, checking out ancient holy sites, movie sets, and brilliant vistas. Less sweat and more ground covered, but both are still a little stinky.

Finally, there is the ancient sport of Scotland. Why merely hike into the rain forest when you can slice a 280-yard drive through it and then hunt for your Titleist in the bushy leaves instead? Almost 40 courses cover this tiny expanse, ranging from the target jungle golf of Luana Hills to the pro-style links of Turtle Bay. There is no off-season in the tropics, and no one here knows your real handicap.

Ka'ena Point on the North Shore is windy and dry, and is where the rare, native Hawaiian plants grow.

AERIAL TOURS

An aerial tour of the Islands opens up a world of perspective. Looking down from the sky at the outline of the USS *Arizona* where it lays in its final resting place below the waters of Pearl Harbor or getting a glimpse of how Mother Nature carved a vast expanse of volcanic crater are the kinds of views only seen by an "eye in the sky." If you go, don't forget your camera.

★ **Island Seaplane Service.** Harking back to the days of the earliest air visitors to Hawai'i, the seaplane has always had a special spot in island lore. The only seaplane service still operating in Hawai'i takes off from Ke'ehi Lagoon. Flight options are either a half-hour south and eastern O'ahu shoreline tour or an hour island circle tour. The *Pan Am Clipper* may be gone, but you can revisit the experience for $135 to $250. ⊠ *85 Lagoon Dr., Honolulu* ☎ *808/836–6273* ⊕ *www.islandseaplane.com.*

Makani Kai Helicopters. This may be the best way to see the infamous and now closed Sacred Falls park, where a rock slide killed 20 people and injured dozens more; Makani Kai dips their helicopter down to show you one of Hawai'i's former favorite hikes. The Schuman family, who run Makani, have been in the transportation business on Oahu for more than a century, and offer tours on all four major islands. Half-hour tour rates begin at $155 per person, and customized private charters are available starting at $1,500 per hour. ⊠ *130 Iolana Pl., Honolulu* ☎ *808/834–5813* ⊕ *www.makanikai.com.*

★ **The Original Glider Rides.** "Mr. Bill" has been offering piloted glider (sailplane) rides over the northwest end of O'ahu's North Shore since 1970.

These are piloted scenic rides for one or two passengers in sleek, bubble-top, motorless aircraft. You'll get aerial views of mountains, shoreline, coral pools, windsurfing sails, and, in winter, humpback whales. For the more adventurous, we recommend the acrobatic ride where the veteran pilot has you drawing shamrocks in the sky during a vertical dive while approaching 4 Gs. Reservations are recommended; 10-, 15-, 20-, and 30-minute flights leave every 20 minutes daily 10–5. The charge for one passenger is $79 to $145, depending on the length of the flight; two people fly for $170 to $260. ⊠ *Dillingham Airfield, Mokulē'ia* ☎ *808/677–3404* ⊕ *www.honolulusoaring.com.*

BIKING

O'ahu's coastal roads are flat, well paved, and unfortunately, awash in vehicular traffic. Frankly, biking is no fun in either Waikīkī or Honolulu, but things are a bit better outside the city.

Honolulu City and County Bike Coordinator (☎ *808/768–8335*) can answer all your biking questions concerning trails, permits, and state laws. For information on mountain biking go to ⊕ *hawaiitrails.ehawaii.gov/ home.php* to find detailed maps and descriptions of dozens of trails you can ride on the Island.

BEST SPOTS

Fodor's Choice Our favorite ride is in central O'ahu on the **'Aiea Loop Trail** (⊠ *Central*
★   *O'ahu, just past Kea'iwa Heiau State Park, at end of 'Aiea Heights Dr.*). There's a little bit of everything you expect to find in Hawai'i—wild pigs crossing your path, an ancient Hawaiian *heiau* (holy ground), and the remains of a World War II crashed airplane. Campsites and picnic tables are available along the way and, if you need a snack, strawberry guava trees abound. Enjoy watching the foliage change from bamboo to Norfolk pine in your climb along this 4½-mi track.

If going up a mountain is not your idea of mountain biking, then perhaps **Ka'ena Point Trail** (⊠ *West O'ahu, end of Farrington Hwy.*) is better suited to your needs. A longer ride (10 mi) but much flatter, this trail takes you oceanside around the westernmost point on the island. You pass sea arches and a mini-blowhole, then finish up with some moto-cross jumps right before you turn around. There's no water on this ride either, but at least at the end you have the Yokohama beach showers to cool you off.

Locals favor biking the **Waimānalo Demonstration Trail** (⊠ *Begins at the Pali Lookout on the blacktop of Old Pali Road.*). It's a 10-mile trail with breathtaking views that can be seen as you descend into Waimānalo. There are many flat portions but also some uneven ground to negotiate unless you're willing to carry your bike for small stretches.

EQUIPMENT AND TOURS

Blue Sky Rentals & Sports Center. Known more for motorcycles than for man-powered bikes, Blue Sky does have bicycles for $25 for eight hours, $30 for a day, and $100 per week—no deposit is required. The prices include a bike, a helmet, and a lock. ⊠ *1920 Ala Moana Blvd., across from Hilton Hawaiian Village, Waikīkī, Honolulu* ☎ *808/947–0101.*

Continued on page 146

HAWAI'I'S PLANTS 101

Hawai'i is a bounty of rainbow-colored flowers and plants. The evening air is scented with their fragrance. Just look at the front yard of almost any home, travel any road, or visit any local park and you'll see a spectacular array of colored blossoms and leaves. What most visitors don't know is that the plants they are seeing are not native to Hawai'i; rather, they were introduced during the last two centuries as ornamental plants, or for timber, shade, or fruit.

Hawai'i boasts nearly every climate on the planet, excluding the two most extreme: arctic tundra and arid desert. The Islands have wine-growing regions, cactus-speckled ranchlands, icy mountaintops, and the rainiest forests on earth.

Plants introduced from around the world thrive here. The lush lowland valleys along the windward coasts are predominantly populated by non-native trees including yellow- and red-fruited **guava**, silvery-leafed **kukui**, and orange-flowered **tulip trees**.

The colorful **plumeria flower**, very fragrant and commonly used in lei making, and

the giant multicolored **hibiscus flower** are both used by many women as hair adornments, and are two of the most common plants found around homes and hotels. The umbrella-like **monkeypod tree** from Central America provides shade in many of Hawai'i's parks including Kapiolani Park in Honolulu. Hawai'i's largest tree, found in Lahaina, Maui, is a giant **banyan tree**. Its canopy and massive support roots cover about two-thirds of an acre. The native **o'hia tree**, with its brilliant red brush-like flowers, and the **hapu'u**, a giant tree fern, are common in Hawai'i's forests and are also used ornamentally in gardens and around homes.

Bougainville	Guava	Monkeypod
Banyan	Ohia Lehua	Tulip Tree
Plumeria	Pandanus	Hibiscus
Anthurium	Kukui	Hapu'u

*endemic to Hawai'i

DID YOU KNOW?

Over 2,200 plant species are found in the Hawaiian Islands, but only about 1,000 are native. Of these, 282 are so rare, they are endangered. Hawai'i's endemic plants evolved from ancestral seeds arriving on the islands over thousands of years as baggage on birds, floating on ocean currents, or drifting on winds from continents thousands of miles away. Once here, these plants evolved in isolation creating many new species known nowhere else in the world.

Boca Hawai'i LLC. This is your first stop if you want to do intense riding. The triathlon shop, owned and operated by top athletes, has full-suspension Trek 4500s for mountain bikes or Trek 1000 for street bikes, both for $35 a day, but that drops to $25 a day if you rent it for more than one day. Call ahead and reserve a bike as supplies are limited. ⊠ *330 Cooke St., next to Bike Factory, Kaka'ako, Honolulu* ☎ *808/591–9839.*

Hawai'i Bicycling League. Not much for riding by yourself? Visit this shop online, and you can get connected with rides and contests. ⌂ *Box 4403, Honolulu 96813* ☎ *808/735–5756* ⊕ *www.hbl.org.*

Bike Hawaii. Whether it's road tours of the North Shore or muddy off-road adventures in Ka'a'awa Valley, this is the company to get you there. They also offer combination packages including snorkeling or hiking. Three-hour road tours start out at $58, with the six-hour mountain-biking foray running $120. ⌂ *Box 240170, Honolulu 96824* ☎ *877/682–7433* ⊕ *www.bikehawaii.com.*

CAMPING

Camping has always been the choice of cost-conscious travelers who want to be vacationing for a while without spending a lot of money. But now, with the growth of ecotourism and the skyrocketing cost of gas, it has become more popular than ever. Whatever your reasons for getting back to nature, O'ahu has plenty to offer year-round.

■ TIP→ Camping here is not as highly organized as it is on the Mainland: expect few marked sites, scarce electrical outlets, and nary a ranger station. What you find instead are unblemished spots in the woods and on the beach. With price tags ranging from free to $5, it's hard to complain about the lack of amenities.

STATE PARKS

There are four state recreation areas at which you can camp, one in the mountains and three on the beach. All state parks require 30 days' advance notice and a $5 fee a day.

To obtain a camping permit as well as rules and regulations for state parks, write to the **Department of Land and Natural Resources, State Parks Division** (⌂ *Box 621, Honolulu 96809* ☎ *808/587–0300* ⊕ *www. hawaiistateparks.org*).

Keaīwa Heiau State Recreation Area (⊠ *End of Aiea Heights Rd.* ☎ *808/ 483–2511*), the mountain option, consists of nearly 400 acres of forests and hiking trails in the foothills of the Ko'olaus. The park is centered around an ancient Hawaiian holy site, known as a *heiau*, that is believed to be the site of many healings. Proper respect is asked of campers in the area.

Of the beach sites, **Kahana Valley State Park** (⊠ *Kamehameha Hwy. near Kahana Bay*) is the choice for a true Hawaiian experience. You camp alongside a beautiful Windward bay, a short walk away from the Huilua Fishpond, a national historic landmark. There are rain-forest hikes chock-full of local fruit trees, a public hunting area for pigs, and a coconut grove for picnicking. The water is suitable for swimming and body surfing, though it's a little cloudy for snorkeling.

COUNTY CAMPSITES

As for the county spots, there are 15 currently available and they all do require a permit. The good news is that the permits are free and are easy to obtain.

Contact the **Department of Parks and Recreation** (✉ *650 S. King St., Honolulu* ☎ *808/768–3440*), or any of the satellite city halls (Ala Moana Mall, Fort St. Mall, and Kapolei Hale), for permits and rules and regulations. Permits become available two weeks ahead of the camping date, making it difficult for visitors to the Islands to camp on Saturdays. Also note that there is no beach camping on Wednesdays or Thursdays.

Fodor's Choice
★

For beach camping we suggest Bellows and Kualoa. **Bellows Field Beach Park** (✉ *220 Tinker Rd.* ☎ *808/259–8080*) has the superior beach as well as excellent cover in the grove of ironwood trees. The Windward beach is over 3 mi long, and both pole fishing and campfires in designated areas are allowed here. You can feel secure with the kids as there are lifeguards and public phones. The only downside is that camping is permitted only on the weekends.

The beach at **Kualoa Regional Park** (✉ *49-479 Kamehameha Hwy.* ☎ *808/237–8525*) isn't the magnificent giant that Bellows is, but the vistas are both magnificent and historic. Near Chinaman's Hat (Mokoli'i Island) at the northern end of Kāne'ohe Bay, the park is listed on the National Registry of Historic Places due to its significance to the Hawaiians. The park is expansive, with large grassy areas, picnic tables, and comfort stations. Although the beach is just a bit of a sandy strip, the swimming and snorkeling are excellent.

Camping is not just all about the beach, however.

Nestled in the foothills of the Ko'olaus is the serene **Hoomaluhia Botanical Garden** (✉ *End of Luluku Rd. in Kāne'ohe* ☎ *808/233–7323*). The 400-acre preserve has catch-and-release fishing, extensive hiking trails, and a large selection of tropical shrubs and trees. There are five fire circles. Though it is a beautiful area, they do caution campers to be prepared for rain, mud, and mosquitoes.

CAMPING INDOORS

If tent camping sounds a little too rugged, consider cabin camping on the beach. These spots do not offer the amenities of the island's hotels and resorts, but they do provide oceanfront rooms for those on smaller budgets.

★ The least expensive is **The Friends of Malaekahana** (✉ *56-335 Kamehameha Hwy.* ☎ *808/293–1736* ⊕ *www.malaekahana.net*) just outside the North Shore's Laie. The complex was originally a series of oceanfront cottages built 60 years ago, but they were taken over by the state and now are run by The Friends as a private venture in what they call "indoor camping." We recommend two price-friendly alternatives. Their eco-cabins come with a gas grill and double beds, and can accommodate up to six people from $80 to $150 a night with a two-night minimum. Another option is their "Li'l Grass Shacks," which are just that, and come with a picnic table and tiki torches on the side for only $40 a night. All the shacks have ocean views.

For a little step up there is the YMCA's **Camp Erdman** (✉ *69-385 Farrington Hwy.* ☎ *808/637–4615* ⊕ *www.camperdman.net*), also on the North Shore. It is a youth camp, but they almost always have extra cabins available for the public. The cabins are in much better condition than Malaekahana, and they offer nicer facilities, including volleyball and basketball, and serve hot meals. The beach is nearly deserted, and there is an amazing ropes course for those without a fear of heights. Though $105 a person for two nights seems a bit steep for camping, keep in mind that the fee also covers six meals. Just try to eat in Waikīkī for two days on that budget!

Finally, if you have a big group to house, there is **Camp Mokulē'ia** (✉ *68-729 Farrington Hwy.* ☎ *808/637–6241* ⊕ *www.campmokuleia.org*). This privately-run operation has wide-open beach space, a monstrous fire pit, and camp sites that can accommodate 30. While the camp sites are a bargain at $15 a night, the cabins are a bit pricey unless you have a troop. Their studio cottages are $90 a night, but the 14-bed cottages are only $238. Located just up the road from Camp Erdman, they offer fewer kids and more privacy, but you are on your own as far as cooking is concerned.

GOLF

Unlike on the Neighbor Islands, the majority of O'ahu's golf courses are not associated with hotels and resorts. In fact, of the island's three-dozen-plus courses, only five are tied to lodging and none of them is in the tourist hub of Waikīkī.

Green fees listed here are the highest course rates per round on weekdays and weekends for U.S. residents. (Some courses charge non-U.S. residents higher prices.) Discounts are often available for resort guests and for those who book tee times on the Web. Twilight fees are usually offered; call individual courses for information.

WAIKĪKĪ

There is only one spot to golf in Waikīkī and it is only the busiest course in America. While not a very imaginative layout, the price is right and the advantage of walking from your hotel to the course is not to be overlooked. Just make sure you bring a newspaper because it will be a little while before you tee off.

Ala Wai Municipal Golf Course. Just across the Ala Wai Canal from Waikīkī, Ala Wai is said to host more rounds than any other U.S. course. Not that it's a great course, just really convenient, being Honolulu's only public "city course." Although residents can obtain a city golf card that allows automated tee-time reservations over the phone, the best bet for a visitor is to show up and expect to wait at least an hour. The course itself is flat. Robin Nelson did some redesign work in the 1990s, adding mounding, trees, and a lake. The Ala Wai Canal comes into play on several holes on the back nine, including the treacherous 18th. ✉ *404 Kapahulu Ave., Waikīkī, Honolulu* ☎ *808/733–7387; 808/739–1900 golf shop* ⏳ *18 holes. 5,861 yds. Par 70. Green Fee: $45* ☞ *Facilities:*

TIPS FOR THE GREEN

Before you head out to the first tee, there are a few things you should know about golf in Hawai'i:

■ All resort courses and many daily fee courses provide rental clubs. In many cases, they're the latest lines from Titleist, Ping, Callaway, and the like. This is true for both men and women, as well as lefthanders, which means you don't have to schlep clubs across the Pacific.

■ Most courses offer deals varying from twilight discount rates to frequent-visitor's discounts, even for tourists. Ask questions when calling pro shops, and don't just accept their first quotes—deals abound if you persist.

■ Pro shops at most courses are well stocked with balls, tees, and other accoutrements, so even if you bring your own bag, it needn't weigh a ton.

■ Come spikeless—very few Hawai'i courses still permit metal spikes.

■ Sunscreen. Buy it, apply it (minimum 30 SPF). The subtropical rays of the sun are intense, even in December.

■ Resort courses, in particular, offer more than the usual three sets of tees, sometimes four or five. So bite off as much or little challenge as you can chew. Tee it up from the tips and you'll end up playing a few 600-yard par-5s and see a few 250-yard forced carries.

■ In theory, you can play golf in Hawai'i 365 days a year. But there's a reason the Hawaiian islands are so green. Better to bring an umbrella and light jacket and not use them than not to bring them and get soaked.

■ Unless you play a muni or certain daily fee courses, plan on taking a cart. Riding carts are mandatory at most courses and are included in the green fees.

5

Driving range, putting green, golf carts, pull carts, rental clubs, pro shop, lessons, restaurant, bar.

HONOLULU

Moanalua Country Club. Said to be (but not without dispute) the oldest golf club west of the Rockies, this 9-holer is private but allows public play except on weekend and holiday mornings. It's a bit quirky, but the final two holes, a par-3 off a cliff to a smallish tree-rimmed green and a par-4 with an approach to a green set snugly between stream and jungle, are classic. ⊠ *1250 Ala Aolani St.* ☏ *808/839–2411* ⸓ *9 holes. ,3062 yds. Par 36. Green Fee: $25* ☞ *Facilities: Putting green, golf carts, restaurant, bar.*

SOUTHEAST O'AHU

Prepare to keep your ball down on this windy corner of Oahu. You will get beautiful ocean vistas, but you may need them to soothe you once your perfect drive gets blown 40 yards off course by a gusting tradewind.

Hawai'i Kai Golf Course. The Championship Golf Course (William F. Bell, 1973) winds through a Honolulu suburb at the foot of Koko Crater. Homes (and the liability of a broken window) come into play on many holes, but that is offset by views of the nearby Pacific and a crafty routing of holes. With several lakes, lots of trees, and bunkers in all the wrong places, Hawai'i Kai really is a "championship" golf

course, especially when the trade winds howl. The **Executive Course** (1962), a par-55 track, is the first of only three courses in Hawai'i built by Robert Trent Jones Sr. Although a few changes have been made to his original design, you can find the usual Jones attributes, including raised greens and lots of risk-reward options. ✉ *8902 Kalaniana'ole Hwy., Hawai'i Kai* ☎ *808/395–2358* ⊕ *www.hawaiikaigolf.com* ⚑ *Championship Course: 18 holes. 6,222 yds. Par 72. Green Fee: $100. Executive Course: 18 holes. 2,223 yds. Par 54. Green Fee: $37/$42* ⚐ *Facilities: Driving range, putting green, golf carts, pull carts, rental clubs, pro shop, lessons, restaurant, bar.*

WINDWARD O'AHU

Windward O'ahu is what you expect when you think of golfing in the Islands. Lush, tropical foliage will surround you with towering mountains framing one shot and the crystal blue Pacific framing the next. While it is a bit more expensive to golf on this side, and a good deal wetter, the memories and pictures you take on these courses will last one a lifetime.

Ko'olau Golf Club. Ko'olau Golf Club is marketed as the toughest golf course in Hawai'i and one of the most challenging in the country. Dick Nugent and Jack Tuthill (1992) routed 10 holes over jungle ravines that require at least a 110-yard carry. The par-4 18th may be the most difficult closing hole in golf. The tee shot from the regular tees must carry 200 yards of ravine, 250 from the blue tees. The approach shot is back across the ravine, 200 yards to a well-bunkered green. Set at the Windward base of the Ko'olau Mountains, the course is as much beauty as beast. Kāne'ohe Bay is visible from most holes, orchids and yellow ginger bloom, the shama thrush (Hawai'i's best singer since Don Ho) chirrups, and waterfalls flute down the sheer, green mountains above. ✉ *45-550 Kionaole Rd., Kāne'ohe* ☎ *808/236–4653* ⊕ *www.koolaugolfclub.com* ⚑ *18 holes. 7,310 yds. Par 72. Green Fee: $110* ⚐ *Facilities: Driving range, putting green, golf carts, rental clubs, pro shop, restaurant, bar.*

Fodor's Choice **Luana Hills Country Club.** In the cool, lush Maunawili Valley, Pete and
★ Perry Dye created what can only be called target jungle golf. In other words, the rough is usually dense jungle, and you may not hit driver on three of the four par-5s, or several par-4s, including the perilous

18th that plays off a cliff to a narrow green protected by a creek. Mt. Olomana's twin peaks tower over Luana Hills. ■TIP➜ **The back nine wanders deep into the valley, and includes an island green (par-3 11th) and perhaps the loveliest inland hole in Hawai'i (par-4 12th).** ✉ *770 Auloa Rd., Kailua* ☎ *808/262–2139* ⊕ *www.luanahills.com* ⅃. *18 holes. 6,164 yds. Par 72. Green Fee: $125* ☞ *Facilities: Driving range, putting green, golf carts, rental clubs, pro shop, restaurant, bar.*

★ **Olomana Golf Links.** Bob and Robert L. Baldock are the architects of record for this layout, but so much has changed since it opened in 1969 that they would recognize little of it. A turf specialist was brought in to improve fairways and greens, tees were rebuilt, new bunkers added, and mangroves cut back to make better use of natural wetlands. But what really puts Olomana on the map is that this is where wunderkind Michelle Wie learned the game. ✉ *41-1801 Kalaniana'ole Hwy., Waimānalo* ☎ *808/259–7926* ⊕ *www.olomanagolflinks.com* ⅃. *18 holes. 6,326 yds. Par 72. Green Fee: $95* ☞ *Facilities: Driving range, putting green, golf carts, pull carts, rental clubs, pro shop, lessons, restaurant, bar.*

NORTH SHORE

The North Shore sports both the cheapest and most expensive courses on the Island, so if you feel like playing nine holes in your bare feet you can do that. If you want to chunk up the course played by both the LPGA and Champions Tour, that is available as well. Just don't try to go barefoot on the LPGA course or the only course you may be allowed on in the Islands will be the Kahuku muni.

Turtle Bay Resort & Spa. When the Lazarus of golf courses, the **Fazio Course** at Turtle Bay (George Fazio, 1971), rose from the dead in 2002, Turtle Bay on O'ahu's rugged North Shore became a premier golf destination. Two holes had been plowed under when the **Palmer Course** at Turtle Bay (Arnold Palmer and Ed Seay, 1992) was built, while the other seven lay fallow, and the front nine remained open. Then new owners came along and recreated holes 13 and 14 using Fazio's original plans, and the Fazio became whole again. It's a terrific track with 90 bunkers. The gem at Turtle Bay, though, is the Palmer Course. The front nine is mostly open as it skirts Punaho'olapa Marsh, a nature sanctuary, while the back nine plunges into the wetlands and winds along the coast. The short par-4 17th runs along the rocky shore, with a diabolical string of bunkers cutting diagonally across the fairway from tee to green. ✉ *57-049 Kuilima Dr., Kahuku* ☎ *808/293–8574* ⊕ *www.turtlebayresort. com* ⅃. *Fazio Course: 18 holes. 6,535 yds. Par 72. Green Fee: $125. Palmer Course: 18 holes. 7,199 yds. Par 72. Green Fee: $175* ☞ *Facilities: Driving range, putting green, golf carts, rental clubs, pro shop, lessons, restaurant, bar.*

Kahuku Municipal Golf Course. The only true links course in Hawai'i, this 9-hole muni is not for everyone. Maintenance is an ongoing issue, and in summer it can look a bit like the Serengeti. It's walking-only (a few pull-carts are available for rent); there's no pro shop, just a starter who sells lost-and-found balls; and the 19th hole is a soda machine and a covered picnic bench. And yet the course stretches out along the blue Pacific where surf crashes on the shore, the turf underfoot is spongy, sea mist drifts across the links, and wildflowers bloom in the rough. ⊠ *56-501 Kamehameha Hwy., Kahuku* ☎ *808/293–5842* ⚑ *9 holes. 2,699 yds. Par 35. Green Fee: $11.50 for 9 holes* ☞ *Facilities: putting green, pull carts.*

KAPOLEI AND CENTRAL O'AHU

The most densely populated area of golf courses is to be found here in Central Oahu as plantation spaces were changed into track housing and golf courses were added to anchor communities. The vegetation is much more sparse on this side, but some of the best greens around can be found here. Try to play this side early as it does get hot in the afternoons. But if you don't mind the heat, most offer substantial discounts for their twilight rates.

★ **Coral Creek Golf Course.** On the 'Ewa Plain, 4 mi inland, Coral Creek is cut from ancient coral—left from when this area was still under water. Robin Nelson (1999) does some of his best work in making use of the coral, and some dynamite, blasting out portions to create dramatic lakes and tee and green sites. They could just as easily call it Coral Cliffs, thanks to the 30- to 40-foot cliffs Nelson created. These include the par-3 10th green's grotto and waterfall, and the vertical drop-off on the right side of the par-4 18th green. An ancient creek meanders across the course, but there's not much water, just enough to be a babbling nuisance. ⊠ *91-1111 Geiger Rd., 'Ewa Beach* ☎ *808/441–4653* ⊕ *www.coralcreekgolfhawaii.com* ⚑ *18 holes. 6,818 yds. Par 72. Green Fee: $130* ☞ *Facilities: Driving range, putting green, golf carts, rental clubs, pro shop, lessons, restaurant, bar.*

Hawai'i Country Club. Also known as Kunia, but not to be confused with Royal Kunia a few miles away, this course is in the middle of sugarcane fields and dates to plantation times. Several par-4s are driveable, including the 9th and 18th holes. This is a fun course, but a bit rough around the edges. ⊠ *94-1211 Kunia Rd., Wahiawā* ☎ *808/621–5654* ⊕ *www.hawaiicc.com* ⚑ *18 holes. 5,910 yds. Par 72. Green Fee: $65/$75* ☞ *Facilities: Driving range, putting green, rental clubs, pro shop, restaurant, bar.*

Hawai'i Prince Golf Course. Affiliated with the Hawai'i Prince Hotel in Waikīkī, the Hawai'i Prince Golf Course (not to be confused with the Prince Course at Princeville, Kaua'i) has a links feel to it, and it is popular with local charity fund-raiser golf tournaments. Arnold Palmer and Ed Seay (1991) took what had been flat, featureless sugarcane fields and sculpted 27 challenging, varied holes. Mounding breaks up the landscape, as do 10 lakes. Water comes into play on six holes of the A course, three of B, and seven of C. The most difficult combination is A and C (A and B from the forward tees). ⊠ *91-1200 Fort Weaver Rd., 'Ewa Beach* ☎ *808/944–4567* ⊕ *www.princeresortshawaii.com* ⚑ *A Course: 9 holes. 3,138 yds. Par 36. B Course: 9 holes. 3,099 yds. Par 36. C Course: 9 holes. 3,076 yds. Par 36. Green Fee: $120* ☞ *Facilities: Driving range, putting green, golf carts, pull carts, rental clubs, pro shop, golf academy/lessons, restaurant, bar.*

Kapolei Golf Course. This is a Ted Robinson water wonderland with waterfalls and four lakes—three so big they have names—coming into play on 10 holes. Set on rolling terrain, Kapolei is a serious golf course, especially when the wind blows. ✉ *91-701 Farrington Hwy., Kapolei* ☎ *808/674–2227* 🏌 *www.kapoleigolfcourse.com* 🏌 *18 holes. 7,001 yds. Par 72. Green Fee: $150/$160* ☞ *Facilities: Driving range, putting green, golf carts, rental clubs, pro shop, lessons, restaurant, bar.*

Mililani Golf Course. Located on O'ahu's central plain, Mililani is usually a few degrees cooler than downtown, 25 minutes away. The eucalyptus trees through which the course plays add to the cool factor and stands of Norfolk pines give Mililani a "mainland course" feel. Bob and Robert L. Baldock (1966) make good use of an old irrigation ditch reminiscent of a Scottish burn. ✉ *95-176 Kuahelani Ave., Mililani* ☎ *808/623–2222* ⊕ *www.mililanigolf.com* 🏌 *18 holes. 6,455 yds. Par 72. Green Fee: $99* ☞ *Facilities: Driving range, putting green, golf carts, rental clubs, pro shop, lessons, restaurant, bar.*

New 'Ewa Beach Golf Club. A private course open to the public, New 'Ewa is one of the delightful products of the too brief collaboration of Robin Nelson and Rodney Wright (1992). Trees are very much part of the character here, but there are also elements of links golf, such as a double green shared by the 2nd and 16th holes. ✉ *91-050 Fort Weaver Rd., 'Ewa Beach* ☎ *808/689–6565* 🏌 *www.ewabeachgc.com* 🏌 *18 holes. 6,124 yds. Par 72. Green Fee: $140* ☞ *Facilities: Putting green, golf carts, rental clubs, pro shop, restaurant.*

Pearl Country Club. Carved in the hillside high above Pearl Harbor, the 18 holes here are really two courses. The front nine rambles out along gently sloping terrain, while the back nine zigzags up and down a steeper portion of the slope as it rises into the Ko'olau Mountains. ■TIP➔ The views of Pearl Harbor are breathtaking. ✉ *98-535 Kaonohi St., 'Aiea* ☎ *808/487–3802* ⊕ *www.pearlcc.com* 🏌 *18 holes. 6,230 yds. Par 72. Green Fee: $80/$90* ☞ *Facilities: Driving range, putting green, golf carts, rental clubs, pro shop, lessons, restaurant, bar.*

Royal Kunia Country Club. At one time the PGA Tour considered buying Royal Kunia Country Club and hosting the Sony Open there. It's that good. ■TIP➔ Every hole offers fabulous views from Diamond Head to Pearl Harbor to the nearby Wai'anae Mountains. Robin Nelson's eye for natural sight lines and dexterity with water features adds to the visual pleasure. ✉ *94-1509 Anonui St., Waipahu* ☎ *808/688–9222* ⊕ *www. royalkuniacc.com* 🏌 *18 holes. 7,007 yds. Par 72. Green Fee: $140* ☞ *Facilities: Driving range, putting green, golf carts, rental clubs, pro shop, restaurant.*

Waikele Golf Course. Outlet stores are not the only bargain at Waikele. The adjacent golf course is a daily-fee course that offers a private club-like atmosphere and a terrific Ted Robinson (1992) layout. The target off the tee is Diamond Head, with Pearl Harbor to the right. Robinson's water features are less distinctive here but define the short par-4 4th hole, with a lake running down the left side of the fairway and guarding the green, and the par-3 17th, which plays across a lake. The par-4 18th is a terrific closing hole, with a lake lurking on the right side

5

of the green. ✉ *94-200 Paioa Pl., Waipahu* ☎ *808/676–9000* ⊕ *www. golfwaikele.com* ⅃. *18 holes. 6,261 yds. Par 72. Green Fee: $130 ☞ Facilities: Driving range, putting green, golf carts, rental clubs, pro shop, lessons, restaurant, bar.*

West Loch Municipal Golf Course. The best of Honolulu's municipal courses, this Robin Nelson (1991) design plays along Pearl Harbor's West Loch. In the process of building the course, wetlands were actually expanded, increasing bird habitat. ✉ *91-1126 Okupe St., 'Ewa Beach* ☎ *808/675– 6076* ⅃. *18 holes. 6,335 yds. Par 72. Green Fee: $45 ☞ Facilities: Driving range, putting green, golf carts, rental clubs, restaurant.*

WEST O'AHU

A long drive from town but if you enjoy a resort setup on a course, the three on the Westside will suit your fancy. They are all built around their resorts, and if you're planning on playing all the way out at Makaha you may want to consider staying out there for a day or two. The beaches are magnificent, and deals are to be had combining a room with a round or two on the course.

Ko Olina Golf Club. Hawai'i's golden age of golf-course architecture came to O'ahu when Ko Olina Golf Club opened in 1989. Ted Robinson, king of the water features, went splash-happy here, creating nine lakes that come into play on eight holes, including the par-3 12th, where you reach the tee by driving behind a Disney-like waterfall. Tactically, though, the most dramatic is the par-4 18th, where the approach is a minimum 120 yards across a lake to a two-tiered green guarded on the left by a cascading waterfall. Today, Ko Olina, affiliated with the adjacent 'Ihilani Resort and Spa (guests receive discounted rates), has matured into one of Hawai'i's top courses. You can niggle about routing issues—the first three holes play into the trade winds (and the morning sun), and two consecutive par-5s on the back nine play into the trades—but Robinson does enough solid design to make those of passing concern. ✉ *92-1220 Ali'inui Dr., Kapolei* ☎ *808/676–5300* ⊕ *www.koolinagolf.com* ⅃. *18 holes. 6,867 yds. Par 72. Green Fee: $179 ☞ Facilities: driving range, putting green, golf carts, rental clubs, pro shop, golf academy, restaurant, bar.*

★ **Makaha Resort Golf Club.** Known locally as Makaha West, this William F. Bell classic design (1969) remains one of the island's true gems, and a serious golf course where subtle elevation changes, if not duly noted, can significantly affect scores. The back nine plays up into Makaha Valley. Roving peacocks make Makaha West one of the island's most colorful layouts. ✉ *84-626 Makaha Valley Rd., Wai'anae* ☎ *808/695–7519* ⊕ *www.makaharesort.com* ⅃. *18 holes. 7,077 yds. Par 72. Green Fee: $120 ☞ Facilities: Driving range, putting green, golf carts, rental clubs, pro shop, lessons, restaurant, bar.*

Makaha Valley Country Club. This course (William F. Bell, 1968), known locally as Makaha East, is indeed a valley course, taking great advantage of the steep valley walls and natural terrain. It's shorter than the nearby West course, but offers plenty of challenge from the back tees. The double-dogleg, downhill-uphill, par-5 18th is a doozy of a closer.

✉ *84-627 Mākaha Valley Rd., Waiʻanae* ☎ *808/695–9578* ⊕ *www. makahavalleycc.com* ⚲. *18 holes. 6,091 yds. Par 71.* Green Fee: *$65/$75* ☞ Facilities: *Driving range, putting green, golf carts, rental clubs, pro shop, restaurant, bar.*

MUNICIPAL GOLF COURSES

We don't have room to mention every muni on Oʻahu, so here are three more you may want to consider. Your best bet for a tee time is to call the day-of and inquire about walk-on availability. Green fees are standard at city courses, walking rate $45, riding cart $9.50 per person, pull carts $4.

ʻEwa Villages Golf Course Municipal. ✉ *91-1760 Park Row St., ʻEwa Beach* ☎ *808/681–0220* ⚲. *18 holes. 6,455 yds. Par 73.*

Pali Golf Course Municipal. ✉ *45-050 Kamehameha Hwy., Kāneʻohe* ☎ *808/ 266–7612* ⚲. *18 holes. 6,524 yds. Par 72.*

Ted Makalena Golf Course Municipal. ✉ *93-059 Waipio Pt. Access Rd., Waipahu* ☎ *808/675–6052* ⚲. *18 holes. 5,946 yds. Par 71.*

HIKING

The trails of Oʻahu cover a full spectrum of environments: desert walks through cactus, slippery paths through bamboo-filled rain forest, and scrambling rock climbs up ancient volcanic calderas. The only thing you won't find is an overnighter, as even the longest of hikes won't take you more than half a day. In addition to being short in length, many of the prime hikes are within 10 minutes of downtown Waikīkī, meaning that you won't have to spend your whole day getting back to nature.

To obtain a Oʻahu recreation map that outlines the island's 33 major trails ($3.95), contact the **Hawaiʻi State Department of Land and Natural Resources** (✉ *1151 Punchbowl St., Room 130, Honolulu* ☎ *808/587– 0300* ⊕ *www.hawaii.gov*).

Contact the City and County of Honolulu **Trails and Access Manager** (☎ *808/973–9782*) for a free hiking-safety guide. Ask for a copy of *Hiking on Oʻahu: The Official Guide*, or go online to ⊕ *www.hawaiitrails.org*.

BEST SPOTS

Every vacation has requirements that must be fulfilled so that when your neighbors ask, you can say, "Yeah, did it." **Diamond Head Crater** is high on that list of things to do on Oʻahu. It's a hike easy enough that even Grandma can do it, as long as she takes a water bottle because it's hot and dry. Only a mile up, a clearly marked trail with handrails scales the inside of this extinct volcano. At the top, the fabled 99 steps take you up to the pill box overlooking the Pacific Ocean and Honolulu. It's a breathtaking view and a lot cheaper than taking a helicopter ride for the same photo op. ✉ *Diamond Head Rd. at 18th Ave. Enter on east of crater; there's limited parking inside, most park on street and walk in.*

Fodorʻs Choice   Travel up into the valley beyond Honolulu to make the **Mānoa Falls** hike.
★   Though only a mile long, this path passes through so many different

ecosystems that you feel as if you're in an arboretum. Walk among the elephant ear ape plants, ruddy fir trees, and a bamboo forest straight out of China. At the top are 150-foot falls with a small pool not quite suited for swimming but good for wading. This hike is more about the journey than the destination. Make sure you bring some mosquito repellent because they grow 'em big up here. ✛ *Behind Mānoa Valley in Paradise Park. Take West Mānoa Rd. to end, park on side of road, and follow trail signs in.*

★ Need more waterfall action that you can actually swim in? Then **Maunawili Falls** is your trip. In fact, even if you don't want to get wet, you're going to have to cross Maunawili Stream several times to get to the falls. Along the 1½-mi trek enjoy the ginger, vines, and heliconia before greeting fern-shrouded falls that are made for swimming. The water is not the clearest, but it's cool and refreshing after battling the bugs to get here. ✛ *Take Pali Hwy., Rte. 61, from Honolulu through the tunnels, take 3rd right onto Auloa Rd., then take left fork immediately. At dead end, climb over vehicle gate for trailhead.*

For the less adventurous hiker and anyone looking for a great view, there is the **Makapu'u Lighthouse Trail**. The paved trail runs up the side of Makapu'u Point in Southeast O'ahu. Early on, the trail is surrounded by lava rock, but, as you ascend, foliage—the tiny white koa haole flower and the cream-tinged spikes of the kiawe—starts to take over the barren rock. Once atop the point, you begin to understand how alone these Islands are in the Pacific. The easternmost tip of O'ahu, this is where the island divides the sea, giving you a spectacular view of the cobalt ocean meeting the land in a cacophony of white caps. To the south are several tide pools and the lighthouse. The eastern view looks down upon Rabbit and Kāohikaipu Islands, two bird sanctuaries just off the coast. The 2-mi round-trip hike is a great break on a circle-island trip. ✛ *Take Kalaniana'ole Hwy. to the base of Makapu'u Pt. Look for the asphalt strip snaking up the mountain.*

Fodor's Choice ★ **Ka'ena Point** trail is a little longer (at 5 mi round-trip) and hotter than Makapu'u Point, but it is right next to the beach, and there are spots where you can get in and cool off. Sea-carved cliffs give way to lava-rock beaches and sea arches. Halfway to the point, there is a double blowhole, which is a good indicator of sea conditions. If it is blowing good, stay out of the water. Though the area is hot and dry, there is still much wildlife here, as it is the only nesting ground for many rare sea birds. ■TIP→ Keep a lookout for the Laysan albatrosses; these enormous

TIPS FOR THE TRAIL

■ When hiking the waterfall and rain-forest trails, use insect repellent. The dampness draws huge swarms of blood suckers that can ruin a walk in the woods real quick.

■ Volcanic rock is very porous and therefore likely to be loose. Rock climbing is strongly discouraged, as you never know which little ledge is going to go.

■ Always let someone know where you are going and never hike alone. The foliage gets very dense, and, small as the island is, many hikers have gotten lost for a week or longer.

birds have recently returned to the area. Don't be surprised if they come in for a closer look at you, too. There has been a cave-in of an old lava tube, so be careful when crossing it, but enjoy the view in its enormous mouth. ✛ *Take Farrington Hwy. to its end at Yokohamas. Hike in on the old 4WD trail.*

When on the North Shore, check out the **Trails at Turtle Bay Resort** (✉ *57-091 Kamehameha Hwy.* ☎ *808/293–8811* ⊕ *www.turtlebayresort.com*), with more than 12 mi of trails and oceanside pathways on the 880-acre resort. You can pick up a trail and ocean guide for a self-guided tour of the 5 mi of coastline and its exotic plants and trees.

GOING WITH A GUIDE

Hawai'i Nature Center. A good choice for families, the center in upper Makīkī Valley conducts a number of programs for both adults and children. There are guided hikes into tropical settings that reveal hidden waterfalls and protected forest reserves. They don't run tours every day, so it is good to get advance reservations. ✉ *2131 Makīkī Heights Dr., Makīkī Heights,* ☎ *808/955–0100* ⊕ *www.hawaiinaturecenter.org.*

O'ahu Nature Tours. Guides explain the native flora and fauna that is your companion on glorious sunrise, hidden-waterfall, mountain-forest, rain-forest, and volcanic walking tours. ☎ *808/924–2473* ⊕ *www.oahunaturetours.com.*

HORSEBACK RIDING

★ **Happy Trails Hawai'i.** Take a guided horseback ride through the verdant Waimea Valley on the North Shore along trails that offer panoramic views from Ka'ena Point to the famous surfing spots. Rates for a 90-minute trail ride begin at $65. ✉ *1 mi mauka up Pupukea Rd. on right, Pupukea* ☎ *808/638–7433.*

Kualoa Ranch. This ranch across from Kualoa Beach Park on the Windward side leads trail rides in the Ka'a'awa Valley. Rates for a one-hour trail ride begin at $63. Kualoa has other activities such as bus and Jeep tours, all-terrain-vehicle trail rides, and children's activities, which may be combined for half- or full-day package rates. ✉ *49-560 Kamehameha Hwy., Ka'a'awa* ☎ *808/237–8515* ⊕ *www.kualoa.com.*

Turtle Bay Stables. This is the only spot on the island where you can take the horses on the beach. The stables here are part of the North Shore resort but can be utilized by nonguests. The sunset ride is a definite must if you are a friend of our four-legged friends. Rates for a 45-minute trail ride begin at $55; a 90-minute evening ride is $90. ✉ *4 mi north of Kahuku in the Turtle Bay Resort* ☎ *808/293–8811.*

JOGGING

The "Honolulu Walking Map" and "The Fitness Fun Map" are free from the **Hawai'i State Department of Health Community Resources Section** (✉ *1250 Punchbowl St., Room 422, Honolulu* ☎ *808/586–4488*). These list more than two dozen routes and suggested itineraries.

DID YOU KNOW?

Manoa Falls is about 150 feet high, and is the gem at the end of a mile-long hike. At its top, you'll find a small pool perfect for wading.

In Honolulu, the most popular places to jog are the two parks, **Kapi'olani** and **Ala Moana**, at either end of Waikīkī. In both cases, the loop around the park is just under 2 mi. You can run a 4½-mi ring around **Diamond Head crater**, past scenic views, luxurious homes, and herds of other joggers.

Once you leave Honolulu, it gets trickier to find places to jog that are scenic as well as safe. It's best to stick to the well-traveled routes, or ask the experienced folks at the **Running Room** (⊠ *819 Kapahulu Ave., Kapahulu, Honolulu* ☎ *808/737–2422*) for advice.

TENNIS

While tennis has given way to golf as the biggest resort attraction, and many of the hotel courts have closed, there are still locations in Waikīkī to get your tennis-jones on. Both sides of Waikīkī are framed by tennis complexes, with Ala Moana Park containing a 12-court spread and two different sets at Kapi'olani Park. The play is free at the public courts, with open courts readily available during the day, but they tend to fill up after the sun goes down and the asphalt cools off.

The **Diamond Head Tennis Center** (⊠ *3908 Pākī Ave.* ☎ *808/971–7150*), near Kapi'olani Park, has nine courts open to the public.

There are more than a dozen courts for play at **Kapi'olani Tennis Courts** (⊠ *2748 Kalākaua Ave.* ☎ *808/971–2510*). The closest public courts to the 'Ewa end of Waikīkī are in **Ala Moana Park** (⊠ *Ala Moana Blvd.* ☎ *808/592–7031*).

The **Pacific Beach Hotel** (⊠ *2490 Kalākaua Ave., Waikīkī, Honolulu* ☎ *808/922–1233*) has rooftop tennis courts that are open to nonguests for a fee.

VOLLEYBALL

Volleyball is an extremely popular spectator sport on the Islands, and no wonder.

Both the men's and women's teams of the **University of Hawai'i** have blasted to a number-one ranking in years past. Crowded, noisy, and exciting home games are played from September through December (women's) and from January through April (men's) in the university's 10,000-seat Stan Sheriff Arena. ⊠ *Lower Campus Rd., Honolulu* ☎ *808/956–4481* 🎫 *$8*.

BEST SPOTS

There are sand volleyball courts in Waikīkī near Fort DeRussy. They are open to the public, so talent levels vary. However, with a winner-plays-on policy, you won't be disappointed with the level as the day progresses. For more advanced play, there is an area at Queen's Beach, but you have to bring your own nets, which leads to a little more court possessiveness. But this is the area where you will find the college kids and pros hitting it while they are in town.

Shops and Spas

WORD OF MOUTH

"Aaaah as a super shopper, I would go to O'ahu to shop. Assuming you are staying in Waikīkī or the Ala Moana area, you could easily do two or three days with shopping and sightseeing."

—MelissaHI

Updated By
Chad Pata

Eastern and Western traditions meet on O'ahu, where savvy shoppers find luxury goods at high-end malls and scout tiny boutiques and galleries filled with pottery, blown glass, woodwork, and Hawaiian-print clothing by local artists. This blend of cultures is pervasive in the wide selection of spas as well. Hawaiian lomi lomi and hot-stone massages are as omnipresent as the orchid and plumeria flowers decorating every treatment room.

Exploring downtown Honolulu, Kailua on the Windward side, and the North Shore often yields the most original merchandise. Some of the small stores carry imported clothes and gifts from around the world—a reminder that, on this island halfway between Asia and the United States, shopping is a multicultural experience.

If you're getting a massage at a spa, there's a spiritual element to the lomi lomi that calms the soul while the muscles release tension. During a hot-stone massage, smooth rocks, taken from the earth with permission from Pele, the goddess of volcanoes, are heated and placed at focal points on the body. Others are covered in oil and rubbed over tired limbs, feeling like powerful fingers. For an alternative, refresh skin with mango scrubs so fragrant they seem edible. Savor the unusual sensation of bamboo tapped against the arches of the feet. Indulge in a scalp massage that makes the entire body tingle. Day spas provide additional options to the self-indulgent services offered in almost every major hotel on the island.

SHOPS

There are two distinct types of shopping experiences for visitors: vast malls with the customary department stores and tiny boutiques with specialty items. Three malls in Honolulu provide a combination of the standard department stores and interesting shops showcasing original paintings and woodwork from local artists and craftsmen. Shoppers who know where to look in Honolulu will find everything from designer merchandise to unusual Asian imports.

Possibilities are endless, but a bit of scouting is usually required to get past the items you'll find in your own hometown. Industrious bargain hunters can detect the perfect gift in the sale bin of a slightly hidden store at every mall.

You'll find that shops stay open fairly late in Waikīkī. Stores open at around 9 AM and many don't close until 10 or even 11 PM.

BUYING TROPICAL FLOWERS AND FRUIT

Bring home fresh pineapple, papaya, or coconut to share with friends and family. Orchids also will brighten your home and remind you of your trip to the Islands. By law, all fresh-fruit and plant products must be inspected by the Department of Agriculture before export. Be sure to inquire at the shop about the Department of Agriculture rules so a surprise confiscation doesn't spoil your departure. In most cases, shipping to your home is best.

Kawamoto Nursery. Kawamoto grows all flowers on its three-acre orchid farm near downtown Honolulu. Their specialty is the Cattleylea, a favorite for Mother's Day, and they have decades of experience

shipping temperamental orchids to the Mainland. ⊠ *2630 Waiomao Rd.* ☎ *808/732–5808* ⊕ *www. kawamotoorchids.com.*

Tropical Fruits Distributors of Hawai'i. Avoid the hassle of airport inspections. This company specializes in packing inspected pineapple and papaya; they will deliver to your hotel and to the airport check-in counter, or ship to the mainland United States and Canada. Think about ordering on the Web, unless you are planning a trip to the North Shore. ⊠ *64-1551 Kamehameha Hwy.* ☎ *808/847–3234* ⊠ *Ilalo St., Wahiawa* ☎ *800/697–9100* ⊕ *www. dolefruithawaii.com.*

6

DOWNTOWN HONOLULU AND CHINATOWN

Downtown shopping is an entirely different, constantly changing experience. Focus on the small galleries—which are earning the area a strong reputation for its arts and culture renaissance—and the burgeoning array of hip, home-decor stores tucked between ethnic restaurants. ■ TIP→ Don't miss the festive atmosphere on the first Friday of every month, when stores, restaurants, and galleries stay open from 5 PM to 9 PM for the "Downtown Gallery Walk."

Chinatown offers the typical mix of the tacky and unique, depending on individual taste, but it is an experience not to be missed. The vital, bright colors of fresh fruits and vegetables blend with the distinct scent of recently killed pigs and poultry. Tucked in between are authentic shops with Asian silk clothing at reasonable prices. The bustling, ethnic atmosphere adds to the excitement. If you're hungry for a local experience you should at least walk through the area, even if you don't plan to purchase the mysterious herbs in the glass jars lining the shelves.

SHOPPING CENTERS

Getting to the Ala Moana shopping centers from Waikīkī is quick and inexpensive thanks to **TheBus** and the **Waikīkī Trolley.**

Ala Moana Shopping Center. One of the nation's largest open-air malls is five minutes from Waikīkī by bus. Designer shops in residence include Gucci, Louis Vuitton, Gianni Versace, and Emporio Armani. All of Hawai'i's major department stores are here, including Neiman Marcus, Sears, and Macy's. More than 240 stores and 60 restaurants make up this 50-acre complex. One of the most interesting shops is Shanghai Tang. First opened in Hong Kong, the store imports silks and other fine fabrics, and upholds the tradition of old-style Shanghai tailoring. To get to the mall from Waikīkī, catch TheBus lines 8, 19, or 20; a one-way ride is $2.50. Or hop aboard the Waikīkī Trolley's pink line, which comes through the area every half hour. ⊠ *1450 Ala Moana Blvd., Ala Moana* ☎ *808/955–9517 special events and shuttle service.*

Aloha Tower Marketplace. Billing itself as a festival marketplace, Aloha Tower cozies up to Honolulu Harbor. Along with restaurants and entertainment venues, it has 80 shops and kiosks selling mostly visitor-oriented merchandise, from expensive sunglasses to exceptional local artwork to souvenir refrigerator magnets. Don't miss the aloha shirts and fancy hats for dogs at Pet Gear, and the curious mix of furniture, stationery, and clothing in Urban Rejuvenation. To get there from Waikīkī take the E-Transit Bus, which goes along TheBus routes every 15 minutes. ⊠ *1 Aloha Tower Dr., at Piers 8, 9, and 10, Downtown* ☎ *808/566–2337* ⊕ *www.alohatower.com.*

Ward Centers. Heading west from Waikīkī toward Downtown Honolulu, you'll run into a section of town with five distinct shopping-complex areas; there are more than 120 specialty shops and 20 restaurants here. The Entertainment Complex features 16 movie theaters. ■TIP➔ A "shopping concierge" can assist you in navigating your way through the center, which spans four city blocks. For distinctive Hawaiian gift stores, visit Nohea Gallery and Native Books/Na Mea Hawaii, carrying quality work from Hawai'i artists, including mu'umu'u, lauhala products, and unparalleled Niihau shell necklaces. Island Soap and Candle Works (☎ *808/591–0533*) makes all of its candles and soaps on-site with Hawaiian flower scents. Take TheBus routes 19 or 20; fare is $2 one-way. Or follow the Waikīkī Trolley yellow line, which comes through the area every 45 minutes. ⊠ *1050–1200 Ala Moana Blvd., Ala Moana.*

BOOKS

Bestsellers. Hawai'i's largest independent bookstore has its flagship shop in Downtown Honolulu on Bishop Square. They carry books by both local and national authors. There are also locations of Bestsellers at the Honolulu International Airport and in Waikīkī at the Hilton Hawaiian Village. ⊠ *1001 Bishop St., Downtown* ☎ *808/528–2378.*

Borders Books. Borders stocks more than 200 books in its Hawaiian section; learn about Hawaiian plants, hula, or surfing. This two-story location has books, music, movies, and a café. ⊠ *Ward Centre, 1200 Ala Moana Blvd.* ☎ *808/591–8995.*

★ **Native Books/Na Mea Hawai'i.** In addition to clothing for adults and children and unusual artwork such as Niihau shell necklaces, this boutique's book selection covers Hawaiian history and language, and offers children's books set in the Islands. ⊠ *Ward Warehouse, 1050 Ala Moana Blvd.* ☎ *808/596–8885.*

CLOTHING

★ **Anne Namba Designs.** Anne Namba brings the beauty of classic kimonos to contemporary fashions. In addition to women's apparel, she's also designed a men's line and a wedding couture line. ⊠ *324 Kamani St., Downtown* ☎ *808/589–1135.*

Hilo Hattie. Busloads of visitors pour in through the front doors of the world's largest manufacturer of Hawaiian and tropical aloha wear. Once shunned by Honolulu residents for its three-shades-too-bright tourist-wear, it has become a favorite source for Island gifts, macadamia nut and chocolate packages, and clothing for elegant Island functions. Free shuttle service is available from Waikīkī. ⊠ *700 N. Nimitz Hwy., Iwilei* ☎ *808/535–6500.*

Reyn's. Reyn's is a good place to buy the aloha-print fashions residents wear. Look for the limited-edition Christmas shirt, a collector's item manufactured each holiday season. Reyn's has 13 locations statewide and offers styles for men, women, and children. ⊠ *Ala Moana Shopping Center, 1450 Ala Moana Blvd., Ala Moana* ☎ *808/949–5929* ⊠ *Kāhala Mall, 4211 Wai'alae Ave., Kāhala* ☎ *808/737–8313.*

★ **Shanghai Tang.** First opened in Hong Kong, Shanghai Tang now has its 11th branch at Ala Moana. An emphasis on workmanship and the luxury of fine fabrics upholds the tradition of old-Shanghai tailoring. They do custom work for men, women, and children. ⊠ *Ala Moana Shopping Center, Ala Moana* ☎ *808/942–9800.*

FOOD SPECIALTIES

Hilo Hattie. This shop is another source for packaged food items, including guava jam, macadamia-nut cookies and chocolates, coconut-macadamia coffee, pineapples, and anthurium and gift baskets stocked with Island specialty snacks. ⊠ *Ala Moana Shopping Center, 1450 Ala Moana Blvd., Suite 1037 Ala Moana,.*

Honolulu Chocolate Company. To really impress those back home, pick up a box of gourmet chocolates here. They dip the flavors of Hawai'i, from Kona coffee to macadamia nuts, in fine chocolate. ⊠ *Ward Centre, 1200 Ala Moana Blvd., Downtown Honolulu* ☎ *808/591–2997.*

Longs Drugs. For gift items in bulk, try one of the many outposts of Longs, the perfect place to stock up on chocolate-covered macadamia nuts—at reasonable prices—to carry home. ⊠ *Ala Moana Shopping Center, 1450 Ala Moana Blvd., 2nd level, Ala Moana* ☎ *808/941–4433* ⊠ *Kāhala Mall, 4211 Wai'alae Ave., Kāhala* ☎ *808/732–0784.*

GALLERIES

Jeff Chang Pottery & Fine Crafts. With locations downtown and in Waikīkī, Jeff Chang has become synonymous with excellent craftsmanship and originality in Raku pottery, blown glass, and koa wood. Gift ideas include petroglyph stoneware coasters, photo albums covered in

KOA KEEPSAKES

Items handcrafted from native Hawaiian wood make beautiful gifts. Koa and milo have a distinct color and grain. The scarcity of koa forests makes the wood extremely valuable. That's why you'll notice a large price gap between koa wood veneer products and the real thing.

UNDER $20 AND PACKABLE

- Hawaiian-print dish towels
- Hawaiian music CDs
- Small wooden serving bowls
- Coffee grown in Hawai'i
- Humuhumunukunukuāpua'a fish (Hawai'ian state fish) Christmas ornaments
- Soaps, oils, lotions, and candles made in Hawai'i, with scents of pīkake and tuberose
- Eye pillow filled with lavender from Maui

- Island-themed T-shirts
- Kukui-nut or shell lei
- Macadamia nuts (chocolate-covered or regular)
- Koa wood pen, bracelet, ring, or bookmark
- Ceramic flip-flop (slipper) magnet
- Dolphin suncatcher
- Hawaiian-print cocktail napkins
- Ceramic dishes in the shape of Hawaiian flowers

Hawaiian-print fabric, blown-glass penholders and business-card holders, and Japanese Aeto chimes. The owners choose work from 300 different local and national artists. ⊠ *Ward Center, 1200 Ala Moana Blvd., Downtown Honolulu* ☎ *808/262–4060.*

Louis Pohl Gallery. Modern works from some of Hawai'i's finest artists. ⊠ *1111 Nu'uanu Ave., Downtown* ☎ *808/521–1812.*

★ **Nohea Gallery.** These shops are really galleries representing more than 450 artists who specialize in koa furniture, bowls, and boxes, as well as art glass and ceramics. Original paintings and prints—all with an Island theme—add to the selection. They also carry unique handmade Hawaiian jewelry with ti leaf, maile, and coconut-weave designs. ■TIP→ The koa photo albums in these stores are easy to carry home and make wonderful gifts. ⊠ *Ward Warehouse, 1050 Ala Moana Blvd., Ala Moana* ☎ *808/596–0074.*

HAWAIIAN ARTS AND CRAFTS

Hawaiian Quilt Collection. Traditional Island comforters, wall hangings, pillows, and other Hawaiian-print quilt items are the specialty here. ⊠ *Ala Moana Center, 1450 Ala Moana Blvd., Ala Moana* ☎ *808/946–2233.*

Indich Collection. Bring home some aloha you can sink your bare feet into. Designs from this exclusive Hawaiian rug collection depict Hawaiian petroglyphs, banana leafs, and heliconia. ⊠ *Gentry Pacific Design Center, 560 N. Nimitz Hwy., Downtown* ☎ *808/524–7769.*

My Little Secret. The word is out that this is a wonderful selection of Hawaiian arts, crafts, and children's toys. ⊠ *Ward Warehouse, 1050 Ala Moana Blvd., Ala Moana* ☎ *808/596–2990.*

Na Hoku. If you look at the wrists of *kama'aina* (local) women, you're apt to see Hawaiian heirloom bracelets fashioned in either gold or silver in a number of Island-inspired designs. Na Hoku sells jewelry in designs that capture the heart of the Hawaiian lifestyle in all its elegant diversity. ⊠ *Ala Moana Center, 1450 Ala Moana Blvd., Ala Moana* 🕾 *808/946–2100.*

HOME DECOR

INTO. The newest and hippest home-decor shop downtown features decorative pillows and Escama handbags and messenger bags. These products are hand-crocheted in Brazil using recycled aluminum tabs. The inventory is always innovative and fresh here. ⊠ *40 N. Hotel St., Downtown* 🕾 *808/536–2211.*

Robyn Buntin Galleries. Chinese nephrite-jade carvings, Japanese lacquer and screens, and Buddhist sculptures are among the international pieces displayed here. ⊠ *848 S. Beretania St., Downtown* 🕾 *808/523–5913.*

SPORTING GOODS

Boca Hawai'i. This triathlon shop near the Bike Factory offers training gear, racing- and mountain-bike rentals ($25 per day with a two-day minimum, $125 per week), yoga and Spinning classes, and nutritional products. ■ TIP→ Inquire directly about the latest schedule of fitness and strength sessions at the store, which is owned and operated by top athletes. ⊠ *330 Cooke St., Kaka'ako* 🕾 *808/591–9839.*

WAIKĪKĪ

Most hotels and shops are clustered along a relatively short strip in Waikīkī, which can be convenient or overwhelming, depending on one's sensibilities. Clothing, jewelry, and handbags from Europe's top designers sit across the street from the International Marketplace, a conglomeration of booths reminiscent of New York City's Canal Street—with a tropical flair. It's possible to find interesting items at reasonable prices in Waikīkī, but shoppers have to be willing to search beyond the $4,000 purses and the tacky wooden tikis to find innovation and quality.

SHOPPING CENTERS

DFS Galleria Waikīkī. Hermès, Cartier, and Van Cleef are among the shops at this enclosed mall, as well as Hawai'i's largest beauty and cosmetics store. An exclusive boutique floor caters to duty-free shoppers only. Amusing and authentic Hawaiian-style shell necklaces, soaps, and printed wraps are rewards for anyone willing to wade through the pervasive tourist schlock along the Waikīkī Beach Walk, this is truly an area of fashions, arts and crafts, and gifts. It's much less crowded than surrounding malls and is designed almost like a maze to keep you browsing forward. ⊠ *Kalākaua and Royal Hawaiian Aves., Waikīkī* 🕾 *808/931–2655.*

Royal Hawaiian Shopping Center. Completely renovated in 2006 with a more open and inviting facade, this three-block-long center is the largest shopping plaza in Waikīkī. The final tenant mix has more than 100 stores, including Hawaiian Heirloom Jewelry Collection by Phillip Rickard, which also has a museum with Victorian pieces. Bike buffs can check out the Harley-Davidson Motor Clothes and Collectibles Boutique, and the Ukelele House may inspire musicians to learn a new instrument. There are restaurants as casual as Señor Frogs, nightclubs

6

as exclusive as Level 4, and even a post office. ⊠ *2201 Kalākaua Ave., Waikīkī* ☎ *808/922–0588.*

2100 Kalakaua. Tenants of this elegant, town-house-style center include Chanel, Coach, Tiffany & Co., Yves Saint Laurent, Gucci, and Tod's. ⊠ *2100 Kalākaua Ave., Waikīkī* ☎ *808/541–5136.*

Waikīkī Beach Walk. What was once the down-and-dirty heart of Waikīkī has become a must-stop for visitors. The revitalization of Lewers St. is now complete and is the largest development in Waikīkī's history. It features nine new restaurants including Roy's, Ruth Chris, and The Yardhouse, as well as 50 new stores. ⊠ *Lewers St, Waikīkī* ☎ *808/931–3593.*

Waikīkī Town Center. Free hula shows liven up this open-air complex on Monday, Wednesday, Friday, and Saturday at 7 PM. Shops carry everything from fashions to jewelry. ⊠ *2301 Kūhiō Ave., Waikīkī* ☎ *808/922–2724.*

BOOKS

Bestsellers. This shop in the Hilton's Rainbow Bazaar is a branch of the local independent bookstore chain. They stock novelty Hawai'i memorabilia as well as books on Hawaiian history, local maps and travel guides, and Hawaiian music. ⊠ *Hilton Hawaiian Village Beach Resort and Spa, 2005 Kālia Rd., Waikīkī* ☎ *808/953–2378.*

CLOTHING

Blue Ginger. Look inside this little shop across from The Yardhouse for beach-casual clothing and accessories, soft cotton prints, and alohaware. *227 Lewers St* ☎ *808/942–2829.*

Moonbow Tropics. An elegant selection of silk Tommy Bahama Aloha shirts, as well as tropical styles for women. ⊠ *Outrigger Reef Hotel, 2169 Kalia Rd., Waikīkī* ☎ *808/924–1496.*

Newt in the Village. Newt is known for Panama hats and tropical sportswear. ⊠ *Hilton Hawaiian Village Beach Resort and Spa, 2005 Kālia Rd.* ☎ *808/949–4321.*

Reyn's. Reyn's is a good place to buy the aloha-print fashions residents wear. This company manufacturers its own label in the Islands, has 13 locations statewide, and offers styles for men, women, and children. ⊠ *Sheraton Waikīkī, 2255 Kalākaua Ave., Waikīkī* ☎ *808/923–0331.*

GALLERIES

Gallery Tokusa. *Netsuke* is a toggle used to fasten small containers to obi belts on a kimono. Gallery Tokusa specializes in intricately carved netsuke, both antique and contemporary, and one-of-a-kind necklaces. ⊠ *Halekūlani, 2199 Kālia Rd., Waikīkī* ☎ *808/923–2311.*

Noeha Gallery. A smaller version of the stores located in Ward Center and Ward Warehouse carries koa bowls and boxes, ceramics, and art glass. ⊠ *Westin Moana Surfrider, 2365 Kalākaua Ave.* ☎ *808/923–6644.*

GIFTS

★ **Sand People.** This little shop stocks easy-to-carry gifts, such as fish-shaped Christmas ornaments, Hawaiian-style notepads, charms in the shape of flip-flops (known locally as "slippers"), soaps, and ceramic clocks. Also

Continued on page 172

ALL ABOUT LEI

Leis brighten every occasion in Hawai'i, from birthdays to bar mitz-vahs to baptisms. Creative artisans weave nature's bounty—flowers, ferns, vines, and seeds—into gorgeous creations that convey an array of heartfelt messages: "Welcome," "Congratulations," "Good luck," "Farewell," "Thank you," "I love you." When it's difficult to find the right words, a lei expresses exactly the right sentiments.

WHERE TO BUY THE BEST LEIS

The best selections and prices are at the lei shops in Honolulu's Chinatown. Three favorites are: **Cindy's Lei & Flower Shop** (1034 Maunakea St., 808/536–6538); **Lin's Lei Shop** (1017-A Maunakea St., 808/537–4112); and **Lita's Leis** (59 N. Beretania St., 808/521–9065). In Mō'ili'ili, a 10-minute drive from Waikīkī, check out **Flowers by Jr., Lou & T** (2652 S. King St., 808/941–2022); and **Rudy's Flowers** (2357 S. Beretania St., 808/944–8844).

LEI ETIQUETTE

■ To wear a closed lei, drape it over your shoulders, half in front and half in back. Open leis are worn around the neck, with the ends draped over the front in equal lengths.

■ Pīkake, ginger, and other sweet, delicate blossoms are "feminine" leis. Men opt for cigar, crown flower, and ti leaf, which are sturdier and don't emit as much fragrance.

■ Leis are always presented with a kiss, a custom that supposedly dates back to World War II when a hula dancer fancied an officer at a U.S.O. show. Taking a dare from members of her troupe, she took off her lei, placed it around his neck, and kissed him on the cheek.

■ You shouldn't wear a lei before you give it to someone else. Hawaiians believe the lei absorbs your *mana* (spirit); if you give your lei away, you'll be giving away part of your essence.

ORCHID

Growing wild on every continent except Antarctica, orchids—which range in color from yellow to green to purple—comprise the largest family of plants in the world. There are more than 20,000 species of orchids, but only three are native to Hawai'i—and they are very rare. The pretty lavender vanda you see hanging by the dozens at local lei stands has probably been imported from Thailand.

MAILE

Maile, an endemic twining vine with a heady aroma, is sacred to Laka, goddess of the hula. In ancient times, dancers wore maile and decorated hula altars with it to honor Laka. Today, "open" maile leis usually are given to men. Instead of ribbon, interwoven lengths of maile are used at dedications of new businesses. The maile is untied, never snipped, for doing so would symbolically "cut" the company's success.

'ILIMA

Designated by Hawai'i's Territorial Legislature in 1923 as the official flower of the island of O'ahu, the golden 'ilima is so delicate it lasts for just a day. Five to seven hundred blossoms are needed to make one garland. Queen Emma, wife of King Kamehameha IV, preferred 'ilima over all other leis, which may have led to the incorrect belief that they were reserved only for royalty.

PLUMERIA

This ubiquitous flower is named after Charles Plumier, the noted French botanist who discovered it in Central America in the late 1600s. Plumeria ranks among the most popular leis in Hawai'i because it's fragrant, hardy, plentiful, inexpensive, and requires very little care. Although yellow is the most common color, you'll also find plumeria leis in shades of pink, red, orange, and "rainbow" blends.

PĪKAKE

Favored for its fragile beauty and sweet scent, pīkake was introduced from India. In lieu of pearls, many brides in Hawai'i adorn themselves with long, multiple strands of white pīkake. Princess Kaiulani enjoyed showing guests her beloved pīkake and peacocks at Āinahau, her Waikīkī home. Interestingly, pīkake is the Hawaiian word for both the bird and the blossom.

KUKUI

The kukui (candlenut) is Hawai'i's state tree. Early Hawaiians strung kukui nuts (which are quite oily) together and burned them for light; mixed burned nuts with oil to make an indelible dye; and mashed roasted nuts to consume as a laxative. Kukui nut leis may not have been made until after Western contact, when the Hawaiians saw black beads from Europe and wanted to imitate them.

located in Kailua. ⊠ *Westin Moana Surfrider, 2369 Kalākaua, Waikīkī* ☎ *808/924–6773.*

JEWELRY

Bernard Hurtig's. Antique jade and 18-karat gold are the specialties at this fine jeweler. ⊠ *Hilton Hawaiian Village Aliʻi Tower, 2005 Kālia Rd., Waikīkī* ☎ *808/947–9399.*

Philip Rickard. The heirloom design collection of this famed jeweler features custom Hawaiian wedding jewelry. ⊠ *Royal Hawaiian Shopping Center, 2201 Kalākaua Ave., Waikīkī* ☎ *808/924–7972.*

SURF SHOPS

Hawaii Five-O. Beach rentals add to a wide array of T-shirts, footwear, bathing suits, and accessories in the store named after the locally filmed television show that ran from 1968 to 1980. ⊠ *Aston Waikīkī Beach Hotel, 2570 Kalākaua Ave.* ☎ *808/923–1243.*

Local Motion. If you plan on surfing or just want to look like a surfer, check out this outfitter's flagship store. They have it all—from surfboards to surf wear. ⊠ *2255 Kalakaua Ave., Waikīkī* ☎ *808/924–4406.*

This neighborhood, while considered separate from the University of Hawaiʻi's Manoa campus, has a distinct college-town feel. About 3 mi from Waikīkī, the area is extremely tired in some sections and needs updating. However, a look past the exterior reveals a haven for excellent family-owned restaurants, health food stores, and shops that have a loyal following in the residential community.

KAPAHULU

Kapahulu begins at the Diamond Head end of Waikīkī and continues up to the H1 freeway. Shops and restaurants are located primarily on Kapahulu Avenue, which like many older neighborhoods, should not be judged at first glance. It is full of variety.

CLOTHING

Bailey's Antiques & Aloha Shirts. Vintage aloha shirts are the specialty at this kitschy store. Prices start at $3.99 for the 10,000 shirts in stock, and the tight space and musty smell are part of the thrift-shop atmosphere. ■TIP→ Antiques hunters can also buy old-fashioned postcards, authentic military clothing, funky hats, and denim jeans from the 1950s. ⊠ *517 Kapahulu Ave., Kapahulu* ☎ *808/734–7628.*

SURF SHOPS AND SPORTING GOODS

Go Bananas. Staffers make sure that you rent the appropriate kayak for your abilities, and they outfit the rental car with soft racks to transport it to the beach. Full-day rates begin at $30 for single kayaks and $45 for doubles. The store also carries clothing and kayaking accessories. ⊠ *799 Kapahulu Ave., Kapahulu* ☎ *808/737–9514.*

Downing Hawaii. Look for old-style Birdwell surf trunks here, along with popular labels such as Quiksilver, which supplement Downing's own line of surf wear. ⊠ *3021 Waialae Ave., Kaimukī* ☎ *808/737–9696.*

Hawaiian Fire. Some of the best-looking firefighters in Honolulu teach surf lessons out of this tiny shop; they transport beginners to the less crowded west side of the island. The store also sells T-shirts and backpacks. ⊠ *3318 Campbell Ave., Kapahulu* ☎ *808/737–3473.*

Island Paddler. Fashionable beach footwear, clothing, bathing suits, fun beach bags, and rash guards supplement a huge selection of canoe paddles. ■TIP→ Check out the wooden steering paddles: they become works of art when mounted on the wall at home. ⊠ *716 Kapahulu Ave., Kapahulu* ☎ *808/737–4854.*

Island Triathlon & Bike. Another source for bikes, sports bathing suits, water bottles, and active clothing. However, they don't rent bicycles. ⊠ *569 Kapahulu Ave., Kapahulu* ☎ *808/732–7227.*

Snorkel Bob's. This is a good place to seek advice about the best snorkel conditions, which vary considerably with the season. The company, popular throughout the Islands, sells or rents necessary gear, including fins, snorkels, wet suits, and beach chairs, and even schedules activities with other suppliers. ⊠ *700 Kapahulu Ave., Kapahulu* ☎ *808/735–7944.*

> **GOOD ENOUGH TO EAT**
>
> You don't necessarily have to buy a whole pineapple to enjoy Hawai'i's fruit flavors back home. Jams are easy to pack and don't spoil. They come in flavors such as pohā, passion fruit, and guava. Coffee is another option. Kona- and O'ahu-grown Waialua coffee beans have an international following. There are also dried-food products such as saimin, haupia, and teriyaki barbecue sauce. All kinds of cookies are available, as well as exotic teas, drink mixes, and pancake syrups. And don't forget the macadamia nuts, from plain to chocolate-covered and brittled.

KĀHALA AND HAWAI'I KAI

The upscale residential neighborhood of Kāhala, near the slopes of Diamond Head, is 10 minutes by car from Waikīkī.

SHOPPING CENTERS

Kāhala Mall. The only shopping of note in the area is located at the indoor mall, which has 90 stores, including Macy's, Gap, Reyn's Aloha Wear, and Barnes & Noble. **Don't miss fashionable boutiques such as Ohelo Road** (☎ *808/735–5525*), **where contemporary clothing for all occasions fills the racks. Eight movie theaters** (☎ *808/593–3000*) **provide post-shopping entertainment.** ⊠ *4211 Wai'alae Ave., Kāhala* ☎ *808/732–7736.*

GIFTS

Island Treasures. Local residents come here to shop for gifts that are both unique and within reach of almost every budget, ranging in price from $1 to $5,000. Located next to Zippy's and overlooking the ocean, the store has handbags, toys, jewelry, home accessories, soaps and lotions, and locally made original artwork. Certainly the most interesting shop in Hawai'i Kai's suburban mall atmosphere, this store is also a good place to purchase CDs of some of the best Hawaiian music. ⊠ *Koko Marina Center, 7192 Kalaniana'ole Hwy., Hawai'i Kai* ☎ *808/396–8827.*

WINDWARD O'AHU

Shopping on the Windward side is one of O'ahu's best-kept secrets. A half-hour by car or about an hour on TheBus, it's definitely a shopping/activity destination. At Windward Mall in Kāne'ohe, stop by the Lomi Shop for authentic Tahitian oils and a 10-minute foot massage in the entrance built to resemble a voyaging canoe. The real treats, however, lie in the small boutiques and galleries in the heart of Kailua—the perfect place to gather unique gifts. After shopping, enjoy the outdoors in one of the most beautiful beach towns in the world. Kailua is the best place to rent kayaks and paddle out to the Mokulua Islands with a guide, take a windsurfing lesson, or watch the expert kiteboarders sailing across the bay.

■TIP→ Stop by Kalapawai Market in Lanikai—the only shop in Lanikai, which is right next to Kailua—for sandwiches and cold drinks and souvenirs, and finish the day relaxing on a sparsely populated white-sand beach. The surf here is minimal, making it a perfect picnic spot with the kids, but not the place to learn to ride waves. Save that for Waikīkī.

ARTS AND CRAFTS

BOOKS

FodorśChoice ★

Bookends. The perfect place to shop for gifts, or just take a break with the family, this bookstore feels more like a small-town library, welcoming browsers to linger for hours. The large children's section is filled with toys and books to read. ⊠ *600 Kailua Rd., Kailua* ☎ *808/261–1996.*

CLOTHING

FodorśChoice ★

Global Village. Tucked into a tiny strip mall near Maui Tacos, this boutique features contemporary apparel for women, Hawaiian-style children's clothing, and unusual jewelry and gifts from all over the world. Look for Kula Cushions eye pillows (made with lavender grown on Maui), coasters in the shape of flip-flops, a wooden key holder shaped like a surfboard, and placemats made from lauhala and other natural fibers, plus accessories you won't find anywhere else. ⊠ *Kailua Village Shops, 539 Kailua Rd., Kailua* ☎ *808/262–8183.*

GALLERIES

The Balcony Gallery. Known almost exclusively to Kailua residents, this small, out-of-the-way gallery features contemporary paintings, photographs, glass, woodwork, ceramics, and jewelry from artists in the Islands. ■TIP→ Join them from 2 to 5 PM on the second Sunday of every month for a tour of 15 art venues in the area. Gallery hours are limited; call before you go. ⊠ *442A Uluniu St., Kailua* ☎ *808/475–5381* ☉ *Closed Sun. and Mon.*

HOME DECOR

FodorśChoice ★

Under a Hula Moon. Exclusive tabletop items and Pacific home decor, such as shell wreaths, shell night lights, Hawaiian-print kitchen towels, and Asian silk clothing, define this eclectic shop. ⊠ *Kailua Shopping Center, 600 Kailua Rd., Kailua* ☎ *808/261–4252.*

SURF SHOPS AND SPORTING GOODS

Kailua Sailboard and Kayaks Company. Beginners and experts will find everything they need here. Windsurfing lessons start at $129 for a two-hour group lesson, or $109 for a one-hour individual lesson. Transporting gear to the nearby beach is no problem with their help. ⊠ *130 Kailua Rd., Kailua* ☎ *808/262–2555.*

Twogood Kayaks Hawai'i. Explore Kailua from the ocean alone or with skilled tour guides who deliver the boats right to the beach (or load them on your car, if you want to go elsewhere on the island), free of charge. Guides are trained in history, geology, and birdlife of the area. Kayak a full day with a guide for $119; this includes lunch, snorkeling gear, and transportation from Waikīkī. The shop is in an open-air market next to O'ahu Dive Center, where scuba divers can rent or buy whatever they need for a successful underwater excursion. ⊠ *345 Hahani St., Kailua* ☎ *808/262–5656.*

NORTH SHORE

A drive to the North Shore takes about one hour from Waikīkī, but allot a full day to explore the beaches and Hale'iwa, a burgeoning attraction that has managed to retain its surf-town charm. The occasional makeshift stand selling delicious fruit or shrimp beside the road adds character to the beach, farm, and artist-colony atmosphere. Eclectic shops are the best place to find skin-care products made on the North Shore, Hawaiian music CDs, sea glass and shell mobiles, coffee grown in the Islands, and clothing items unavailable anywhere else. Be sure to chat with the owners in each shop. North Shore residents are an animated, friendly bunch with multiple talents. Stop in for coffee and the shop's owner might reveal a little about his or her passion for creating distinguished pieces of artwork.

SHOPPING CENTERS

North Shore Marketplace. While playing on the North Shore, check out this open-air plaza that includes North Shore Custom and Design Swimwear for mix-and-match bikinis off the rack, as well as Jungle Gems, where they make almost all of the precious and semiprecious gemstone jewelry on the premises. And don't miss the Silver Moon Emporium or Outrigger Trading Company upstairs. ⊠ *66-250 Kamehameha Hwy., Hale'iwa* ☎ *808/637–7000.*

CLOTHING

★ **The Growing Keiki.** Frequent visitors return to this store year after year. They know they'll find a fresh supply of original, hand-picked, Hawaiian-style clothing for youngsters. ⊠ *66-051 Kamehameha Hwy., Hale'iwa* ☎ *808/637–4544.*

Fodor'sChoice **Silver Moon Emporium.** This small boutique carries everything from
★ Brighton accessories and fashionable T-shirts to Betsy Johnson formal wear, and provides attentive yet casual personalized service. Their stock changes frequently, and there's always something wonderful on sale. No matter what your taste, you'll find something for everyday wear or

special occasions. ⊠ *North Shore Marketplace, 66-250 Kamehameha Hwy., Haleʻiwa* ☎ *808/637–7710.*

GIFTS

★ **Global Creations Interiors.** Look for Hawaiian bath products, pīkake perfume, locally made jewelry, and a carefully chosen selection of Hawaiian music CDs. Fun gifts include chip-and-dip plates and spreaders shaped like ʻukuleles. ⊠ *66-079 Kamehameha Hwy., Haleʻiwa* ☎ *808/637–1780:*

★ **Outrigger Trading Company.** Though this shop has been in business since 1982, its upstairs location in the North Shore Marketplace often gets bypassed when it shouldn't. Look for Jam's World patchwork tablecloths with an aloha flair, shell boxes, mobiles made of ceramic fish and driftwood, stained-glass ornaments, and beach-glass wind chimes. Other novelties include hula-girl and bamboo lamps and silk-screened table runners. ⊠ *North Shore Marketplace, 66-250 Kamehameha Hwy., Haleʻiwa* ☎ *808/637-4737.*

FOOD SPECIALTIES

Matsumoto Shave Ice. Actor Tom Hanks, sumo wrestler Konishiki, and ice skater Kristi Yamaguchi have all stopped in for a cold flavored cone at Matsumoto's. If you're going to the North Shore, it's a must to stop by this legendary shack established in 1951. On average, they produce 1,000 shave ices a day. Matsumoto's also has T-shirts and souvenirs. ⊠ *66-087 Kamehameha Hwy., Haleʻiwa* ☎ *808/637–4827.*

★ **Surf Town Coffee Roasters.** Luscious chocolate is made right here in the store, and owners Dave and JulieAnn Hoselton buy coffee beans from Kauaʻi, Molokaʻi, and the Big Island. Look for their own secret blend called "Dawn Patrol," with a picture of their dog on the package. The Hoseltons are also artists. She creates decorative feather *kahili* (a Hawaiian ceremonial staff), and he makes Hawaiian wooden bowls. Enjoy sipping coffee while shopping for art. ⊠ *66-470 Kamehameha Hwy., Haleʻiwa* ☎ *808/637–3000.*

SURF SHOPS AND SPORTING GOODS

Surf ʻN Sea. A North Shore water-sports store with everything under one roof. Purchase rash guards, bathing suits, T-shirts, footwear, hats, and shorts. Rent kayaks, snorkeling or scuba gear, spears for free diving, windsurfing equipment, surfboards, and bodyboards. Experienced surfing instructors will take beginners to the small breaks on the notoriously huge (winter) or flat (summer) North Shore beaches. Warning to fishing enthusiasts: a fishing pole is the one ocean apparatus they don't carry. ⊠ *62-595 Kamehameha Hwy.* ☎ *808/637–9887.*

WEST OʻAHU

Shopping on this part of the island is at two extremes—an outdoor market that literally sells everything under the sun, and a high-end shopping outlet with all the big designer names.

SHOPPING CENTERS

Aloha Stadium Swap Meet. This thrice-weekly outdoor bazaar attracts hundreds of vendors and even more bargain hunters. Every Hawaiian souvenir imaginable can be found here, from coral-shell necklaces to bikinis, as well as a variety of ethnic wares, from Chinese brocade dresses to Japanese pottery. There are also ethnic foods, silk flowers, and luggage in aloha-floral prints. Shoppers must wade through the typical sprinkling of used goods to find value. Wear comfortable shoes, use sunscreen, and bring bottled water. The flea market takes place in the Aloha Stadium parking lot Wednesday and weekends from 6 to 3. Admission is $1. Several shuttle companies serve Aloha Stadium for the swap meet, including VIP Shuttle ☎ *808/839–0911*; Rabbi Shuttle ☎ *808/922–4900*; Reliable Shuttle ☎ *808/924–9292*; and Hawaii Supertransit ☎ *808/841–2928*. The average cost is $11 per person, round-trip. For a cheaper but slower ride, take TheBus. Check routes at ⊕ *www.thebus.org.* ✉ *99-500 Salt Lake Blvd., 'Aiea* ☎ *808/486–6704.*

Waikele Premium Outlets. Anne Klein Factory, Donna Karan Company Store, Kenneth Cole, and Saks Fifth Avenue Outlet anchor this discount destination. You can take a shuttle to the outlets, but the companies do change over frequently. One to try: Moha Shuttle ☎ *808/216–8006*; $10 round-trip. ✉ *H1, 30 mins west of Downtown Honolulu, Waikele* ☎ *808/676–5656.*

SPAS

Day spas provide additional options to the self-indulgent services offered in almost every major hotel on the island.

Abhasa Spa. Natural organic skin and body treatments highlight this spa tucked away in the Royal Hawaiian Hotel's coconut grove. Vegetarian-lifestyle spa therapies, color-light therapy, an Ayurveda-influenced Bamboo Facial using Sundari products, and body cocooning are all available. You can choose to have your treatment in any of Abhasa's eight indoor rooms or in one of their three garden cabanas. ✉ *Royal Hawaiian Hotel, 2259 Kalākaua Ave., Waikīkī* ☎ *808/922–8200* ⊕ *www.abhasa.com* ☞ *$152, 50-min lomi lomi massage. Hair salon, indoor hot tub, sauna, showers. Services: massage, body cocoons and scrubs, hydrotherapy, waxing, facials.*

Ampy's European Facials and Body Spa. This 30-year-old spa has kept its prices reasonable over the years thanks to its "no frills" way of doing business. All of Ampy's facials are 75 minutes, and the spa has become famous for custom aromatherapy treatments. Call at least a week in advance because the appointment book fills up quickly here. It's in the Ala Moana Building, adjacent to the Ala Moana Shopping Center. ✉ *1441 Kapi'olani Blvd., Suite 377, Ala Moana* ☎ *808/946–3838* ☞ *$85, 60-min lomi lomi massage. Sauna. Services: massage, body treatments, facials, hand and foot care.*

Aveda Salon and Spa. Aveda offers hydrotherm massage, where water-filled cushions cradle your body as a therapist works out your body's kinks. This spa has everything from Vichy showers to hydrotherapy rooms to customized aromatherapy. Ladies, they'll even touch-up your makeup for free before you leave. ✉ *Ala Moana Shopping Center, 3rd fl., 1450 Ala Moana Blvd., Ala Moana* ☎ *808/947–6141* ⊕ *www.aveda. com* ☞ *$160, 75-min lomi lomi massage. Hair salon, eucalyptus steam room. Services: massage, waxing, facials, body treatments.*

Fodor'sChoice **J. W. Marriott 'Ihilani Resort & Spa.** Soak in warm seawater among vel-
★ vety orchid blossoms at this unique Hawaiian hydrotherapy spa. Thalassotherapy treatments combine underwater jet massage with color therapy and essential oils. Specially designed treatment rooms have a hydrotherapy tub, a Vichy-style shower, and a needle shower with 12 heads. The spa's Pua Kai line of natural aromatherapy products includes massage and body oil, bath crystals and body butter, which combine ingredients such as ginger, jasmine, rose petals, and coconut and grapeseed oil. ✉ *J. W. Marriott 'Ihilani Resort & Spa, 92-1001 'Ōlani St., Kapolei* ☎ *808/679–0079* ⊕ *www.ihilani.com* ☞ *$145, 50-min lomi lomi massage. Hair salon, hot tubs (indoor and outdoor), sauna, steam room. Gym with: cardiovascular machines, free weights, weight-training equipment. Services: aromatherapy, body wraps and scrubs, facials, massage, thalassotherapy. Classes and programs: aerobics, body sculpting, dance classes, fitness analysis, guided walks, personal training, Pilates, tai chi, yoga.*

Mandara Spa at the Hilton Hawaiian Village Beach Resort & Spa. From its perch in the Kalia Tower, Mandara Spa, an outpost of the chain that originated in Bali, overlooks the mountains, ocean, and downtown Honolulu. Fresh Hawaiian ingredients and traditional techniques headline an array of treatments. Try an exotic upgrade, such as eye treatments using Asian silk protein and reflexology. The delicately scented, candlelit foyer can fill up quickly with robe-clad conventioneers, so be sure to make a reservation. There are spa suites for couples, a private infinity pool, and a café. ✉ *Hilton Hawaiian Village Beach Resort and Spa, 2005 Kālia Rd., Waikīkī* ☎ *808/949–4321* ⊕ *www. hiltonhawaiianvillage.com* ☞ *$130, 50-min lomi lomi massage. Hair salon, hot tubs (indoor and outdoor), sauna, steam room. Gym with: cardiovascular machines, free weights, weight-training equipment. Services: aromatherapy, body wraps and scrubs, facials, massages.*

Nā Hō'ola at the Hyatt Regency Waikīkī Resort & Spa. Nā Hō'ola is the largest spa in Waikīkī, sprawling across the 5th and 6th floors of the Hyatt, with 19 treatment rooms, jet baths, and Vichy showers. Arrive early for your treatment to enjoy the postcard views of Waikīkī Beach. Four packages identified by Hawai'i's native healing plants—noni, kukui, awa, and kalo—combine various body, face, and hair treatments and span 2½ to 4 hours. The Champagne of the Sea body treatment employs a self-heating mud wrap to release tension and stress. The small exercise room is for use by hotel guests only. ✉ *Hyatt Regency Waikīkī Resort and Spa, 2424 Kalākaua Ave., Waikīkī* ☎ *808/921–6097* ⊕ *www.waikiki.hyatt.com* ☞ *$145, 50-min lomi lomi massage. Sauna, showers. Gym with: cardiovascular machines. Services: aromatherapy, body scrubs and wraps, facials, hydrotherapy, massage.*

Paul Brown's Spa Olakino at the Waikīkī Beach Marriott Resort & Spa. Paul Brown has created a spa facing Waikīkī Beach. Linger with a cup of tea between treatments and gaze through 75-foot-high windows at the activity outside. Lush Hawaiian foliage, sleek Balinese teak furnishings, and a mist of ylang-ylang and nutmeg in the air inspire relaxation. Treatments incorporate Brown's Hapuna line of essential oils, as well as a thermal masking system using volcanic ash. The couples' experience lasts four hours and includes massage, massage instruction, and chocolate-covered strawberries at sunset. ⊠ *Waikīkī Beach Marriott Resort & Spa, 2552 Kalākaua Ave., Waikīkī* ☎ *808/922–6611* ⊕ *www.marriottwaikiki.com* ☞ *$110, 60-min lomi lomi massage. Hair salon, nail care, steam showers. Services: massage, facials, body treatments, waxing.*

Paul Brown Salon and Day Spa. This is one of the few salons where the principal owner still works the floor. Paul Brown's specialized treatments combat everything from cellulite to low energy and dry skin. There's even a facial designed especially for men. ⊠ *Ward Centre, 1200 Ala Moana Blvd., Ala Moana* ☎ *808/591–1881* ⊕ *www.paulbrownhawaii. com* ☞ *$66, 50-min lomi lomi massage. Hair and nail salon. Services: massage, body scrubs, body wraps, makeup, facials, waxing.*

Serenity Spa Hawai'i. Want to jump start your "just back from Hawai'i" tan without burning to a crisp? Consider the Golden Touch tanning massage, which combines a massage with tan accelerators, sunscreen, and scented oils. Only steps off the beach, this day spa provides aromatherapy treatments, massages, and facials. You can mix and match treatments from the menu to create a specialized package. ⊠ *Outrigger Reef on the Beach, 2169 Kālia Rd., Waikīkī* ☎ *808/926–2882* ⊕ *www. serenityspahawaii.com* ☞ *$105, 50-min lomi lomi massage. Showers, nail salon, hair station. Services: massage, facials, body treatments, waxing, makeup.*

Fodor's Choice
★ **SpaHalekulani.** SpaHalekulani mines the traditions and cultures of the Pacific Islands with massages and body and facial therapies. Try the Polynesian Nonu, which uses warm stones and healing nonu gel. The invigorating Japanese Ton Ton Amma massage is another popular choice. The exclusive line of bath and body products is scented by maile, lavender orchid, hibiscus, coconut passion, or Manoa mint. ⊠ *Halekūlani Hotel, 2199 Kālia Rd., Waikīkī* ☎ *808/931–5322* ⊕ *www.halekulani.com* ☞ *$180, 75-min lomi lomi massage. Use of facilities is specific to treatment but may include Japanese furo bath, steam shower, or whirlpool tub. Services: hair salon, nail care, massage, facials, body treatments.*

The Spa Luana at Turtle Bay Resort. Luxuriate at the ocean's edge in this serene spa. Don't miss the tropical Pineapple Pedicure ($65), administered outdoors overlooking the North Shore. Tired feet soak in a bamboo bowl filled with coconut milk before the pampering really begins with Hawaiian algae salt, Island bee honey, kukui nut oil, and crushed pineapple. There are private spa suites, an outdoor treatment cabana that overlooks the surf, an outdoor exercise studio, and a lounge area and juice bar. ⊠ *Turtle Bay Resort, 57-091 Kamehameha Hwy., North Shore* ☎ *808/447–6868* ⊕ *www.turtlebayresort.com* ☞ *$135, 50-min lomi lomi massage. Hair and nail salon, showers, steam room,*

6

outdoor whirlpool. Gym with: free weights, cardio and weight-training machines. Services: facials, massages, body treatments, waxing. Classes and programs: hula aerobics, Pilates, yoga.

Spa Suites at The Kāhala. A footbath begins the pampering process at the elegant yet homey Kāhala property favored by celebrities and U.S. presidents. The new spa suites feature wooden floors, handmade Hawaiian quilts, Kohler infinity-edged whirlpool tubs, private vanity areas, and private gardens in which to relax after treatments with lemongrass-pīkake tea. Custom-designed treatments merge Hawaiian, Asian, and traditional therapies. ✉ *The Kāhala, 5000 Kāhala Ave., Kāhala* 🏨 *808/739–8938 www.kahalaresort.com* ☞ *$185, 60-min lomi lomi massage. Hair salon, hot tub, sauna, steam room. Services: facials, massage, body treatments.*

Entertainment and Nightlife

WORD OF MOUTH

"My husband and I spent a week of our honeymoon on Oʻahu last year. We like lively places, and there is plenty of nightlife in Waikīkī."

—optimystic

Updated By
Chad Pata

Many first-time visitors arrive in the Islands expecting to see scenic beauty and sandy beaches but not much at night. That might be true on some of the other Islands, but not in Oʻahu. Honolulu sunsets herald the onset of the best night-life scene in the Islands.

Local artists perform every night of the week along Waikīkī's Kalākaua and Kūhiō avenues and in Downtown Honolulu; the clubs dance to every beat from Top 40 to alternative to '80s.

The arts also thrive alongside the tourist industry. Oʻahu has an established symphony, a thriving opera company, chamber-music groups, and community theaters. Major Broadway shows, dance companies, and rock stars also make their way to Honolulu. Check the local newspapers—*MidWeek,* the *Honolulu Advertiser,* the *Honolulu Star-Bulletin,* or the *Honolulu Weekly*—for the latest events.

Whether you make it an early night or stay up to watch that spectacular tropical sunrise, there's lots to do in paradise.

ENTERTAINMENT

DINNER CRUISES AND SHOWS

Dinner cruises depart either from the piers adjacent to the Aloha Tower Marketplace in Downtown Honolulu or from Kewalo Basin, near Ala Moana Beach Park, and head along the coast toward Diamond Head. There's usually a buffet-style dinner with a local accent, dancing, drinks, and a sensational sunset. Except as noted, dinner cruises cost approximately $40 to $110, cocktail cruises $25 to $40. Most major credit cards are accepted. In all cases, reservations are essential. Check their Web sites for savings of up to 15%.

Aliʻi Kai Catamaran. Patterned after an ancient Polynesian vessel, this 170-foot catamaran casts off from Aloha Tower with 300 passengers. The deluxe dinner cruise has two bars, a huge dinner, and an authentic Polynesian show with colorful hula music. The food is good, the after-dinner show loud and fun, and everyone dances on the way back to shore. Rates begin at $74 and include round-trip transportation, the dinner buffet, and one drink. ⊠ *Pier 5, street level, Honolulu* ☎ *808/539–9440 Ext. 2.* ⊕ *www.robertshawaii.com.*

★ **Atlantis Cruises.** The sleekly high-tech *Navatek,* a revolutionary craft designed to sail smoothly in rough waters, powers farther along Waikīkī's coastline than its competitors, sometimes making it past Diamond Head and all the way to Hanauma Bay. Choose from sunset dinner or moonlight cruises aboard the 300-passenger boat where you can feast on beef tenderloin and whole lobster or opt for the downstairs buffet. There's also the option of humpback whale–watching cruises December–mid-April. Tours leave from Pier 6, next to Aloha Tower Marketplace. Rates begin at $95 for the buffet, including one drink;

the sit-down dinner, which includes three drinks, starts at $130. ✉ *Honolulu Harbor* ☎ *808/973–1311* ⊕ *www.atlantisadventures.com.*

Blue Hawai'i: The Show. The King loved the Islands. Jonathan Von Brana sings Elvis Presley tunes that showcase this affection. ✉ *Waikīkī Beachcomber Hotel, 2300 Kalākaua Ave., Waikīkī* ☎ *808/923–1245* ⊗ *Shows daily at 6:15.*

Creation: A Polynesian Journey. A daring Samoan fire-knife dancer is the highlight of this show that traces Hawai'i's culture and history, from its origins to statehood. The buffet costs $85, but the show with just cocktails is only $49. ✉ *'Āinahau Showroom, Sheraton Princess Ka'iulani Hotel, 120 Ka'iulani Ave., Waikīkī* ☎ *808/931–4660* ⊗ *Dinner shows Tues. and Thurs.–Sun. at 7.*

★ **Magic of Polynesia.** Hawai'i's top illusionist, John Hirokawa, displays mystifying sleight of hand in this highly entertaining show, which incorporates contemporary hula and island music into its acts. ✉ *Waikīkī Beachcomber Hotel, 2300 Kalākaua Ave., Waikīkī* ☎ *808/971–4321* ⊗ *Nightly at 8.*

Paradise Cruises. Prices vary depending on which deck you choose on the 1,600-passenger, four-deck *Star of Honolulu*. For instance, a seven-course French-style dinner and live jazz on the top deck starts at $177. A steak-and-crab feast on level two starts at $86. This ship also features daily Hawaiiana Lunch cruises that offer lei-making and 'ukulele and hula lessons starting at $55. Evening excursions also take place on the 340-passenger *Starlet I* and 230-passenger *Starlet II*, which offer three-course dinners beginning at $43. You can bring your bathing suits for a morning cruise for $73 complete with ocean fun on a water trampoline and slide, and feast on a barbecue lunch before heading back to shore. ✉ *1540 S. King St., Honolulu* ☎ *808/983–7827* ⊕ *www.starofhonolulu.com.*

☺ **Polynesian Cultural Center.** Easily one of the best on the Islands, this show has soaring moments and an "erupting volcano." The performers are students from Brigham Young University's Hawai'i campus. Plan a whole day out here to visit the eight island villages, representing the varied groups of peoples in the South Pacific. Interactive games and crafts make this a must for the whole family. ✉ *55-370 Kamehameha Hwy., Lā'ie* ☎ *808/293–3333 or 800/367–7060* ⊕ *www.polynesia.com* ⊗ *Mon.–Sat. 12:30–9:30.*

Society of Seven. This lively, popular septet has great staying power and, after more than 25 years, continues to put on one of the best shows in Waikīkī. They sing, dance, do impersonations, play instruments, and, above all, entertain with their contemporary sound. ✉ *Outrigger Waikīkī on the Beach, 2335 Kalākaua Ave., Waikīkī* ☎ *808/922–6408* ⊕ *www.outrigger.com* ⊗ *Wed.–Sat. at 8:30.*

7

LŪʻAU

The lūʻau is an experience that everyone, both local and tourist, should have. Today's lūʻau still adhere to traditional foods and entertainment, but there's also a fun, contemporary flair. With most, you can even watch the roasted pig being carried out of its ʻimu, a hole in the ground used for cooking meat with heated stones.

Lūʻau cost anywhere from $56 to $195. Most that are held outside of Waikīkī offer shuttle service so you don't have to drive. Reservations are essential.

Germaine's Lūʻau. Widely regarded as the most folksy and local, this lūʻau is held in Kalaeloa in Leeward Oʻahu. The food is the usual multicourse, all-you-can-eat buffet, but it's very tasty. It's a good lūʻau for first-timers and at a reasonable price. Expect a lively crowd on the 35-minute bus ride from Waikīkī. Admission includes buffet, Polynesian show, and shuttle transport from Waikīkī. ☏ *808/949–6626 or 800/367–5655* ⊕ *www.germainesluau.com* ✉ *$72* ◷ *Daily at 6.*

★ **Paradise Cove Lūʻau.** The scenery is the best here—the sunsets are unbelievable. Watch Mother Nature's special-effects show in Kapolei/Ko Olina Resort in Leeward Oʻahu, a good 27 mi from the bustle of Waikīkī. The party-hearty atmosphere is kid-friendly with Hawaiian games, canoe rides in the cove, and lots of pre-dinner activities. The stage show includes a fire-knife dancer, singing emcee, and both traditional and contemporary hula. Basic admission includes buffet, activities, and the show. Shuttle transport from Waikīkī is $12. You pay extra for table service and box seating. ☏ *808/842–5911* ⊕ *www.paradisecovehawaii. com* ✉ *$68–$125* ◷ *Daily at 5:30, doors open at 5.*

Fodor's Choice **Polynesian Cultural Center Aliʻi Lūʻau.** This elaborate lūʻau has the sharp-
★ est production values but no booze (it's a Mormon-owned facility). It's held amid the seven re-created villages at the Polynesian Cultural Center in the North Shore town of Lāʻie, about an hour's drive from Honolulu. The lūʻau includes tours of the park with shows and activities. Package rates vary depending on activities and amenities (personalized tours, reserved seats, buffet vs. dinner service, backstage tours, etc.). Waikīkī transport is available, call for prices. ☏ *808/293–3333 or 800/367–7060* ⊕ *www.polynesia.com* ✉ *$83–$215* ◷ *Mon.–Sat. center opens at noon; lūʻau starts at 5.*

Waikīkī Starlight Luau. The only luau still held in Waikīkī is done spectacularly on the rooftop of the Hilton Hawaiian Village. There isn't an ʻimu ceremony, but the entertainment is top notch and the views are unparalleled—and for less than $100 in the heart of Waikīkī. They have traditional activities, such as hula lessons and conch blowing, but don't miss the fun of the pineapple tossing contest. ☏ *808/941–5828* ⊕ *www.hiltonhawaiianvillage.com/luau* ✉ *$95* ◷ *Sun.–Thurs. Activities start at 5:15* PM.

FILM

Hawaiʻi International Film Festival. It may not be Cannes, but this festival is unique and exciting. During the middle of October, top films from the United States, Asia, and the Pacific are screened day and night at several theaters on Oʻahu to packed crowds. It's a must-see for

film adventurers. ☎ *808/697–2463*
⊕ *www.hiff.org.*

Honolulu Academy of Arts. Art, international, classic, and silent films are screened at the 280-seat Doris Duke theater. Though small, the theater is still classy and comfortable. It also has a great sound system. ✉ *900 S. Beretania St., Downtown Honolulu* ☎ *808/532–8768* ⊕ *www.honoluluacademy.org.*

★ **Sunset on the Beach.** It's like watching a movie at the drive-in, minus the car and the impossible speaker box. Think romantic and cozy; bring a blanket and find a spot on the sand to enjoy live entertainment, food from top local restaurants, and a movie feature on a 40-foot screen. Held twice a month on Waikīikī's Queen's Surf Beach across from the Honolulu Zoo, Sunset on the Beach is a favorite event for both locals and tourists. If the weather is blustery, beware of flying sand. ☎ *808/923–1094* ⊕ *www.waikikiimprovement.com.*

MUSIC

Hawai'i Opera Theater. Better known as "HOT," the Hawai'i Opera Theater has been known to turn the opera-challenged into opera lovers. All operas are sung in their original language with projected English translation. Tickets range from $29 to $120. ✉ *Neil Blaisdell Center Concert Hall, Ward Ave. and King St., Downtown Honolulu* ☎ *808/596–7372* ⊕ *www.hawaiiopera.org.*

Honolulu Symphony Orchestra. In recent years, the Honolulu Symphony has worked hard to increase its appeal to all ages. The orchestra performs at the Neil Blaisdell Concert Hall under the direction of the internationally acclaimed Andreas Delfs. The Honolulu Pops series, with performances under the summer stars at the Waikīkī Shell, features top local and national artists under the direction of talented conductor-composer Matt Cattingub. Tickets are $17–$59. ✉ *Dole Cannery, 650 Iwilei Rd., Suite 202, Iwilei* ☎ *808/792–2000* ⊕ *www. honolulusymphony.com.*

Honolulu Zoo Concerts. For almost two decades, the Honolulu Zoo Society has sponsored Wednesday-evening concerts from June to August on the zoo's stage lawn. Listen to local legends play everything from Hawaiian to jazz to Latin music. ■ **TIP→** At just $2 admission, this is one of the best deals in town. Take a brisk walk through the zoo exhibits before they close at 5:30 PM or join in the family activities; bring your own picnic for the concert, which starts at 6 PM. It's an alcohol-free event, and there's a food concession for those who come unprepared. ✉ *151 Kapahulu Ave., Waikīkī* ☎ *808/926–3191* ⊕ *www.honoluluzoo. org* ⌫ *$2* ☉ *Gates open at 4:30.*

THEATER

Hawai'i can be an expensive gig for touring shows and music artists that depend on major theatrical sets. Not many manage to stop here, and those who do sell out fast. O'ahu has developed several excellent local theater companies, which present first-rate entertainment on an amateur and semiprofessional level all year long. Community support for these groups is strong.

Army Community Theatre. This is a favorite for its revivals of musical theater classics presented in an 800-seat house. The casts are talented, and the fare is great for families. ⊠ *Richardson Theater, Fort Shafter, Downtown Honolulu* ☎ *808/438–4480* ▱ *$15–$20.*

Diamond Head Theater. The repertoire includes a little of everything: musicals, dramas, experimental productions, and classics. This company is in residence five minutes from Waikīkī, right next to Diamond Head. ⊠ *520 Makapuʻu Ave., Kapahulu* ☎ *808/733–0274* ⊕ *www.diamondheadtheater.com* ▱ *$12–$42.*

Hawaiʻi Theatre Center. Beautifully restored, this Downtown Honolulu theater, built in the 1920s in a neoclassic Beaux-Arts style, hosts a wide variety of performing-arts events, including international theatrical productions, international touring acts, festivals, films, and meetings. It's the most beautiful theater in Hawaiʻi. Historic tours are offered Tuesday at 11 AM for $5. Admission for performances varies. ⊠ *1130 Bethel St., Downtown Honolulu* ☎ *808/528–0506* ⊕ *www.hawaiitheatre.com.*

Honolulu Theater for Youth. This group stages delightful productions for children around the Islands from September through May. Call for a schedule. ⊠ *2846 Ualena St., Downtown Honolulu* ☎ *808/839–9885* ▱ *$10.*

Kumu Kahua. This is the only troupe presenting shows and plays written by local playwrights about the Islands. It stages five or six productions a year in a small venue that's perfect for getting up close and personal with the cast. ⊠ *46 Merchant St., Downtown Honolulu* ☎ *808/536–4441* ⊕ *www.kumukahua.org* ▱ *$12–$15.*

NIGHTLIFE

Oʻahu is the best of all the Islands for nightlife. The locals call it *pau hana,* but you might call it "off the clock and ready for a cocktail." The literal translation of the Hawaiian phrase means "done with work." On weeknights, it's likely that you'll find the working crowd still in their casual business attire sipping a few gin and tonics even before the sun goes down. Those who don't have to wake up in the early morning should change into a fresh outfit and start the evening closer to 10 PM.

On the weekends, it's typical to have dinner at a restaurant before hitting the clubs around 9:30. Some bar hoppers start as early as 7, but

Continued on page 192

MORE THAN A FOLK DANCE

Hula has been called "the heartbeat of the Hawaiian people" and also "the world's best-known, most misunderstood dance." Both are true. Hula isn't just dance. It is storytelling. No words, no hula.

Chanter Edith McKinzie calls it "an extension of a piece of poetry." In its adornments, implements, and customs, hula integrates every important Hawaiian cultural practice: poetry, history, genealogy, craft, plant cultivation, martial arts, religion, protocol. So when 19th century Christian missionaries sought to eradicate a practice they considered depraved, they threatened more than just a folk dance.

With public performance outlawed and private hula practice discouraged, hula went underground for a generation, to rural villages. The fragile verbal link by which culture was transmitted from teacher to student hung by a thread. Even increasing literacy did not help because hula's practitioners were a secretive and protected circle.

As if that weren't bad enough, vaudeville, Broadway, and Hollywood got hold of the hula, giving it the glitz treatment in an unbroken line from "Oh, How She Could Wicky Wacky Woo" to "Rock-A-Hula Baby." Hula became shorthand for paradise: fragrant flowers, lazy hours. Ironically, this development assured that hundreds of Hawaiians could make a living performing and teaching hula. Many danced 'auana (modern form) in performance; but taught kahiko (traditional), quietly, at home or in hula schools.

Today, 30 years after the cultural revival known as the Hawaiian Renaissance, language immersion programs have assured a new generation of proficient—and even eloquent—chanters, songwriters, and translators. Visitors can see more, and more authentic, traditional hula than at any other time in the last 200 years.

Like the culture of which it is the beating heart, hula has survived.

Lei *po'o*. Head lei. In kahiko, greenery only. In 'auana, flowers.

Face emotes appropriate expression. Dancer should not be a smiling automaton.

Shoulders remain relaxed and still, never hunched, even with arms raised. No bouncing.

Eyes always follow leading hand.

Lei. Hula is rarely performed without a shoulder lei.

Arms and hands remain loose, relaxed, below shoulder level—except as required by interpretive movements.

Traditional hula skirt is loose fabric, smocked and gathered at the waist.

Hip is canted over weight-bearing foot.

Knees are always slightly bent, accentuating hip sway.

Kupe'e. Ankle bracelet of flowers, shells, or—traditionally—noise-making dog teeth.

In kahiko, feet are flat. In 'auana, they may be more arched, but not tiptoes or bouncing.

BASIC MOTIONS

Speak or Sing

Moon or Sun

Grass Shack or House

Mountains or Heights

Love or Caress

At backyard parties, hula is performed in bare feet and street clothes, but in performance, adornments play a key role, as do rhythm-keeping implements.

In hula kahiko (traditional style), the usual dress is multiple layers of stiff fabric (often with a pellom lining, which most closely resembles *kapa*, the paperlike bark cloth of the Hawaiians). These wrap tightly around the bosom but flare below the waist to form a skirt. In pre-contact times, dancers wore only kapa skirts. Monarchy-period hula is performed in voluminous Mother Hubbard muʻumuʻu or high-necked muslin blouses and gathered skirts. Men wear loincloths or, for monarchy period, white or gingham shirts and black pants—sometimes with red sashes.

In hula ʻauana (modern), dress for women can range from grass skirts and strapless tops to contemporary tea-length dresses. Men generally wear aloha shirts, but sometimes grass skirts over pants or even everyday gear. (One group at a recent competition wore wetsuits to do a surfing song!)

SURPRISING HULA FACTS

■ Grass skirts are not traditional; workers from Kiribati (the Gilbert Islands) brought this custom to Hawaiʻi.

■ In olden-day Hawaiʻi, *mele* (songs) for hula were composed for every occasion—name songs for babies, dirges for funerals, welcome songs for visitors, celebrations of favorite pursuits.

■ Hula *maʻi* is a traditional hula form in praise of a noble's genitals; the power of the *aliʻi* (royalty) to procreate gave *mana* (spiritual power) to the entire culture.

■ Hula students in old Hawaiʻi adhered to high standards: scrupulous cleanliness, no sex, daily cleansing rituals, certain food prohibitions, and no contact with the dead. They were fined if they broke the rules.

WHERE TO WATCH

■ House Without a Key: Live music, graceful solo hula, relaxed seaside stage. Halekūlani, ☎ 808/923–2311.

■ Two worthwhile commercial shows: "Creation-A Polynesian Journey," Sheraton Princess Kaʻiulani, ☎ 808/922–5811; Polynesian Cultural Center, ☎ 808/293–3333.

■ Free hula shows: Bishop Museum, ☎ 808/847–3511. Frequent performances and free hula lessons: Royal Hawaiian Shopping Center, ☎ 808/922–0588.

■ Festivals and hōʻike: To find authentic amateur hula, check local media and the gohawaii.com calendar for annual hula school hōʻike (recital/fundraisers) and hula festivals and competitions.

partygoers typically don't patronize more than two establishments a night. That's because getting from one O'ahu nightspot to the next usually requires packing your friends into the car and driving. You can find a bar in just about any area on O'ahu. Most of the clubs, however, are in Waikīkī, Ala Moana, and Downtown Honolulu. The drinking age is 21 on O'ahu and throughout Hawai'i. Many bars will admit younger people but will not serve them alcohol. By law, all establishments that serve alcoholic beverages must close by 2 AM. The only exceptions are those with a cabaret license, which have a 4 AM curfew.

24-HOUR EATERIES

If it's 3 AM and you're desperate for a snack, avoid the fast-food drive-through and opt to satisfy your munchies the local way. There are several 24-hour eateries on O'ahu that pack in the after-hours crowd: Wailana Coffee House in Waikīkī, Like Like Drive-In by Ala Moana Shopping Center, and Zippy's, of which there are 20 locations open all night. Try Like Like's fried rice and Portuguese sausage or Zippy's saimin, chili frank plate, or an apple napple from the bakery.

■TIP→ Most places have a cover charge of $5 to $10, but with some establishments, getting there early means you don't have to pay.

DOWNTOWN HONOLULU

BARS

Chai's Island Bistro. Chai's welcomes some of Hawai'i's top entertainers, such as the Brothers Cazimero (on Wednesday evening), Hapa, and Jake Shimabukuro. Chai's is the perfect place if you're looking to enjoy the signature sounds of Hawai'i while dining on Pacific Rim cuisine. ⊠ *Aloha Tower Marketplace, 1 Aloha Tower Dr., Downtown* ☎ *808/585–0011.*

🕯 **Dave and Buster's.** Located in the Ward Centers, this restaurant features a stocked bar and lots of amusements ranging from classic billiards to shuffleboard and the latest in video-arcade games. On Wednesday, Friday, and Saturday a DJ spins hip-hop music on the rooftop Sunset Bar starting at 10 PM. ⊠ *Ward Entertainment Complex, 1030 Auahi St., Ala Moana* ☎ *808/589–2215.*

Don Ho's Grill. This popular waterfront restaurant in the Aloha Tower Marketplace houses the Tiny Bubbles Bar, famous for its "suck 'em up" mai tai, a Don Ho classic. The dinner hour features Hawaiian musicians like Jerry Santos and Robert Cazimero. On the weekend, live bands play reggae music from 10 PM to 2 AM. ⊠ *Aloha Tower Marketplace, 1 Aloha Tower Dr., Downtown* ☎ *808/528–0807.*

Gordon Biersch Brewery Restaurant. This outside bar flanks Honolulu Harbor. Live bands serenade patrons with everything from funk to jazz to rock and roll. Those who feel inspired have been known to strut their stuff in front of the stage, while their friends enjoy a pint of the restaurant's own brew from the sidelines. ⊠ *Aloha Tower Marketplace, 1 Aloha Tower Dr., Downtown* ☎ *808/599–4877.*

Fodor's Choice
★

Mai Tai Bar at Ala Moana Center. After a long day of shopping, the Mai Tai Bar on the third floor of Ala Moana Center is a perfect spot to relax. There's live entertainment and two nightly happy hours: one for food items and another strictly for specialty drinks. There's never a cover charge and no dress code, but to avoid waiting in line, get there before 9 PM. ⊠ *1450 Ala Moana Blvd., Ala Moana* ☎ *808/947–2900.*

Murphy's Bar & Grill. When you need a taste of home, this 120-year-old pub in the heart of downtown will transport you there. It features award-winning steaks and burgers and was voted the best bar in Hawaii in popular polls four of the past five years. Locals love it because it's a getaway from the mai tais and grass shacks, with 16 premium beers on draft and the longest shuffleboard table on the Islands. ⊠ *2 Merchant St., Downtown* ☎ *808/531–0422* ⊕ *www.gomurphys.com.*

Pipeline Cafe and Sports Bar. This is two stories of fun with pool, darts, and more. The upstairs sports bar has TVs galore and a skybox view of the dancing below. Music includes both live acts and seasoned DJs. ⊠ *805 Pohukaina St., Kaka'ako* ☎ *808/589–1999* ⊕ *www.pipelinecafehawaii.com.*

thirtyninehotel. This loft and art gallery is on the cutting edge of what's hot downtown. Every three months it gets a new "art installation" where a local artist repaints and configures the entire space. Their bartenders and their "market-fresh" cocktails have become the stuff of local legend, using Hawaiian produce to recreate classic turn-of-the-century libations. Entertainment varies from jazz groups to DJs depending on the night. Come any night of the week for happy hour from 4–8 PM, when their specialty cocktails are half off. ⊠ *39 N. Hotel St., Downtown* ☎ *808/599–2552.*

The Varsity. This bar has had several names over the years but there's always been one constant: cheap beer. Located just south of the University of Hawaii, students flock here for the pizza, big-screen TVs, and 50 beers on tap. In a town where a pint of beer costs an average of $6, a bar that has $6 pitchers will seem darn well refreshing. Luckily the open-air design allows the smell of beer to waft outside. ⊠ *1015 University Ave., Mo'ili'ili* ☎ *808/447–9244.*

CLUBS

Fodor's Choice
★

Rumours. The after-work crowd loves this spot, which has dance videos, disco, and throbbing lights. On Saturday "Little Chill" nights, the club plays oldies from the '70s, '80s, and '90s and serves free pūpū. ⊠ *Ala Moana Hotel, 410 Atkinson St., Ala Moana* ☎ *808/955–4811.*

Tsunami. While this club has moved locations a couple times, it seems to have found a permanent home on King Street. It has a cool, modern atmosphere, with its sleek black couches and sharply dressed waitresses.

BLUE HAWAI'I

In 1957 Harry Yee, a bartender at the Hilton Hawaiian Village, created the Blue Hawai'i using the Bols company's newest liqueur, Blue Curaçao. It may turn your tongue a tasty shade of blue, but this sweet beverage goes down smoothly. Mix ¾ ounce light rum, ¾ ounce vodka, ½ ounce blue curaçao, 3 ounces pineapple juice, and 1 ounce sweet-and-sour mix.

7

The food is quite good and the happy hour specials are reasonable, but things don't get going until after 10 PM when lines form and the DJs get the place hopping. ⊠ *1272 S. King St., Mo'ili'ili* ☎ *808/951–8885.*

WAIKĪKĪ

BARS

Banyan Veranda. The Banyan Veranda is steeped in history. From this location the radio program *Hawai'i Calls* first broadcast the sounds of Hawaiian music and the rolling surf to a U.S. mainland audience in 1935. Today, a variety of Hawaiian entertainment continues to provide the perfect accompaniment to the sounds of the waves. ⊠ *Sheraton Moana Surfrider, 2365 Kalākaua Ave., Waikīkī* ☎ *808/922–3111.*

★ **Duke's Canoe Club.** If you're picking one spot to stop for a drink on the island, this should be it. Making the most of its oceanfront spot on Waikīkī Beach, Duke's presents "Concerts on the Beach" every Friday, Saturday, and Sunday with contemporary Hawaiian musicians like Henry Kapono. National musicians like Jimmy Buffett have also performed here. At Duke's Barefoot Bar, solo Hawaiian musicians take the stage nightly, and it's not unusual for surfers to leave their boards outside to step in for a casual drink after a long day on the waves. ⊠ *Outrigger Waikīkī, 2335 Kalākaua Ave., Waikīkī* ☎ *808/922–2268.*

Formaggio Wine and Cheese Bar. Only people in the know, know where Formaggio is. There's no flashy signage for this establishment on the outskirts of Waikīkī—only the word "Formaggio" painted on the door. This tinted door cloaks a dimly lighted bar, where young professionals and baby boomers enjoy live jazz Wednesday to Saturday. There are more than 40 wines by the glass or taste and a Mediterranean menu with everything from pizzas to panini. ⊠ *Market City Shopping Center, 2919 Kapi'olani Blvd., lower level, Waikīkī* ☎ *808/739–7719* ☉ *Tues.–Sun.*

Irish Rose Saloon. This Waikīkī rock-and-roll club feels like a modern-day version of a speakeasy. The owners found a loophole in Hawaii's smoking laws, and so along with their sister bar Kelly O'Neil's, smokers here can still enjoy their drinks and cigarettes simultaneously. Come for live rock and roll seven nights a week. ⊠ *478 Ena Rd., Waikīkī* ☎ *808/947–3414.*

★ **Level 4.** This Vegas-style nightclub, located in the Royal Hawaiian Shopping Center, will give you the ultimate VIP experience, with bottle service, top international DJs, and plenty of celebs to rub elbows with. It's where the beautiful people go on Oahu to mingle late at night and relax inside its 7,000-square-foot lanai overlooking Waikīkī. ⊠ *Royal Hawaiian Shopping Center 2233 Kalākaua Ave., Waikīkī* ☎ *808/926–4441* ☉ *Wed. –Sat. 10:30 PM–4 AM.*

★ **Mai Tai Bar at the Royal Hawaiian.** The bartenders sure know how to make one killer mai tai—just one could do the trick. This is, after all, the establishment that came up with the famous drink in the first place. The pink, umbrella-covered tables at the outdoor bar are front-row seating for Waikīkī sunsets and an unobstructed view of Diamond

Head. Contemporary Hawaiian music is usually on stage starting at 6 PM, and the staff is extremely friendly. ✉ *Royal Hawaiian Hotel, 2259 Kalākaua Ave., Waikīkī* ☎ *808/923–7311.*

Fodor's Choice
★

Moana Terrace. Three floors up from Waikīkī Beach, this open-air terrace was the home of Aunty Genoa Keawe, the "First Lady of Hawaiian Music," before she passed in 2008. The Bar has kept her tradition alive though with falsetto sessions and slack-key guitar work performed by some of the finest of Hawai'i's musicians. ✉ *Waikīkī Beach Marriott Resort, 2552 Kalākaua Ave., Waikīkī* ☎ *808/922–6611.*

Moose McGillycuddy's Pub and Cafe. Loud bands play for the beach-and-beer gang in a blue-jeans-and-T-shirt setting. Bikini contests are the thrill on Sunday nights; live bands play late '80s and '90s music the rest of the week. ✉ *310 Lewers St., Waikīkī* ☎ *808/923–0751.*

Tiki's Grill and Bar. Get in touch with your primal side at this restaurant/bar overlooking Kūhiō Beach. Tiki torches, tiki statues, and other South Pacific art set the mood. A twentysomething mix of locals and tourists comes on the weekends to get their fill of kitschy-cool. There's nightly entertainment featuring contemporary Hawaiian musicians. Don't leave without sipping on a "lava flow." It's served in a whole coconut, which is yours to keep at the end of the night. ✉ *Aston Waikīkī Beach Hotel, 2570 Kalākaua Ave., Waikīkī* ☎ *808/923–8454.*

CLUBS

Hula's Bar and Lei Stand. Hawai'i's oldest and best-known gay-friendly nightspot offers calming panoramic outdoor views of Diamond Head and the Pacific Ocean by day and a high-energy club scene by night. Check out the soundproof, glassed-in dance floor. ✉ *Waikīkī Grand Hotel, 134 Kapahulu Ave., 2nd fl., Waikīkī* ☎ *808/923–0669.*

Hush Boutique. If thumping clubs make your head hurt, try out this intimate little jazz and blues spot, where you can enjoy the perks of a classy club with bottle service. Relax on the white leather couches and enjoy one of their private rooms' plasma-screen TVs. ✉ *444 Niu St. Waikīkī* ☎ *808/479–9152.*

Lotus Soundbar. This three-story, five-room club booms with everything from trance to hip-hop to drum n' bass. Check out the dance floor upstairs or gab with a friend in the comfort of one of the Lotus loungers. Boasting the best sound system in the state, even the most meager partier won't be able to resist moving once the speakers start thumping. ✉ *2301 Kuhio Ave., Waikīkī* ☎ *808/924–1688* ◷ *Open 7 days a week.*

MAI TAIS

The cocktail known around the world as the mai tai recently celebrated its 50th birthday. While the recipe has changed slightly over the years, the original formula, created by bar owner Victor J. "Trader Vic" Bergeron, included two ounces of 17-year-old J. Wray & Nephew rum over shaved ice, ½ ounce Holland Dekuyper orange curaçao, ¼ ounce Trader Vic's rock candy syrup, ½ ounce French Garier orgeat syrup, and the juice of one fresh lime. Done the right way, this tropical drink still lives up to the name "mai tai!" meaning, "out of this world!"

7

Nashville Waikīkī. Country music in the tropics? You bet! Put on your *paniolo* (Hawaiian cowboy) duds and mosey on out to the giant dance floor. There are pool tables, dartboards, line dancing, and free dance lessons (Wednesday at 6:30 PM) to boot. Look for wall-to-wall crowds on the weekends, and this is a favorite late nightspot for the more easygoing 4 AM crowd. ⊠ *Ohana Waikīkī West Hotel, 2330 Kūhiō Ave., Waikīkī* ☏ *808/926–7911.*

Zanzabar. Traverse a winding staircase and make an entrance at Zanzabar where DJs spin top hits, from hip-hop to soul and techno to trance. It's easy to find a drink at this high-energy nightspot with its three bars. Not exactly sure how to get your groove on? Zanzabar offers free Latin dance lessons every Tuesday at 8 PM. Some nights are 21 and over; Sunday, Tuesday, Wednesday, and Thursday allow 18 and over in for $15. ⊠ *Waikīkī Trade Center, 2255 Kūhiō Ave., Waikīkī* ☏ *808/924–3939.*

GREATER O'AHU

BARS

Boardrider's Bar & Grill. Tucked away in Kailua Town, this spot has long been the venue for local bands to strut their stuff. Renovations have spruced up the space, which now includes pool tables, dart boards, foosball, and eight TVs for sports-viewing with the local and military crowd. Look for live entertainment—reggae to alternative rock to good old-fashioned rock and roll—Wednesday through Saturday from 10:30 PM to 1:30 AM. Cover ranges from $3 to $10. ⊠ *201-A Hamakua Dr., Kailua* ☏ *808/261–4600.*

Breaker's Restaurant. Just about every surf contest post-party is celebrated at this family-owned establishment, as the owner's son, Benji Weatherly, is a pro surfer himself. Surfing memorabilia, including surfboards hanging from the ceiling, fill the space. The restaurant/bar is open from 11 AM to 9:30 PM with a late-night menu until midnight. But things start to happen around 9 PM on Thursday for the 18-and-over crowd, who cruise while the DJ spins; there's live music on Saturday. The party goes until 2 AM. ⊠ *Marketplace Shopping Center, 66-250 Kamehameha Hwy., Hale'iwa* ☏ *808/637–9898.*

The Shack. This sports bar and restaurant is about the only late-night spot you can find in Southeast O'ahu. After a day of snorkeling at Hanauma Bay, stop by to kick back, have a beer, eat a burger, watch some sports, or play a game of pool. ⊠ *Hawai'i Kai Shopping Center, 377 Keahole St., Hawai'i Kai* ☏ *808/396–1919* ⊙ *Nightly until 2 AM.*

Where to Eat

WORD OF MOUTH

"Make sure you have a shrimp plate lunch from one of the shrimp trucks. YUM YUM YUM! You will find them along the roadside in the North Shore area."

—annikany

WHERE TO EAT PLANNER

Eating-Out Strategy

Where should we eat? With dozens of island eateries competing for your attention, it may seem like a daunting question. But our expert writers and editors have done most of the legwork—the dozens of selections here represent the best eating experience this island has to offer. Search "Best Bets" for top recommendations by price, cuisine, and experience. Or find a restaurant quickly—reviews are ordered alphabetically within their geographic area.

Where to Park

In Waikīkī, walk or take a cab; it's cheaper than parking or valet rates. Elsewhere on O'ahu, free, validated, and reasonably priced parking is widely available. Exceptions: Parking downtown during the day is hideously expensive—take the trolley or TheBus; Chinatown at night is somewhat dicey—use valet parking or park in lighted lots such as Mark's Garage or municipal lots.

Smoking

Smoking is prohibited except in places where liquor revenues exceed food sales.

Reservations

If you expect to dine at Alan Wong's, Chef Mavro, or Roy's, book your table from home weeks in advance. Also beware the brand-new restaurants: they get slammed by migratory hordes for the first few weeks. Otherwise, reserve when you get into town.

With Kids

Hawai'i is a kid-friendly destination in many regards, and that includes taking the little ones out to eat with you. That said, there are probably a few places in Waikīkī that you're better off dining at sans kids and taking advantage of your hotel's child care.

What to Wear

You'll find people dress up for dinner on O'ahu—especially in Waikīkī and Honolulu—more so than on any other Hawaiian Island. Even so, casual reigns supreme here; most top restaurants abide by the "dressy causal" standard, where dark jeans are acceptable as long as they're not worn with sneakers.

Hours and Prices

The most sought-after dinner reservations are between 6 and 7, but you can often have your pick of tables at 8. Exceptions: sushi bars and Japanese taverns, a few 24-hour diners, and some younger-spinning restaurants. Takeout places still open at dawn and close shortly after midday. Standard tipping for good service is 20%.

WHAT IT COSTS

	¢	$	$$	$$$	$$$$
AT DINNER	under $10	$10–$17	$18–$26	$27–$35	over $35

Restaurant prices are for a main course at dinner.

BEST BETS FOR O'AHU DINING

Where can I find the best food the island has to offer? Fodor's writers and editors have selected their favorite restaurants by price, cuisine, and experience in the lists below. In the first column, the Fodor's Choice properties represent the "best of the best" across price categories. You can also search by area for excellent eats—just peruse our complete reviews on the following pages.

Fodor's Choice ★

Alan Wong's, p. 215
Buzz's Original Steakhouse, p. 227
Chef Mavro, p. 216
Little Village Noodle House, p. 209
Ola at Turtle Bay Resort, p. 230

By Price

¢

Bac Nam, p. 209
To Chau, p. 209
Wailana Coffee House, p. 225

$

Little Village Noodle House, p. 209
Kaka'ako Kitchen, p. 210
Kalapawai Café and Deli, p. 227
'Ono Hawaiian Foods, p. 215
Pasta & Basta, p. TK

$$

Buzz's Original Steakhouse, p. 227
Keo's in Waikiki, p. 222
Pah Ke's Chinese Restaurant, p. 228
Sam Choy's Breakfast Lunch & Crab and Brewery, p. 217

$$$

3660 on the Rise, p. 214
Nobu, p. 222
Ola at Turtle Bay Resort, p. 230
Roy's, p. 225

$$$$

Alan Wong's, p. 215
Chef Mavro, p. 216
Hoku's at the Kāhala, p. 212

By Cuisine

HAWAIIAN

Alan Wong's, p. 215
Chef Mavro, p. 216
Hoku's at the Kāhala, p. 212
Roy's, p. 225

PLATE LUNCH

Keneke's BBQ, p. 228
L&L Drive Inn, p. 211
'Ono Hawaiian Foods, p. 215
Ted's Bakery, p. 230

SUSHI

Mitch's Sushi Restaurant, p. 230
Nobu, p. 222
Sansei, p. 223
Sushi Sasabune, p. 216
Yanagi Sushi, p. 207

By Experience

MOST KID-FRIENDLY

3660 on the Rise, p. 214
Big City Diner, p. 214
'Ono Hawaiian Foods, p. 215
Sam Choy's Breakfast, Lunch & Crab and Brewery, p. 217
Wailana Coffee House, p. 225

MOST ROMANTIC

Hau Tree Lānai, p. 221
Hoku's at the Kāhala, p. 212
La Mer, p. 222
Michel's at the Colony Surf, p. 211
Sarento's Top of the "I", p. 224

BEST VIEW

John Dominis, p. 210
La Mer, p. 222
Orchids, p. 223
Sarento's Top of the "I", p. 224
Top of Waikiki, p. 225

8

Updated
By Melissa
Chang

O'ahu, where the majority of the Islands' 2,000-plus restaurants are located, offers the best of all worlds: it has the exoticness and excitement of Asia and Polynesia, but when the kids need McDonald's, or when you just have to have a Starbucks latte, they're here, too.

Budget for a pricey dining experience at the very top of the restaurant food chain, where chefs Alan Wong, Roy Yamaguchi, George Mavrothalassitis, and others you've read about in *Bon Appétit* put a sophisticated and unforgettable spin on local foods and flavors. Savor seared 'ahi tuna in sea urchin beurre blanc or steak marinated in Korean kimchee sauce.

Spend the rest of your food dollars where budget-conscious locals do: in plate-lunch places and small ethnic eateries, at roadside stands and lunchwagons, or at window-in-the-wall delis. Snack on a *musubi* (a hand-held rice ball wrapped with seaweed and often topped with Spam), slurp shave ice with red-bean paste, or order up Filipino pork adobo with two scoops of rice and macaroni salad.

In Waikīkī, where most visitors stay, you can find choices from gracious rooms with a view to surprisingly authentic Japanese noodle shops. But hop in the car, or on the trolley or bus, and travel just a few miles in any direction, and you can save your money and get in touch with the real food of Hawai'i.

Kaimukī's Wai'alae Avenue, for example, offers one of the city's best espresso bars, a hugely popular Chinese bakery, a highly recommended patisserie, an exceptional Italian bistro, a dim-sum restaurant, Mexican food (rare here), and a Hawai'i regional cuisine standout, 3660 on the Rise—all in three blocks, and 10 minutes from Waikīkī. Chinatown, 10 minutes in the other direction and easily reached by the Waikīkī Trolley, is another dining (and shopping) treasure, not only for Chinese but also Vietnamese, Filipino, Malaysian, and Indian food, and even a chic little tea shop.

HONOLULU

There's no lack of choices when it comes to dining in Honolulu, where everything from the haute cuisine of heavy-hitting top-notch chefs to a wide variety of Asian specialties to reliable and inexpensive American favorites can be found.

ALA MOANA

$–$$ ✕ **Akasaka.** Step inside this tiny sushi bar tucked behind the Ala Moana
JAPANESE   Hotel, and you'll swear you're in an out-of-the-way Edo neighborhood in some indeterminate time. Greeted with a cheerful "Iraishaimasu!" (Welcome!), sink down at a diminutive table or perch at the handful of seats at the sushi bar. It's safe to let the sushi chefs here decide (omakase-

Continued on page 205

LŪ'AU: A TASTE OF HAWAI'I

The best place to sample Hawaiian food is at a backyard lū'au. Aunts and uncles are cooking, the pig is from a cousin's farm, and the fish is from a brother's boat.

But even locals have to angle for invitations to those rare occasions. So your choice is most likely between a commercial lū'au and a Hawaiian restaurant.

Most commercial lū'au will offer you little of the authentic diet; they're more about umbrella drinks, laughs, spectacle, and fun. Expect to spend some time and no small amount of cash.

For greater authenticity, folksy experiences, and rock-bottom prices, visit a Hawaiian restaurant (most are in anonymous storefronts in residential neighborhoods). Expect rough edges and some effort negotiating the menu.

In either case, much of what is known today as Hawaiian food would be as foreign to a 16th-century Hawaiian as risotto or chow mien. The pre-contact diet was simple and healthy–mainly raw and steamed seafood and vegetables. Early Hawaiians used earth ovens and heated stones to cook seafood, taro, sweet potatoes, and breadfruit and seasoned their food with sea salt and ground kukui nuts. Seaweed, fern shoots, sweet potato vines, coconut, banana, sugarcane, and select greens and roots rounded out the diet.

Successive waves of immigrants added their favorites to the ti leaf–lined table. So it is that foods as disparate as salt salmon and chicken long rice are now Hawaiian—even though there is no salmon in Hawaiian waters and long rice (cellophane noodles) is Chinese.

AT THE LŪ'AU: KĀLUA PORK

The heart of any lū'au is the *imu*, the earth oven in which a whole pig is roasted. The preparation of an imu is an arduous affair for most families, who tackle it only once a year or so, for a baby's first birthday or at Thanksgiving, when many Islanders prefer to imu their turkeys. Commercial lū'au operations have it down to a science, however.

THE ART OF THE STONE

The key to a proper imu is the *pohaku*, the stones. Imu cook by means of long, slow, moist heat released by special stones that can withstand a hot fire without exploding. Many Hawaiian families treasure their imu stones, keeping them in a pile in the backyard and passing them on through generations.

PIT COOKING

The imu makers first dig a pit about the size of a re-frigerator, then lay down *kiawe* (mesquite) wood and stones, and build a white-hot fire that is allowed to burn itself out. The ashes are raked away, and the hot stones covered with banana and ti leaves. Well-wrapped in ti or banana leaves and a net of chicken wire, the pig is lowered onto the leaf-covered stones. *Laulau* (leaf-wrapped bundles of meats, fish, and taro leaves) may also be placed inside. Leaves—ti, banana, even ginger—cover the pig followed by wet burlap sacks (to create steam). The whole is topped with a canvas tarp and left to steam for the better part of a day.

OPENING THE IMU

This is the moment everyone waits for: The imu is unwrapped like a giant present and the imu keep-ers gingerly wrestle out the steaming pig. When it's unwrapped, the meat falls moist and smoky-flavored from the bone, looking and tasting just like Southern-style pulled pork, but without the barbecue sauce.

WHICH LŪ'AU?

Paradise Cove. Party-hearty atmosphere, kid-friendly.

Polynesian Cultural Center. The sharpest production values but no booze.

Royal Hawaiian Hotel. Gracious and relaxed, famous mai tais.

MEA ʻAI ʻONO.
GOOD THINGS TO EAT.

LAULAU
Steamed meats, fish, and taro leaf in ti-leaf bundles: fork-tender, a medley of flavors; the taro resembles spinach.

LOMI LOMI SALMON
Salt salmon in a piquant salad or relish with onions, tomatoes.

POI (DON'T CALL IT LIBRARY PASTE.)
Islanders are beyond tired of jokes about poi, a paste made of pounded taro root.

Laulau

Consider: The Hawaiian Adam is descended from *kalo* (taro). Young taro plants are called "keiki"—children. Poi is the first food after mother's milk for many Islanders. ʻAi, the word for food, is synonymous with poi in many contexts.

Not only that, we like it. "There is no meat that doesn't taste good with poi," the old Hawaiians said.

Lomi Lomi Salmon

But you have to know how to eat it: with something rich or powerfully flavored. "It is salt that makes the poi go in," is another adage. When you're served poi, try it with a mouthful of smoky kālua pork or salty lomi lomi salmon. Its slightly sour blandness cleanses the palate. And if you don't like it, smile and say something polite. (And slide that bowl over to a local.)

Poi

E HELE MAI ʻAI! COME AND EAT!

Hawaiian restaurants tend to be inconveniently located in well-worn storefronts with little or no parking, outfitted with battered tables and clattering Melmac dishes, open odd (and usually limited) hours and days, and often so crowded you have to wait. But they personify aloha, invariably run by local families who welcome tourists who take the trouble to find them.

Many are cash-only operations and combination plates are a standard feature: one or two entrées, a side such as chicken long rice, choice of poi or steamed rice and—if the place is really old-style—a tiny portion of coarse Hawaiian salt and some raw onions for relish.

Most serve some foods that aren't, strictly speaking, Hawaiian, but are beloved of

kamaʻāina, such as salt meat with watercress (preserved meat in a tasty broth), or *akubone* (skipjack tuna fried in a tangy vinegar sauce).

Our two favorite: **ʻOno Hawaiian Foods** and **Helena's Hawaiians Food**.

MENU GUIDE

Much of the Hawaiian language encountered during a stay in the Islands will appear on restaurant menus and lists of lū'au fare. Here's a quick primer.

'ahi: *yellowfin tuna.*

aku: *skipjack, bonito tuna.*

'ama'ama: *mullet; it's hard to get but tasty.*

bento: *a box lunch.*

chicken lū'au: *a stew made from chicken, taro leaves, and coconut milk.*

haupia: *a light, pudding-like sweet made from coconut.*

imu: *the underground ovens in which pigs are roasted for lū'au.*

kālua: *to bake underground.*

kaukau: *food. The word comes from Chinese but is used in the Islands.*

kimchee: *Korean dish of pickled cabbage made with garlic and hot peppers.*

Kona coffee: *coffee grown in the Kona district of the Big Island.*

laulau: *literally, a bundle. Laulau are morsels of pork, chicken, butterfish, or other ingredients wrapped with young taro leaves and then bundled in ti leaves for steaming.*

liliko'i: *passion fruit, a tart, seedy yellow fruit that makes delicious desserts, juice, and jellies.*

lomi lomi: *to rub or massage; also a massage. Lomi lomi salmon is fish that has been rubbed with onions and herbs; commonly served with minced onions and tomatoes.*

lū'au: *a Hawaiian feast; also the leaf of the taro plant used in preparing such a feast.*

lū'au leaves: *cooked taro tops with a taste similar to spinach.*

mahimahi: *mild-flavored dolphinfish, not the marine mammal.*

mai tai: *potent rum drink with orange and lime juice, from the Tahitian word for "good."*

malasada: *a Portuguese deep-fried doughnut without a hole, dipped in sugar.*

manapua: *dough wrapped around diced pork or other fillings.*

manō: *shark.*

niu: *coconut.*

'ōkolehao: *a liqueur distilled from the ti root.*

onaga: *pink or red snapper.*

ono: *a long, slender mackerel-like fish; also called wahoo.*

'ono: *delicious; also hungry.*

'opihi: *a tiny shellfish, or mollusk, found on rocks; also called limpets.*

pāpio: *a young ulua or jack fish.*

pohā: *Cape gooseberry. Tasting a bit like honey, the pohā berry is often used in jams and desserts.*

poi: *a paste made from pounded taro root, a staple of the Hawaiian diet.*

poke: *chopped, pickled raw tuna or other fish, tossed with herbs and seasonings.*

pūpū: *Hawaiian hors d'oeuvre.*

saimin: *long thin noodles and vegetables in broth, often garnished with small pieces of fish cake, scrambled egg, luncheon meat, and green onion.*

sashimi: *raw fish thinly sliced and usually eaten with soy sauce.*

tī leaves: *a member of the agave family. The fragrant leaves are used to wrap food while cooking and removed before eating.*

uku: *deep-sea snapper.*

ulua: *a member of the jack family that also includes pompano and amberjack. Also called crevalle, jack fish, and jack crevalle.*

style) or you can go for the delicious grilled specialties, such as scallop *battayaki* (grilled in butter). Reservations are accepted for groups only. ⊠ *1646 B Kona St., Ala Moana* ☎ *808/942–4466* ⊟ *AE, D, DC, MC, V* ⊗ *No lunch Sun.*

$–$$ ✕ **Alan Wong's Pineapple Room.** This is not your grandmother's depart-
PACIFIC RIM ment-store restaurant. It's über-chef Alan Wong's more casual second spot, where the chef de cuisine plays intriguing riffs on local food themes. Warning: the spicy chili-fried soybeans are addictive. Their house burger, made with locally raised grass-fed beef, bacon, ched-dar cheese, hoisin-mayonnaise spread, and avocado, won a local tast-ing hands-down. For a twist on an old favorite, try the salmon with ochazuke (rice and tea) risotto, served with green tea on the side to pour into the bowl. Surroundings are pleasant and service is very pro-fessional. ⊠ *Macy's, Ala Moana Center, 1450 Ala Moana Blvd., Ala Moana* ☎ *808/945–6573* ⊟ *AE, D, DC, MC, V.*

¢–$ ✕ **Big City Diner.** Part of a chain of unfussy retro diners, Big City offers a
AMERICAN short course in local-style breakfasts—rice instead of potatoes, fish or Portuguese sausage instead of bacon, steaming bowls of noodles—with generous portions, low prices, and pronounced flavors. Lunch and din-ner focus on local-style comfort food—baby back ribs, kimchee fried rice—and burgers. ⊠ *Ward Entertainment Center, 1060 'Auahi St., Ala Moana* ☎ *808/591–8891* ⊟ *AE, D, MC, V.*

$–$$ ✕ **Mariposa.** Yes, the popovers and the wee little cups of bouillon are
PACIFIC RIM here at lunch, but in every other regard, this Neiman-Marcus restaurant menu departs from the classic model, incorporating a clear sense of Pacific place. The veranda, open to the breezes and view of Ala Moana Park, twirling ceiling fans, and life-size hula-girl murals say Hawai'i. The popovers come with a fruit-infused butter spread; the oxtail osso buco is inspired; and local fish are featured nightly in luxuriant specials. ⊠ *Neiman-Marcus, Ala Moana Center, 1450 Ala Moana, Ala Moana* ☎ *808/951–3420* ⨑ *Reservations essential* ⊟ *AE, D, DC, MC, V.*

8

¢–$ ✕ **Side Street Inn.** Famous as the place where celebrity chefs gather after
AMERICAN hours, local boy Colin Nishida's pub is on an obscure side street near Ala Moana Shopping Center. It is worth searching for, despite the some-times-surly staff, because Nishida makes what might be the best darned pork chops and fried rice in the world. Local-style bar food comes in huge, share-plate portions. This is a place to dress any way you like, nosh all night, watch sports on TV, and sing karaoke until they boot you out. Pūpū (in portions large enough for a dinner) are served from 4 PM to 12:30 AM daily. ⊠ *1225 Hopaka St., Ala Moana* ☎ *808/591–0253* ⊟ *AE, D, MC, V* ⊗ *No lunch.*

$–$$ ✕ **Sorabol.** The largest Korean restaurant in the city, this 24-hour eatery,
KOREAN with its impossibly tiny parking lot and maze of booths and private rooms, offers a vast menu encompassing the entirety of day-to-day Korean cuisine, plus sushi. English menu translations are cryptic at best. Still, it's great for wee-hour "grinds" (local slang for food): *bi bim bap* (veggies, meats, and eggs on steamed rice), *kal bi* and *bulgogi* (barbe-cued meats), and meat or fish *jun* (thin fillets fried in batter). ⊠ *805 Ke'eaumoku St., Ala Moana* ☎ *808/947–3113* ⊟ *AE, DC, MC, V.*

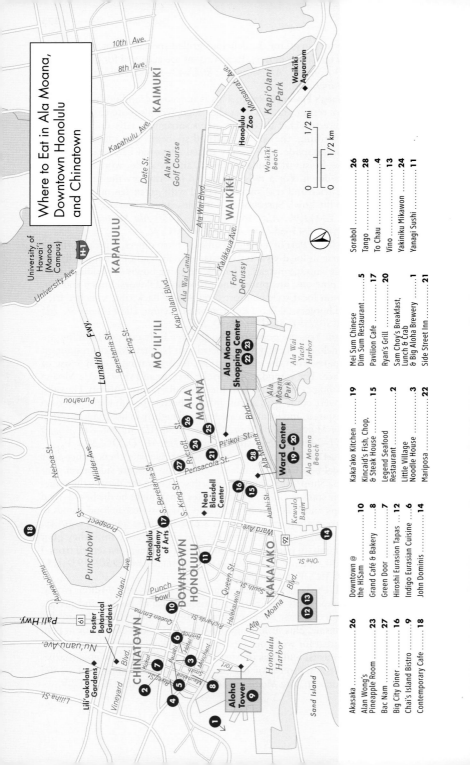

Where to Eat in Ala Moana, Downtown Honolulu and Chinatown

$$–$$$
ECLECTIC

✕ **Tangö.** Long lines of hungry locals are the telltale sign that you've stumbled upon Tangö, the latest dining destination at the swanky Hokua condominiums. Unflappable restaurateur Göran Streng seems to have bypassed the usual growing pains of a new restaurant, instead rewarding his customers' palates with an unfussy menu and polished service. Minimalist yet contemporary decor comes in the form of blond and birch woods, earthy complements to the cloud-like white lampshades. Silver birch branches divide spaces. Göran's dishes pay homage to his Scandinavian background, with touches of Pacific Rim and Asian influences. Dinner standouts include Swedish gravlax with crispy skin, moi (or Pacific Threadfin), a flaky white fish served with fennel coulis, and a burger that stands heads above usual unremarkable bovine renditions. Dinner prices are reasonable (especially by Hawaii standards), but for an additional $6.50, diners can tack on a soup or salad, and a dessert, like *lilikoi* (passion fruit) sorbet. Reservations are only available only for dinner, and don't expect a super-touristy experience—Streng caters mostly to his discriminating city-dwelling clientele. ⊠ *Hokua Building, 1288 Ala Moana Blvd., O'ahu* ☎ *808/593–7288* ⊟ *MC, V.*

$–$$
KOREAN

✕ **Yakiniku Mikawon.** Korean is spoken here, in cooking style and in language, but you can make yourself understood with the help of menu translations and pointing. Mikawon is one of few grill-it-yourself restaurants to use real, charcoal-burning grills, considered the sine qua non of this Korean style of cooking which has been adopted by Japan. Their specialty is *wang galbi*—ribs seasoned in the style of Su Won, Korea, a mellower style than the usual soy sauce–soaked kal bi ribs. ⊠ *1726 Kapi'olani Blvd., Ala Moana* ☎ *808/947–5454* ⊟ *AE, MC, V.*

$–$$
JAPANESE

✕ **Yanagi Sushi.** One of relatively few restaurants to serve its complete menu until 2 AM (Sunday only until 10 PM), Yanagi is a full-service Japanese restaurant offering not only sushi and sashimi around a small bar, but also *teishoku* (combination menus), tempura, stews, and grill-it-yourself shabu-shabu. The fish here can be depended on for freshness and variety. ⊠ *762 Kapi'olani Blvd., Ala Moana* ☎ *808/597–1525* ⊟ *AE, D, DC, MC, V.*

CHINATOWN

¢–$
ECLECTIC

✕ **Grand Café & Bakery.** This well-scrubbed, pleasantly furnished breakfast, brunch, and lunch spot is ideal for taking a break before or after a trek around Chinatown. Its period feel comes from the fact that chef Anthony Vierra's great-grandfather had a restaurant of this name in Chinatown nearly 100 years ago. The delicious and well-presented food ranges from retro diner dishes (chicken potpie) to contemporary creations such as beet-and-goat-cheese salad. ⊠ *31 N. Pauahi, Chinatown* ☎ *808/531–0001* ⊟ *MC, V.*

¢–$
ASIAN

✕ **Green Door.** Closet-size and fronted by a green door and a cluster of welcoming Chinese lanterns, this café has introduced Honolulu to budget- and taste bud–friendly Malaysian and Singaporean foods, redolent of spices and crunchy with fresh vegetables. Favorites include warm roti bread, Malaysian chicken curry, and Singapore basil shrimp. ⊠ *1110 Nu'uanu Ave., Chinatown* ☎ *808/533–0606* ⊟ *No credit cards* ⚑ *Reservations not accepted* ☽ *Closed weekends.*

8

Oahu's Best Takeout

For lunch at the beach, or a movie night in your hotel room, do as Islanders do: get takeout. (And in the Islands, incidentally, the proper term is always takeout or to-go, never take-away.)

The universality of takeout here stems from traditions imported by plantation workers from Asia. The Chinese had their bakeries, the Japanese *okazu-ya*, Asian-style delis. Honolulu is awash in Western-style fast-food joints, Islands-style plate-lunch places, and Asian drive-ins offering Japanese sushi, Korean barbecue, Thai noodles, and Vietnamese spring rolls.

But locals particularly cherish the old-style businesses, now into the third and fourth generation, usually inconveniently located, with no parking and ridiculously quirky hours—and each with a specialty or two that no one else can quite match.

Buy a cheap Styrofoam cooler, pack it with ice to keep the goodies cool, and stop by one of these places. And remember: you'll need cash.

Fukuya Delicatessen. This family operation on the main thoroughfare in charming Mōʻiliʻili, a mile or so mauka out of Waikīkī, offers take-out breakfasts and lunches, Japanese snacks, noodle dishes, even confections. Try *mochi* (sweet rice-flour cakes), *chow fun* (thick, flat noodles flecked with vegetables and barbecue pork), hash patties, garlic chicken, and Asian-style salads. The folks here are particularly patient and helpful to visitors. Open 6 AM to 2 PM. ⊠ *2710 S. King St., Mōʻiliʻili* ☎ *808/946–2073* ⊙ *Closed Mon. and Tues. No dinner* ⊟ *No credit cards.*

Mitsu-Ken. Trust us: Ignore the downscale neighborhood just north of the city and the unpromising, battered exterior. Just line up and order the garlic chicken (either as a plate lunch, with rice and salad, or chicken only). Crispy, profoundly garlicky, and drizzled with some sweetish glaze that sets the whole thing off, Mitsu-Ken chicken will haunt your dreams. But go early; they open at 4 AM, and by 1 PM they're washing down the sidewalks. It's in Kahili, not far from the Bishop Museum. ⊠ *1223 N. School St., Kapālama* ☎ *808/848–5573* ⊟ *No credit cards* ⊙ *Closed Sun. and Mon. No dinner.*

$$–$$$
ECLECTIC
✕ **Indigo Eurasian Cuisine.** Indigo sets the right mood for an evening out on the town: the walls are red brick, the ceilings are high, and from the restaurant's lounge next door comes the sultry sound of late-night jazz. Take a bite of goat-cheese wontons with four-fruit sauce followed by rich Mongolian lamb chops. After dinner, duck into the hip Green Room lounge or Opium Den & Champagne Bar for a nightcap. If you're touring downtown at lunchtime, the Eurasian buffet with a trio of dim sum is a good deal at around $16 per person. ⊠ *1121 Nuʻuanu Ave., Chinatown* ☎ *808/521–2900* ⊟ *AE, D, DC, MC, V.*

¢–$
CHINESE
✕ **Legend Seafood Restaurant.** Do as the locals do: start your visit to Chinatown with breakfast dim sum at Legend. If you want to be able to hear yourself think, get there before 9 AM, especially on weekends. And don't be shy: use your best cab-hailing technique and sign language to make the cart ladies stop at your table and show you their wares.

The pork-filled steamed buns, hearty spare ribs, prawn dumplings, and still-warm custard tarts are excellent pre-shopping fortification. ⊠ *Chinese Cultural Plaza, 100 N. Beretania St., Chinatown* ☎ *808/532–1868* ▤ *AE, D, DC, MC, V.*

¢–$ ✕ **Little Village Noodle House.** Unassuming and budget-friendly, Little Village sets a standard of congenial and attentive service. We have roamed the large, pan-China menu and found a new favorite in everything we've tried: steamed *basa* (white fish), spinach with garlic, Shanghai mochi noodles, honey-walnut shrimp, lamb stew, dried green beans. Two words: go there. ■ TIP→ Two hours of free parking is available next door. ⊠ *1113 Smith St., Chinatown* ☎ *808/545–3008* ▤ *AE, DC, MC, V.*

CHINESE
Fodor'sChoice
★

¢   ✕ **Mei Sum Chinese Dim Sum Restaurant.** In contrast to the sprawling and noisy halls in which dim sum is generally served, Mei Sum is compact and shiny bright. It's open daily, serving small plates from 7:45 AM to 8:45 PM in addition to full-sized special dishes. Be ready to guess and point at the color photos of dim-sum favorites as not much English is spoken, but the delicate buns and tasty bits are exceptionally well prepared and worth the charades. ⊠ *65 N. Pauahi St., Chinatown* ☎ *808/531–3268* ▤ *No credit cards.*

CHINESE

¢   ✕ **To Chau.** If you need proof that To Chau is highly regarded for its authentic *pho* (Vietnamese beef noodle soup), just check the lines that form in front every morning of the week. It's said that the broth is the key, and it won't break the bank for you to find out, as the average check is less than $10. Open only until 12:30 PM. ⊠ *1007 River St., Chinatown* ☎ *808/533–4549* ▤ *No credit cards* ◎ *No dinner.*

VIETNAMESE

DOWNTOWN

8

¢–$ ✕ **Bac Nam.** Tam and Kimmy Huynh's menu is much more extensive than that of most Vietnamese restaurants, ranging far beyond the usual *pho* (beef noodle soup) and *bun* (cold noodle dishes). Coconut-milk curries, an extraordinary crab noodle soup, and other dishes hail from both North and South Vietnam. The atmosphere is welcoming and relaxed, and they'll work with you to make choices. Reservations are not accepted for groups of fewer than six. ⊠ *1117 S. King St., Downtown Honolulu* ☎ *808/597–8201* ▤ *MC, V.*

VIETNAMESE

$$$ ✕ **Chai's Island Bistro.** Chai Chaowasaree's stylish, light-bathed, and orchid-draped lunch and dinner restaurant expresses the sophisticated side of this Thai-born chef. He plays East against West on the plate in signature dishes such as *kataifi* (baked and shredded phyllo), macadamia-crusted prawns, 'ahi *katsu* (tuna steaks dredged with crisp Japanese bread crumbs and quickly deep-fried), crispy duck confetti spring rolls, and seafood risotto. Some of Hawai'i's best-known contemporary Hawaiian musicians play dinner shows here nightly. ⊠ *Aloha Tower Marketplace, 1 Aloha Tower Dr., Downtown Honolulu* ☎ *808/585–0011* ▤ *AE, D, DC, MC, V* ◎ *No lunch Sat.–Mon.*

ECLECTIC

¢–$ ✕ **Downtown @ the HiSam.** Chef-owner Ed Kenny, who presides over the popular restaurant town, has contributed this new restaurant at the Hawai'i State Art Museum to the downtown business-lunch crowd. Contemporary furnishings and art provide just the right frame for the variety of lunch options inspired by Kenny's philosophy of "local first,

AMERICAN

organic whenever possible, with aloha always." You'll find salads with organic local produce, Mediterranean-inspired sandwiches and even filet mignon for those with a bit more time to linger at this casual, contemporary local favorite. ⊠ *Hawai'i State Art Museum, 250 Hotel St., Downtown Honolulu* ☎ *808/586–5900* ⚐ *Reservations essential* ▤ *AE, MC, V* ⊗ *No dinner.*

$$–$$$ ✕ **Hiroshi Eurasion Tapas.** Built around chef Hiroshi Fukui's signature style
ASIAN   of "West & Japan" cuisine, this sleek dinner house focuses on small plates to share (enough for two servings each), with an exceptional choice of hard-to-find wines by the glass selected by Hawaii's first master sommelier. Do not miss Hiroshi's braised veal cheeks (he was doing them before everyone else), the locally raised kampachi fish carpaccio, or the best-ever *misoyaki* butterfish (marinated in a rich miso-soy blend, then grilled). ⊠ *Restaurant Row, 500 Ala Moana Blvd., Downtown Honolulu* ☎ *808/533–4476* ▤ *AE, D, MC, V* ⊗ *No lunch.*

$$$–$$$$ ✕ **John Dominis.** "Legendary" is the word for the Sunday brunch buffet
SEAFOOD   at this long-established restaurant, named for a Hawaiian kingdom chamberlain who became the consort of the last queen, Lili'uokalani. With a network of koi ponds running through the multilevel restaurant, a view of Diamond Head and a favorite surfing area, and over-the-top seafood specials, it's the choice of Oahuans with something to celebrate. An appetizer-and-small-plates menu is available in the bar. ⊠ *43 Ahui St., Downtown Honolulu* ☎ *808/523–0955* ▤ *AE, D, DC, MC, V.*

$ ✕ **Pavilion Cafe.** The cool courtyards and varied galleries of the Hono-
AMERICAN   lulu Academy of Arts are well worth a visit and, afterward, so is Mike Nevin's popular lunch restaurant. The café overflows onto a lānai from which you can ponder Asian statuary and a burbling-water feature while you wait for your salade niçoise or signature Piadina Sandwich (fresh-baked flatbread rounds stuffed with arugula, tomatoes, basil, and cheese). ⊠ *Honolulu Academy of Arts, 900 S. Beretania St., Downtown Honolulu* ☎ *808/532–8734* ▤ *AE, D, DC, MC, V* ⊗ *No dinner. Closed Sun. and Mon.*

$$–$$$ ✕ **Vino.** Small plates of Italian-inspired appetizers are creatively incor-
ITALIAN   porated with local ingredients that often change with the seasons. Add to this a wine list selected by the state's first master sommelier, a relaxed atmosphere, and periodic special tastings, and you have the formula for success at this wine bar. ■ TIP➔ Vino is well situated for stopping off between downtown sightseeing and a return to your Waikīkī hotel. ⊠ *Restaurant Row, 500 Ala Moana Blvd., Downtown Honolulu* ☎ *808/524–8466* ▤ *AE, D, DC, MC, V* ⊗ *Closed Sun.–Tues.*

¢–$ ✕ **Kaka'ako Kitchen.** Russell Siu was the first of the local-boy fine dining
MODERN   chefs to open a place of the sort he enjoys when he's off-duty, serv-
HAWAIIAN   ing high-quality plate lunches (house-made sauce instead of from-a-mix brown gravy, for example). Here you can get your two scoops of either brown or white rice, green salad instead of the usual macaroni salad, grilled fresh fish specials, and vegetarian fare. Breakfast is especially good, with combos like corned-beef hash and eggs, and exceptional baked goods. ⊠ *Ward Centre, 1200 Ala Moana Blvd., Kaka'ako* ☎ *808/596–7488* ⚐ *Reservations not accepted* ▤ *AE, MC, V.*

$$$ ✕**Kincaid's Fish, Chop & Steak House.** Known for Copper River salmon in
AMERICAN season, consistently well-made salads and seafood specials, efficient ser-
vice, and appropriate pricing, Kincaid's is business-lunch central. But,
with its tired, window-fronted room overlooking Kewalo Basin harbor,
it's also a relaxing place for a post-shopping drink or intimate din-
ner. ✉ *Ward Warehouse, 2nd level, 1050 Ala Moana Blvd., Kaka'ako*
☎ *808/591–2005* ▭ *AE, D, DC, MC, V.*

$–$$ ✕**Ryan's Grill.** An all-purpose food and drink emporium, lively and pop-
AMERICAN ular Ryan's has an exceptionally well-stocked bar, with 20 beers on tap,
an outdoor deck, and TVs broadcasting sports. Lunch, dinner, and small
plates are served from 11 AM to 2 AM. The eclectic menu ranges from an
addictive hot crab-and-artichoke dip with focaccia to grilled fresh fish,
pasta, salads, and sophisticated versions of local favorites, such as the
Kobe beef hamburger steak. ✉ *Ward Centre, 1200 Ala Moana Blvd.,
Kaka'ako* ☎ *808/591–9132* ▭ *AE, D, DC, MC, V.*

¢–$ ✕**Contemporary Café.** This tasteful lunch spot in the Contemporary
AMERICAN Museum offers light and healthful food from a short but well-selected
menu of house-made soups, crostini of the day, innovative sandwiches
garnished with fruit, and a hummus plate with fresh pita. In the exclusive Makīkī Heights neighborhood above the city, the restaurant spills
out of the ground floor of the museum onto the lawn. ✉ *The Contemporary Museum, 2411 Makīkī Heights Dr., Makīkī* ☎ *808/523–3362*
▭ *AE, DC, MC, V* ☽ *No dinner.*

EAST HONOLULU AND DIAMOND HEAD

DIAMOND HEAD

8

¢–$ ✕**Diamond Head Market & Grill.** Kelvin Ro's one-stop spot is a plate-lunch
AMERICAN place, a gourmet market, a deli and bakery and espresso bar, too—and
it's a five-minute hop from Waikīkī hotels. A take-out window offers
grilled sandwiches or plates ranging from teriyaki beef to portobello
mushrooms. The market's deli case is stocked with a range of heat-
and-eat entrées from risotto cakes to lamb stew; specials change daily.
There are packaged Japanese bento lunchboxes, giant scones, enticing desserts, and even a small wine selection. ✉ *3158 Monsarrat Ave.,
Diamond Head* ☎ *808/732–0077* ⌕ *Reservations not accepted* ▭ *AE,
D, MC, V.*

¢ ✕**L&L Drive Inn.** On Monsarrat Avenue in Waikīkī and at more than 60
ECLECTIC neighborhood locations on the island of O'ahu, the Drive Inn serves up
an impressive mix of Asian-American and Hawaiian-style plate lunches.
Chicken *katsu* (cutlet), shrimp curry, and seafood mix plates include
two scoops of rice-and-macaroni salad. There are also "mini" versions
of the large-portion plates that include just one scoop of each starch.
It's a quick take-out place to pick up lunch before heading to the nearest
beach or park. ✉ *3045 Monsarrat Ave., Diamond Head* ☎ *808/735–
1388* ⌕ *Reservations not accepted* ▭ *No credit cards.*

$$$–$$$$ ✕**Michel's at the Colony Surf.** With its wide-open windows so close to the
FRENCH water that you feel the soft mist at high tide, this is arguably the most
romantic spot in Waikīkī for a sunset dinner for two. Venerable Michel's
is synonymous with fine dining in the minds of Oahuans who have

been coming here for more than 40 years. The menu is très, très French with both classic choices (escargot, foie gras) and contemporary items (Hardy's Hawaiian Bouillabaisse—named after the chef who created a Hawaiian twist on a French classic). There's a Sunday brunch. ✉ *Colony Surf, 2895 Kalākaua Ave., Waikīkī* ☎ *808/923–6552* ⚠ *Reservations essential* ⊟ *AE, D, DC, MC, V* ⊗ *No lunch.*

¢–$ ✕ **South Shore Grill.** Just a couple of minutes out of Waikīkī proper on
AMERICAN trendy Monsarrat, South Shore Grill is a great place to stoke up before or after sightseeing or beach time. It's inexpensive and portions are ample. The food, a cut above the usual plate lunch or burgers, includes ciabatta-bread sandwiches, entrée salads, and stuffed burritos. ✉ *3114 Monsarrat Ave., Waikīkī* ☎ *808/734–0229* ⚠ *Reservations not accepted* ⊟ *AE, DC, MC, V.*

KĀHALA

¢ ✕ **Antonio's New York Pizzeria.** Thin, crisp, hand-tossed pies sold in 9-inch
PIZZA personal size, cannoli shipped over from New York's Little Italy and filled to order, and even—incongruously—Philly cheesesteaks make this an expat's paradise. Stop on the way back to the hotel from snorkeling at Hanauma Bay. ✉ *4210 Wai'lae Ave., Kāhala* ☎ *808/737–3333* ⚠ *Reservations not accepted* ⊟ *No credit cards.*

¢–$ ✕ **Himalayan Kitchen.** The sign claims to serve authentic Nepali and
ASIAN Indian cuisine, but many dishes incorporate a blend of cultures, including Chinese and Hawaiian. Start with Himalayan spring rolls or garlic naan bread, try the mahi Nepali masala—which is a Nepalese curry with Hawaii mahimahi—and don't miss the mango kulfi, which is like a creamy mango dessert. The extensive menu appeals to a wide range of tastes—some that soothe the palate, others that excite—which may be why this little restaurant tucked away in a business/residential area is packed every night. Perhaps it helps that this place is BYOB with no corkage fee, as well. ✉ *1137 11th Ave., Kaimukī* ☎ *808/735–1122* ⚠ *Reservations essential* ⊟ *MC, V* ⊗ *No lunch.*

$$$–$$$$ ✕ **Hoku's at the Kāhala.** Everything about this room speaks of quality
MODERN and sophistication: the wall of windows with their beach views, the
HAWAIIAN avant-garde cutlery and dinnerware, the solicitous staff, and Pacific Rim cuisine. Though the prices are eye-popping, you get good value in such dishes as the melting salt-crusted rack of lamb for two ($94) and the warm Tristan de Cunha Salad ($27). An excellent choice for special occasions. The dress code is collared shirts, no beachwear. ✉ *The Kāhala Hotel & Resort, 5000 Kāhala Ave., Kāhala* ☎ *808/739–8780* ⊟ *AE, D, MC, V* ⊗ *No lunch Sat.*

¢–$ ✕ **Olive Tree.** Mediterranean food is scarce in the Islands, so Olive Tree
MEDITERRANEAN keeps insanely busy; expect a wait for your hummus, fish souvlaki, Greek egg-and-lemon soup, and other specialties at this small spot behind Kāhala Mall. An added bonus: This place is BYOB. ✉ *4614 Kīlauea Ave., Kāhala* ☎ *808/737–0303* ⚠ *Reservations not accepted* ⊟ *No credit cards* ⊗ *No lunch.*

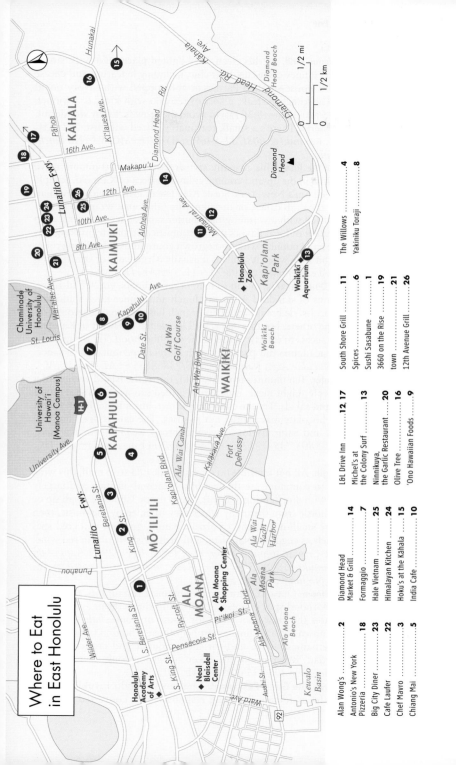

Where to Eat in East Honolulu

KAIMUKĪ

$$ ✕**12th Avenue Grill.** At this clean, well-lighted place on a back street,
MODERN   chef Kevin Hanney dishes up diner chic, including macaroni-and-cheese
HAWAIIAN   glazed with house-smoked Parmesan and topped with savory bread
crumbs. The kimchee steak, a sort of teriyaki with kick, is a winner.
Go early (5 PM) or late (8:30 PM) to avoid the crowds. Enjoy wonderful,
homey desserts. There's a small, reasonably priced wine list. ⊠ *1145C
12th Ave., Kaimukī* ☎ *808/732–9469* 🍴 *BYOB* ▭ *MC, V* ☺ *No lunch.
Closed Sun.*

$$$ ✕**3660 on the Rise.** This casually stylish eatery is a 10-minute drive
ECLECTIC   from Waikīkī in the up-and-coming culinary mecca of Kaimukī. Sample
Chef Russell Siu's New York Steak Alae (steak grilled with Hawaiian
clay salt), the crab cakes, or the signature 'ahi katsu wrapped in nori
and deep-fried with a wasabi-ginger butter sauce. Siu combines a deep
understanding of local flavors with a sophisticated palate, making this
place especially popular with homegrown gourmands. The dining room
can feel a bit snug when it's full (as it usually is); go early or late. ⊠ *3660
Waiʻalae Ave., Kaimukī* ☎ *808/737–1177* ▭ *AE, DC, MC, V.*

¢   ✕**Big City Diner.** At this, one in a chain of retro diners, you'll find gener-
AMERICAN   ous portions of standard American lunch and dinner fare in addition
to great local-style breakfasts. This branch has the same generous portions as the others, but this one is well located in the heart of Kaimukī
with easy access to eclectic shops in the neighborhood. Try the gigantic
roasted macadamia nut pancakes with *haupia* (coconut) crème sauce.
⊠ *3569 Waiʻalae Ave., Kaimukī* ☎ *808/738–8855* ▭ *AE, D, MC, V.*

$–$$ ✕**Cafe Laufer.** Ten minutes from Waikīkī, this is the Island version of a
AMERICAN   Viennese café. Light meals range from grilled sausage with sauerkraut
to soups and salads. Try the classic apple tart, linzer torte, Black Forest
cake, or chocolate macadamia-nut pastries. The café is open until 10
PM Friday and Saturday for a sweet nightcap. ⊠ *3565 Waiʻalae Ave.,
Kaimukī* ☎ *808/735–7717* 🍴 *Reservations not accepted* ▭ *AE, DC,
MC, V.*

¢–$ ✕**Formaggio.** All but invisible on the back side of a strip mall, this wine
ITALIAN   bar seeks to communicate the feel of a catacomb in Italy and largely
succeeds, with dim lighting and soft, warm tones. Choose a small sip or
an entire bottle from the many wines they offer, enjoy the music, then
ponder the small-dish menu of pizzas, panini, and hot and cold specialties such as eggplant Napoléon and melting short ribs in red wine.
⊠ *Market City Shopping Center, rear, lower level, 2919 Kapiʻolani
Blvd., Kaimukī* ☎ *808/739–7719* 🍴 *Reservations not accepted* ▭ *AE,
MC, V* ☺ *No lunch. Closed Sun.*

$–$$ ✕**Hale Vietnam.** One of Oʻahu's first Vietnamese restaurants, this popu-
VIETNAMESE   lar neighborhood spot expresses its friendly character in a name that
incorporates the Hawaiian word for house or home: *hale* (hah-lay).
They're known for a willingness to help those who don't know much
about Vietnamese food, and for their piquant and crunchy green-
papaya salad. Reservations are taken for groups only. ⊠ *1140 12th
Ave., Kaimukī* ☎ *808/735–7581* ▭ *AE, MC, V.*

$$–$$$ ✕**Ninnikuya, the Garlic Restaurant.** Chef-owner Endo Eiyuki picked a
JAPANESE   powerful focus for his charming restaurant in a converted Kaimukī

bungalow: garlic. He calls the menu Euro-Asian but the spicing and approach—except for the prevalence of garlic—are distinctly Japanese. Don't miss the Black Angus steak served on a sizzling stone. ⊠ *3196 Waīalae Ave., Kaimukī* ☎ *808/735–0784* 🍴 *Reservations essential* 🖃 *AE, D, DC, MC, V* ⊗ *No lunch. Closed Sun.*

$$ ✕ **town.** Pretty much everyone agrees that chef-owner Ed Kenney's
PACIFIC RIM Mediterranean-eclectic menu ranges from just fine (pastas and salads) to just fabulous (polenta with egg and asparagus or buttermilk panna cotta). But the over-40 crowd tends to be put off by the minimalist decor, the shrieking-level acoustics, and the heedlessly careless wait-staff, who have a tendency to get lost. The predominantly 20- and 30-something clientele doesn't seem bothered by these circumstances. The restaurant serves an inexpensive Continental breakfast, as well as lunch and dinner. ⊠ *3435 Wai'alae Ave., Kaimukī* ☎ *808/735–5900* 🖃 *MC, V* ⊗ *Closed Sun.*

KAPAHULU

¢–$ ✕ **'Ono Hawaiian Foods.** The adventurous in search of a real local food
HAWAIIAN experience should head to this no-frills hangout. You know it has to be good if residents are waiting in line to get in. Here you can sample *poi* (a paste made from pounded taro root), *lomi lomi* salmon (salmon mas-saged until tender and served with minced onions and tomatoes), laulau, *kālua* pork (roasted in an underground oven), and *haupia* (a light, gelatinlike dessert made from coconut milk). Appropriately enough, the Hawaiian word *'ono* means "delicious." ⊠ *726 Kapahulu Ave., Kapahulu* ☎ *808/737–2275* 🍴 *Reservations not accepted* 🖃 *No credit cards* ⊗ *Closed Sun.*

¢ ✕ **India Cafe.** At this restaurant owned by Indians of Malaysian ori-
INDIAN gin, *dosai*, griddle breads made of rice and lentil flour, are filled vari-ously with savory and sweet ingredients. Like most such restaurants, this one is very vegetarian-friendly, serving up *dals* (lentil stews), cur-ries, and samosas. ⊠ *Kilohana Square, 1016 Kapahulu Ave., Kapahulu* ☎ *808/737–4600* 🖃 *AE, DC, MC, V* ⊗ *No lunch Mon.–Thurs.*

$–$$ ✕ **Yakiniku Toraji.** Trendy Yakiniku Toraji resembles a Japanese country
JAPANESE inn and features, in addition to the usual meats and vegetables grilled at the table, *ishikyaki*, which are meats and vegetables baked on a bed of rice in a stone bowl heated to broiling, forming a delicious crust. This is a particularly visitor-friendly spot, as the menus offer a car-toon to explain yakiniku how-tos. ⊠ *949 Kapahulu Ave., Kapahulu* ☎ *808/732–9996* 🖃 *AE, D, MC, V* ⊗ *No lunch.*

MŌ'ILI'ILI

$$$–$$$$ ✕ **Alan Wong's.** This not-to-be-missed restaurant is like that very rare
PACIFIC RIM shell you stumble upon on a perfect day at the beach—well polished and
Fodor's Choice without a flaw. The "Wong Way," as it's not-so-jokingly called by his
★ staff, includes an ingrained understanding of the aloha spirit, evident in the skilled but unstarched service, and creative and playful interpreta-tions of Island cuisine. Try Da Bag (seafood steamed in an aluminum pouch), Chinatown Roast Duck Nachos, and Poki Pines (rice-studded seafood wonton appetizers). With a view of the Ko'olau Mountains, warm tones of koa wood, and lauhala woven mats, you forget you're

8

OAHU'S BEST SHAVE ICE

Island-style shave ice (never shaved ice—it's a pidgin thing) is said to have been born when neighborhood kids hung around the ice house, waiting to pounce on the shavings from large blocks of ice, carved with ultrasharp Japanese planes that created an exceptionally fine-textured granita.

In the 1920s, according to the historian for syrup manufacturer Malolo Beverages Co., Chinese vendors developed sweet fruit concentrates to pour over the ice.

The evolution continued with mom-and-pop shops adding their own touches, such as hiding a nugget of sweet bean paste, Japanese-style, in the center; placing a small scoop of ice cream at the bottom; adding *li hing* powder (a sweet spice); or using multitoned cones.

There's nothing better on a sticky hot day. Try **Waiola** (⌂ *525 Kapahulu Ave., Kapahulu*) or **Aoki's** (⌂ *66-117 Kamehameha Hwy., Hale'iwa*).

on the third floor of an office building. ⌂ *McCully Court, 1857 S. King St., 3rd fl., Mō'ili'ili* ☎ *808/949–2526* ▭ *AE, MC, V* ⊗ *No lunch.*

$$$$

PACIFIC RIM

Fodor'sChoice

★

✕ **Chef Mavro.** George Mavrothalassitis, who took two hotel restaurants to the top of the ranks before founding this James Beard Award–winning restaurant, admits he's crazy. Crazy because of the care he takes to draw out the truest and most concentrated flavors, to track down the freshest fish, to create one-of-a-kind wine pairings that might strike others as mad. But for this passionate Provençal transplant, there's no other way. The menu changes quarterly, every dish (including dessert) matched with a select wine. We recommend the multicourse tasting menus (beginning at $65 for three courses without wine; up to $250 for 11 courses with wine). Etched-glass windows screen the busy street-corner scene, and all within is mellow and serene with starched white tablecloths, fresh flowers, wood floors, and contemporary Island art. ⌂ *1969 S. King St., Mō'ili'ili* ☎ *808/944–4714* ⚑ *Reservations essential* ▭ *AE, DC, MC, V* ⊗ *No lunch.*

¢–$

THAI

✕ **Chiang Mai.** Long beloved for its Thai classics based on family recipes, such as spicy curries and stir-fries and sticky rice in woven grass baskets, Chiang Mai is just a short cab ride from Waikīkī. Some dishes, like the signature Cornish game hen in lemongrass and spices, show how acculturation can create interesting pairings. The cozy space is decorated with Thai fabrics and artwork. ⌂ *2239 S. King St., Mō'ili'ili* ☎ *808/941–1151* ▭ *AE, D, DC, MC, V* ⊗ *No lunch weekends.*

$

THAI

✕ **Spices.** Created by a trio of well-traveled friends who enjoy the foods of Southeast Asia, Spices is alluringly decorated in spicelike oranges and reds and offers a lunch and dinner menu far from the beaten path, even in a city rich in the cuisine of this region. They claim inspiration but not authenticity and use Island ingredients to everyone's advantage. The menu is vegetarian friendly. ⌂ *2671 S. King St., Mō'ili'ili* ☎ *808/949–2679* ⚑ *Reservations not accepted* ▭ *MC, V* ⊗ *Closed Mon.*

$–$$

JAPANESE

✕ **Sushi Sasabune.** Meals here are unforgettable, though you may find the restaurant's approach exasperating and a little condescending. It's possible to order from the menu, but you're strongly encouraged to order omakase-style (oh-*mah*-ka-*say*, roughly, "trust me"), letting the chef send out his choices for the night. The waiters keep up a steady mantra to instruct patrons in the proper way to eat their delicacies: "Please, no shoyu on this one." "One piece, one bite." But any trace of annoyance vanishes with the first bite of California baby squid stuffed with Louisiana crab, or unctuous *toro* ('ahi belly) smeared with a light soy reduction, washed down with a glass of the smoothest sake you've ever tasted. A caution: the courses come very rapidly—ask the server to slow down the pace a bit. An even bigger caution: the courses, generally two pieces of sushi or six to eight slices of sashimi, add up fast. ✉ *1419 S. King St., Mōʻiliʻili* ☎ *808/947–3800* ⟐ *Reservations essential* ▭ *AE, D, DC, MC, V* ⊙ *Closed Sun. No lunch Sat. and Mon.*

$$–$$$ ✕ **The Willows.** An island dream, this buffet restaurant is made up of
HAWAIIAN pavilions overlooking a network of ponds (once natural streams flowing from mountain to sea). The Island-style comfort food includes the trademark Willows curry along with Hawaiian dishes such as *laulau* (a steamed bundle of ti leaves containing pork, butterfish, and taro tops) and local favorites such as Korean barbecue ribs. ✉ *901 Hausten St., Mōʻiliʻili* ☎ *808/952–9200* ⟐ *Reservations essential* ▭ *AE, D, MC, V.*

GREATER HONOLULU

$–$$ ✕ **La Mariana Restaurant & Sailing Club.** Just past downtown Honolulu,
AMERICAN tucked away in the industrial area of Sand Island, is this friendly South Seas–style restaurant. Over the past 50 years, nonagenarian owner Annette Nahinu has bought up kitsch from other restaurants, so it's tikis to the max here. The food—grilled seafood, steaks—is just okay, but go for the sing-along fun and the feeling that Don the Beachcomber might walk in any minute. ✉ *50 Sand Island Rd., Iwilei* ☎ *808/848–2800* ▭ *AE, D, DC, MC, V.*

¢ ✕ **Nico's at Pier 38.** Lyon-born chef Nico Chaiz opened Nico's because
SEAFOOD he wanted to create a place where he could work the hours he likes and serve people like himself, who love good food at reasonable prices. Where better than a few steps from the city's fish auction? Though its chief clientele is rough-hewn dock workers and fishermen, the café has received universal critical acclaim for its upscale plate lunches of seaweed-crusted tuna steaks, and fish or egg breakfasts. ✉ *1133 N. Nimitz Hwy., Pier 38, Downtown* ☎ *808/540–1377* ⟐ *Reservations not accepted* ▭ *AE, D, MC, V.*

$$–$$$ ✕ **Sam Choy's Breakfast, Lunch & Crab and Big Aloha Brewery.** In this casual,
SEAFOOD family-friendly setting, diners can down crab and lobster—but since these come from elsewhere, we recommend the catch of the day, the *char siu* (Chinese barbecue), baby back ribs, or Sam's special fried *poke* (flash-fried tuna). This eatery's warehouse size sets the tone for its *bambucha* (huge) portions. An on-site microbrewery brews six varieties of Big Aloha beer. Sam Choy's is in Iwilei past Downtown Honolulu on the highway heading to Honolulu International Airport. ✉ *580 N. Nimitz Hwy., Iwilei* ☎ *808/545–7979* ▭ *AE, D, DC, MC, V.*

8

WAIKĪKĪ

There are several notable steak-houses and grills in Waikīkī as well, serving upscale American cuisine. But thanks to the many Japanese nationals who stay here, Waikīkī is blessed with lots of cheap, filling, authentic Japanese food, particularly noodle housess. Plastic representations of food in the window outside are an indicator of authen-

ticity and a help in ordering. It's not uncommon for a server to accompany a guest outside so the selection can be pointed to.

$–$$
ITALIAN
✕ **Arancino di Mare.** Arancino offers fresh seafood, hand-trimmed beef, pastas cooked to order, handmade pizza dough and bread, and home-made desserts, and meats and cheese imported from Italy. Locals as well as tourists like to come here to enjoy dishes that use only fresh, authentic ingredients. Customer favorites include Pescatore and a pizza with shrimp and Maui onions, which is the owner's favorite pizza. ✉ *2552 Kalakaua Ave., Waikīkī* ☎ *808/931–6273* ⚄ *Reservations recommended* ▭ *AE, MC, V.*

$$$–$$$$
ECLECTIC
✕ **Bali by the Sea.** This many-windowed, multilevel room takes delightful advantage of the restaurant's perch above the beach, facing Diamond Head. Chef Francois Bougard creates uncomplicated contemporary cuisine—grilled fish, steaks, and chops accented with East–West fusion flavors. The experienced staff, often called on to serve the VIPs who favor this hotel, extends unruffled and gracious service. ✉ *Hilton Hawaiian Village, 2005 Kālia Rd., Waikīkī* ☎ *808/941–2254* ⚄ *Reservations essential* ▭ *AE, D, DC, MC, V* ☺ *Closed Sun. No lunch.*

$$$–$$$$
STEAKHOUSE
✕ **d.k Steakhouse.** Around the country, the steak house has returned to prominence as chefs rediscover the art of dry-aging beef and of preparing the perfect béarnaise sauce. D.K. Kodama's chic 2nd-floor restaurant characterizes this trend with such presentations as a 22-ounce Paniolo ("cowboy") rib-eye steak, dry-aged 30 days on the bone with house-made rub, grilled local onions, and creamed corn. The restaurant shares space, but not a menu, with Kodama's Sansei Seafood Restaurant & Sushi Bar; sit at the bar perched between the two and you can order from either menu. ✉ *Waikīkī Beach Marriott Resort and Spa, 2552 Kalākaua Ave., Waikīkī* ☎ *808/931–6280* ▭ *AE, D, MC, V* ☺ *No lunch.*

$$–$$$
JAPANESE
✕ **Doraku Sushi.** This contemporary fusion sushi bar was started in Miami by Kevin Aoki, son of famous restaurateur Rocky Aoki. As a result, you'll find some Cuban-influenced fusion dishes on the mostly-traditional sushi menu that are as exceptional as they are unique, like the nigiri with slices of Cuban beef or the spicy lobster roll with cucumber and a spicy cream sauce. Chef Hide Yoshimoto is constantly coming up with new creations to show off the freshness of Hawaii's fish and other island ingredients. This is a hot spot at night for local club goers and scensters, but for meals, it's outstanding. Be sure to try the Emperor Roll,

Izakaya

Japanese pub-restaurants, called *izakaya* (ee-ZAH-ka-ya), are sprouting up all over the Islands like *matsutake* mushrooms in a pine forest. They began as oases for homesick Japanese nationals but were soon discovered by adventurous locals, who appreciated the welcoming atmosphere, sprawling menus, and later dining hours.

Expect to be greeted by a merry, full-staff cry of "Irashaimase!", offered an *oshibori* (hot towel) and a drink, and handed a menu of dozens of small-plate, made-to-order dishes.

You can find *yakitori* (grilled dishes), tempura (deep-fried dishes), *donburi* (rice bowls), sushi and sashimi, *nabemono* and *shabu-shabu* (hot pots), noodles (both soup and fried), *okonomiyaki* (chop suey–type omelets), and a bizarre assortment of *yoshoku* dishes (Western foods prepared in Japanese style, such as hamburgers in soy-accented gravy, fried chicken with a mirin glaze, odd gratins, and even pizza).

Full bars are usual; a wide choice of lager-type beers and good-to-great sakes are universal. Many specialize in single-malt scotch, but wine lists are generally short.

Izakaya menus are often confusing, many staff speak marginal English, and outings can get expensive fast (liquor plus small-plate prices equals eyes bigger than stomach). Prices range from $5 for a basket of edamame (steamed and salted soybeans) to $20 or more for *wafu* (seasoned, grilled steak, sliced for sharing). Start by ordering drinks and edamame or silky-textured braised *kabocha* pumpkin. This will keep the waiter happy. Then give yourself a quarter of an hour to examine the menu, ogle other people's plates, and seek recommendations. Start with one dish per person and one for the table; you can always call for more.

Imanas Tei. Go early to this cozy, out-of-the-way restaurant for its tasteful, simple decor and equally tasteful and simply perfect sushi, sashimi, *nabe* (hot pots prepared at the table), and grilled dishes; reservations are taken from 5 to 7 PM; after that, there's always a line. ⊠ *2626 S. King St., Mōʻiliʻili* ☎ *808/941–2626 or 808/934–2727* ▤ *AE, DC, MC, V* ⟳ *$8–$25.*

Izakaya Nonbei. Teruaki Mori designed this pub to put you in mind of a northern inn in winter in his native Japan; dishes not to miss— *karei kara-age* (delicate deep-fried flounder) and *dobinmushi* (mushroom consommé presented in a teapot). ⊠ *3108 Olu St., Kapahulu* ☎ *808/734– 5573* ▤ *AE, D, DC, MC, V* ⟳ *$7–$20.*

Tokkuri-Tei. This is a favorite of locals for the playful atmosphere that belies the excellence of the food created by chef Hideaki "Santa" Miyoshi, famous for his quirky menu names (Nick Jagger, Spider Poke); just say "Moriwase, kudasai" ("chef's choice, please"), and he'll order for you. ⊠ *611 Kapahulu Ave., Kapahulu* ☎ *808/739–2800* ▤ *AE, D, DC, MC, V* ⟳ *$13–$25.*

Also worth a visit:

Mr. Oji-san (⊠ *1018 Kapahulu Ave., Kapahulu* ☎ *808/735–4455*) for family-style izakaya specialties.

Kaiwa (⊠ *Waikiki Beachwalk, 2nd Floor, 226 Lewers St., Waikīkī* ☎ *808/924–1555* for Osaka-style omelets.

8

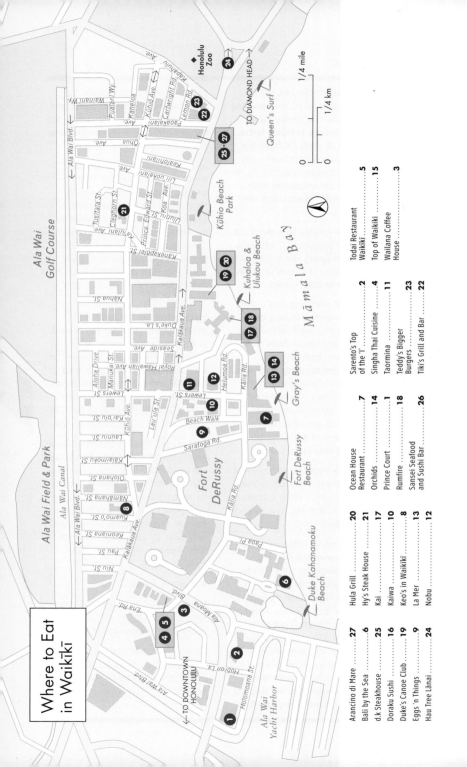

Where to Eat in Waikīkī

Arancino di Mare **27**
Bali by the Sea **6**
d.k Steakhouse **25**
Doraku Sushi **16**
Duke's Canoe Club **19**
Eggs 'n Things **9**
Hau Tree Lānai **24**

Hula Grill **20**
Hy's Steak House **21**
Kai **17**
Kaiwa **10**
Keo's in Waikīkī **8**
La Mer **13**
Nobu **12**

Ocean House
Restaurant **20**
Orchids **14**
Prince Court **1**
Rumfire **18**
Sansei Seafood
and Sushi Bar **26**

Sarento's Top
of the 'I' **2**
Singha Thai Cuisine **4**
Taormina **11**
Teddy's Bigger
Burgers **23**
Tiki's Grill and Bar **22**

Todai Restaurant
Waikīkī **5**
Top of Waikiki **15**
Wailana Coffee
House **3**

which Hide created specifically for Kevin, and the New Style Doraku Roll, which is like a California roll topped with tuna, radish, shiso, and a special sauce. ⊠ *Royal Hawaiian Center, 2233 Kalākaua Ave., Waikīkī* 🖀 *808/922–2268* ⚓ *Reservations essential* ▤ *AE, DC, MC, V.*

\$\$–\$\$\$
AMERICAN
✕ **Duke's Canoe Club.** Named for the father of modern surfing, and outfitted with much Duke Kahanamoku memorabilia, Duke's is both an open-air bar and a very popular steak-and-seafood grill. It's known for its Big Island pork ribs, *huli-huli* (rotisserie) chicken, and grilled catch of the day, as well as for a simple and economical Sunday brunch. A drawback is that it's often loud and crowded, and the live contemporary Hawaiian music can stymie conversation. ⊠ *Outrigger Waikīkī on the Beach, 2335 Kalākaua Ave., Waikīkī* 🖀 *808/922–2268* ⚓ *Reservations essential* ▤ *AE, DC, MC, V.*

¢–\$
AMERICAN
✕ **Eggs 'n Things.** This perennially popular breakfast spot has moved from its original location in the Hawaiian Monarch Hotel to a side street on Waikīkī's west end. The second floor perch gives diners the option of balcony seating so they can watch the world go by as they eat. The food isn't fancy, but it is good, solid food that will satisfy your grumbling stomach morning or night, as they are now open for breakfast, lunch, and dinner. ⊠ *343 Saratoga Rd. , Waikīkī* 🖀 *808/923–3447* ▤ *MC, V* ⊗ *6 AM–2 PM and 5–10 PM.*

\$\$\$–\$\$\$\$
ECLECTIC
✕ **Hau Tree Lānai.** The vinelike hau tree is ideal for sitting under, and it's said that the one that spreads itself over this beachside courtyard is the very one that shaded Robert Louis Stevenson as he mused and wrote about Hawai'i. In any case, diners are still enjoying the shade, though the view has changed—the gay-friendly beach over the low wall is paved with hunky sunbathers. The food is unremarkable island casual, but we like the place for late-afternoon or early-evening drinks, *pūpū*, and people-watching. ⊠ *New Otani Kaimana Beach Hotel, 2863 Kalākaua Ave., Waikīkī* 🖀 *808/921–7066* ⚓ *Reservations essential* ▤ *AE, D, DC, MC, V.*

\$\$–\$\$\$
AMERICAN
✕ **Hula Grill.** The placid younger sister of boisterous Duke's, downstairs, this restaurant and bar resembles a plantation-period summer home: open to the air, outfitted with kitschy decor, stone-flagged floors, warm wood, and floral prints. The food is carefully prepared and familiar— standard breakfast items, steaks and grilled seafood at dinner—but with local and Asian touches that add interest. There's a fabulous Diamond Head view. ⊠ *Outrigger Waikīkī on the Beach, 2335 Kalākaua Ave., Waikīkī* 🖀 *808/923–4852* ▤ *AE, D, DC, MC, V* ⊗ *No lunch.*

\$\$\$–\$\$\$\$
STEAKHOUSE
✕ **Hy's Steak House.** If the Rat Pack reconvened for big steaks and a bigger red, they'd feel right at home at Hy's, which has changed little in the last 30 years. The formula: prime-grade beef, old-style service, a men's-club atmosphere (but ladies very welcome), and a wine list recognized for excellence by *Wine Spectator.* Specialties include Beef Wellington, Caesar salad, and those tableside flambéed desserts rarely seen these days. ⊠ *Waikīkī Park Heights Hotel, 2440 Kūhiō Ave., Waikīkī* 🖀 *808/922– 5555* ⚓ *Reservations essential* ▤ *AE, DC, MC, V* ⊗ *No lunch.*

\$\$\$–\$\$\$\$
PACIFIC RIM
✕ **Kai Market.** This is the first "farm-to-table" buffet on Oahu (or the other Islands), and it's quite a surprise to find it in a hotel like the Sheraton Waikiki. Local chef Darren Demaya helped to bring this

8

concept to life, creating recipes that use as much local produce as possible. The dinner menu changes daily, and you get the added bonus of an open-air luau-style show. Be sure to take a look at their "living wall" of herbs, which are plucked as needed during the preparation of very small buffet servings such as kurobuta pork loin with lehua honey mustard glaze or Chinese salt and pepper head-on Kahuku shrimp. Kai has created a following with locals as well as tourists for the high quality of food and friendliness of the service. ⊠ *Sheraton Waikiki Hotel, 2255 Kalakaua Ave., Waikīkī* ☎ *808/922–4422* ⌕ *Reservations recommended* ⊟ *AE, DC, MC, V* ⊙ *No lunch.*

¢–$

JAPANESE

✕ **Kaiwa.** This casual little spot introduced Honolulu to *okonomiyaki,* the famous savory pancakes that are a specialty of Osaka, with mix-and-match ingredients scrambled together on a griddle, then drizzled with various piquant sauces. They also specialize in unusual appetizers such as fried lotus root with cheese and a cracker-like crust or a wasabi-tinged tossed salad with crab and avocado. The combinations may at times strike you as bizarre, but you can always order simpler grilled dishes such as sliced pork wrapped around enoki mushrooms, slices of Wagyu beef, or eggplant with shaved bonito (dried mackerel). ⊠ *Waikiki Beachwalk226 Lewers St., Waikiki* ☎ *808/924–1555* ⊟ *AE, D, DC, MC, V.*

$–$$

THAI

✕ **Keo's in Waikīkī.** Many Islanders—and many Hollywood stars—got their first taste of pad thai noodles, lemongrass, and coconut-milk curry at one of Keo Sananikone's restaurants. This one, perched right at the entrance to Waikīkī, characterizes his formula: a bright, clean space awash in flowers, with intriguing menu titles and reasonable prices. Evil Jungle Prince, a stir-fry redolent of Thai basil, flecked with chilies and rich with coconut milk, is a classic; also try the apple bananas (smaller, sweeter variety of banana) in coconut milk. ⊠ *2028 Kūhiō Ave., Waikīkī* ☎ *808/951–9355* ⊟ *AE, D, DC, MC, V.*

$$$$

FRENCH

✕ **La Mer.** Like the hotel in which it's housed (Halekūlani, or "House Befitting Heaven"), La Mer is pretty much heavenly: a softly lighted, low-ceiling room with windows open to the breeze, a perfectly framed vista of Diamond Head, and the faint sound of music wafting up from a courtyard below. The food captures the rich and sunny flavors of the south of France in one tiny, exquisite course after another. We recommend the degustation menu. Place yourself in the sommelier's hands for wine choices from the hotel's exceptional cellar. ■ TIP→ Long sleeves or a jacket is required for men. ⊠ *Halekūlani, 2199 Kālia Rd., Waikīkī* ☎ *808/923–2311* ⌕ *Reservations essential* ⊟ *AE, DC, MC, V* ⊙ *No lunch.*

$$$–$$$$

JAPANESE

✕ **Nobu.** Famed chef Nobu Matsuhisa is the master of innovative Japanese cuisine, and his Hawaiian outpost is definitely a Waikīkī hot spot. Fish is the obvious centerpiece, with entrées such as Tasmanian ocean trout with crispy spinach and *yuzu* (citrus) soy, seafood *harumaki* (spring roll) with caviar and Maui onion salsa, and even Nobu's version of fish-and-chips. Cold dishes include tuna tataki with ponzu, yellowtail sashimi with jalapeño, and whitefish sashimi with dried miso. The warm decor and sexy lighting means there isn't a bad seat in the house.

✉ *Waikiki Parc Hotel, 2233 Helumoa Rd., Waikīkī* ☎ *808/237–6999* ▭ *AE, MC, V.*

$$–$$$
SEAFOOD
✕ **Ocean House Restaurant.** Guests are greeted on the front porch at this re-creation of a 1900s plantation home. Tables and booths are spaced for views. The menu puts forth the bounty of the Pacific with such dishes as crusted opah, coconut lobster skewers, and seared peppered scallops. For beef lovers, there's the slow-roasted prime rib. If you're an early riser, you can also enjoy their daily breakfast or Sunday brunch offerings. ✉ *Outrigger Reef on the Beach, 2169 Kālia Rd., Waikīkī* ☎ *808/923–2277* ▭ *AE, D, DC, MC, V* ☉ *No lunch.*

$$$–$$$$
SEAFOOD
✕ **Orchids.** Perched along the seawall at historic Gray's Beach, Orchids is beloved by power-breakfasters, ladies who lunch, and family groups celebrating at the elaborate Sunday brunch. La Mer, upstairs, is better known for the evening, but we have found dinner at Orchids equally enjoyable. The louvered walls are open to the breezes, the orchids add splashes of color, the seafood is perfectly prepared, and the wine list is intriguing. Plus, it is more casual and a bit less expensive than La Mer. Whatever your meal, finish with the hotel's signature coconut layer cake. ✉ *Halekūlani, 2199 Kālia Rd., Waikīkī* ☎ *808/923–2311* ⌕ *Reservations essential* ▭ *AE, D, MC, V.*

$$$$
ECLECTIC
✕ **Prince Court.** This restaurant overlooking Ala Wai Yacht Harbor is a multifaceted success, with exceptional high-end lunches and dinners, daily breakfast buffets, weekly dinner seafood buffets, and sold-out weekend brunches. With a truly global mix of offerings, the overall style is Eurasian. Their ever-changing prix-fixe menu includes offerings such as Australian rack of lamb, Kahuku prawns, and medallions of New York Angus. ✉ *Hawai'i Prince Hotel, 100 Holomoana St., Waikīkī* ☎ *808/944–4494* ⌕ *Reservations essential* ▭ *AE, D, DC, MC, V.*

$–$$
PACIFIC RIM
✕ **Rumfire Waikiki.** This beachfront restaurant offers indoor and outdoor dining for the full oceanside dining experience; even while sitting indoors, you can view the horizon through floor-to-ceiling windows. You can get a full meal here, but it's the ideal setting for noshing on appetizers while you enjoy an exotic tropical drink: try the kalua pig quesadillas and the ahi poke (raw fish) chips, which come with freshly-made condiments, including guacamole, salsa, and a special hot sauce. At night, Rumfire is a popular club/lounge for young locals. ✉ *Sheraton Waikiki Hotel, 2255 Kalakaua Ave., Waikīkī* ☎ *808/922–4422* ⌕ *Reservations recommended* ▭ *AE, DC, MC, V.*

$$$
JAPANESE
✕ **Sansei Seafood Restaurant & Sushi Bar.** D. K. Kodama's Japanese-based Pacific Rim cuisine is an experience not to be missed, from early-bird dinners (from 5:30 PM) to late-night appetizers and sushi (until 1 AM Friday and Saturday, with karaoke). The specialty sushi here—mango-crab roll, foie gras nigiri with eel sauce, and more—leaves California rolls far behind. We fantasize about the signature calamari salad with spicy Korean sauce and crisp-tender squid. Cleverly named and beautifully prepared dishes come in big and small plates or in a multicourse tasting menu. Finish with tempura-fried ice cream or Mama Kodama's brownies. ✉ *Waikīkī Beach Marriott Resort and Spa, 2552 Kalākaua Ave., Waikīkī* ☎ *808/931–6286* ▭ *AE, DC, MC, V* ☉ *No lunch.*

8

$$-$$$ ╳ **Sarento's Top of the "I".** Among restaurants with the best views in
ITALIAN   Honolulu, 30th-floor Sarento's, looking toward both the Ko'olau
Mountains and the South Shore, is an especially favored date-night
venue. Regional Italian cuisine is the specialty, and the wild tiger
shrimp–stuffed potato ravioli and osso buco are local favorites. The
wine cellar contains some gems, and there may not be more attentive
service staff in the city. ⊠ *Renaissance 'Ilikai Waikīkī Hotel, 1777
Ala Moana, top fl., Waikīkī* ☎ *808/955–5559* ⌖ *Reservations essential*
═ *AE, D, DC, MC, V* ⊘ *No lunch.*

$$ ╳ **Singha Thai Cuisine.** Chai and Joy Chaowasaree's devotion to their
THAI   native Thailand is evident in the gilt model of the Thai royal palace
that graces the entryway of this restaurant just below street level on a
busy Waikīkī corner. This is also the only Thai restaurant in the city
to showcase Thai dance each evening. We especially like Singha Thai's
way with seafood—Siamese Fighting Fish, a whole fish sizzling in garlic-
chili oil, or fish in Thai chili, ginger, and black-bean sauce—and the
contemporary additions to the menu, such as blackened 'ahi summer
rolls. ⊠ *1910 Ala Moana Blvd., Waikīkī* ☎ *808/941–2898* ═ *AE, D,
DC, MC, V* ⊘ *No lunch.*

$$$ ╳ **Taormina.** Dishes inspired by the romantic Mediterranean resort
ITALIAN   town of Taormina are served at this elegant restaurant on the Waikīkī
Beach Walk. In addition to Sicilian-inspired *primi piatti* (first-course
dishes, usually pasta) such as *uni* (sea urchin) pasta and a light cream
risotto with grilled scallops and prawns, the menu features a variety of
local fish done with Italian flair. The artfully presented antipasti *misti*
(mixed appetizers) should not be missed. Try the cannoli with a touch
of coconut in the filling to round out your meal. The wine list is extensive. ⊠ *Waikīkī Beach Walk, 227 Lewers St., Waikīkī* ☎ *808/926–5050*
⌖ *Reservations essential* ═ *AE, MC, V.*

¢–$ ╳ **Teddy's Bigger Burgers.** Though the focus at Teddy's is on the burg-
AMERICAN   ers, fries, and shakes, their success has inspired them to add a chicken,
veggie, and fish sandwich to their menu. But, for those who like a classic, the burgers are beefy, the fries crisply perfect, the shakes rich and
sweet. The original location in Waikīkī combines burger shack simplic-
ity with surf-boy cool—there's even a place to store your surfboard
while you have your burger. This popular location has given birth to
two others in Kailua and Hawai'i Kai. ⊠ *134 Kapahulu Ave., Waikīkī*
☎ *808/926–3444* ═ *MC, V.*

$–$$ ╳ **Tiki's Grill and Bar.** On the second floor of a busy hotel, Tiki's is the kind
AMERICAN   of place people come to Waikīkī for: a retro–South Pacific spot designed
for fun. It has a back-of-the-bar faux volcano, an open-air lounge with
live local-style music, indoor-outdoor dining, and a view of the beach
across the street. The menu of contemporary island cuisine includes
Asian-influenced seven-spice salmon, sophisticated interpretations of
plate-lunch standards, and exceptional desserts. There's a late-night
bar menu. ⊠ *Aston Waikīkī Beach Hotel, 2570 Kalākaua Ave., Waikīkī*
☎ *808/923–8454* ═ *AE, D, DC, MC, V.*

$$-$$$ ╳ **Todai Restaurant Waikīkī.** Bountiful buffets and menus that feature sea-
SEAFOOD   food are popular with Islanders, so this Japan-based restaurant is a local
favorite. It's popular with budget-conscious travelers as well, for the

wide range of hot dishes, sushi, and the 160-foot seafood spread. The emphasis here is more on quantity than quality. ✉ *1910 Ala Moana Blvd., Waikīkī* ☎ *808/947–1000* ⬧ *Reservations essential* ⊟ *AE, D, DC, MC, V.*

WORD OF MOUTH

"For the one nice dinner—Alan Wong's Pineapple Room if you can swing it."   —DebitNM

$$$
CONTINENTAL

✕ **Top of Waikiki.** The three-tiered Top of Waikiki has amazing 360-degree views of Honolulu, but unlike many revolving restaurants it also has an award-winning menu that features delicious new American cuisine with island flavor. The lobster-crab cake salad or the coconut shrimp are great ways to start the evening. For dinner, although it sounds basic, their seafood pasta and garlic rib eye are the most popular entrées because they're just that good. To get a sunset view, grab dinner from 5 to 6 PM and enjoy the added early-bird $16.95 dishes. ✉ *Waikiki Business Plaza, 2270 Kalakaua Ave. Waikīkī* ☎ *808/923–3877* ⬧ *Reservations recommended* ⊟ *AE, DC, MC, V.*

¢–$
AMERICAN

✕ **Wailana Coffee House.** Budget-conscious snowbirds, night owls with a yen for karaoke, all-day drinkers of both coffee and the stronger stuff, hearty eaters, and lovers of local-style plate lunches contentedly rub shoulders at this venerable diner and cocktail lounge at the edge of Waikīkī. Most checks are under $9; there's a $1.95 children's menu. It's open 24 hours a day, 7 days a week, 365 days a year, but the place fills up and a line forms around the corner at breakfast time, so arrive early or late. ✉ *Wailana Condominium, ground floor, 1860 Ala Moana Blvd., corner of 'Ena Rd. and Ala Moana, Waikīkī* ☎ *808/955–1674* ⬧ *Reservations not accepted* ⊟ *AE, MC, V.*

8

ELSEWHERE ON O'AHU

Outside of Honolulu and Waikiki, there are fewer dining options, of course, but restaurants also tend to be filled with locals, more casual, and less expensive. Cuisine is mainly American—great if you're traveling with kids—but there are a handful of Italian and Asian places worth trying as well.

SOUTHEAST O'AHU

HAWAI'I KAI

$$–$$$
PACIFIC RIM

✕ **BluWater Grill.** Time your drive along Honolulu's South Shore to allow for a stop at this relaxed restaurant on Kuapa Pond. The savvy chef-manager team left a popular chain restaurant to found this eatery, serving wok-seared moi fish, mango and guava ribs, and lots of other interesting small dishes for $5 to $10. They're open until 11 PM Monday through Thursday and on Sunday, and until midnight Friday and Saturday. ✉ *Hawai'i Kai Shopping Center, 377 Keahole St., Hawai'i Kai* ☎ *808/395–6224* ⊟ *AE, DC, MC, V.*

$$–$$$
PACIFIC RIM

✕ **Roy's.** Roy Yamaguchi's flagship restaurant across the highway from Maunalua Bay attracts food-savvy visitors like the North Shore attracts surfers. But it also has a strong following among well-heeled Oahuans from surrounding neighborhoods, who consider the place an extension

YAKINIKU

A Korean technique with a Japanese name, *yakiniku* restaurants—where diners grill their own marinated meats and sliced vegetables on braziers set in the middle of the table— is one of the few happy results of the Japanese occupation of Korea.

A yakiniku restaurant may be a chic contemporary pub (Yakiniku Toraji), but it can also be a homey family buffet. A few, like Yakiniku Mikawon, employ well-vented charcoal braziers to infuse the ingredients with rich,

smoky flavor. Most, however, use gas grills.

Budget yakiniku places charge a flat rate; you serve yourself from a raw buffet. In upscale yakiniku, you order from a menu.

■TIP➔ Appoint one griller to prevent mid-table traffic jams. Order or fill your plate in stages to avoid waste and a big bill.

of their homes and Roy's team their personal chefs. Part of the appeal is the open kitchen in the main dining area, which adds to the energy of the place. For this reason, Roy's is always busy and sometimes overly noisy. The first-floor dining area is quieter, but reservations aren't taken in this section. It's best to visit later in the evening if you're sensitive to pressure to turn the table. The wide-ranging and ever-interesting Hawaiian-fusion menu changes daily, except for signature dishes like Roy's Original blackened 'ahi with soy-mustard-butter sauce, and a legendary meat loaf. There's an exceptional wine list. ⊠ *Hawai'i Kai Corporate Plaza, 6600 Kalaniana'ole Hwy., Hawai'i Kai* ☎ *808/396–7697* ⌲ *Reservations essential* ▭ *AE, D, DC, MC, V.*

WINDWARD O'AHU

KAILUA

$–$$ ╳ **Baci Bistro.** Baci Bistro is a favorite for intimate dinners and good-
ITALIAN value lunches. Join Windward locals for generous portions of Italian classics such as pappardelle del campo (wide pasta noodles with veal, chicken, sausage, sun-dried tomatoes, and mushrooms) or pollo piccata (chicken breast in a lemon, white wine, and caper sauce). You won't leave the table hungry. Service is friendly, and dining is available in their intimate dining room or alfresco on their leafy lānai. ⊠ *30 Aulike St., Kailua* ☎ *808/262–7555* ▭ *AE, MC, V* ⊗ *No lunch weekends.*

¢ ╳ **Big City Diner.** This outlet of the popular retro diner chain has outdoor
AMERICAN lānai seating, a bar, and is across the street from a small bird sanctuary. It's a hot spot for breakfast; popular dinner items include grilled steak with onions and mushrooms, baby back ribs, meat loaf, and salads. ⊠ *108 Hekili St., Kailua* ☎ *808/263–8880* ▭ *AE, D, MC, V.*

¢ ╳ **Boots & Kimo's Homestyle Kitchen.** If you're wondering what aloha spirit
AMERICAN is all about, check out this family-owned, local-style restaurant in the industrial backwaters of Kailua where brothers Ricky and Jesse Kiakona treat their guests like family. At breakfast, the signature dish is macadamia-nut pancakes; at lunch, *pulehu* (grilled) ribs. Then again,

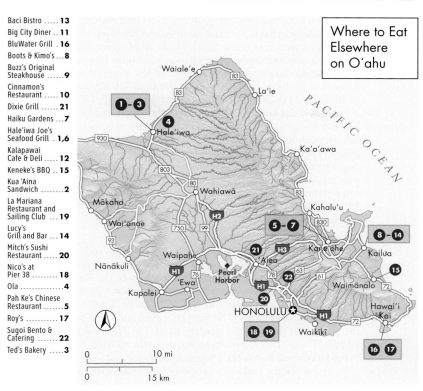

Where to Eat
Elsewhere
on O'ahu

8

the pulehu ribs are pretty popular at breakfast, too. Portions are generous. There is a line outside almost any time of day, so budget some time for the wait. ⊠ *151 Hekili St., Ste. 102., Kailua* ☎ *808/263–7929* ⌦ *Reservations not accepted* ▭ *No credit cards.*

$–$$
AMERICAN
Fodor's Choice
★

✕ **Buzz's Original Steakhouse.** Virtually unchanged since it opened in 1967, this cozy maze of rooms opposite Kailua Beach Park is filled with the enticing aroma of grilling steaks. It doesn't matter if you're a bit sandy (but bare feet are not allowed). Stop at the salad bar, order up a steak, a burger, teriyaki chicken, or the fresh fish special. If you sit at the bar, expect to make friends. ⊠ *413 Kawailoa Rd., Kailua* ☎ *808/261–4661* ▭ *No credit cards.*

¢
AMERICAN

✕ **Cinnamon's Restaurant.** Known for uncommon variations on common breakfast themes (pancakes, eggs Benedict, French toast, home fries, and eggs), this neighborhood favorite is tucked into a hard-to-find Kailua office park; call for directions. Lunch and dinner feature local-style plate lunch and a diner-style menu (meat loaf, baked beans), which are good, but the main attraction is breakfast. Don't miss the guava chiffon pancakes. ⊠ *315 Uluniu St., Kailua* ☎ *808/261–8724* ▭ *D, DC, MC, V* ⊗ *No dinner Sun.–Wed.*

¢–$
ECLECTIC

✕ **Kalapawai Café and Deli.** Rarely do you find a café that serves as a wine bar, breakfast spot, gourmet takeout deli, tapas bar, and restaurant with a wide variety of Mediterranean entrées, but owner Don Dymond of

Kalapawai Café and Deli has established just that with this green-and-white landmark that is a central meeting spot for Windward residents. Come in on your way to the beach for a cup of coffee and bagel, stop back for a gourmet sandwich or salad at lunchtime. Happy-hour tapas plates include hummus and flat bread or figs wrapped in bacon. All dinner entrées have suggested wine pairings. ⊠ *750 Kailua Rd., Kailua* ☎ *808/262–3354* ⌖ *Reservations not accepted* ⊟ *AE, DC, MC, V.*

$$
AMERICAN

✕ **Lucy's Grill and Bar.** This Windward eatery offers outdoor lānai seating and an open-air bar that shakes up a mean martini to go with its eclectic and innovative menu. The indoor seating, though attractive, gets very noisy. Begin with the deep-fried kālua pig (pork roasted in an underground oven) pastry triangles with a mandarin orange–plum dipping sauce. Seafood offerings include daily fish specials with your choice of preparations. For meat lovers, there are Indonesian lamb chops or rib-eye steak. ⊠ *33 Aulike St., Kailua* ☎ *808/230–8188* ⊟ *MC, V* ⊗ *No lunch Sat. and Sun.*

KĀNE'OHE

$$–
AMERICAN

✕ **Hale'iwa Joe's Haiku Gardens.** Like the more famous restaurant on the North Shore, Hale'iwa Joe's serves standard surf-and-turf favorites in a casual and friendly atmosphere, but the view of the Haiku Gardens directly behind the restaurant makes the difference at this Kane'ohe location. Come for an early dinner or fantastic Sunday brunch and enjoy the stunning views. Be sure to leave time for a stroll around the pond and through the garden. ⊠ *44-336 Haiku Rd., Kane'ohe* ☎ *808/247–6671* ⌖ *Reservations not accepted* ⊟ *MC, V.*

¢–$
CHINESE

✕ **Pah Ke's Chinese Restaurant.** Chinese restaurants tend to be interchangeable, and while the ambience here may be standard, this one—named for the local pidgin term for Chinese (literally translated this is Chinese's Chinese Restaurant)—is worth the drive from Honolulu for its focus on healthier cooking techniques and use of local ingredients, its seasonal specials such as cold soups and salads made from locally raised produce, and its exceptional East–West desserts. The menu offers all the usual suspects, some with a distinct Hawaiian flourish, but ask the owner and chef Raymond Siu, a former hotel pastry cook, if he's got anything different and interesting in the kitchen, or call ahead to ask for a special menu. ⊠ *46-018 Kamehameha Hwy., Kāne'ohe* ☎ *808/235–4505* ⊟ *AE, DC, MC, V.*

WAIMĀNALO

¢
FAST FOOD

✕ **Keneke's BBQ.** When you're sightseeing between Hanauma Bay and Makapu'u, the food pickings are slim. But every day, 365 days a year, there's Keneke's in Waimānalo town. It's the home of inexpensive plate lunches, shave ice, and Scriptural graffiti on the walls (Keith "Keneke" Ward, the burly, weight-lifting, second-generation owner of the place, is a born-again Christian). The food is diet-busting, piled high, and mostly pretty good, particularly the Asian-style barbecue (including teriyaki chicken or beef and Korean *kalbi* (barbecue), Filipino *guisantes* (pork and peas in tomato gravy), and adobo (piquant pork stew). If you want a treat, try the shave ice with ice cream. ⊠ *41-855 Kalaniana'ole Hwy., Waimānalo* ☎ *808/259–9800* ⊟ *No credit cards.*

CLOSE UP

Shrimp Snacks

No drive to the North Shore is complete without a shrimp stop. Shrimp stands dot Kamehameha Highway from Kahalu'u to Kahuku. For about $12, you can get a shrimp plate lunch or a snack of chilled shrimp with cocktail sauce, served from a rough hut or converted van (many permanently parked), with picnic-table seating.

The shrimp-shack phenomenon began with a lost lease and a determined restaurateur. In 1994, when Giovanni and Connie Aragona couldn't renew the lease on their Hale'iwa deli, they began hawking their best-selling dish—an Italian-style scampi preparation involving lemon, butter, and lots of garlic—from a truck alongside the road. About the same time, aquaculture was gaining a foothold in nearby Kahuku, with farmers raising sweet, white shrimp and huge, orange-whiskered prawns in shallow freshwater ponds. The ready supply and the success of the first shrimp truck led to many imitators.

Though it's changed hands, that first business lives on as Giovanni's Original Shrimp Truck, parked in Kahuku town. Signature dishes include the garlic shrimp and a spicy shrimp sauté, both worth a stop.

But there's plenty of competition—at least a dozen stands, trucks, or stalls are operating at any given time, with varying menus (and quality).

Don't be fooled that all of the shrimp comes fresh from the ponds; much of it is imported. The only way you can be sure you're buying local farm-raised shrimp is if the shrimp is still kicking. Romy's Kahuku Prawns and Shrimp Hut (Kamehameha Hwy., near Kahuku) is an arm of one of the longest-running aquaculture farms in the area; they sell live shrimp and prawns and farm-raised fish along with excellent plate lunches. The award-winning Mackey's serves some of the juiciest, tastiest plates on the North Shore; if you're lucky, you will be greeted by the gregarious Mackey Chan himself.

8

THE NORTH SHORE

HALE'IWA

$$
AMERICAN
✕ **Hale'iwa Joe's Seafood Grill.** After the long drive to the North Shore, it's a treat to while away the afternoon on the covered open-air lānai at Hale'iwa Joe's, scoring a couple of cute souvenir glasses, watching the boats and surfers in the harbor, and munching crunchy coconut shrimp, a mahi burger, or whatever's the freshest fish special. It's just past the Anahulu Stream Bridge. A Kāne'ohe location overlooks lush Haiku Gardens. ✉ *66-011 Kamehameha Hwy., Hale'iwa* ☎ *808/637–8005* ⌚ *Reservations not accepted* ▭ *AE, DC, MC, V.*

¢
AMERICAN
✕ **Kua 'Aina Sandwich.** A must-stop spot during a drive around the island, this North Shore eatery specializes in large, hand-formed burgers heaped with bacon, cheese, avocado, and pineapple; or try the grilled mahimahi sandwich. The crispy shoestring fries alone are worth the trip. Kua 'Aina also has a south-shore location across from the Ward Centre in Honolulu. ✉ *66-160 Kamehameha Hwy., Hale'iwa* ☎ *808/637–6067* ✉ *1200 Ala Moana Blvd., Ala Moana* ☎ *808/591–9133* ⌚ *Reservations not accepted* ▭ *No credit cards.*

AMERICAN ✕ **Ola at Turtle Bay Resort.** In a pavilion literally on the sand, this casual
Fodor'sChoice but refined restaurant wowed critics from the moment it opened, both
★ with its idyllic location on Kuilima Cove and with chef Fred DeAngelo's reliably wonderful food. Ola means "life, living, healthy," an apt name for a place that combines a commitment to freshness and wholesomeness with a discriminating and innovative palate in such dishes as a vegan risotto made with local mushrooms and orzo pasta, slow-poached salmon with caramelized cane sugar and Okinawan sweet potatoes. It is absolutely worth the drive. ⊠ *57-091 Kamehameha Hwy., Kahuku* ☎ *808/293–0801* ▤ *DC, MC* ⚱ *Reservations essential.*

¢ ✕ **Ted's Bakery.** Across from Sunset Beach and famous for its chocolate *haupia* pie (layered coconut and chocolate puddings topped with whipped cream), Ted's Bakery is also favored by surfers and area residents for quick breakfasts, sandwiches, or plate lunches—to-go or eaten at the handful of umbrella-shaded tables outside. ⊠ *59-024 Kamehameha Hwy., Hale'iwa* ☎ *808/638–8207* ⚱ *Reservations not accepted* ▤ *DC, MC, V.*

CENTRAL AND LEEWARD O'AHU

¢–$ ✕ **Dixie Grill.** Casual and family-friendly, the Dixie Grill, just off the
AMERICAN freeway in Pearl City, brings a taste of the South to the Islands with barbecue (including a variety of spicy sauces to choose from), seafood specialties (creole mahimahi, fried catfish), coleslaw, and hush puppies. ■ TIP→ This place is convenient if you're visiting Pearl Harbor or the swap meet. ⊠ *99-016 Kamehameha Hwy., 'Aiea* ☎ *808/485–2722* ⚱ *Reservations not accepted* ▤ *AE, D, DC, MC, V.*

$$–$$$ ✕ **Mitch's Sushi Restaurant.** This microscopic sushi bar (15 seats) is an
JAPANESE adjunct of a wholesale seafood market operated by gregarious South African expatriate Douglas Mitchell, who oversees the sushi chefs and keeps customers chatting. The fish, air-freighted from around the world, is ultrafresh, well cut, and nicely presented. You can spend as much or as little as you like—$40 for a half-dozen pieces of prime bluefin tuna belly, or just a few dollars for pickled plum sushi. ⊠ *524 Ohohia St., near Honolulu International Airport, Airport area* ☎ *808/837–7774* ⚱ *Reservations essential* ▤ *MC, V.*

¢ ✕ **Sugoi Bento & Catering.** Sugoi was among the first of a new wave of
AMERICAN plate-lunch places to take particular care with quality and to recognize that some plate-lunch eaters are interested in good health. They serve, for example, brown rice and green salad instead of the usual white rice and macaroni loaded with mayonnaise. Garlic chicken and *mochiko* (batter-dipped and fried) chicken, both adapted from traditional Japanese dishes, are specialties. Service is quick and cheerful. Primarily a takeout place, Sugoi is in a strip mall in industrial Kalihi, north of town. ⊠ *City Square Shopping Center, 1286 Kalani St., Kalihi* ☎ *808/841–7984* ⚱ *Reservations not accepted* ▤ *No credit cards* ☯ *No dinner. Closed Sun.*

Where to Stay

WORD OF MOUTH

"The simplest thing would be to stay in Waikīkī. The beach there is beautiful and everything in Waikīkī is within walking distance of the beach. There are hotels in all price ranges."

—aloha

WHERE TO STAY PLANNER

Hotels and Resorts

O'ahu boasts more accommodation choices than any other Hawaiian island, and for many visitors, staying at a top-notch resort or hotel here—such as the Turtle Bay Resort on the North Shore or Halekūlani in Waikīkī—is the ultimate island-style luxury and pampering experience.

Keep in mind that most Waikīkī hotels charge $10 and up per day for parking. Consider renting a car only on the days that you wish to go exploring, or factor the parking costs into your budget.

B&Bs and Inns

There are about a dozen B&Bs on O'ahu, primarily located in Kailua, on the Windward side of the island. Several are located within walking distance of world-famous Kailua Beach and a handful have pools. A few serve simple continental breakfasts with pastries, coffee, and fresh island fruit and juices, while others provide breakfast items in the units for guests to enjoy at their leisure during their stay. In addition to the listings below, check the OVB Web site for additional B&B options.

Condos and Vacation Rentals

Vacation rentals give you the convenience of staying at a home away from home—and you should be able to find the perfect getaway on O'ahu. Properties managed by individual owners can be found on online vacation-rental directories such as CyberRentals and Vacation Rentals By Owner, as well as on the O'ahu Visitors Bureau Web site. There also are several O'ahu-based management companies with vacation rentals. Compare companies, as some offer Internet specials and free nights when booking.

Reservations

After your online research but before you book a room, try calling the hotels directly. Sometimes on-property reservationists can hook you up with the best deals, and they usually have the most accurate information about rooms and hotel amenities. If you use a toll-free number, ask for the location of the calling center you've reached. If it's not in O'ahu, double-check information and rates by calling the hotel's local number.

Prices

The lodgings we list are the cream of the crop in each price category. Assume that hotels have private bath, phone, and TV and that they do not serve meals unless we state otherwise. We always list facilities but not whether you'll be charged an extra fee to use them, so when pricing accommodations, find out what's included.

WHAT IT COSTS					
	¢	$	$$	$$$	$$$$
For two people	under $100	$100–$180	$181–$260	$261–$340	over $340

Hotel prices are for two people in a standard double room in high season. Condo price categories reflect studio and one-bedroom rates.

BEST BETS FOR O'AHU LODGING

Fodor's writers and editors have selected their favorite hotels, resorts, condos, vacation rentals, and B&Bs by price and experience. Fodor's Choice properties represent the "best of the best" across price categories. You can also search by area for excellent places to stay—check out our reviews on the following pages.

Fodor's Choice ★

Halekūlani, p. 240
The Kāhala, p. 235
The Turtle Bay Resort, p. 257

By Price

¢

Backpacker's Vacation Inn and Plantation Village, p. 256
Royal Grove Hotel, p. 252
Schrader's Windward Country Inn, p. 256

$

The Breakers, p. 238
Diamond Head Bed and Breakfast, p. 238
Doubletree Alana Hotel, p. 239
Ke Iki Beach Bungalows, p. 257
Winston's Waikīkī Condos, p. 255

$$

Ala Moana Hotel, p. 234
Aqua Aloha Surf, p. 237

Aqua Palms at Waikīkī, p. 237
Hotel Equus, p. 240
ResortQuest Waikīkī Beach Hotel, p. 250

$$$

Hilton Hawaiian Village, p. 243
Outrigger Reef on the Beach, p. 249
Waikīkī Parc, p. 254

$$$$

Embassy Suites Hotel Waikīkī Beach Walk, p. 239
Halekulani, p. 240
J.W. Marriott 'Ihilani Resort & Spa, p. 259
The Kāhala, p. 235
Marriott's Ko Olina Beach Club, p. 259
Moana Surfrider, p. 246
The Royal Hawaiian, p. 253

By Experience

MOST KID-FRIENDLY

Aqua Aloha Surf, $$–$$$, p. 237

Embassy Suites Hotel Waikīkī Beach Walk, $$$$, p. 239
Hilton Hawaiian Village, $$, p. 243
Marriott's Ko Olina Beach Club, $$$$, p. 259
ResortQuest Waikīkī Beach Hotel, $$$–$$$$, p. 250

BEST FOR ROMANCE

Halekūlani, $$$$, p. 246
J.W. Marriott 'Ihilani Resort & Spa, $$$$, p. 259
The Kāhala, $$$$, p. 235
Moana Surfrider, $$$$, p. 246
The Royal Hawaiian, $$$$, p. 253

BEST HOTEL BAR

Hilton Hawaiian Village, $$, p. 243
J.W. Marriott 'Ihilani Resort & Spa, $$$$, p. 259
Moana Surfrider, $$$$, p. 246

Outrigger Waikīkī on the Beach, $$$$, p. 249
The Royal Hawaiian, $$$$, p. 253

BEST SPA

Halekūlani, $$$$, p. 240
Hilton Hawaiian Village, $$, p. 243
J.W. Marriott 'Ihilani Resort & Spa, $$$$, p. 259
The Kāhala, $$$$, p. 235
Waikīkī Beach Marriott Resort & Spa, $$$–$$$$, p. 254

BEST B&BS & INNS

Diamond Head Bed and Breakfast, $, p. 238
Ingrid's $, p. 256
Ke Iki Beach Bungalows $–$$, p. 257
Schrader's Windward Country Inn, ¢–$, p. 256

BEST BEACH

J.W. Marriott 'Ihilani Resort and Spa, $$$$, p. 259
The Kāhala, $$$$, p. 235
Marriott's Ko Olina Beach Club, $$$$, p. 259
Moana Surfrider, $$$$, p. 246
The Turtle Bay Resort, $$$$, p. 257

9

Updated By
Chad Pata

The 2½-mi stretch of sand known as Waikīkī Beach is a 24-hour playground and the heartbeat of Hawai'i's tourist industry. Waikīkī has a lot to offer—namely, the beach, shopping, restaurants, and nightlife, all within walking distance of your hotel.

Business travelers stay on the western edge, near the Hawai'i Convention Center, Ala Moana, and downtown Honolulu. As you head east, Ala Moana Boulevard turns into Kalākaua Avenue, Waikīkī's main drag. This is hotel row (mid-Waikīkī), with historic boutique hotels, newer high-rises, and megaresorts. Bigger chains like Sheraton, Outrigger, ResortQuest, and Ohana have multiple properties along the strip, which can be confusing. Surrounding the hotels and filling their lower levels is a flurry of shopping centers, restaurants, bars, and clubs. As you get closer to Diamond Head Crater, the strip opens up again, with the Honolulu Zoo and Kapi'olani Park providing green spaces. This end has a handful of smaller hotels and condos for those who like their Waikīkī with a "side of quiet."

Waikīkī is still the resort capital of this island, and the lodging landscape is constantly changing. The Waikīkī Beach Walk opened in 2007 on eight acres within the confines of Beach Walk, Lewers and Saratoga streets, and Kālia Road. It comprises a multitiered entertainment complex, cultural center, hotels, and vacation ownership properties, all accented by lush tropical landscaping. Ko Olina Resort and Marina, about 15 minutes from the airport in West O'ahu, looms large on the horizon—this ongoing development already contains the J. W. Marriott 'Ihilani Resort, Marriott's Ko Olina Beach Club, and some outstanding golf courses, but it is slated, over the coming decade, to see the construction of an extensive planned resort community and marina, an aquarium, dozens of restaurants and shops, more hotels, and yet more vacation-ownership rentals.

Casual Windward and North Shore digs are shorter on amenities but have laid-back charms all their own. O'ahu offers a more limited list of B&Bs than other islands because the state stopped licensing them here in the 1980s; many of those operating here now do so under the radar.

DOWNTOWN HONOLULU

The majority of tourists who come to O'ahu stay in Waikīkī, but choosing accommodations downtown affords you the opportunity to be close to shopping and restaurants at Ala Moana. It also provides easy access to the airport.

$$ **Ala Moana Hotel.** Shoppers might wear out their Manolos here; this
HOTEL   renovated condo-hotel is connected to O'ahu's biggest mall, the Ala Moana Shopping Center, by a pedestrian ramp, and it's a four-block stroll away from the Victoria Ward Centers. Business travelers can walk

one block in the opposite direction to the Hawai'i Convention Center. Fresh off a multi-million -dollar renovation, the lobby is now a soothing entry with a piano bar and modern furnishings. Swimmers, surfers, and beachgoers make the two-minute walk to Ala Moana Beach Park across the street. Rooms are like small, comfortable apartments, with cherrywood furnishings, a soothing blue color scheme, kitchenettes, flat-screen TVs, and balconies with outdoor seating. The recreation deck features a pool with cabanas and a bar, outdoor yoga and Pilates studios, and a fitness center. **Pros:** adjacent to Ala Moana shopping center, ; rooms nicely appointed. **Cons:** beach across busy Ala Moana Boulevard. ⊠ *410 Atkinson Dr., Ala Moana* ☎ *808/955–4811 or 888/367–4811* 🖷 *808/944–6839* ⊕ *www.alamoanahotel.com* ⇲ *1,150 studios, 67 suites* ♿ *In-room: safe, refrigerator. In-hotel: 4 restaurants, room service, bars, pool, gym, laundry facilities, parking (paid), no-smoking rooms* ▤ *AE, DC, MC, V.*

$$$$
RESORT
Fodor's Choice
★

🖫 **The Kāhala.** Hidden away in the wealthy residential neighborhood of Kāhala (on the other side of Diamond Head from Waikīkī), this elegant oceanfront hotel has played host to both presidents and princesses as one of Hawai'i's very first luxury resorts. The Kāhala is flanked by the exclusive Wai'alae Golf Links and the Pacific Ocean—surrounding it in a natural tranquility. Pathways meander out along a walkway with benches tucked into oceanfront nooks for lazy viewing offering an "outer island" experience only 10 minutes from Waikīkī and Honolulu. The expansive oceanfront Chi Fitness Center offers outdoor yoga and Pilates. Fine dining is available at Hoku's, or the poolside bar and grill will serve at your lounge chair on the beach. The reef not far from shore makes the waters here calm enough for young kids. You can also sign up for dolphin interactions in the 26,000-square-foot-lagoon. The rooms, decorated in an understated Island style with mahogany furniture, are spacious (550 square feet), with bathrooms with two vanities, and lānai big enough for a lounge chair. If you're a golf-lover visiting the second week of January, ask for a room overlooking the course for a bird's-eye view of the PGA Sony Open from your lānai. **Pros:** away from hectic Waikīkī, ; beautiful rooms and public spaces, ; heavenly spa. **Cons:** Waikīkī is a drive away. ⊠ *5000 Kāhala Ave., Kāhala* ☎ *808/739–8888 or 800/367–2525* 🖷 *808/739–8800* ⊕ *www. kahalaresort.com* ⇲ *306 rooms, 32 suites* ♿ *In-room: safe, refrigerator, Internet. In-hotel: 5 restaurants, room service, bars, pool, gym, spa, beachfront, bicycles, children's programs (ages 5–12), parking (paid), no-smoking rooms* ▤ *AE, D, DC, MC, V.*

$$$
HOTEL

🖫 **ResortQuest at the Executive Centre Hotel.** Downtown Honolulu's only hotel is an all-suites high-rise in the center of the business district, within walking distance of the historic Capitol District, Honolulu's Chinatown, and a 10-minute drive from Honolulu International Airport. It's also three blocks from Aloha Tower Marketplace and the cruise-ship terminal at Pier 10. Accommodations occupy the top top-10 floors of a 40-story glass tower, and have magnificent views of downtown Honolulu and Honolulu Harbor. Many hotels offer their guests free continental breakfast each morning, but here it's served in the top-floor Executive Club with views so mesmerizing, you might linger over your

9

The Kāhala

morning coffee past sunset. The slew of amenities is a boon to those staying for several days or longer. Each spacious suite has a separate living area, three phones, deep whirlpool tubs, and kitchenette stocked with cold beverages. Some units have washer-dryers. It is also within walking distance to the newly revitalized Chinatown area that's burgeoning with new restaurants, bars, and art galleries. **Pros:** central to downtown businesses, transportation, and sights. **Cons:** no beach within walking distance. ⊠ *1088 Bishop St., Downtown* ☎ *808/539–3000 or 866/774–2924* 🖷 *808/523–1088* ⊕ *www.rqexecutivecentre.com* ⟿ *116 suites* ♿ *In-room: safe, kitchen. In-hotel: restaurant, pool, gym, laundry facilities, parking (paid), no-smoking rooms* ⊟ *AE, DC, MC, V.*

WAIKĪKĪ

Hotels in Waikīkī range from super-luxe resorts to small, beachy places where surfers hang out in the lobby. It's where the heart of the action is on O'ahu. Those traveling with families might want to consider easy access to the Waikīkī Beach Walk, as parking can sometimes be difficult. For those looking to be slightly removed from the scene, choose accommodations on the 'ewa end of Waikīkī.

$$–$$$
HOTEL

🏨 **Aqua Aloha Surf.** This boutique property in the heart of Waikīkī is surfer cool with a lobby and interior spaces reflecting the theme. The cool blue-and-green color scheme, surfing videos on flat-screen TVs behind the check-in desk, and lounge chairs throughout don't leave any doubt about where you are and why this hotel appeals to the young and young at heart. It's a great value: most rooms have lānai and there are many freebies, including Wi-Fi in the lobby, high-speed Internet in rooms, continental breakfast, and newspapers. As with all the Aqua properties, they use dynamic pricing here, meaning the hotel charges according to occupancy, so rates can vary greatly from week to week. Asking for a few different travel times can often net you a great deal of savings with them. **Pros:** fun lobby; great beachy decor and friendly atmosphere. **Cons:** no view; traffic noise; 10-minute walk to beach. ⊠ *444 Kanekapolei St., Waikīkī* ☎ *866/406–2782 or 808/923–0222* ⊕ *www.aquaresorts.com* ⟿ *202 rooms* ♿ *In-room: safe, refrigerator. In-hotel: pool, spa, public Wi-Fi, parking (paid)* ⊟ *AE, DC, MC, V.*

¢–$
RENTAL

🏨 **Aqua Palms at Waikīkī.** Across from the Hilton Hawaiian Village on Ala Moana Boulevard just as it curves toward Waikīkī's Kalākaua Avenue, the 12-story Aqua Palms completed a $15 million transformation into a "condotel" in 2005 and now has studio and luxury one-bedroom suite accommodations. The studios include kitchenettes and the suites have full kitchens; both have tiled entryways, private lānai, and in-room DVD players. One-bedroom penthouse suites are elegant and spacious enough to make you want to move in. ■**TIP→** The minimal cost difference between the studio and penthouse suite is well worth the "splurge." **Pros:** excellent full kitchens in suites; comfortable furnishings; trolley stop directly in front of hotel. **Cons:** closest beach access is through Hilton Hawaiian Village across the street. ⊠ *1850 Ala Moana Blvd., Waikīkī* ☎ *808/947–7256 or 866/406–2782* 🖷 *808/947–7002* ⊕ *www. aquaresorts.com* ⟿ *263 units* ♿ *In-room: safe, kitchen (some), DVD.*

9

In-hotel: Wi-Fi, pool, gym, spa, laundry facilities, parking (paid) ☰ *AE, DC, MC, V.*

$–$$
HOTEL
▣ **Best Western Coconut Plaza.** Overlooking the Ala Wai Canal, this reasonably priced boutique hotel is more residential than a typical resort, with a cobblestone driveway, a lobby with rattan, living room–style furnishings, and a wall of French doors that open up to a gazebo garden and a tiny "two-stroke" swimming pool tucked in a backyard. Accommodations—either hotel rooms or studios with kitchenettes—are compact but functional with tile flooring instead of carpets. Views from your lānai include the canal and its canoers by day and the lights of Honolulu's skyline by night. Complimentary continental breakfast is served in the lobby overlooking the hotel garden. It's a three-block walk to the beach. **Pros:** a small and economical hotel in Waikīkī. **Cons:** the walk through busy Waikīkī gets tiring when you're carrying all of your beach equipment. ✉ *450 Lewers St., Waikīkī,* ☎ *866/406–2782 or 808/923–8828* ⊕ *www.aquaresorts.com* ⌁ *81 rooms* ♿ *In-room: safe, kitchen (some), Internet. In-hotel: pool, laundry facilities, spa, public Wi-Fi, parking (paid), no-smoking rooms* ☰ *AE, D, DC, MC, V.*

$–$$
RENTAL
▣ **The Breakers.** Despite an explosion of high-rise construction all around it, the low-rise Breakers continues to offer a taste of '60s Hawai'i in this small complex a mere half block from Waikīkī Beach. The Breakers' six two-story buildings surround its pool and overlook gardens filled with tropical flowers. Guest rooms have Japanese-style shoji doors that open to the lānai, plus kitchenettes, and bathrooms with showers only. Some have views of the Urasenke Teahouse. The Breakers enjoys enviable proximity to the Waikīkī Beach Walk entertainment, dining, and retail complex. The resort is very popular thanks to its reasonable prices and great location. **Pros:** intimate atmosphere; great location. **Cons:** parking space is limited. ✉ *250 Beach Walk, Waikīkī* ☎ *808/923–3181 or 800/426–0494* 🖷 *808/923–7174* ⊕ *www.breakers-hawaii.com* ⌁ *63 units* ♿ *In-room: kitchen. In-hotel: restaurant, pool, parking (free)* ☰ *AE, DC, MC, V.*

$$$–$$$$
RENTAL
▣ **Castle Waikīkī Shore.** Nestled between Fort DeRussy Beach Park and the Outrigger Reef on the Beach, this is the only condo right on Waikīkī Beach. Units include studios and one- and two-bedroom suites, each with private lānai and panoramic views of the Pacific Ocean. All units have washers and dryers, and many have full kitchens, but some have only kitchenettes, so be sure to inquire when booking. Families love this place for its spaciousness, while others love it for its quiet location on the 'ewa (west) end of Waikīkī. However, through 2008 and into 2009, there will be construction on the new Trump Towers directly across Kālia Road. **Pros:** great security; great views; great management. **Cons:** ongoing construction on Diamond Head side of property. ✉ *2161 Kālia Rd., Waikīkī* ☎ *808/952–4500 or 800/367–2353* 🖷 *808/952–4580* ⊕ *www.castleresorts.com* ⌁ *168 units* ♿ *In-room: safe, kitchen (some), Internet. In-hotel: beachfront, parking (paid), no-smoking rooms* ☰ *AE, D, DC, MC, V.*

$
B&B/INN
▣ **Diamond Head Bed and Breakfast.** Many a traveler and resident would love to own a home like this art-filled B&B at the base of Waikīkī's famous Diamond Head crater, one of the city's most exclusive neighborhoods.

All three guest rooms feature koa-wood furnishings and private bath, and they open to a lānai and a big backyard filled with the sounds of birds and rustling trees. The more private ground-floor suite has a separate living room and a bedroom with a queen bed. To experience a bit of Hawaiian history, request the room that includes the extra-large

hand-carved koa bed that once belonged to a Hawaiian princess. The closest beach is the intimate Sans Souci near the Natatorium; it's hard to believe that the hustle and bustle of Waikīkī is a short stroll from the house. Reserve three to four months in advance. **Pros:** secluded and peaceful. **Cons:** small and therefore difficult to book. ⊠ *3240 Noela Dr., Waikīkī* ⊕ *Reservations: Hawai'i's Best Bed and Breakfasts, Box 485, Laupahoehoe 96767* ☎ *808/923–3360; 800/262–9912 reservations* 🖷 *808/962–6360* ⊕ *www.diamondheadbnb.com* ⤹ *2 rooms, 1 suite* ⚿ *In-room: no a/c, no phone. In-hotel: no-smoking rooms* ▭ *No credit cards.*

$$ ⬚ **Doubletree Alana Waikīkī.** The location (a 10-minute walk from the
HOTEL Hawai'i Convention Center), three phones in each room, and the 24-hour business center and gym meet the requirements of the Doubletree's global business clientele, but the smallness of the property, the staff's attention to detail, and the signature Doubletree chocolate-chip cookies upon arrival, resonate with vacationers. All rooms in the 19-story high-rise have lānai, but they overlook the city and busy Ala Moana Boulevard across from Fort DeRussy. To get to the beach, you either cross Fort DeRussy or head through the Hilton Hawaiian Village. **Pros:** professional staff; pleasant public spaces. **Cons:** beach is a bit of a walk. ⊠ *1956 Ala Moana Blvd., Waikīkī* ☎ *808/941–7275 or 800/222–8733* 🖷 *808/949–0996* ⊕ *www.alana-doubletree.com* ⤹ *272 rooms, 45 suites* ⚿ *In-room: safe, Internet. In-hotel: restaurant, room service, bar, pool, gym, parking (paid), no-smoking rooms* ▭ *AE, D, MC, V.*

$$$$ ⬚ **Embassy Suites Hotel–Waikīkī Beach Walk.** In a place where space is at a
RESORT premium, the only all-suites resort in Hawai'i offers families and groups traveling together a bit more room to move about, with two 21-story towers housing one- and two-bedroom suites. All rooms have at least two balconies, some with ocean views; most overlook the 1,965-square-foot Grand Lānai with its pool, bar, restaurant, and meeting areas. The experience begins with a sit-down check-in and a manager's reception with free appetizers and drinks, and ends with an aloha lei ceremony. Rooms are done in Tommy Bahama–meets–Island beach home style (carved-wood tables, pineapple-print upholstery, hula-dancer artwork) and have relaxing earth tones, with amenities like pull-out beds and wet bars with microwaves and mini-refrigerators inviting longer stays. Developed by locally based Outrigger Enterprises, the hotel is steeped in Hawaiiana, with tapa-pattern murals adorning the exterior and cultural programs available for adults and youth. **Pros:** great location

9

next to Waikīkī Beach Walk; great vibe; nice pool deck. **Cons:** no direct beach access. ☒ *201 Beachwalk St., Waikīkī* ☎ *800/362–2779* ⊕ *www. embassysuiteswaikiki.com* ☞ *353 1-bedroom suites, 68 2-bedroom suites* ♿ *In-room: safe, refrigerator, Internet. In-hotel: 4 restaurants, room service, bar, pool, parking (paid)* ⊟ *AE, D, MC, V.*

$–$$
HOTEL

🖥 **The Equus.** This small hotel, now part of the Aqua Resorts chain, fronts busy Ala Moana Boulevard, on the 'ewa end of Waikīkī and is one block from both Ala Moana shopping center and Ala Moana Beach Park. All rooms are equipped with refrigerators, microwaves, and TVs that can access any channel in the world; some have balconies and partial ocean views; daily continental breakfast is included. The front-desk staff is happy to assist with driving directions to the polo-playing fields at Mokuleia and Waimānalo, where guests receive free tickets in season—pack a picnic if you go. **Pros:** casual, fun atmosphere; attentive staff; nicely furnished rooms. **Cons:** on a very busy road you must cross to get to the beach. ☒ *1696 Ala Moana Blvd., Waikīkī* ☎ *808/949–0061 or 800/535–0085* 🖨 *808/949–4906* ⊕ ☞ *69 rooms* ♿ *In-room: safe. In-hotel: pool, laundry facilities, public Wi-Fi, parking (paid)* ⊟ *AE, DC, MC, V.*

$$$$
RESORT
Fodor's Choice
★

🖥 **Halekūlani.** Honeymooners, and others seeking seclusion amid the frenetic activity of the Waikīkī scene, find it here. Halekūlani exemplifies the translation of its name—the "house befitting heaven." From the moment you step inside the lobby, the attention to detail and service wraps you in luxury. It begins with private registration in your guest room and extends to the tiniest of details, such as complimentary tickets to the Honolulu Symphony, Contemporary Art Museum, and Honolulu Academy of Arts. Spacious guest rooms, artfully appointed in marble and wood, have ocean views and extra-large lānai. If you want to honeymoon in the ultimate style, consider the 4,300-square-foot Vera Wang Suite, created by the noted wedding-dress designer herself. It's entirely Vera, right down to the signature soft-lavender color scheme. For a day of divine pampering, check into the Halekūlani Spa. Outside, the resort's freshwater pool has an orchid design created from more than 1½ million glass mosaic tiles. Gray's Beach, which fronts the hotel just beyond the pool, is small and has been known to disappear at high tide. **Pros:** heavenly interior spaces and wonderful dining opportunities in house. **Cons:** might feel a bit formal for Waikīkī. ☒ *2199 Kālia Rd., Waikīkī* ☎ *808/923–2311 or 800/367–2343* 🖨 *808/926–8004* ⊕ *www. halekulani.com* ☞ *412 rooms, 43 suites* ♿ *In-room: safe, DVD, Internet. In-hotel: 3 restaurants, room service, bars, pool, spa, beachfront, laundry service, Internet terminal, public Wi-Fi, parking (paid), no-smoking rooms* ⊟ *AE, DC, MC, V.*

$$$$
RESORT

🖥 **Hawai'i Prince Hotel & Golf Club Waikīkī.** This slim high-rise fronts Ala Wai Yacht Harbor at the 'ewa edge of Waikīkī, close to Honolulu's downtown business districts, the convention center, and Ala Moana's outdoor mall. There's no beach here, but Ala Moana Beach Park is a 10-minute stroll away along the harbor, and the hotel also offers complimentary shuttle service around Waikīkī and its surrounding beaches. It's the only resort in Waikīkī with a golf course—the 27-hole Arnold Palmer–designed course is in 'Ewa Beach, about a 45-minute ride via

Halekūlani

complimentary shuttle from the hotel. The sleek, modern Prince looks to Asia both in its high-style decor and such pampering touches as the traditional *oshiburi* (chilled hand towel) for refreshment upon check-in. Floor-to-ceiling windows overlooking the harbor—ideal for sunsets— make up for the lack of lānai. **Pros:** fantastic views, all very elegant, easy exit from complicated-to-maneuver Waikīkī. **Cons:** can feel a bit stuffy as it caters more to business travelers. ⊠ *100 Holomoana St., Waikīkī* ☎ *808/956–1111 or 866/774–6236* 🖷 *808/946–0811* ⊕ *www. hawaiiprincehotel.com* ⬎ *521 rooms, 57 suites* ⚲ *In-room: safe, refrigerator, Internet. In-hotel: 3 restaurants, room service, bar, golf course, pool, gym, spa, parking (paid), no-smoking rooms* ▭ *AE, DC, MC, V.*

$$
RESORT
⬚ **Hilton Hawaiian Village Beach Resort and Spa.** Location, location, location: this megaresort and convention destination sprawls over 22 acres on Waikīkī's widest stretch of beach, with the green lawns of neighboring Fort DeRussy creating a buffer zone from the high-rise lineup of central Waikīkī. The Hilton makes the most of its prime real estate— surrounding the six hotel towers with lavish gardens, an aquatic playground of pools, a five-acre lagoon, cascading waterfalls, koi ponds, penguins, and pink flamingos. Rainbow Tower, with its landmark 31-story mural, has knockout views of Diamond Head. Rooms in all towers have lānai with ocean, city, or Waikīkī Beach views. More of a city than a village, the HHV has an ABC sundries store, a bookstore, a Louis Vuitton store, and a post office. Culture comes in the form of an outpost of the Bishop Museum and the contemporary Hawaiian art gracing the public spaces. It even has its own pier, docking point for the Atlantis submarine. The sheer volume of options, including free activities (lei-making, 'ukulele lessons, and fireworks), makes the HHV a good choice for families. **Pros:** activities and amenities can keep you busy for weeks; big-resort perks like check-in kiosks (complete with room keys) in the baggage-claim area at the airport. **Cons:** temptation to stay on-site, missing out on the "real" Hawai'i; frequent renovations and construction; size of property can be overwhelming. ⊠ *2005 Kālia Rd., Waikīkī* ☎ *808/949–4321 or 800/221–2424* 🖷 *808/951–5458* ⊕ *www.hiltonhawaiianvillage.com* ⬎ *3,432 rooms, 365 suites, 264 condominiums* ⚲ *In-room: safe, refrigerator. In-hotel: 20 restaurants, room service, bars, pools, gym, spa, beachfront, children's programs (ages 5–12), laundry service, public Wi-Fi, parking (paid), no-smoking rooms* ▭ *AE, D, DC, MC, V.*

$$
HOTEL
⬚ **Hilton Waikīkī Prince Kūhiō.** You enter through a lobby of rich wood detailing, contemporary fabrics, and magnificent tropical floral displays whose colors match the hibiscus reds of the carpeting. Two blocks from Kūhiō Beach, this 37-story high-rise is on the Diamond Head end of Waikīkī. The lobby bar mixes up tropical cocktails and an island-style pūpū menu and has wireless access and a wide-screen plasma TV for sports fans and news junkies, while their restaurant MAC 24-7 offers their version of modern comfort food 24 hours a day, 7 days a week. If marriage is on your mind, note the wedding gazebo anchoring the hotel gardens. Book on an upper floor for an ocean view from your lānai. **Pros:** good value; central location; pleasant, comfortable public spaces. **Cons:** a bit of a distance to the beach; very few rooms with

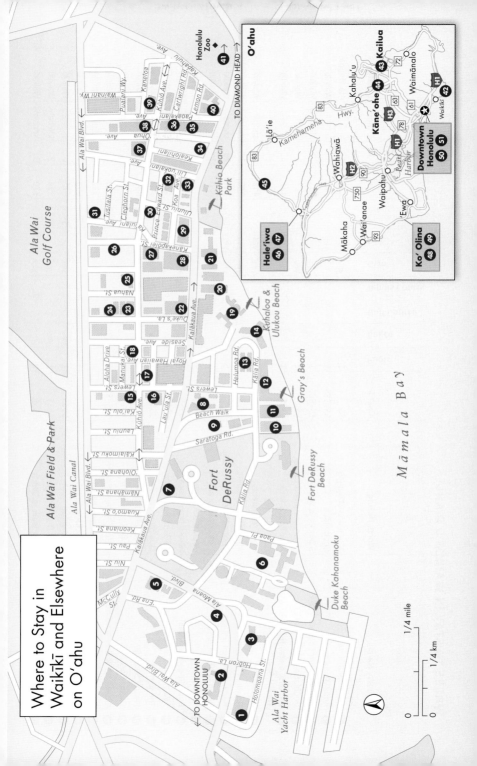

	Property Name	Worth Noting	Cost $	Pools	Beach	Golf Course	Tennis Courts	Gym	Spa	Children's Programs	Rooms	Restaurants	Other	Location
	Hotels and Resorts													
50	Ala Moana Hotel	Ala Moana Shopping	$$	1				yes			1,217	4		Ala Moana
18	Aqua Aloha Surf	Good value	$$-$$$	1					yes		202			Waikīkī
15	Best Western Coconut Plaza	3 blocks to beach	$$-$$$	1							80		kitchens	Waikīkī
5	Doubletree Alana Waikīkī	Near Convention Center	$$	1				yes			317	1		Waikīkī
8	Embassy Suites Hotel—Waikīkī Beach Walk	Near Beach Walk	$$$$	1							421	4		Waikīkī
12	Halekūlani	Great restaurants	$$$$	1	yes			yes	yes		455	3	shops	Waikīkī
1	Hawai'i Prince Hotel	Ala Moana Shopping	$$$$	1		yes		yes	yes		578	3	shops	Waikīkī
6	Hilton Hawaiian Village	Bishop Museum, fireworks	$$	5	yes			yes	yes	5-12	3,787	20	shops	Waikīkī
37	Hilton Waikīkī Prince K.	2 blocks to beach	$$	1				yes			620	1		Waikīkī
2	The Equus	Good value	$-$$	1									laundry	Waikīkī
29	Hyatt Regency Waikīkī	Across from beach	$$$$	1	yes			yes	yes	5-12	1,248	5	shops	Waikīkī
49	J.W. Marriott 'Ihilani	Ko'Olina Resort, spa	$$$$	2	yes	yes	6	yes	yes	5-12	423	3	shops	West O'ahu
42	The Kāhala	Oceanfront view	$$$$	1	yes			yes	yes		343	3	shops	East Honolulu
21	Moana Surfrider	Landmark historic wing	$$$$	1	yes					5-12	839	2	shops	Waikīkī
27	Ohana East	2 blocks to beach	$$$	1				yes			440	3	kitchens	Waikīkī
22	Ohana Waikīkī Beachcomber	1 block to beach, shows	$$$-$$$$	1						5-12	500	1		Waikīkī
17	Ohana Waikīkī Malia	3 blocks to beach	$$				1				332	1	kitchens	Waikīkī
25	Ohana Waikīkī West	2 blocks to beach	$$	1							665	1	kitchens	Waikīkī
11	Outrigger Reef on the Beach	Good value	$$$$	1	yes			yes		5-12	675	2		Waikīkī
20	Outrigger Waikīkī on the Beach	Near Duke's Canoe Club	$$$$	1	yes			yes	yes	5-13	554	3	kitchens	Waikīkī
3	Renaissance 'Ilikai Waikīkī	Short walk to beach	$$$$	2			1	yes			779	3	kitchens	Waikīkī

#	Name	Location	Price						Units		Amenities	Area
51	ResortQuest Executive Centre Hotel	Near Chinatown	$$$	1			yes		116	1	kitchens	Downtown Honolulu
40	ResortQuest Waikīkī Beach	Across from beach	$$$–$$$$	1					684	3	shops	Waikīkī
33	ResortQuest Waikīkī Circle	Across from beach	$$						104	3		Waikīkī
16	ResortQuest Waikīkī Joy	2 blocks to beach	$	1			yes		94	1	kitchens	Waikīkī
32	Royal Grove Hotel	Good value	¢	1					85		no A/C	Waikīkī
19	Royal Hawaiian Hotel	Near Coconut Grove	$$$$	1		yes		yes	5-12	528	2	shops	Waikīkī
28	Sheraton Princess Kaiulani	1 block to beach	$$	1			yes		5-12	1,164	2		Waikīkī
14	Sheraton Waikīkī	Cobalt Lounge	$$$$	2		yes	yes		5-12	1,823	2	shops	Waikīkī
45	Turtle Bay Resort	Beach cottages, trails	$$$$	2	10	yes	yes	yes	5-12	511	4	shops	North Shore
35	Waikīkī Beach Marriott	Great sushi, spa	$$$–$$$$	2			yes	yes		1,323	6		Waikīkī
13	Waikīkī Parc	1 block to beach	$$$–$$$$	1			yes	yes		297	1		Waikīkī
31	Waikīkī Sand Villa	3 blocks to beach	$	1			yes			214	1	no A/C	Waikīkī

Condos

#	Name	Location	Price						Units		Amenities	Area
4	Aqua Palms at Waikīkī	Near Hilton Hawaiian	$	1			yes		263	1	kitchens	Waikīkī
9	The Breakers	2 blocks to beach	$–$$	1					63		kitchens	Waikīkī
10	Castle Waikīkī Shore	Great value	$$$–$$$$	1	yes				168		kitchens	Waikīkī
24	Ilima Hotel	3 blocks to beach	$$–$$$	1			yes		98		kitchens	Waikīkī
7	Outrigger Luana	2 blocks to beach	$$$–$$$$	1			yes		218	1	kitchens	Waikīkī
30	ResortQuest Pacific Monarch	3 blocks to beach	$$–$$$	1					152	1	kitchens	Waikīkī
34	ResortQuest Waikīkī Beach Tower	Across from beach	$$$$	1	1				140	1	kitchens	Waikīkī
38	ResortQuest at the Waikīkī Banyan	1 block to beach	$$–$$$	1	1				876	1	kitchens	Waikīkī
39	ResortQuest Waikīkī Sunset	3 blocks to beach	$$–$$$	1	1				307	1	kitchens	Waikīkī
23	Winston's Waikīkī Condos	2 blocks to beach	$–$$	1					10	1	kitchens	Waikīkī

BθBs & Vacation Rentals

#	Name	Location	Price						Units		Amenities	Area
47	Backpackers Vacation Inn	Near Waimea Bay	$						25		no A/C	North Shore
41	Diamond Head Bed-and-Breakfast	Near Crater	$						3		no A/C	Waikīkī
43	Ingrid's	Near Kailua, Japanese garden	$	1					1		kitchens	Windward O'ahu
46	Ke Iki Beach Bungalows	Near Waimea Bay	$–$$	1		yes			11		no A/C	North Shore
48	Marriot Ko'Olina Beach Club	Near Ko'Olina Resort, spa	$$$$	2	6	yes	yes	yes	5-12	200	2	kitchens	Windward O'ahu
44	Schrader's Windward Country Inn	Near Kāne'ohe Bay	$	1			yes			57	1	no A/C	Windward O'ahu

views. ⊠ *2500 Kūhiō Ave., Waikīkī* ☎ *808/922–0811 or 800/445–8667* 🖷 *808/921–5507* ⊕ *www.princekuhiohotel.com* ⟿ *620 rooms* ⟐ *In-room: safe, Internet. In-hotel: restaurant, room service, bar, pool, gym, laundry facilities, parking (paid), no-smoking rooms* ▭ *AE, D, DC, MC, V.*

$$$$
RESORT

🏨 **Hyatt Regency Waikīkī Resort and Spa.** Though it's across the street from the Kūhiō Beach section of Waikīkī, the Hyatt is actually on the oceanfront, as there's no resort between it and the Pacific Ocean. A pool-deck staircase leads directly to street level, for easy beach access. An open-air atrium with three levels of shopping, a two-story water-fall, and free nightly live entertainment make this one of the liveliest lobbies anywhere. An activity center offers kids' programs, including lei-making lessons, 'ukulele lessons, and field trips to the aquarium and zoo. **Pros:** public spaces are airy and waterfall is spectacular. **Cons:** in a very busy and crowded part of Waikīkī. ⊠ *2424 Kalākaua Ave., Waikīkī* ☎ *808/923–1234 or 800/633–7313* 🖷 *808/923–7839* ⊕ *www.waikiki.hyatt.com* ⟿ *1,230 rooms, 18 suites* ⟐ *In-room: safe, refrigerator, Wi-Fi. In-hotel: 5 restaurants, room service, bars, pool, gym, spa, children's programs (ages 5–12), parking (paid), no-smoking rooms* ▭ *AE, D, DC, MC, V.*

$$–$$$
RENTAL

🏨 **'Ilima Hotel.** Tucked away on a residential side street near Waikīkī's Ala Wai Canal, this locally owned 17-story condominium-style hotel is a gem. The glass-wall lobby with koa-wood furnishings, original Hawaiian artwork, and friendly staff create a Hawaiian home away from home. Rates are decent for the spacious studios with kitchenettes and the one- and two-bedroom suites with full kitchens, Jacuzzi baths, cable TV with free HBO and Disney channels, multiple phones, and spacious lānai. It's a two-block walk to Waikīkī Beach, shopping, and Kalākaua Avenue restaurants. The parking is free but limited. When the spots are full, you park on the street. **Pros:** big rooms are great for families. **Cons:** limited hotel parking, and street parking can be difficult to find. ⊠ *445 Nohonani St., Waikīkī* ☎ *808/923–1877 or 800/801–9366* 🖷 *808/924–2617* ⊕ *www.ilima.com* ⟿ *98 units* ⟐ *In-room: safe, kitchen. In-hotel: pool, gym, laundry facilities, parking (free), no-smoking rooms* ▭ *AE, DC, MC, V.*

$$$$
RESORT

🏨 **Moana Surfrider.** Outrageous rates of $1.50 per night were the talk of the town when the "First Lady of Waikīkī" opened her doors in 1901. The Hawai'i Calls radio program was broadcast from the veranda during the 1940s and '50s. Today this historic beauty is still a wedding and honeymoon favorite with a sweeping main staircase and period furnishings in its main wing, the Moana. In the late 1950s, the hotel's Diamond Head Tower was built. In the '70s, the Surfrider hotel went up next door; all three merged into one hotel in the 1980s. The newly refurbished Surfrider has oceanfront suites with two separate lānai, one for sunrise and one for sunset viewing. Relax on the private beach or in a cabana by the pool. Enjoy live music and hula at the Banyan Court each evening or dine at the Beach House restaurant. **Pros:** elegant, historic property; best place on Waikīkī Beach to watch hula and have a drink. **Cons:** you might feel you have to tiptoe around formal public spaces. ⊠ *2365 Kalākaua Ave., Waikīkī* ☎ *808/922–3111,*

888/488–3535, or 866/500–8313 📠 *808/923–0308* ⊕ *www.moana-surfrider.com* ↻ *793 rooms, 46 suites* ⚲ *In-room: safe, Internet. In-hotel: 2 restaurants, room service, bars, pool, spa, beachfront, children's programs (ages 5–12), laundry service, parking (paid), no-smoking rooms* ▭ *AE, DC, MC, V.*

$$$
HOTEL

🖾 **Ohana East.** If you want to be in central Waikīkī and don't want to pay beachfront lodging prices, consider the flagship property for Ohana Hotels in Waikīkī. Next to the Sheraton Princess Kaiulani on the corner of Kaiulani and Kūhiō avenues, it's a mere two blocks from the beach and within walking distance of shopping, restaurants, and nightlife. Its location and reasonable rates tend to attract plenty of group travelers. Don't expect any fancy lobbies or outdoor gardens here. Certain rooms on lower floors have no lānai, and some rooms have showers only. Suites have kitchenettes. **Pros:** close to the beach and reasonable rates. **Cons:** no lānai and very basic public spaces. ⊠ *150 Kaiulani Ave., Waikīkī* 📞 *808/922–5353 or 800/462–6262* 📠 *808/926–4334* ⊕ *www.ohanahotels.com* ↻ *420 rooms, 20 suites* ⚲ *In-room: safe, kitchen (some), refrigerator. In-hotel: 3 restaurants, bar, pool, gym, laundry facilities, parking (paid)* ▭ *AE, D, DC, MC, V.*

$$$–$$$$
HOTEL

🖾 **Ohana Waikīkī Beachcomber Hotel.** Ohana took over the beloved old Beachcomber in 2005 and has given her a comprehensive face lift while retaining the Polynesian theme. At this and other Ohana hotels, the Ohana Waikīkī Connection offers several free services: unlimited rides on the Waikīkī Trolley Pink Line, long-distance phone service to the United States and Canada, and a daily newspaper. Early check-in guests can leave their bags, pick up a pager, and hit the beach; they'll be alerted when their rooms are ready. This Ohana hotel hosts the popular Blue Hawai'i show and is almost directly across from the Royal Hawaiian Shopping Center and next door to the International Marketplace. It's also home to Jimmy Buffet's massive Margaritaville restaurant. The third-floor pool deck is front-row seating for any of Waikīkī's year-round parades or Ho'olaulea street-party festivals. It's a family-friendly place, with cultural activities that include 'ukulele and hula lessons as well as arts and crafts. On the hotel's ground level is an entrance to Macy's, and across the street is a public access-way that opens up to the beach fronting the Royal Hawaiian hotel. **Pros:** lots of freebees, in the thick of Waikīkī action. **Cons:** very busy area, no direct beach access. ⊠ *2300 Kalākaua Ave., Waikīkī* 📞 *808/922–4646 or 800/462–6262* 📠 *808/923–4889* ⊕ *www.ohanahotels.com* ↻ *493 rooms, 7 suites* ⚲ *In-room: refrigerator. In-hotel: restaurant, bar, pool, laundry facilities, public Wi-Fi, parking (paid), no-smoking rooms* ▭ *AE, DC, MC, V.*

9

$$
HOTEL

⌘ **Ohana Waikīkī Malia.** Close to the ʻewa end of Waikīkī, this older hotel comprises a pair of buildings, one with standard rooms, the other with one-bedroom suites that have kitchenettes. Although almost all rooms and suites here have lānai, the views are more city and concrete than foliage and ocean. Guests who return here year after year are those who fancy the property's proximity to restaurants and shopping, and its easygoing "come as you are" vibe. During major sporting events on Oʻahu, don't be surprised if you share the elevator with a triathlete and his bicycle or a marathoner just back from her run. There is a coffee shop on the lobby level, and stops for TheBus and trolley lines are right outside the front door. The hotel's tennis court is on the roof so think carefully before chasing after

> **HOTELS' CULTURAL PROGRAMS**
>
> Once upon a time, hotel lobbies were filled with lei-makers and Hollywood-style hula lessons. Today, there's a renaissance of Hawaiian culture, and you can often connect with free programs celebrating this movement without leaving your hotel. Check out hotel music venues featuring some of Hawaiʻi's most talented musical artists. Watch a revered master *kumu* (teacher) sharing the art of ancient hula. Meet by the ocean for a lesson in the craft of canoe-making or join marine reef experts spotting *honu* (Hawaiian sea turtles). Check with your concierge for daily Hawaiiana activities.

the longer lobs. **Pros:** central to shopping and dining in Waikīkī. **Cons:** views not much to speak of. ✉ *2211 Kūhiō Ave., Waikīkī* ☎ *808/923–7621 or 800/462–6262* 🖶 *808/921–4804* ⊕ *www.ohanahotels.com* ⇱ *285 rooms, 47 suites* ♿ *In-room: safe, kitchen (some), refrigerator, Internet. In-hotel: restaurant, tennis court, laundry facilities, parking (paid), no-smoking rooms* ➭ *AE, D, DC, MC, V.*

$$
HOTEL

⌘ **Ohana Waikīkī West.** Just behind the International Marketplace, this economical hotel offers a 3rd-floor pool and sundeck overlooking all the action of busy Kūhiō Avenue. You can choose a standard room or one with a kitchenette. There are also standard/kitchenette combos consisting of two connecting rooms with either one king and two double beds or four double beds—these sleep a maximum of six. Rooms have showers only. Views from private lānai overlook bustling Kūhiō Avenue or face neighboring high-rises. From the higher-floor rooms, you can catch glimpses of the ocean. Favored by group travelers, airline crews, and visiting military, the hotel is just two blocks from the beach and handy for shopping and dining. **Pros:** an economy property, by Waikīkī standards; clean rooms; centrally located. **Cons:** no bathtubs. ✉ *2330 Kūhiō Ave., Waikīkī* ☎ *808/922–5022 or 800/462–6262* 🖶 *808/924–6414* ⊕ *www.ohanahotels.com* ⇱ *645 rooms, 16 suites* ♿ *In-room: safe, kitchen (some), refrigerator, Internet. In-hotel: restaurant, bar, pool, laundry facilities, public Wi-Fi, parking (paid), no-smoking rooms* ➭ *AE, D, DC, MC, V.*

$$$–$$$$
RENTAL

⌘ **Outrigger Luana.** At the entrance to Waikīkī near Fort DeRussy is this welcoming hotel offering both rooms and condominium units. Luana's two-story lobby is appointed in rich, Hawaiian-wood furnishings with Island-inspired fabrics, and the mezzanine lounge is as comfortable as any living room back home. Units are furnished with a mix of rich woods with etched accents of pineapples and palm trees. At bedside, hula-dancer and beach-boy lamps add another Hawaiian residential touch. The recreational deck has a fitness center, pool, and barbecue area with tables that can be enclosed cabana-style for privacy when dining outdoors. Each one-bedroom suites has two lānai. If you like Hawaiiana and appreciate a bit of kitsch this is a great option. **Pros:** two lānai in suites; barbecue area (rare for Waikīkī). **Cons:** no direct beach access. ✉ *2045 Kalākaua Ave., Waikīkī* ☎ *808/955–6000 or 800/688–7444* 🖨 *808/943–8555* ⊕ *www.outrigger.com* 🛏 *218 units* ♿ *In-room: safe, kitchen (some), Internet. In-hotel: pool, gym, laundry facilities, public Wi-Fi, parking (paid)* ▭ *AE, D, DC, MC, V.*

$$$–$$$$
RESORT
🖳 **Outrigger Reef on the Beach.** Recent renovations have drastically updated this location. The new entrance incorporates a Hawaiian voyaging-design theme, expanded room size, larger and more contemporary bathrooms—including full-size bathtubs in what was previously an all-shower hotel—and a new signature restaurant, though the Shore Bird and Ocean House remain. What had been a plain but pleasant oceanfront bargain now offers polished elegance in keeping with its prime location. Though the inland Pacific Tower has been renovated more recently, it's worthwhile to go for an ocean view or oceanfront accommodation in the Ocean Tower; other rooms have less enchanting views, and noisy construction on the Trump Towers across the street will continue into 2010. New features include smoke-free rooms, flat-screen TVs, and free long distance to the U.S. mainland and Canada. **Pros:** on beach, direct access to Waikīkī Beach Walk. **Cons:** proximity to Trump Tower construction. ✉ *2169 Kālia Rd., Waikīkī* ☎ *808/923–3111 or 800/688–7444* 🖨 *808/924–4957* ⊕ *www.outrigger.com* 🛏 *631 rooms, 44 suites* ♿ *In-room: refrigerator, Internet. In-hotel: 2 restaurants, bar, pool, gym, beachfront, children's programs (ages 5–12), laundry facilities, Internet terminal, public Wi-Fi, parking (paid), no-smoking rooms* ▭ *AE, D, DC, MC, V.*

$$$$
RESORT
🖳 **Outrigger Waikīkī on the Beach.** This star jewel of Outrigger Hotels & Resorts sits on one of the finest strands of Waikīkī Beach. The guest rooms in the 16-story no-smoking resort have rich dark-wood furnishings, Hawaiian art, and lānai that offer either ocean or Waikīkī-skyline views. The popular Duke's Canoe Club has beachfront concerts under the stars. Waikīkī Plantation Spa offers Hawaiian seaweed wraps, hot-stone massages, and wedding packages. **Pros:** the best bar on the beach is downstairs; free Wi-Fi in lobby. **Cons:** the lobby feels a bit like an airport with so many people using it as a throughway to the beach. ✉ *2335 Kalākaua Ave., Waikīkī* ☎ *808/923–0711 or 800/688–7444* 🖨 *808/921–9798* ⊕ *www.outrigger.com* 🛏 *524 rooms, 30 suites* ♿ *In-room: safe, kitchen (some), refrigerator, Internet. In-hotel: 3 restaurants, room service, bars, pool, gym, beachfront, children's programs (ages 5–13), laundry facilities, laundry service, public Wi-Fi, parking (paid), no-smoking rooms* ▭ *AE, D, DC, MC, V.*

$$$$
RESORT
🖳 **Renaissance 'Ilikai Waikīkī.** At the 'ewa edge of Waikīkī overlooking the Ala Wai Harbor, this resort has both standard rooms and units with full kitchens, which can save you some bucks if you self-cater occasionally.

9

The atmosphere here is casual thanks to an open-air lobby, cascading waterfalls, and torch-lighted walkways perfect for romantic, evening strolls above the harbor. At sunset the lighting of the torches and blowing of the conch prepare you for a romantic evening in paradise. The place is in need of renovation and sometimes feels like there is a convention going on in the lobby, but the two freshwater pools and a tennis court offer a welcome respite. Unfortunately, the nearest beach, at Ala Moana Beach Park, is a five-minute walk. Most rooms have lānai and there's a 24-hour fitness center. ■ TIP➔ While riding the glass elevator to the top of the "I", note the uppermost penthouse balcony to the west—it's where Jack Lord's character Steve McGarrett turns to face the camera at the beginning of each episode of Hawaii 5-0. **Pros:** views of sunset from most rooms on the 'ewa side; comfortable beds. **Cons:** sometimes surly service; very slow elevators; in need of renovations. ✉ *1777 Ala Moana Blvd., Waikīkī* ☎ *808/949–3811 or 800/245–4524* 🖷 *808/947–4523* ⊕ *www.ilikaihotel.com* ⟿ *728 rooms, 51 suites* ♿ *In-room: kitchen (some), refrigerator. In-hotel: 3 restaurants, room service, bars, tennis court, pools, gym, laundry facilities, parking (paid), no-smoking rooms* ▭ *AE, D, DC, MC, V.*

$$–$$$

RENTAL

⚏ ResortQuest at the Waikīkī Banyan. The recreation deck at this family-oriented property has outdoor grills, a heated swimming pool, two hot tubs, a playground, a mini putting green, and volleyball, basketball, and tennis courts. The welcoming lobby is decorated in warm tropical woods with plenty of seating to enjoy the trade winds. There is also a koi pond and mini-waterfall. One-bedroom suites contain island-inspired decor and have complete kitchens and lānai that offer Diamond Head or ocean views. **Pros:** many rooms have great views. **Cons:** trekking to the beach with all your gear. ✉ *201 Ohua Ave., Waikīkī* ☎ *808/922–0555 or 866/774–2924* 🖷 *808/922–0906* ⊕ *www. rqwaikikibanyan.com* ⟿ *876 units* ♿ *In-room: kitchen, Internet. In-hotel: tennis court, pool, laundry facilities, parking (paid), no-smoking rooms* ▭ *AE, D, DC, MC, V.*

$$–$$$

RENTAL

⚏ ResortQuest Pacific Monarch. One block from Waikīkī Beach on the 'ewa end of Waikīkī, this 34-story high-rise condominium resort features a rooftop deck—with a freshwater pool, hot tub, and sauna—affords a panoramic view spanning the length of Waikīkī. Studio and one-bedroom suites are available, plus some larger units with full kitchens. All accommodations have lānai. There's a hospitality lounge with showers available to early arrivals and late departures. The one drawback here is that the rooftop-pool deck is accessible only via a single flight of stairs after you exit the elevator on the top floor; however, the view is worth the climb. **Pros:** fantastic view from rooftop pool; hospitality lounge. **Cons:** stairs to the pool deck are fairly steep and may be difficult for some. ✉ *2427 Kūhiō Ave., Waikīkī* ☎ *808/923–9805 or 866/774–2924* 🖷 *808/924–3220* ⊕ *www.rqpacificmonarch.com* ⟿ *152 units* ♿ *In-room: kitchen (some). In-hotel: pool, laundry facilities, parking (paid), no-smoking rooms* ▭ *AE, D, DC, MC, V.*

$$$–$$$$

HOTEL

⚏ ResortQuest Waikīkī Beach Hotel. A three-story volcano, backlighted in a faux eruption, crawls up the side of this hotel opposite Kūhiō Beach and near Kapi'olani Park. Rooms are furnished in dark tropical woods with lava-red floral-print fabrics. The Tiki Bar and Grill completes the tropical-island experience. Breakfast, evening music, and gatherings take place on the third-floor pool deck. In the early mornings, there's an international food court where guests can choose complimentary breakfast munchies to pack in a take-out cooler bag and head to the beach across the street to catch some early-morning wave action. A good choice for families, it is directly across the street from a protected stretch of Kūhiō Beach, and there are in-room movies and games and free hula lessons twice weekly. In the evenings, the poolside bar breaks out with Hawaiian music that ranges from traditional to Jawaiian (Hawaiian sound with a reggae beat). **Pros:** fun for families; great beach access. **Cons:** active lobby area and crowded elevators. ⊠ *2570 Kalākaua Ave., Waikīkī* ☎ *808/922–2511 or 877/997–6667* 🖷 *808/923–3656* ⊕ *www.rqwaikikibeachhotel.com* ⥲ *644 rooms, 40 suites* ⚒ *In-room: safe, refrigerator, Internet. In-hotel: 3 restaurants, pool, gym, laundry facilities, public Wi-Fi, parking (paid), no-smoking rooms* ▭ *AE, D, DC, MC, V.*

\$\$\$\$
RENTAL ⛾ **ResortQuest Waikīkī Beach Tower.** You'll find the elegance of a luxury all-suite condominium combined with the intimacy and service of a boutique hotel at this Kalākaua Avenue address. Facing Kūhiō Beach, this 40-story resort offers spacious (1,100- to 1,400-square-foot) one- and two-bedroom suites with gourmet kitchens and windows that open to sweeping views of Waikīkī and the Pacific Ocean. Amenities include twice-daily maid service, washer-dryers, and spacious private lānai. **Pros:** very large rooms—big enough to move into. **Cons:** no on-site restaurants; you must cross a busy street to get to the beach. ⊠ *2470 Kalākaua Ave., Waikīkī* ☎ *808/926–6400 or 866/774–2924* 🖷 *808/926–7380* ⊕ *www.rqwaikikibeachtower.com* ⥲ *140 units* ⚒ *In-room: safe, kitchen, DVD, Internet. In-hotel: room service, tennis court, pool, laundry facilities, parking (free), no-smoking rooms* ▭ *AE, D, DC, MC, V.*

\$\$
HOTEL ⛾ **ResortQuest Waikīkī Circle Hotel.** This unusual 14-story circular hotel is a Waikīkī landmark. A charming interior design scheme brings the Pacific inside, beginning at check-in beneath a seascape mural in the open-air lobby. The elevators are painted a bright sea blue–green, and hallway floors are textured to mimic the sandy beach, complete with appliquéd seashells and sea creatures dotting the circular walkways. Rooms here are small, with tiny bathrooms with showers only—every bit of space is utilized, hence the flat-screen TVs. A sand pail and shovel sit on the counter, just begging you to go out and play. You won't have far to walk: Waikīkī Beach is right down the front stairs and across the street. Honeymooners, snowbirds, and old-timers love this little hotel with a front-desk staff that takes the time to get to know you. **Pros:** great location and views. **Cons:** interior design, though charming to some, may feel dated to others. ⊠ *2464 Kalākaua Ave., Waikīkī* ☎ *808/923–1571 or 866/774–2924* 🖷 *808/926–8024* ⊕ *www.rqwaikikicirclehotel.com* ⥲ *104 rooms* ⚒ *In-room: safe, Internet. In-hotel: restaurant, laundry facilities, parking (paid), no-smoking rooms* ▭ *AE, D, DC, MC, V.*

9

$ ⊤ **ResortQuest Waikīkī Joy.** A trellised open-air lobby of Italian marble,

HOTEL   a koi pond, and a guava smoothie greet you on arrival at this Lewers Street hideaway. In-room Jacuzzi tubs and slick stereo-entertainment systems add appeal to basic rooms. One of the hotel's towers contains standard rooms; the other is all suites. Request a room close to the top of the hotel's 11 stories if you want to see the ocean from your lānai. It's about a five-minute stroll to Kalākaua Avenue and through one of the many public access-ways to the beach, which can be a bit of a haul if you're carrying beach chairs. Continental breakfast on the lobby veranda is included, and Cappuccino's Cafe offers a mix of Asian, American, and Hawaiian treats as well as Internet access. Cappuccino's will also cater meals for you and your groupies if you're busy recording your first hit at the hotel's GS Karaoke Studio. **Pros:** a bit of old Waikīkī; rooms are spotless; attentive staff. **Cons:** rooms are slightly dated. ⊠ *320 Lewers St., Waikīkī* ☎ *808/923–2300 or 866/774–2924* 🖨 *808/922–885* ⊕ *www.waikikijoy.com* ➭ *50 rooms, 44 suites* ⟐ *In-room: safe, kitchen (some), refrigerator, Internet. In-hotel: restaurant, bar, pool, gym, laundry facilities, parking (paid), no-smoking rooms* ▭ *AE, D, DC, MC, V.*

$$–$$$ ⊤ **ResortQuest Waikīkī Sunset.** This 38-story high-rise condominium

RENTAL   resort is near Diamond Head, one block from Waikīkī Beach and on TheBus line. Without leaving the property, you can swim, take a sauna break, throw some steaks on the outdoor grill, have access to a computer in the hospitality lounge, and end your day with night play on the condo's tennis courts. One- and two-bedroom suites are light, bright, and airy with tropical furnishings, complete kitchens, daily maid service, private lānai, and terrific views through floor-to-ceiling windows. There are coin-operated washers and dryers on each guest floor. **Pros:** spectacular views. **Cons:** noise from outdoor activities can be a distraction. ⊠ *229 Paoakalani Ave., Waikīkī* ☎ *808/922–0511 or 866/774–2924* 🖨 *808/922–8580* ⊕ *www.rqwaikikisunset.com* ➭ *307 units* ⟐ *In-room: kitchen, Internet. In-hotel: tennis court, pool, laundry facilities, no-smoking rooms* ▭ *AE, D, DC, MC, V.*

¢   ⊤ **Royal Grove Hotel.** Two generations of the Fong family have put their

HOTEL   heart and soul into the operation of this tiny (by Waikīkī standards), six-story hotel that feels like a throwback to the days of boarding houses, where rooms were outfitted for function, not style, and served up with a wealth of home-style hospitality at a price that didn't break the bank. During the hot summer months, seriously consider splurging on the highest-end accommodations, which have air-conditioning, lānai, and small kitchens. The hotel's pool is its social center in the evenings, when you can usually find one or more members of the Fong family strumming a 'ukulele, dancing hula, and singing songs in the old Hawaiian style. On special occasions, the Fongs host a potluck dinner by the pool. Little touches that mean a lot include free use of boogie boards, surfboards, beach mats, and beach towels. The hotel is two blocks from Waikīkī's Kūhiō Beach. On property are a tiny sushi bar, a natural foods deli, and an authentic Korean barbecue plate-lunch place. For extra value, inquire about the Grove's weekly rates. Parking is available in a public lot down the street. **Pros:** very economical Waikīkī option;

lots of character. **Cons:** no air-conditioning in some rooms. ✉ *151 Uluniu Ave., Waikīkī* ☎ *808/923–7691* 🖷 *808/922–7508* 🌐 *www.royalgrovehotel.com* ⬦ *78 rooms, 7 suites* ♿ *In-room: kitchen. In-hotel: pool* ⊟ *AE, D, DC, MC, V.*

$$$$
RESORT

📺 **The Royal Hawaiian Hotel.** Fresh off its $85 million makeover the Pink Palace of the Pacific is young again. The newly designed entrance is airy and welcoming and the outdoor Mai Tai bar is reopened with its world-famous concoction. Orig-

LOOKING FOR A PRIVATE BEACH?

The Royal Hawaiian Hotel and Moana Surfrider are the only hotels in Waikīkī with property lines that extend out into the sand. They have created private roped-off beach areas that can only be accessed by hotel guests. The areas are adjacent to the hotel properties at the top of the beach.

inally built for luxury-cruise passengers, this icon on Waikīkī Beach is now outfitted with modern comfort in historical elegance. A modern tower has since been added, but we're partial to the romance and architectural detailing of the historic wing, with its canopy beds, Queen Anne–style desks, and color motifs that range from soft mauve to soothing sea foam. If you want a lānai for sunset viewing, rooms in the oceanfront tower are your best bet. **Pros:** can't be beat for history; mai tais and sunsets are amazing. **Cons:** history is not cheap. ✉ *2259 Kalākaua Ave., Waikīkī* ☎ *888/488–3535, 808/923–7311, or 866/500–8313* 🖷 *808/924–7098* 🌐 *www.royal-hawaiian.com* ⬦ *528 rooms, 53 suites* ♿ *In-room: refrigerator, Internet. In-hotel: 1 restaurant, room service, bar, pool, spa, beachfront, children's programs (ages 5–12), Internet terminal, parking (paid), no-smoking rooms* ⊟ *AE, DC, MC, V.*

$$
HOTEL

📺 **Sheraton Princess Kaiulani.** This hotel sits across the street from its sister property, the Sheraton Moana Surfrider. You can sleep at the Princess Kaiulani, taking advantage of the lower rates of a non-beachfront hotel, oversee the bustle of Waikīkī from your private lānai, and dine at any of the more-pricey oceanfront Sheratons, charging everything back to your room at the Princess Kaiulani. Rooms are in two towers—some peer at the ocean over the Moana's low-rise historic wing. It's a two-minute stroll to the beach. The hotel's pool is street-side, facing Kalākaua Avenue. **Pros:** in the heart of everything in Waikīkī. **Cons:** no direct beach access; kid's activities off-site. ✉ *120 Kaiulani Ave., Waikīkī* ☎ *808/922–5811, 888/488–3535, or 866/500–8313* 🖷 *808/931–4577* 🌐 *www.princesskaiulani.com* ⬦ *1,150 rooms, 14 suites* ♿ *In-room: Internet. In-hotel: 2 restaurants, room service, bars, pool, gym, children's programs (ages 5–12), no-smoking rooms* ⊟ *AE, D, DC, MC, V.*

$$$$
RESORT

📺 **Sheraton Waikīkī.** Towering over its neighbors on the prow of Waikīkī's famous sands, the Sheraton is center stage on Waikīkī Beach. Designed for the convention crowd, it's big and busy; the ballroom, one of O'ahu's largest, hosts convention expos, concerts, and boxing matches. A glass-wall elevator, with magnificent views of Waikīkī, ascends 30 stories to the Hano Hano Room's skyline Cobalt lounge and restaurant in the sky. The resort's best beach is on its Diamond Head side, fronting the Royal Hawaiian Hotel. Lānai afford views of

9

the ocean, Waikīkī, or mountains. If you don't shy away from crowds, this could be the place for you. It's so large that even the walk to your room could hike off a few of those calories consumed in mai tais. The advantage here is that you have at your vacation fingertips a variety of amenities, venues, and programs, as well as a location smack-dab in the middle of Waikīkī. **Pros:** location in the heart of everything. **Cons:** busy atmosphere clashes with laid-back Hawaiian style. ⊠ *2255 Kalākaua Ave., Waikīkī* ☎ *888/488–3535, 808/922–4422, or 866/500–8313* 🖨 *808/923–8785* ⊕ *www.sheraton-waikiki.com* ⟟ *1,695 rooms, 128 suites* ☖ *In-room: refrigerator. In-hotel: 2 restaurants, room service, bars, pools, beachfront, children's programs (ages 5–12), laundry service, parking (paid), no-smoking rooms* ⊟ *AE, DC, MC, V.*

$$$–$$$$

RESORT

🛏 **Waikīkī Beach Marriott Resort & Spa.** On the eastern edge of Waikīkī, this flagship Marriott sits across from Kūhiō Beach and close to Kapiʻolani Park, the zoo, and the aquarium. Deep Hawaiian woods and bold tropical colors fill the hotel's two towers, which have ample courtyards and public areas open to ocean breezes and sunlight. Rooms in the Kealohilani Tower are some of the largest in Waikīkī, and the Paoakalani Tower's Diamond Head–side rooms offer breathtaking views of the crater and Kapiʻolani Park. All rooms have private lānai. The hotel's Spa Olakino, owned by Honolulu celebrity stylist Paul Brown, is one of the largest in Waikīkī and specializes in use of Hawaiʻi-based materials and treatments. Daily activities are offered for children and adults alike, and surf lessons are available from surfer Tony Moniz at the Faith Surf School. **Pros:** stunning views of Waikīkī; professional service; airy tropical public spaces. **Cons:** noise from Kalākaua Avenue can drown out surf below. ⊠ *2552 Kalākaua Ave., Waikīkī* ☎ *808/922–6611 or 800/367–5370* 🖨 *808/921–5222* ⊕ *www.marriottwaikiki.com* ⟟ *1,310 rooms, 13 suites* ☖ *In-room: Internet, Wi-Fi. In-hotel: 6 restaurants, room service, bars, pools, gym, spa, parking (paid), no-smoking rooms* ⊟ *AE, D, MC, V.*

$$$–$$$$

HOTEL

🛏 **Waikīkī Parc.** Contrasting the stately vintage-Hawaiian elegance of her sister hotel, the Halekūlani, the Waikīkī Parc makes a chic and contemporary statement to its Gen-X clientele, offering the same attention to detail in service and architectural design but lacking the beachfront location and higher prices. The guest rooms in this high-rise complex have modern minimalist furnishings but give a nod to the tropics by keeping plantation-style shutters that open out to the lānai. A complimentary evening manager's reception features wine specially made for the hotel. Its heated pool and sundeck are eight floors up, affording a bit more privacy and peace for sunbathers, and guests can take advantage of the spa at the Halekūlani across the street. Nobu Waikīkī, of the world-renowned Nobu restaurant family, opened here in 2007, serving Japanese food with a South American accent. **Pros:** stunningly modern, high-design rooms; great access to Waikīkī Beach Walk. **Cons:** no direct beach access. ⊠ *2233 Helumoa Rd., Waikīkī* ☎ *808/921–7272 or 800/422–0450* 🖨 *808/923–1336* ⊕ *www.waikikiparc.com* ⟟ *297 rooms* ☖ *In-room: safe, Internet. In-hotel: restaurant, room service, pool, gym, parking (paid)* ⊟ *AE, D, DC, MC, V.*

$ **Waikīkī Sand Villa.** Families and
HOTEL others looking for a good rate
without sacrificing proximity to
Waikīkī's beaches, dining, and
shopping return to the Waikīkī
Sand Villa year after year. It's on
the corner of Kaiulani Avenue and
Ala Wai Boulevard, a three-block
walk to restaurants and the beach.
There's a high-rise tower and a
three-story building (no elevator) of
studio accommodations with kitchenettes. Rooms are small but well
planned. Corner deluxe units with lānai overlook Ala Wai Canal and
the golf course. The fitness center has 24-hour access. Complimentary
continental breakfast is served poolside beneath shady coconut trees,
and the hotel's Sand Bar comes alive at happy hour with a great mix of
hotel guests and locals who like to hang out and "talk story." The Sand
Bar also has computers and Web cams, so that you not only can keep in
touch with family by e-mail, you can also taunt them with your developing tan. **Pros:** fun bar; economical choice. **Cons:** the noise from the bar
might annoy some; 10-minute walk to the beach. ⊠ *2375 Ala Wai Blvd.,
Waikīkī* ☎ *808/922–4744 or 800/247–1903* 🖷 *808/923–2541* ⊕ *www.
waikikisandvillahotel.com* ⇋ *214 rooms* ⚭ *In-room: safe, refrigerator.
In-hotel: restaurant, bar, gym, parking (paid)* ▭ *AE, D, DC, MC, V.*

$–$$ **Winston's Waikīkī Condos.** This five-story condominium complex spe-
RENTAL cializing in monthly rates is just off Kūhiō Avenue near the International
Marketplace and two blocks from Waikīkī Beach. All units have full
kitchens, ceiling fans, sofa beds, and lānai. Interior designs vary, with
units to accommodate families, honeymooners, business travelers, and
nostalgia buffs (check out the *Hawaii 5-0* suite). Owner Pat Winston
provides everything from rice cookers to tips on the best places to
dine on the island. There's no maid service, but basic cleaning supplies are provided. Parking ($14) is available at a condo on Ala Wai
Boulevard. To save a substantial amount, ask for monthly and other
specials. **Pros:** Pat Winston is a slice of 1960s Hawaii; suites are all
unique; careful attention to details. **Cons:** not many suites; check-in
can be confusing due to a desk for other properties nearby; credit cards
not accepted for payment (only to hold reservations). ⊠ *417 Nohonani St., Waikīkī* ☎ *808/924–3332 or 800/545–1948* 🖷 *808/924–3332*
⊕ *www.winstonswaikikicondos.com* ⇋ *10 units* ⚭ *In-room: kitchen.
In-hotel: pool, laundry facilities, public Wi-Fi, parking (paid)* ▭ *No
credit cards.*

> ## WORD OF MOUTH
>
> "If you decide to stay on O'ahu,
> try Kailua. You can rent a house
> on or near the beach…From
> Kailua you can explore Lanikai
> and the north shore. This area is
> totally different from Honolulu."
> —rpowell

9

ELSEWHERE ON O'AHU

Away from the hopping scene of Waikīkī or busy downtown, accommodations on the rest of O'ahu range quiet and romantic bed-and-
breakfasts and cottages to less expensive hotels that are a great value.
There are a handful of luxury resorts as well, where you'll truly feel as
if you're getting away from it all.

WINDWARD O'AHU

$ ⛨ **Ingrid's.** This B&B in the Wind-
B&B/INN   ward bedroom community of
Kailua features a one-bedroom
upstairs studio with decor that
mimics that of a traditional Japanese inn, with shoji screen doors
and black-tile counters. Ingrid is
one of the island's most popular
hosts, and she has created a space
of Zen-like tranquility in this unit,
which also has a kitchenette and

deep soaking tub, and a private entrance. Guests have access to the
pool, and Kailua Beach is less than 1 mi away. Three- to four-month
advance reservations are advised. **Pros:** in Kailua, one of the most desir-
able locations on O'ahu. **Cons:** you'll need a car or bike to get to
the beach; must reserve months ahead. ⊠ *Pauku St., Kailua* ⌂ *Reservations: Hawai'i's Best Bed and Breakfasts, Box 485, Laupahoehoe
96767* ☎ *808/962–0100, 800/262–9912 reservations* 🖷 *808/962–6360*
⊕ *www.bestbnb.com* ⏍ *1 2-room unit* ⛲ *In-room: no phone, kitchen,
DVD. In-hotel: pool* ⊟ *No credit cards.*

¢–$ ⛨ **Schrader's Windward Country Inn.** If you're looking for an alterna-
B&B/INN   tive to staying in Waikīkī and you aren't fussy about amenities, consider Schrader's in Kāne'ohe, 30 minutes from both Waikīkī and the
North Shore. Though billed as "cottages by the sea," the setting is
actually more roadside motel than resort. However, Schrader's provides
a moderately priced lodging option with amenities you won't find in
Waikīkī, like complimentary biweekly ocean-reef tours that include
snorkeling and kayaking the scenic Windward coastline. One- to four-
bedroom accommodations are available. Units have microwaves and
refrigerators; some have full kitchens. Complimentary breakfast on the
main building's veranda is included. Ask for the units that open onto
Kāne'ohe Bay if you relish the possibility of fishing right off your lānai.
Pros: what views of Kane'ohe Bay! **Cons:** not all units are bayside; rental
car is a necessity. ⊠ *47-039 Lihikai Dr., Kāne'ohe* ☎ *800/735–5071
or 808/239–5711* 🖷 *808/239–6658* ⊕ *www.hawaiiscene.com/schrader*
⏍ *57 units* ⛲ *In-room: kitchen. In-hotel: pool, public Wi-Fi* ⊟ *AE, D,
DC, MC, V.*

NORTH SHORE

¢   ⛨ **Backpackers Vacation Inn and Plantation Village.** Laid-back Hale'iwa
B&B/INN   surfer chic at its best, Backpackers is Spartan in furnishings, rustic
in amenities, and definitely very casual in spirit. At Pūpūkea Beach
Marine Sanctuary, otherwise known as Three Tables Beach, it's a short
stroll to Waimea Bay. This is the place to catch z's between wave sets.
Accommodations in this property's 10 buildings include hostel-type
dorm rooms, double rooms (some with a double bed, others with two
single beds), studios, and cabins. Some have kitchenettes while others have full kitchens. TVs are available in every building, and pay

CONDO COMFORTS

The local **Foodland** grocery-store chain has two locations near Waikīkī. ⊠ *Market City, 2939 Harding Ave., near intersection with Kapahulu Ave. and highway overpass, Kaimukī* ☏ *808/734–6303* ✉ *Ala Moana Center, 1450 Ala Moana Blvd., ground level, Ala Moana* ☏ *808/949–5044.*

A smaller version of larger Foodland, **Food Pantry** also has apparel, beach stuff, and tourist-oriented items. ⊠ *2370 Kūhiō Ave.,* *across from Miramar hotel, Waikīkī* ☏ *808/923–9831* ✉ *2370 Kūhiō Ave., across from Miramar hotel, Waikīkī* ☏ *808/923–9831.*

Blockbuster Video. ⊠ *Ala Moana Shopping Center, 451 Piikoi St., Ala Moana* ☏ *808/593–2595.*

Pizza Hut. ☏ *808/643–1111 for delivery statewide.*

phones and barbecues are on the property. It's a three-minute walk to the supermarket. **Pros:** friendly, laid-back staff; prices you won't find anywhere else. **Cons:** many rooms are plainly furnished. ⊠ *59-788 Kamehameha Hwy., Hale'iwa* ☏ *808/638–7838* ⊕ *www.backpackers-hawaii.com* ⇆ *25 rooms* ⚭ *In-room: no a/c, no phone, kitchen (some), no TV (some). In-hotel: laundry facilities* ▭ *DC, MC, V.*

$–$$
B&B/INN

⚏ **Ke Iki Beach Bungalows.** Ke Iki Road runs parallel to Kamehameha Highway and is the site of this 1½-acre sloped beachfront lot with six duplex beach bungalows operated by Greg Gerstenberger and his wife, Annie. You can choose from studios to one- or two-bedroom units outfitted with breezy beach-house furnishings, individual grills and picnic tables, and access to a 200-foot strand of creamy white-sand beach running between the North Shore's famous Waimea Bay and Banzai Pipeline. Swimming is best here in summer, as the rest of the year the North Shore is slammed with monster waves best tackled only by professional surfers. There are outdoor showers, an outdoor meditation area, and beachfront seating for nightly stargazing. Ke Iki is popular with families for reunions and weddings. A bike path fronting the property meanders along the ocean to Sunset Beach and Waimea Bay. If you want more surf than street sounds, reserve one of the beachside bungalows. **Pros:** helpful and friendly staff; great prices. **Cons:** a bit far from restaurants and shopping. ⊠ *59-579 Ke Iki Rd., Hale'iwa* ☏ *808/638–8829* ⊕ *www.keikibeach.com* ⇆ *11 units* ⚭ *In-room: no a/c, kitchen. In-hotel: beachfront, laundry facilities, parking (paid)* ▭ *AE, MC, V.*

$$$$
RESORT
Fodor's Choice
★

⚏ **The Turtle Bay Resort.** Some 880 acres of raw natural Hawai'i landscape are your playground at this glamorous resort on O'ahu's scenic North Shore. On the edge of Kuilima Point, the Turtle Bay has spacious guest rooms averaging nearly 500 square feet, with lānai that showcase stunning peninsula views. In winter, when the big waves roll ashore, you get a front-row seat for the powerful surf. The sumptuous oceanfront beach cottages have Brazilian-walnut floors, teak rockers on the lānai, and beds you can sink right into while listening to the sounds of the ocean. Turtle Bay has a Hans Heidemann Surf School, horse stables,

The Turtle Bay Resort

a spa, and the only 36-hole golf facility on O'ahu to keep you busy. There are two swimming pools, one with an 80-foot waterslide. While out exploring Turtle Bay's 12 mi of nature trails, don't be surprised if you suddenly find yourself *Lost.* The hit television series has been known to frequent the resort's beaches, coves, and natural forests

for location filming. **Pros:** great open, public spaces in a secluded area of O'ahu. **Cons:** very far from anything else—even Hale'iwa is a 20-minute drive. ✉ *57-091 Kamehameha Hwy., Box 187, Kahuku* ☎ *808/293–8811 or 800/203–3650* 🖷 *808/293–9147* ⊕ *www.turtlebayresort.com* ⇱*373 rooms, 31 suites, 42 beach cottages, 56 ocean villas* ⚭ *In-room: refrigerator. In-hotel: 4 restaurants, room service, bars, golf courses, tennis courts, pools, gym, spa, beachfront, children's programs (ages 5–12), no-smoking rooms* ⊟ *AE, D, DC, MC, V.*

WEST (LEEWARD) O'AHU

$$$$
RESORT

🖵 **J. W. Marriott 'Ihilani Resort & Spa.** Forty-five minutes and a world away from the bustle of Waikīkī, this sleek, 17-story resort anchors the still-developing Ko Olina Resort and Marina on O'ahu's Leeward coastline. Honeymooners, NFL Pro-Bowlers, and even local residents looking for a Neighbor Island experience without the hassle of catching a flight come to 'Ihilani for first-class R&R. The resort sits on one of Kō'Ōlina's seven lagoons and has a lū'au cove, tennis garden, wedding chapel, yacht marina, spa, and a Ted Robinson–designed 18-hole championship golf facility. The 650-square-foot rooms are luxurious, with lulling color schemes, marble bathrooms with deep soaking tubs, spacious private lānai with teak furnishings; and high-tech control systems for lighting and temperature. Introduced in 2007, Hawai'i's only allergy-friendly rooms are equipped with tea-tree-oil-infused air purifiers that remove allergens from the room within 15 minutes and with hypoallergenic fabrics, specially treated to reduce contaminants and irritants. Most rooms have views. **Pros:** beautiful property; impeccable service; pool is stunning at night. **Cons:** a bit of a drive from Honolulu; rental car a necessity. ✉ *92-1001 'Olani St., Kapolei* ☎ *808/679–0079 or 800/626–4446* 🖷 *808/679–0080* ⊕ *www.ihilani.com* ⇱*387 rooms, 36 suites* ⚭ *In-room: safe. In-hotel: 3 restaurants, room service, golf course, tennis courts, pools, spa, beachfront, children's programs (ages 5–12), no-smoking rooms* ⊟ *AE, DC, MC, V.*

$$$$
RESORT

🖵 **Marriott's Ko Olina Beach Club.** If you have your heart set on getting away to O'ahu's western shores, check out this hotel and (primarily) vacation-ownership property. Rooms range from hotel-style standard guest rooms to expansive and elegantly appointed one- or two-bedroom apartments. Interior decor soothes in rich reds, greens, and creamy soft yellows, with furnishings made of rare Hawaiian koa wood. The larger villas (1,240 square feet) have three TVs, full kitchens, and separate living and dining areas. On 30 acres of Kō'Ōlina , fronting a lagoon, this

9

resort has two pools (one with sandy-beach bottom), a fitness center, barbecue areas, and four outdoor hot tubs, including one overlooking the ocean that's ideal for sunset soaks. Guests can choose from two restaurants on the property or purchase groceries at The Market, on-site. **Pros:** suites are beautifully decorated and ample for families; nice views. **Cons:** 40-minute drive to Honolulu; ongoing construction at other properties nearby. ⊠ *92-161 Waipahe Pl., Kapolei* ☎ *808/679–4900 or 877/229–4484* 🖷 *808/679–4910* ⊕ *www.marriottvacationclub.com* ↩ *300 units* ⅛ *In-room: safe, kitchen, DVD, In-room Wi-Fi. In-hotel: 2 restaurants, bar, golf course, tennis courts, pools, gym, beachfront, children's programs (ages 5–12), parking (paid)* ⊟ *AE, DC, MC, V.*

HAWAIIAN VOCABULARY

HAWAIIAN VOCABULARY

Although an understanding of Hawaiian is by no means required on a trip to the Aloha State, a *malihini*, or newcomer, will find plenty of opportunities to pick up a few of the local words and phrases. Traditional names and expressions are widely used in the Islands. You're likely to read or hear at least a few words each day of your stay.

With a basic understanding and some uninhibited practice, anyone can have enough command of the local tongue to ask for directions and to order from a restaurant menu. One visitor announced she would not leave until she could pronounce the name of the state fish, the *humuhumunukunukuāpua'a*.

Simplifying the learning process is the fact that the Hawaiian language contains only eight consonants—H, K, L, M, N, P, W, and the silent *'okina*, or glottal stop, written '—plus one or more of the five vowels. All syllables, and therefore all words, end in a vowel. Each vowel, with the exception of a few diphthongized double vowels such as *au* (pronounced "ow") or *ai* (pronounced "eye"), is pronounced separately. Thus *'Iolani* is four syllables (ee-oh-la-nee), not three (yo-la-nee). Although some Hawaiian words have only vowels, most also contain some consonants, but consonants are never doubled.

Pronunciation is simple. Pronounce *A* "ah" as father; *E* "ay" as in weigh; *I* "ee" as in marine; *O* "oh" as in no; *U* "oo" as in true.

Consonants mirror their English equivalents, with the exception of W. When the letter begins any syllable other than the first one in a word, it is usually pronounced as a V. *'Awa*, the Polynesian drink, is pronounced "ava," *'ewa* is pronounced "eva."

Almost all long Hawaiian words are combinations of shorter words; they are not difficult to pronounce if you segment them. *Kalaniana'ole*, the highway running east from Honolulu, is easily understood as *Kalani ana 'ole*. Apply the standard pronunciation rules—the stress falls on the next-to-last syllable of most two- or three-syllable Hawaiian words—and Kalaniana'ole Highway is as easy to say as Main Street.

Now about that fish. Try *humu-humu nuku-nuku āpu a'a*.

The other unusual element in Hawaiian language is the *kahakō*, or macron, written as a short line (ˉ) placed over a vowel. Like the accent (´) in Spanish, the kahakō puts emphasis on a syllable that would normally not be stressed. The most familiar example is probably *Waikīkī*. With no macrons, the stress would fall on the middle syllable; with only one macron, on the last syllable, the stress would fall on the first and last syllables. Some words become plural with the addition of a macron, often on a syllable that would have been stressed anyway. No Hawaiian word becomes plural with the addition of an S, since that letter does not exist in the language.

What follows is a glossary of some of the most commonly used Hawaiian words. Hawaiian residents appreciate visitors who at least try to pick up the local language.

'a'ā: rough, crumbling lava, contrasting with *pāhoehoe*, which is smooth.

'ae: yes.

aikane: friend.

āina: land.

akamai: smart, clever, possessing savoir faire.

akua: god.

ala: a road, path, or trail.

ali'i: a Hawaiian chief, a member of the chiefly class.

aloha: love, affection, kindness; also a salutation meaning both greetings and farewell.

'ānuenue: rainbow.

'a'ole: no.

'apōpō: tomorrow.

'auwai: a ditch.

auwē: alas, woe is me!

'ehu: a red-haired Hawaiian.

'ewa: in the direction of 'Ewa plantation, west of Honolulu.

hala: the pandanus tree, whose leaves (*lau hala*) are used to make baskets and plaited mats.

hālau: school.

hale: a house.

hale pule: church, house of worship.

ha mea iki or ha mea 'ole: you're welcome.

hana: to work.

haole: ghost. Since the first foreigners were Caucasian, *haole* now means a Caucasian person.

hapa: a part, sometimes a half; often used as a short form of *hapa haole,* to mean a person who is part-Caucasian.

hau'oli: to rejoice. *Hau'oli Makahiki Hou* means Happy New Year. *Hau'oli lā hānau* means Happy Birthday.

heiau: an outdoor stone platform; an ancient Hawaiian place of worship.

holo: to run.

holoholo: to go for a walk, ride, or sail.

holokū: a long Hawaiian dress, somewhat fitted, with a yoke and a train. Influenced by European fashion, it was worn at court, and at least one local translates the word as "expensive mu'umu'u."

holomū: a post–World War II cross between a *holokū* and a mu'umu'u, less fitted than the former but less voluminous than the latter, and having no train.

honi: to kiss; a kiss. A phrase that some tourists may find useful, quoted from a popular hula, is *Honi Ka'ua Wikiwiki:* Kiss me quick!

honu: turtle.

ho'omalimali: flattery, a deceptive "line," bunk, baloney, hooey.

huhū: angry.

hui: a group, club, or assembly. A church may refer to its congregation as a *hui* and a social club may be called a *hui.*

hukilau: a seine; a communal fishing party in which everyone helps to drive the fish into a huge net, pull it in, and divide the catch.

hula: the dance of Hawai'i.

iki: little.

ipo: sweetheart.

ka: the. This is the definite article for most singular words; for plural nouns, the definite article is usually *nā.* Since there is no *S* in Hawaiian, the article may be your only clue that a noun is plural.

kahuna: a priest, doctor, or other trained person of old Hawai'i, endowed with special professional skills that often included prophecy or other supernatural powers; the plural form is kāhuna.

kai: the sea, saltwater.

kalo: the taro plant from whose root *poi* (paste) is made.

kamā'aina: literally, a child of the soil; it refers to people who were born in the Islands or have lived there for a long time.

kanaka: originally a man or humanity, it is now used to denote a male Hawaiian or part-Hawaiian, but is occasionally taken as a slur when used by non-Hawaiians. *Kanaka maoli,* originally a full-blooded Hawaiian person, is used by some native Hawaiian rights activists to embrace part-Hawaiians as well.

kāne: a man, a husband. If you see this word on a door, it's the men's room. If you see *kane* on a door, it's probably a misspelling; that is the Hawaiian name for the skin fungus tinea.

kapa: also called by its Tahitian name, *tapa,* a cloth made of beaten bark and usually dyed and stamped with a repeat design.

kapakahi: crooked, cockeyed, uneven. You've got your hat on *kapakahi.*

kapu: keep out, prohibited. This is the Hawaiian version of the more widely known Tongan word *tabu* (taboo).

kapuna: grandparent; elder.

kēia lā: today.

keiki: a child; *keikikāne* is a boy, *keiki-wahine* a girl.

kona: the leeward side of the Islands, the direction (south) from which the *kona* wind and *kona* rain come.

kula: upland.

kuleana: a homestead or small plot of ground on which a family has been installed for some generations without necessarily owning it. By extension, *kuleana* is used to denote any area or department in which one has a special interest or prerogative. You'll hear it used this way: If you want to hire a surfboard, see Moki; that's his *kuleana*.

lā: sun.

lamalama: to fish with a torch.

lānai: a porch, a balcony, an outdoor living room. Almost every house in Hawai'i has one. Don't confuse this two-syllable word with the three-syllable name of the island, Lāna'i.

lani: heaven, the sky.

lau hala: the leaf of the *hala,* or pandanus tree, widely used in handicrafts.

lei: a garland of flowers.

limu: sun.

lolo: stupid.

luna: a plantation overseer or foreman.

mahalo: thank you.

makai: toward the ocean.

malihini: a newcomer to the Islands.

mana: the spiritual power that the Hawaiian believed inhabited all things and creatures.

manō: shark.

manuwahi: free, gratis.

mauka: toward the mountains.

mauna: mountain.

mele: a Hawaiian song or chant, often of epic proportions.

Mele Kalikimaka: Merry Christmas (a transliteration from the English phrase).

Menehune: a Hawaiian pixie. The *Menehune* were a legendary race of little people who accomplished prodigious work, such as building fishponds and temples in the course of a single night.

moana: the ocean.

mu'umu'u: the voluminous dress in which the missionaries enveloped Hawaiian women. Now made in bright printed cottons and silks, it is an indispensable garment. Culturally sensitive locals have embraced the Hawaiian spelling but often shorten the spoken word to "mu'u." Most English dictionaries include the spelling "muumuu."

nani: beautiful.

nui: big.

ohana: family.

'ono: delicious.

pāhoehoe: smooth, unbroken, satiny lava.

Pākē: Chinese. This *Pākē* carver makes beautiful things.

palapala: document, printed matter.

pali: a cliff, precipice.

pānini: prickly pear cactus.

paniolo: a Hawaiian cowboy, a rough transliteration of *español,* the language of the Islands' earliest cowboys.

pau: finished, done.

pilikia: trouble. The Hawaiian word is much more widely used here than its English equivalent.

puka: a hole.

pupule: crazy, like the celebrated Princess Pupule. This word has replaced its English equivalent in local usage.

pu'u: volcanic cinder cone.

waha: mouth.

wahine: a female, a woman, a wife, and a sign on the ladies' room door; the plural form is *wāhine.*

wai: freshwater, as opposed to saltwater, which is *kai.*

wailele: waterfall.

wikiwiki: to hurry, hurry up (since this is a reduplication of *wiki,* quick, neither *W* is pronounced as a *V*).

Note: Pidgin is the unofficial language of Hawai'i. It is a Creole language, with its own grammar, evolved from the mixture of English, Hawaiian, Japanese, Portuguese, and other languages spoken in 19th-century Hawai'i, and it is heard everywhere.

Travel Smart O'ahu

WORD OF MOUTH

"Sometimes I stay in Waikīkī for a couple of nights and I never rent a car. Hotels charge a fortune for parking, and many of the hotel garages are a block or two away from the lodging. Taxis are plentiful and it's easy to hop a bus to Ala Moana or Chinatown."

—Barbara5353

GETTING HERE AND AROUND

Yes, O'ahu is a wonderful tourist destination, and on any given day there are more than 100,000 visitors on the island. It's also home to about 75% of the 1.3 million people who live in Hawai'i. And, as the capital of the state and the financial crossroads to Asia and the Pacific, Honolulu is among the nation's largest cities. So, needless to say, you'll find lots of cars and traffic, especially during the morning and afternoon drive times. Visitors may be able to navigate more easily by orienting themselves to a few major landmarks. O'ahu is made up of two extinct volcanoes, which form what is today the island's two mountain ranges: Wai'anae and Ko'olau. The Wai'anae range curves from Ka'ena State Park, on the island's westernmost point, past Makaha, Wai'anae, and Nānākuli to Kō'Ōlina, a growing resort on the sunny Leeward shore. The extinct craters of Diamond Head and Koko Head are usually visible from anywhere along the island's Leeward coast. The Ko'olau Range forms a jagged spine that runs from the island's eastern tip along the Windward coast to the famous surfing center on the North Shore.

The island's volcanic origins have limited O'ahu's developments to tide flats and ridge lines, and as a result the city and county have many one-way streets and limited public parking. Honolulu's public transportation system, TheBus, is a stress-free, affordable, and convenient way to get around. There are routes that will take you to all of the major attractions, neighborhoods, and sightseeing locations around the island.

▌ AIR TRAVEL

Flying time is about 10 hours from New York, 8 hours from Chicago, and 5 hours from Los Angeles.

All of the major airline carriers serving Hawai'i fly direct to Honolulu; some also offer nonstops to Maui, Kaua'i, and the Big Island. Honolulu International Airport, although open-air and seemingly more casual than airports in most major U.S. hubs, can be very busy. Allow extra travel time during morning and afternoon traffic periods.

The least expensive airfares to Honolulu are often priced for round-trip travel and must usually be purchased in advance. Airlines generally allow you to change your return date for a fee; most low-fare tickets, however, are nonrefundable.

Plants and plant products are subject to regulation by the Department of Agriculture, both on entering and leaving O'ahu. Upon leaving, you'll have to have your bags X-rayed and tagged at the airport's agricultural inspection station before you proceed to check-in. Pineapples and coconuts with the packer's agricultural inspection stamp pass freely; papayas must be treated, inspected, and stamped. All other fruits are banned for export to the U.S. mainland. Flowers pass except for gardenia, rose leaves, jade vine, and mauna loa. Also banned are insects, snails, soil, cotton, cacti, sugarcane, and all berry plants.

You'll have to leave dogs and other pets at home. A 120-day quarantine is imposed to keep out rabies, which is nonexistent in Hawai'i. If specific pre- and post-arrival requirements are met, animals may qualify for 30-day or 5-day-or-less quarantine.

Airline Security Issues Transportation Security Administration (⊕ *www.tsa.gov*) has answers for almost every question that might come up.

Air-Travel Resources in O'ahu State of Hawai'i Airports Division Offices (☎ *808/836-6413* ⊕ *www.hawaii.gov/dot/airports*).

AIRPORTS

Honolulu International Airport (HNL) is 20 minutes (9 mi) west of Waikīkī, and is served by most of the major domestic and international carriers. To travel inter-island from Honolulu, you can depart from either the interisland terminal or the commuter-airline terminal, located in two separate structures adjacent to the main overseas terminal building. A free Wiki Wiki shuttle bus operates between terminals.

If you have time after you've checked in for your flight home, visit the Pacific Aerospace Museum, open daily, in the main terminal. It includes a 1,700-square-foot, 3-dimensional, multimedia theater presenting the history of flight in Hawai'i, and a full-scale space-shuttle flight deck. Hands-on exhibits include a mission-control computer program tracing flights in the Pacific.

Airport Information Honolulu International Airport (HNL) (☎ *808/836–6413* ⊕ *www. hawaii.gov/dot/airports*).

GROUND TRANSPORTATION

Some hotels have their own pickup service. Check when you book accommodations.

Taxi service is available on the center median just outside baggage-claim areas. Look for the taxi dispatchers wearing green shirts who will radio for a taxi. The fare to Waikīkī runs approximately $35 to $40, plus $.50 per bag, and tip. If your baggage is oversized, there is an additional charge of $4.60.

Roberts Hawai'i runs a 24-hour airport shuttle from the airport to most of the major hotels in Waikīkī. The fare is $9 one-way, $15 round-trip; paid in cash to your driver. Look for a representative at the baggage claim. Call for return reservations only.

TheBus, the municipal bus, will take you into Waikīkī for only $2, but you are allowed only one bag, which must fit on your lap.

Contacts Roberts Hawai'i (☎ *808/539–9400* w *www.robertshawaii.com*). **TheBus** (☎ *808/848–5555* ⊕ *www.thebus.org*).

FLIGHTS

From the U.S. mainland, Continental, Delta, and United serve Honolulu.

Airline Contacts Continental Airlines (☎ *800/523–3273 for U.S. and Mexico reservations, 800/231–0856 for international reservations* ⊕ *www.continental.com*). **Delta Airlines** (☎ *800/221–1212 for U.S. reservations, 800/241–4141 for international reservations* ⊕ *www.delta.com*).**United Airlines** (☎ *800/864–8331 for U.S. reservations, 800/538–2929 for international reservations* ⊕ *www.united.com*).

CHARTER FLIGHTS

There are three companies that provide charter flights between the Islands, should you want to make one- or multiday trips to the Neighbor Islands. go! Mokulele Airlines offers nonstop charter service from O'ahu to Lāna'i and Maui. In business since 1998, the company also services the Big Island and Moloka'i. Pacific Wings serves O'ahu, Lāna'i, Maui, Moloka'i and the Big Island. Services include premiere (same-day departures on short notice), premium (24-hour notice), group and cargo /courier. Paragon Air offers 24-hour private charter service from any airport in Hawai'i. In business since 1980, the company prides itself on its perfect safety record and its celebrity list of passengers including Bill Gates, Michael Douglas, and Kevin Costner, among others. You also can arrange a customized tour of neighboring islands.

Charter Companies go! Mokulele Airlines (☎ *808/326–7070* ⊕ *www.mokuleleairlines. com*). **Pacific Wings** (☎ *888/575–4546* ⊕ *www.pacificwings.com*).**Paragon Air** (☎ *800/428–1231* ⊕ *www.paragon-air.com*).

INTERISLAND FLIGHTS

If you've allotted more than a week for your vacation, you may want to consider visiting a neighbor island. From Honolulu, there are departing flights to the neighbor islands leaving almost every half hour from early morning until evening. Since each flight is only 30 to 60 minutes in length, you can watch the sunrise on O'ahu and look for the green flash at sunset while on either the Big Island, Kaua'i, Lāna'i, Maui, or Moloka'i. To simplify your vacation, schedule your return flight to O'ahu so that it coincides with your flight home.

Aloha Airlines, Hawaiian Airlines, Island Air, go! Mokulele Airlines, and Pacific Wings/PWExpress offer regular service between the Islands. In addition to offering very competitive rates and online specials, all have frequent-flyer programs that entitle you to rewards and upgrades the more you fly. Be sure to compare prices offered by all of the interisland carriers. If you are somewhat flexible with your dates and times for island-hopping, you should have no problem getting a very affordable round-trip ticket. There are also a number of wholesalers that offer neighbor island packages including air, hotel, rental car, and even visitor attractions or activities.

Interisland Flights Aloha Airlines (☎ *800/367–5250* ⊕ *www.alohaairlines.com).* **go! Mokulele Airlines** (☎ *808/326–7070* ⊕ *www.mokuleleairlines.com).* **Hawaiian Airlines** (☎ *800/367–5320* ⊕ *www.hawaiianair. com).***IslandAir** (☎ *800/323–3345* ⊕ *www. islandair.com).*

▌ BOAT TRAVEL

The City and County of Honolulu runs TheBoat, one-hour passenger ferry service from Kalaeloa on O'ahu's west coast to Aloha Tower in downtown Honolulu. Designed primarily to ease the commute for West O'ahu residents, there are three departures each way in the morning and again in the afternoon/evening. The one-way fare is $2/person. A four-day pass for unlimited rides is $20 and can be purchased at ABC stores in Waikīkī and in the Ala Moana Shopping Center, at selected 7-Eleven stores, and at TheBus Pass Office. This is a great alternative to driving for

visitors staying at Kō'Ōlina who want to spend one or more days in Honolulu, or for those staying in Honolulu who want to spend time at Kō'Ōlina or Hawaiian Waters Adventure Park. There is connecting bus service for most of the trips; check the Web site or call to confirm.

Information TheBoat (☎ *808/848–5555* ⊕ *www.trytheboat.com).*

CRUISES
For information about cruises, see chapter 1, Experience O'ahu.

▌ BUS TRAVEL

Getting around by bus is a convenient and affordable option on O'ahu. In Waikīkī, in addition to TheBus and the Waikīkī Trolley, there are a number of brightly painted private buses, many of which are free, that will take you to such commercial attractions as dinner cruises, garment factories, and the like.

You can go all around the island or just down Kalākaua Avenue for $2 on Honolulu's municipal transportation system, affectionately known as TheBus. It's one of the island's best bargains. Taking TheBus in the Waikīkī and downtown Honolulu areas is especially easy, with buses making stops in Waikīkī every 15 minutes to take passengers to nearby shopping areas, such as Ala Moana Center.

You're entitled to one free transfer per fare if you ask for it when boarding. Exact change is required, and dollar bills are accepted. A four-day pass for visitors costs $20 and is available at ABC convenience stores in Waikīkī and in the Ala Moana Shopping Center. Monthly passes cost $40.

There are no official bus-route maps, but you can find privately published booklets at most drugstores and other convenience outlets. The important route numbers for Waikīkī are 2, 4, 8, 19, 20, 58, and City Express Route B. If you venture farther afield, you can always get back on one of these.

Bus Information TheBus (☎ *808/848–5555* ⊕ *www.thebus.org*).

▌ CAR TRAVEL

O'ahu can be circled except for the roadless west-shore area around Ka'ena Point. Elsewhere, major highways follow the shoreline and traverse the island at two points. Rush-hour traffic (6:30 to 9:30 AM and 3:30 to 6 PM) can be frustrating around Honolulu and the outlying areas, as many thoroughfares allow no left turns due to contra-flow lanes. Parking along many streets is curtailed during these times, and towing is strictly practiced. Read curbside parking signs before leaving your vehicle, even at a meter.

Asking for directions will almost always produce a helpful explanation from the locals, but you should be prepared for an island term or two. Instead of using compass directions, remember that Hawai'i residents refer to places as being either *mauka* (toward the mountains) or *makai* (toward the ocean) from one another. Other directions depend on your location: in Honolulu, for example, people say to "go Diamond Head," which means toward that famous landmark, or to "go '*ewa*," meaning in the opposite direction. A shop on the mauka–Diamond Head corner of a street is on the mountain side of the street on the corner closest to Diamond Head. It all makes perfect sense once you get the lay of the land.

GASOLINE

You can pretty much count on having to pay more at the pump for gasoline on O'ahu than on the U.S. mainland.

ROAD CONDITIONS

O'ahu is a relatively easy island to navigate. Roads and streets, although they may challenge the visitor's tongue, are well marked; just watch out for the many one-way streets in Waikīkī and downtown Honolulu. Keep an eye open for the Hawai'i Visitors and Convention Bureau's red-caped King Kamehameha signs, which mark major attractions and scenic spots.

Ask for a map at the car-rental counter. Free publications containing good-quality road maps can be found at most hotels and resorts and throughout Waikīkī.

ROADSIDE EMERGENCIES

If you find yourself in an emergency or accident, pull over if you can. If you have a cell phone with you, call the roadside assistance number on your rental-car contract or AAA Help. If you find that your car has been broken into or stolen, report it immediately to your rental-car company and they can assist you. If it's an emergency and someone is hurt, call 911 immediately.

Emergency Services AAA Help (☎ *800/222–4357*).

RULES OF THE ROAD

Be sure to buckle up. Hawai'i has a strictly enforced seat-belt law for front-seat passengers. Children under four must be in a car seat (available from car-rental agencies). Children 18 and under, riding in the backseat, are also required by state law to use seat belts. The highway speed limit is usually 55 mph. In-town traffic moves from 25 to 40 mph. Jaywalking is very common, so be particularly watchful for pedestrians, especially in congested areas such as Waikīkī and downtown Honolulu. Unauthorized use of a parking space reserved for persons with disabilities can net you a $150 fine.

O'ahu's drivers are generally courteous, and you rarely hear a horn. People will slow down and let you into traffic with a wave of the hand. A friendly wave back is customary. If a driver sticks a hand out the window in a fist with the thumb and pinky sticking straight out, this is a good thing: it's the *shaka*, the Hawaiian symbol for "hang loose," and is often used to say "thanks," as well.

CAR RENTAL

Depending on where you're staying and what you're planning on seeing and doing while on O'ahu, there are lots of ways to keep your ground transportation costs affordable. If you are staying in Waikīkī,

Car Rental Resources

Automobile Associations		
U.S.: American Automobile Association	☎ 315/797–5000	⊕ www.aaa.com
National Automobile Club	☎ 650/294–7000	⊕ www.thenac.com; CA residents only
Major Agencies		
Alamo	☎ 800/462–5266	⊕ www.alamo.com
Avis	☎ 800/331–1212	⊕ www.avis.com
Budget	☎ 800/527–0700	⊕ www.budget.com
Hertz	☎ 800/654–3131	⊕ www.hertz.com
National Car Rental	☎ 800/227–7368	⊕ www.nationalcar.com
Thrifty Car Rental	☎ 888/400–8877	⊕ www.thrifty.com

you can easily walk or use public or shuttle transportation to get to many of the attractions in and around the resort area. Since hotel parking garages charge upwards of $20 per day, you may want to rent a car only on the days you plan to sightsee around the island.

If you are staying outside of Waikīkī, your best bet is to rent a car. Even though the city bus is a wonderfully affordable way to get around the island, you'll want the flexibility of having your own transportation, especially if you're planning lots of dining and sightseeing adventures.

■TIP➔ Make sure that a confirmed reservation guarantees you a car. Agencies sometimes overbook, particularly for busy weekends and holiday periods.

You can rent anything from an econobox and motorcycle to a Ferrari while on O'ahu. Rates are usually better if you reserve through a rental agency's Web site. It's wise to make reservations far in advance, especially if visiting during peak seasons or for major conventions or sporting events.

Rates in Honolulu begin at about $25 a day for an economy car with air-conditioning, automatic transmission, and unlimited mileage. This does not include the airport concession fee, general excise tax, rental-vehicle surcharge or vehicle-license fee. When you reserve a car, ask about cancellation penalties and drop-off charges, should you plan to pick up the car in one location and return it to another. Many rental companies offer coupons for discounts at various attractions that could save you money later on in your trip.

In Hawai'i you must be 21 years of age to rent a car, and you must have a valid driver's license and a major credit card. Those under 25 will pay a daily surcharge of $15 to $25. Request car seats and extras such as GPS when you make your reservation. Hawai'i's Child Restraint Law requires that all children three years and younger be in an approved child safety seat in the backseat of a vehicle. Children ages four to seven must be seated in a rear booster seat or child restraint such as a lap and shoulder belt. Car seats and boosters range from $8 to $ 12/day.

In Hawai'i your unexpired mainland driver's license is valid for rental for up to 90 days.

Be sure to allow plenty of time to return your vehicle so that you can make your flight. Traffic in Honolulu is terrible during morning and afternoon rush hours, especially between Waikīkī and Honolulu International Airport. Give yourself about

3½ to 4 hours before departure time to return your vehicle if you're traveling during these peak times; otherwise plan on about 2½ to 3 hours.

∎ TAXI TRAVEL

Taxis can be found at the airport, through your hotel doorman, in the more popular resort areas, or by contacting local taxi companies by telephone. Rates are $2.75 at the drop of the flag and each additional mile is $3. Drivers are generally courteous and the cars are in good condition, many of them air-conditioned. In addition, taxi and limousine companies on the island can provide a car and driver for half-day or daylong island tours if you absolutely don't want to rent a car, and a number of companies also offer personal guides. Remember, however, that rates are quite steep for these services, ranging from $100 to $200 or more per day.

Taxi Companies **Carey Hawai'i Chauffeured Services** (☎ 888/563–2888 or 808/572–3400 ⊕ www.careyhawaii.com).**Charley's Taxi & Limousine** (☎ 808/531–1333 ⊕ www. charleystaxi.com). **Elite Limousine Service** (☎ 800/776–2098 or 808/735–2431 ⊕ www. elitelimohawaii.com). **The Cab Hawai'i** (☎ 808/422–2222 ⊕ www.thecabhawaii.com).

∎ TROLLEY TRAVEL

The Waikiki Trolley has four lines and dozens of stops that allow you to design your own itinerary while riding on brass-trimmed, open-air trolleys. The Honolulu City Line (Red Line) travels between Waikīkī and the Bishop Museum and includes stops at Aloha Tower, Ala Moana, and downtown Honolulu, among others. The Ocean Coast Line (Blue Line) provides a tour of O'ahu's southeastern coastline, including Diamond Head Crater, Hanauma Bay, and Sea Life Park. The Blue Line also has an express trolley to Diamond Head which runs twice daily. The Ala Moana Shuttle Line (Pink Line) stops at Ward Warehouse, Ward Centers, and Ala Moana Shopping Center. These trolley lines depart from the DFS Galleria Waikīkī or Hilton Hawaiian Village. The Local Shopping & Dining Line (Yellow Line) starts at Ala Moana Center and stops at Ward Farmers' Market, Ward Warehouse, Ward Centers, and other shops and restaurants. A one-day, four-line ticket costs $25. Four-day tickets, also good for any of the four lines, are $45. You can order online, and there are often online specials including a "buy one adult 4-day pass and get a second for free."

Information **Waikīkī Trolley** (☎ 808/591–2561 or 800/824–8804 ⊕ www.waikikitrolley.com).

ESSENTIALS

▮ BUSINESS SERVICES AND FACILITIES

The Hawai'i Convention Center located at the entrance to Waikīkī is a gorgeous facility that truly captures the spirit of Hawai'i through its open-air spaces, tropical gardens with native plants and water features, and soaring forms that resemble Polynesian sailing canoes. Recognized nationally for its architectural and landscape design, the Center also boasts a $2-million-art collection featuring the work of dozens of local artists. The Hawai'i Visitors & Convention Bureau's meeting and convention Web site has an online directory of products and services, should you be planning for or participating in an event at the Center.

Contacts Hawai'i Convention Center (⊠ 1801 Kalākaua Avenue, Honolulu ☎ 808/943–3500 ⊕ www.hawaiiconvention. com). **Hawai'i Visitors & Convention Bureau** (⊕ www.meethawaii.com).

▮ COMMUNICATIONS

INTERNET

If you've brought your laptop with you to O'ahu, you should have no problem checking e-mail or connecting to the Internet. Most of the major hotels and resorts offer high-speed access in rooms and/or lobbies. You should check with your hotel in advance to confirm that access is wireless; if not, ask whether in-room cables are provided. In some cases there will be an hourly or daily charge posted to your room. If you're staying at a small inn or B&B without Internet access, ask the proprietor for the nearest café or coffee shop with wireless access.

Contacts Cybercafes (⊕ www.cybercafes. com) lists more than 4,000 Internet cafés worldwide. **JiWire** (⊕ www.jiwire.com) features a directory of Wi-Fi hotspots around the world.

▮ EMERGENCIES

To reach the police, fire department, or an ambulance in an emergency, dial 911.

A doctor, laboratory-radiology technician, and nurses are always on duty at Doctors on Call. Appointments are recommended but not necessary. Dozens of medical insurance plans are accepted, including Medicare, Medicaid, and most kinds of travel insurance.

Kūhiō Pharmacy is Waikīkī's only pharmacy and handles prescription requests only until 4:30 PM. Longs Drugs is open evenings at its Ala Moana location and 24 hours at its South King Street location (15 minutes from Waikīkī by car). Pillbox Pharmacy, located in Kaimukī, will deliver prescription medications for a small fee.

Doctors & Dentists Doctors on Call (⊠ Sheraton Princess Kaiulani Hotel, 120 Kaiulani Ave., Waikīkī ☎ 808/971–6000).

General Emergency Contacts Coast Guard Rescue Center (☎ 808/541–2450).

Hospitals & Clinics Castle Medical Center (⊠ 640 Ulukahiki, Kailua ☎ 808/263–5500). **Kapiolani Medical Center for Women and Children** (⊠ 1319 Punahou St., Makiki Heights, Honolulu ☎ 808/983–6000).**Queen's Medical Center** (⊠ 1301 Punchbowl St., Downtown Honolulu, Honolulu ☎ 808/538–9011).**Saint Francis Medical Center–West** (⊠ 91-2141 Ft. Weaver Rd., 'Ewa Beach ☎ 808/678–7000). **Straub Clinic** (⊠ 888 S. King St., Downtown Honolulu, Honolulu ☎ 808/522–4000).

Pharmacies Kūhiō Pharmacy (⊠ Outrigger West Hotel, 2330 Kūhiō Ave., Waikīkī ☎ 808/923–4466).**Drugs** (⊠ Ala Moana Shopping Center, 1450 Ala Moana Blvd., 2nd level, near Sears Ala Moana ☎ 808/949–4010 ⊠ 2220 S. King St., Mō'ili'ili ☎ 808/947–2651). **Pillbox Pharmacy** (⊠ 1133 11th Ave., Kaimukī ☎ 808/737–1777).

∎ HEALTH

Hawai'i is known as the Health State. The life expectancy here is 79 years, the longest in the nation. Balmy weather makes it easy to remain active year-round, and the low-stress aloha attitude certainly contributes to general well-being. When visiting the Islands, however, there are a few health issues to keep in mind.

The Hawai'i State Department of Health recommends that you drink 16 ounces of water per hour to avoid dehydration when hiking or spending time in the sun. Use sunblock, wear UV–reflective sunglasses, and protect your head with a visor or hat for shade. If you're not acclimated to warm, humid weather, you should allow plenty of time for rest stops and refreshments. When visiting freshwater streams, be aware of the tropical disease leptospirosis, which is spread by animal urine and carried into streams and mud. Symptoms include fever, headache, nausea, and red eyes. If left untreated it can cause liver and kidney damage, respiratory failure, internal bleeding, and even death. To avoid this, don't swim or wade in freshwater streams or ponds if you have open sores and don't drink from any freshwater streams or ponds.

On the Islands, fog is a rare occurrence, but there can often be "vog," an airborne haze of gases released from volcanic vents on the Big Island. During certain weather conditions such as "Kona Winds," the vog can settle over the Islands and wreak havoc with respiratory and other health conditions, especially asthma or emphysema. If susceptible, stay indoors and get emergency assistance if needed.

The Islands have their share of bugs and insects that enjoy the tropical climate as much as visitors do. Most are harmless but annoying. When planning to spend time outdoors in hiking areas, wear long-sleeved clothing and pants and use mosquito repellent containing deet. In very damp places you may encounter the dreaded local centipede. On the

WORD OF MOUTH

Was the service stellar or not up to snuff? Did the food give you shivers of delight or leave you cold? Did the prices and portions make you happy or sad? Rate restaurants and write your own reviews in Travel Ratings or start a discussion about your favorite places in Travel Talk on www.fodors.com. Your comments might even appear in our books. Yes, you, too, can be a correspondent!

Islands they usually come in two colors, brown and blue, and they range from the size of a worm to an 8-inch cigar. Their sting is very painful, and the reaction is similar to bee- and wasp-sting reactions. When camping, shake out your sleeping bag before climbing in, and check your shoes in the morning, as the centipedes like cozy places. If planning on hiking or traveling in remote areas, always carry a first-aid kit and appropriate medications for sting reactions.

∎ HOURS OF OPERATION

Even people in paradise have to work. Generally local business hours are weekdays 8 to 5. Banks are usually open Monday to Thursday 8:30 to 3 and until 6 on Friday. Some banks have Saturday-morning hours.

Many self-serve gas stations stay open around-the-clock, with full-service stations usually open from around 7 AM until 9 PM. U.S. post offices are open weekdays 8:30 to 4:30 and Saturday 8:30 to noon. On O'ahu, the Ala Moana post office branch is the only branch, other than the main Honolulu International Airport facility, that stays open until 4 PM on Saturday.

Most museums generally open their doors between 9 and 10 and stay open until 5 Tuesday to Saturday. Many museums operate with afternoon hours only on Sunday and close on Monday. Visitor-attraction hours vary, but most sights are

LOCAL DOS AND TABOOS

Remember, when in Hawai'i, refer to the contiguous 48 states as "the mainland" and not as the United States. When you do, you won't appear to be such a *malahini* (newcomer).

GREETINGS

Hawai'i is a very friendly place and this is reflected in the day-to-day encounters with friends, family, and even business associates. Women will often hug and kiss one another on the cheek, and men will shake hands and sometimes combine that with a friendly hug. When a man and woman are greeting each other and are good friends, it is not unusual for them to hug and kiss on the cheek. Children are taught to call any elders "auntie" or "uncle," even if they aren't related. It's a way to show respect; it's also reflective of the strong sense of family.

When you walk off a long flight, nothing quite compares with a Hawaiian lei greeting. The casual ceremony ranks as one of the fastest ways to make the transition from the worries of home to the joys of your vacation. Though the tradition has created an expectation that everyone receives this floral garland when they step off the plane, the state of Hawai'i cannot greet each of its nearly seven million annual visitors.

If you've booked a vacation with a wholesaler or tour company, a lei greeting might be included in your package. If not, it's easy to arrange a lei greeting before you arrive into Honolulu International Airport with Kama'aina Leis, Flowers & Greeters. To be really wowed by the experience, request a lei of plumeria, some of the most divine-smelling blossoms on the planet.

Contact **Kama'āina Leis, Flowers & Greeters** (📞 *808/836-3246 or 800/367-5183* 📠 *808/836-1814* ⊕ *www.alohaleigreetings.com*).

LANGUAGE

English is the primary language on the Islands. Making the effort to learn some Hawaiian words can be rewarding, however.

Despite the length of many Hawaiian words, the Hawaiian alphabet is actually one of the world's shortest, with only 12 letters: the five vowels, *a, e, i, o, u,* and seven consonants, *h, k, l, m, n, p, w.* Hawaiian words you are most likely to encounter during your visit to the Islands are *aloha, mahalo* (thank you), *keiki* (child), *haole* (Caucasian or foreigner), *mauka* (toward the mountains), *makai* (toward the ocean), and *pau* (finished, all done). If you'd like to learn more Hawaiian words, visit ⊕ *www.geocities.com/~olelo*, the Hawaiian language Web site.

Hawaiian history includes waves of immigrants, each bringing their own language. To communicate with each other, they developed a sort of slang known as "pidgin." If you listen closely, you will know what is being said by the inflections and by the extensive use of body language. For example, when you know what you want to say but don't know how to say it, just say "you know, da kine." (⇨ *See Hawaiian Vocabulary in Understanding O'ahu.*) For an informative and somewhat-hilarious view of things Hawaiian, check out Jerry Hopkins's series of books titled *Pidgin to the Max* and *Fax to the Max,* available at most local bookstores in the Hawaiiana sections.

VISITING AND ALOHA

If you've been invited to the home of friends living in Hawai'i (an ultimate compliment), bring a small gift and don't forget to take off your shoes when you enter their house. Try to take part in a cultural festival during your stay in the Islands; there is no better way to get a glimpse of Hawai'i's colorful ethnic mosiac.

And finally, remember that "aloha" is not only the word for hello, good-bye, and love, but it also stands for the spirit that is all around the Islands. Take your time (after all you're on vacation and "Hawaiian time"). Respect the *aina* (land) that is not only a precious commodity in this small island state but also stands at the core of the Polynesian belief system.

open daily with the exception of major holidays such as Christmas. Check local newspapers upon arrival for attraction hours and schedules if visiting over holiday periods. The local dailies carry a listing of "What's Open/What's Not" for those time periods.

Stores in resort areas sometimes open as early as 8, with shopping-center opening hours varying from 9 to 10 on weekdays and Saturday, a bit later on Sunday. Bigger malls stay open until 9 weekdays and Saturday and close at 5 on Sunday. Boutiques in resort areas may stay open as late as 11.

▌ MONEY

Prices throughout this guide are given for adults. Substantially reduced fees are almost always available for children, students, and senior citizens.

ATMS & BANKS

Automatic-teller machines, for easy access to cash, can be found at many locations throughout O'ahu, including shopping centers, small convenience and grocery stores, inside hotels and resorts, as well as outside most bank branches. For a directory of locations, call 800/424–7787 for the MasterCard/Cirrus/Maestro network or 800/843–7587 for the Visa/Plus network.

CREDIT CARDS

Throughout this guide, the following abbreviations are used: **AE,** American Express; **D,** Discover; **DC,** Diners Club; **MC,** MasterCard; and **V,** Visa.

It's a good idea to inform your credit-card company before you travel. Otherwise, the credit-card company might put a hold on your card owing to unusual activity—not a good thing halfway through your trip. Record all your credit-card numbers—as well as the phone numbers to call if your cards are lost or stolen—in a safe place, so you're prepared should something go wrong. Both MasterCard and Visa have general numbers you can

call (collect if you're abroad) if your card is lost, but you're better off calling the number of your issuing bank, since MasterCard and Visa usually just transfer you to your bank; your bank's number is usually printed on your card.

Reporting Lost Cards American Express (📠 800/528–4800 in the U.S. or 336/393–1111 collect from abroad ⊕ www.americanexpress. com). **Diners Club** (📠 800/234–6375 in the U.S. or 303/799–1504 collect from abroad ⊕ www.dinersclub.com). **Discover** (📠 800/347–2683 in the U.S. or 801/902–3100 collect from abroad ⊕ www.discovercard.com). **MasterCard** (📠 800/627–8372 in the U.S. or 636/722–7111 collect from abroad ⊕ www. mastercard.com). **Visa** (📠 800/847–2911 in the U.S. or 410/581–9994 collect from abroad ⊕ www.visa.com).

TRAVELER'S CHECKS

Some consider this the currency of the cave man, and it's true that fewer establishments accept traveler's checks these days. Nevertheless, they're a cheap and secure way to carry extra money, particularly on trips to urban areas. Both Citibank (under the Visa brand) and American Express issue traveler's checks in the United States, but Amex is better known and more widely accepted; you can also avoid hefty surcharges by cashing Amex checks at Amex offices. Whatever you do, keep track of all the serial numbers in case the checks are lost or stolen.

Contacts American Express (📠 888/412–6945 in the U.S., 801/945–9450 collect outside of the U.S. to speak to customer service ⊕ www.americanexpress.com).

▌ PACKING

O'ahu is casual: sandals, bathing suits, and comfortable, informal clothing are the norm. In summer synthetic slacks and shirts, although easy to care for, can be uncomfortably warm.

There's a saying that when a man wears a suit during the day, he's either going for a loan or he's a lawyer trying a case. Only

INTERNATIONAL TRAVELERS

CURRENCY

The dollar is the basic unit of U.S. currency. It has 100 cents. Coins are the penny (1¢); the nickel (5¢), dime (10¢), quarter (25¢), half-dollar (50¢), and the very rare golden $1 coin and even rarer silver $1. Bills are denominated $1, $5, $10, $20, $50, and $100, all mostly green and identical in size; designs and background tints vary. You may come across a $2 bill, but the chances are slim.

CUSTOMS

Information U.S. Customs and Border Protection (⊕ *www.cbp.gov*).

DRIVING

Gas costs in Hawai'i range from $3 to $4 a gallon. Driving in the United States is on the right. Speed limits are posted in miles per hour, between 25 *to* 55 mph in the Islands. Watch for lower limits near schools (usually 20 mph). Honolulu's freeways have special lanes, marked with a diamond, for high-occupancy vehicles (HOV)—cars carrying two people or more. Hawa'i has a strict seat-belt law. Passengers in the front seats must be belted. Children under the age of three must be in approved safety seats in the backseat, and those ages four to seven must be in a rear booster seat or child restraint such as a lap and shoulder belt. Morning (between 6:30 and 9:30 AM) and afternoon (between 3:30 and 6:30 PM) rush-hour traffic around major cities on most of the Islands can be bad, so use caution. In rural areas, it's not unusual for gas stations to close early. If you see that your tank is getting low, don't take any chances; fill up when you see a station.

If your car breaks down, pull onto the shoulder and wait for help, or have your passengers wait while you walk to an emergency phone. If you have a cell phone with you, call the roadside-assistance number on your rental-car agreement.

ELECTRICITY

The U.S. standard is AC, 110 volts/60 cycles. Plugs have two flat pins set parallel to each other.

EMBASSIES

Contacts Australia (☎ *202/797–3000* ⊕ *www.austemb.org*).**Canada** (☎ *202/682–1740* ⊕ *www.canadianembassy.org*).**United Kingdom** (☎ *202/588–7800* ⊕ *www.britainusa.com*).

Australia Australian Consulate (✉ *1000 Bishop St., Honolulu* ☎ *808/524–5050*).

Canada Canadian Consulate (✉ *1000 Bishop St., Honolulu* ☎ *808/524–5050*).

New Zealand New Zealand Consulate (✉ *900 Richards St., Room 414, Honolulu* ☎ *808/543–7900*).

United Kingdom British Consulate (✉ *1000 Bishop St., Honolulu* ☎ *808/524–5050*).

EMERGENCIES

For police, fire, or ambulance, dial 911 (0 in rural areas).

HOLIDAYS

New Year's Day (Jan. 1); Martin Luther King Day (3rd Mon. in Jan.); Presidents' Day (3rd Mon. in Feb.); Memorial Day (last Mon. in May); Independence Day (July 4); Labor Day (1st Mon. in Sept.); Columbus Day (2nd Mon. in Oct.); Thanksgiving Day (4th Thurs. in Nov.); Christmas Eve and Christmas Day (Dec. 24 and 25); and New Year's Eve (Dec. 31).

MAIL

You can buy stamps and aerograms and send letters and parcels in post offices. Stamp-dispensing machines can occasionally be found in airports, bus and train stations, office buildings, drugstores, and convenience stores. U.S. mail boxes are stout, dark-blue steel bins; pickup schedules are posted inside the bin (pull down the handle to see them). Parcels weighing more than a pound must be mailed at a post office or at a private mailing center. Within the United States a first-class letter weighing 1 ounce or less costs 41¢; each additional ounce costs 24¢. Postcards cost 24¢. A 1-ounce airmail letter to most countries costs 84¢, an airmail postcard costs 75¢; a 1-ounce letter to Canada or Mexico costs 63¢, a postcard 55¢. To receive mail on the road, have it sent c/o General Delivery at your destination's main post office (use the correct five-digit ZIP code). You must pick up mail in person within 30 days, with a driver's license or passport for identification.

Contacts DHL (☎ *800/225–5345* ⊕ *www. dhl.com*). **Federal Express** (☎ *800/463– 3339* ⊕ *www.fedex.com*). **Mail Boxes, Etc./ The UPS Store** (☎ *800/789–4623* ⊕ *www. mbe.com*). **United States Postal Service** (⊕ *www.usps.com*).

PASSPORTS AND VISAS

Visitor visas aren't necessary for citizens of Australia, Canada, the United Kingdom, or most citizens of European Union countries coming for tourism and staying for fewer than 90 days. If you require a visa, the cost is $100, and waiting time can be substantial, depending on where you live. Apply for a visa at the U.S. consulate in your place of residence; check the U.S. State Department's special visa Web site for further information.

Visa Information Destination USA (⊕ *www.unitedstatesvisas.gov*).

PHONES

Numbers consist of a three-digit area code and a seven-digit local number. The area code for all calls in Hawai'i is 808. For local calls to businesses on the island where you are staying, you only need to dial the seven-digit number (not the 808 area code). If you are calling businesses on other neighboring islands, you will need to use "1-808" followed by the number. Calls to numbers prefixed by "800," "888," "866," and "877"are toll-free and require that you first dial a "1.".

For calls to numbers prefixed by "900" you must pay—usually dearly. For international calls, dial "011," followed by the country code and the local number. For help, dial "0" and ask for an overseas operator. Most phone books list country codes and U.S. area codes. The country code for Australia is 61, for New Zealand 64, for the United Kingdom 44. Calling Canada is the same as calling within the United States, whose country code, by the way, is 1. For operator assistance, dial "0." For directory assistance, call 555–1212 or occasionally 411 (free at many public phones). You can reverse long-distance charges by calling "collect"; dial "0" instead of "1" before the 10-digit number. Instructions are generally posted on pay phones. Usually you insert coins in a slot (usually 25¢–50¢ for local calls) and wait for a steady tone before dialing. On long-distance calls the operator tells you how much to insert; prepaid phone cards, widely available in various denominations, can be used from any phone. Follow the directions to activate the card (there's usually an access number, then an activation code), then dial your number.

CELL PHONES

The United States has several GSM (Global System for Mobile Communications) networks, so multiband mobiles from most countries (except for Japan) work here. Unfortunately, it's almost impossible to buy a pay-as-you-go mobile SIM card in the U.S.—which allows you to avoid roaming charges—without also buying a phone. That said, cell phones with pay-as-you-go plans are available for well under $100. AT&T, T-Mobile, and Virgin Mobile offer affordable, pay-as-you-go service.

a few upscale restaurants require a jacket for dinner. The aloha shirt is accepted dress on O'ahu for business and most social occasions. Shorts are acceptable daytime attire, along with a T-shirt or polo shirt. There's no need to buy expensive sandals on the mainland—here you can get flip-flops for a couple of dollars and off-brand sandals for $20. Golfers should remember that many courses have dress codes requiring a collared shirt; call courses you're interested in for details. If you're not prepared, you can pick up appropriate clothing at resort pro shops. If you're visiting in winter or planning to visit a high-altitude area, bring a sweater or light- to medium-weight jacket. A polar fleece pullover is ideal, and makes a great impromptu pillow. If you're planning on doing any hiking, a good pair of boots is essential.

SHIPPING LUGGAGE AHEAD

Imagine globe-trotting with only a carry-on in tow. Shipping your luggage in advance via an air-freight service is a great way to cut down on backaches, hassles, and stress—especially if your packing list includes strollers, car seats, etc. There are some things to be aware of, though.

First, research carry-on restrictions; if you absolutely need something that isn't practical to ship and isn't allowed in carry-ons, this strategy isn't for you. Second, plan to send your bags several days in advance to U.S. destinations and as much as two weeks in advance to some international destinations. Third, plan to spend some money: it will cost at least $100 to send a small piece of luggage, a golf bag, or a pair of skis to a domestic destination, much more to places overseas.

Some people use Federal Express to ship their bags, but this can cost even more than air-freight services. All these services insure your bag (for most, the limit is $1,000, but you should verify that amount); you can, however, purchase additional insurance for about $1 per $100 of value.

Contacts Luggage Concierge (☎ 800/288–9818 ⊕ www.luggageconcierge.com). **Luggage/Sports Express** (☎ 866/744–7224 ⊕ www.sportsexpress.com) ships luggage and sports equipment including golf clubs and surfboards. **Luggage Free** (☎ 800/361–6871 ⊕ www.luggagefree.com).

▌SAFETY

O'ahu is generally a safe tourist destination, but it's still wise to follow the same common-sense safety precautions you would normally follow in your own hometown. Hotel and visitor-center staff can provide information should you decide to head out on your own to more remote areas. Rental cars are magnets for break-ins, so don't leave any valuables in the car, not even in a locked trunk. Avoid poorly lighted areas, beach parks, and isolated areas after dark as a precaution. When hiking, stay on marked trails, no matter how alluring the temptation might be to stray. Weather conditions can cause landscapes to become muddy, slippery, and tenuous, so staying on marked trails will lessen the possibility of a fall or getting lost.

Be wary of those hawking "too good to be true" prices on everything from car rentals to attractions. Many of these offers are just a lure to get you in the door for time-share presentations. When handed a flyer, read the fine print before you make your decision to participate.

Women traveling alone are generally safe on the Islands, but always follow the safety precautions you would use in any major destination. When booking hotels, request rooms closest to the elevator, and always keep your hotel-room door and balcony doors locked. Stay away from isolated areas after dark; camping and hiking solo are not advised. If you stay out late visiting nightclubs and bars, use caution when exiting night spots and returning to your lodging.

■ TIP→ Distribute your cash, credit cards, I.D.s, and other valuables between a deep front pocket, an inside jacket or vest pocket, and a hidden money pouch. Don't reach for the money pouch once you're in public.

Safety Transportation Security Administration (*TSA;* ⊕ *www.tsa.gov*) .

■ TAXES

As of July 1, 2010, there is a 13.9% tax added onto your hotel bill. A $3-per-day road tax is also assessed on each rental vehicle.

■ TIME

Hawai'i is on Hawaiian Standard Time, 5 hours behind New York, and 2 hours behind Los Angeles.

When the U.S. mainland is on daylight saving time, Hawai'i is not, so add an extra hour of time difference between the Islands and U.S. mainland destinations. You may also find that things generally move more slowly here. That has nothing to do with your watch—it's just the laid-back way called Hawaiian time.

■ TIPPING

As this is a major vacation destination and many of the people who work in the service industry rely on tips to supplement their wages, tipping is not only common, but expected.

■ TOURS

GUIDED TOURS

Whenever you book a guided tour, find out what's included and what isn't. A "land-only" tour includes all your travel (by bus, in most cases) in the destination, but not necessarily your flights to and from or even within it. Also, in most cases prices in tour brochures don't include fees and taxes. And remember that you'll be expected to tip your guide (in cash) at the end of the tour.

TIPPING GUIDELINES FOR O'AHU	
Bartender	$1 to $5 per round of drinks, depending on the number of drinks
Bellhop	$1 to $5 per bag, depending on the level of the hotel and whether you have bulky items like golf clubs and surfboards
Hotel Concierge	$5 or more, depending on the service
Hotel Doorman	$1 to $5 if s/he helps you get a cab or helps with bags, golf clubs, etc.
Hotel Maid	$1 to $3 a day (either daily or at the end of your stay, in cash)
Hotel Room-Service Waiter	$1 to $2 per delivery, even if a service charge has been added
Porter at Airport or Train Station	$1 per bag
Skycap at Airport	$1 to $3 per bag checked
Taxi Driver	15% to 20%, but round up the fare to the next dollar amount
Tour Guide	10% of the cost of the tour
Valet Parking Attendant	$2 to $5, each time your car is brought to you
Waiter	15% to 20%, with 20% being the norm at high-end restaurants; nothing additional if a service charge is added to the bill

Globus has four Hawai'i itineraries that include O'ahu, one of which is an escorted cruise on Norwegian Cruise Line's Pride of America that includes two days on the island. Tauck and Trafalgar offer several land-based Hawai'i itineraries that include two or three nights on O'ahu. Both companies offer similar itineraries with visits to the USS *Arizona* Memorial National Park and plenty of free time to explore the island. Tauck offers 7- and 11-night multi-island tours, including a "Magic Hawai'i" trip for families. Highlights of the Tauck tours include a catamaran sail along Waikīkī Beach and hula and surf lessons. Trafalgar has 7-, 9-, 10- and 12-night multi-island tours.

EscortedHawaiiTours.com, owned and operated by Atlas Cruises & Tours, sells more than a dozen Hawai'i trips ranging from 7 to 12 nights operated by various guided tour companies including Globus, Tauck, and Trafalgar.

Recommended Companies Atlas Cruises & Tours (☎ 800/942–3301 ⊕ www. escortedhawaiitours.com).</R>**Globus** (☎ 866/755–8581 ⊕ www.globusjourneys.com). **Tauck Travel** (☎ 800/788–7885 ⊕ www.tauck. com). **Trafalgar** (☎ 866/544–4434 ⊕ www. trafalgar.com).

SPECIAL-INTEREST TOURS

BIRD-WATCHING
Hawai'i boasts more than 150 species of birds that live in the Hawaiian Islands. Field Guides has a three-island (O'ahu, Kaua'I, and the Big Island), 11-day guided bird-watching trip for 14 birding enthusiasts that focuses on endemic landbirds and specialty seabirds. While on O'ahu, birders will spot Fairy Terns, 'Amakihi (endemic Hawaiian honey creepers), Bristle-thighed Curlews, Japanese Bush-Warblers, white-rumped Shamas and possibly even the rare Oahu 'Elepaio. A highlight of the trip will be a pelagic boat trip to see Great Frigatebirds, Red-footed and Brown boobies, nesting Sooty Black-footed Albatross, and maybe the rare Gray-backed Terns, Christmas Shearwaters, or Hawaiian petrels. Chances are good that participants also will spot fascinating species of marine mammals. The trip costs about $4,200 per person and includes accommodations, meals, ground transportation, interisland air, an eight-hour pelagic boat trip, and guided bird-watching excursions. Field Guides has been offering worldwide birding tours since 1984.

Victor Emanuel Nature Tours, the largest company in the world specializing in birding tours, has a nine-day "Fall Hawai'i"

trip to O'ahu, Kaua'I, and the Big Island. Birders will spend two nights on O'ahu in search of Bristle-thighed Curlews, endangered Hawaiian waterbirds such as Koloa (Hawaiian duck), Hawaiian Coots, and the Hawaiian subspecies of Black-necked Stilts and Common Moorhens. The group will visit the James Campbell National Wildlife Refuge, a breeding site for endangered birds, and one of the best spots to see Hawai'i's migrant shorebirds including Bristle-thighed Curlews, Sharp-tailed Sandpipers, and Black-tailed Godwits. "Fall Hawai'i" is priced at around $4,000 and includes accommodations, meals, interisland air, ground transportation, and guided excursions.

Travelers must purchase their own airfare to and from their gateway city.

Contacts Field Guides (☎ 800/728–4953 ⊕ www.fieldguides.com). **Victor Emanuel Nature Tours** (☎ 800/328–8368 ⊕ www. ventbird.com).

CULTURE
Elderhostel, a nonprofit educational travel organization, offers several guided Hawai'i tours for older adults that provide fascinating in-depth looks into the culture, history, and beauty of the Islands. For all Elderhostel programs, travelers must purchase their own airfare if coming from outside of Hawai'i. Below are a few typical trips; the Web site shows more options.

A *"Tall Ship Sail Training: Sailing the Hawaiian Islands"* is an incredible six-night sailing adventure through the Hawaiian Islands aboard the SSV *Makani Olu*, a Coast Guard–certified, 96-foot, three-masted schooner. Prices for this tour start at about $1,080 per person and include accommodations and meals on board the schooner.

Travelers who want to learn more about the geology and heritage of Hawai'i and its people can book the eight-night "O'ahu and Maui: Experience the Essence of Hawai'i" vacation. During the five nights on O'ahu, you will visit the Bishop

Museum, USS *Arizona*, Punchbowl National Cemetery of the Pacific, and Queen Emma Summer Palace. There will also be special sessions with Hawaiian cultural specialists. Presented in conjunction with Hawai'i Pacific University, the program is priced at $1,440 per person and includes accommodations, meals, tours and activities, ground transportation, and air travel between O'ahu and Maui.

"Hawai'i: The Land & the People" is a six-night vacation on Oahu's North Shore that introduces travelers to the Hawai'i of yesterday and today. Participants visit the Polynesian Cultural Center, Waimea Botanical Garden, USS *Arizona* and USS *Missouri*, among others. Highlights also include a glass-bottom boat ride and day trips to learn modern surfing and the ancient arts of poi pounding and navigation by stars. Priced at $875 per person, the vacation includes accommodations, meals, ground transportation, and activities.

Contacts **Elderhostel** (☎ *800/454–5768* ⊕ *www.elderhostel.org*).

ECOTOURS

Imagine the thrill of working alongside marine biologists and helping with conservation efforts on O'ahu's west coast. Wild Side Specialty Tours offers seven-day Under the Sea Ocean Trekker Expeditions where you can do just that. Each expedition is tailored to groups of up to 12, and every day the group goes out on boat trips to study the ocean and its habitats. Together with scientists and researchers you'll be gathering data and learning more about Hawai'i's fascinating marine life. You'll also visit Hawaiian historical and cultural sites along the coast and learn about the people who settled on these shores. Priced at about $1,900 per person, the trip includes accommodations at Makaha Golf Resort, meals, and all activities. Travelers must purchase their own air from/to their gateway city.

Contacts **Wild Side Specialty Tours** (☎ *808/306–7273* ⊕ *www.sailhawaii.com*).

HIKING

Want to hike through lush rain forests, snorkel at Shark's Cove, discover quiet beaches, and visit historical monuments? Check out the "It's Not Just Waikīkī: Hiking and Touring O'ahu" tour offered by Sierra Club Outings, priced at about $2,000/person. You will spend 10 nights hiking and discovering the joys of O'ahu, nicknamed "the gathering place." Since the 1930s, Sierra Club Outings has been organizing outdoor adventure trips for people of all ages. Included in this tour are condominium accommodations in Honolulu and the North Shore, vegetarian-friendly meals with fresh, local seafood, produce and fruit (each participant will be asked to help prepare meals on one or two days), ground transportation, and activities. The 12 travelers on this tour will also be able to participate in a community-service project on the island. Participants must purchase their own airfare to and from their gateway city.

Contacts **Sierra Club Outings** (☎ *415/977–5522* ⊕ *www.sierraclub.org/outings*).

▌ TRIP INSURANCE

Comprehensive trip insurance is valuable if you're booking a very expensive or complicated trip (particularly to an isolated region) or if you're booking far in advance. Comprehensive policies typically cover trip cancellation and interruption, letting you cancel or cut your trip short because of illness, or, in some cases, acts of terrorism in your destination. Such policies might also cover evacuation and medical care. Some also cover you for trip delays because of bad weather or mechanical problems, as well as for lost or delayed luggage.

Another type of coverage to consider is financial default—that is, when your trip is disrupted because a tour operator, airline, or cruise line goes out of business. Generally you must buy this when you book your trip or shortly thereafter, and it's available to you only if your operator isn't on a list of excluded companies.

Always read the fine print of your policy to make sure that you're covered for the risks that most concern you. Compare several policies to be sure you're getting the best price and range of coverage available.

Insurance Comparison Info Insure My Trip (☎ 800/487–4722 ⊕ www.insuremytrip.com). **Square Mouth** (☎ 800/240–0369 ⊕ www.squaremouth.com).

Comprehensive Insurers Access America (☎ 800/284-8300 ⊕ www.accessamerica.com). **AIG Travel Guard** (☎ 800/826–4919 ⊕ www.travelguard.com). **CSA Travel Protection** (☎ 800/873–9855 or 800/711–1197 ⊕ www.csatravelprotection.com). **Travelex Insurance** (☎ 888/228–9792 or 888/457–4602 ⊕ www.travelex-insurance.com). **Travel Insured International** (☎ 800/243–3174 ⊕ www.travelinsured.com).

▌VISITOR INFORMATION

Before you go, contact the O'ahu Visitors Bureau (OVB) for a free vacation planner and map. You can also request brochures on the island's romance, golf, and family activities. The OVB Web site has an online yellow-pages listing of accommodations,

FODORS.COM CONNECTION

Before your trip, be sure to check out what other travelers are saying in "Travel Ratings" and "Talk" on www.fodors.com.

activities and sports, attractions, dining venues, services, transportation, travel professionals, and wedding information. For general information on all of the Islands, contact the Hawai'i Visitors & Convention Bureau. The HVCB Web site has a calendar section that allows you to see what local events will be taking place during your stay.

Contacts Hawai'i Visitors & Convention Bureau (✉ 2270 Kalakaua Ave., Suite 801, Honolulu ☎ 808/923–1811, 800/464–2924 for brochures ⊕ www.gohawaii.com). **O'ahu Visitors Bureau** (✉ 733 Bishop St., Suite 1520, Honolulu ☎ 808/524-0722, ⊕ www.visit-oahu.com).

ONLINE RESOURCES
Contacts Hawai'i Beach Safety (⊕ www.hawaiibeachsafety.org).

Hawai'i Department of Land and Natural Resources (⊕ www.state.hi.us/dlnr). **Hawai'i Tourism Authority** (⊕ www.travelsmarthawaii.com).

INDEX

ABOUT OUR WRITERS

Melissa Chang is a lifelong Honolulu resident and has worked in public relations for more than 20 years, representing a range of travel, retail, and restaurant clients. She is also a food reviewer for Honolulu's Metromix.com and is a regular contributor to the *Honolulu Advertiser,* the state's most popular daily newspaper.

Trina Kudlacek splits her time between her home in Hawai'i, where she is a faculty member at the University of Hawai'i, and Italy where she is a tour guide. Before moving back to Hawai'i, she spent a year guiding and guidebook writing in Northern Italy and vagabonding throughout Europe.

Chad Pata is a freelance writer who has spent the past fifteen years falling in love with Hawai'i. Originally hailing from Georgia he has gladly traded in Southern hospitality for the Aloha spirit. He married a local girl and has two hapa kids, Honu and Calogero, through whom his life moves and gains its beauty.